Trafficking in Antiblackness

Trafficking in Antiblackness

MODERN-DAY SLAVERY, WHITE INDEMNITY, AND RACIAL JUSTICE

LYNDSEY P. BEUTIN

Duke University Press
Durham and London
2023

Designed by Courtney Leigh Richardson
Typeset in Portrait and Acumin Variable Concept
by Westchester Publishing Services

Library of Congress Cataloging-in-Publication Data
Names: Beutin, Lyndsey P., [date] author.
Title: Trafficking in antiblackness : modern-day slavery, white indemnity,
and racial justice / Lyndsey P. Beutin.
Description: Durham : Duke University Press, 2023. | Includes
bibliographical references and index.
Identifiers: LCCN 2022041324 (print)
LCCN 2022041325 (ebook)
ISBN 9781478019787 (paperback)
ISBN 9781478017073 (hardcover)
ISBN 9781478024354 (ebook)
Subjects: LCSH: Human trafficking. | Racism against Black people. |
Slavery in mass media. | Racism in mass media. | BISAC: SOCIAL SCIENCE /
Black Studies (Global) | SOCIAL SCIENCE / Media Studies
Classification: LCC HQ281 .B5845 2023 (print) | LCC HQ281 (ebook) | DDC
364.15/51—dc23/eng/20221222
LC record available at https://lccn.loc.gov/2022041324
LC ebook record available at https://lccn.loc.gov/2022041325

COVER ART: *Liquid a Place*, 2021. Steel, painted brass, mirror, and graphite.
8 × 12 × 4 ft. © Torkwase Dyson. Photograph by Damian Griffiths, courtesy
Pace Gallery.

For my families, because all kin are chosen:
Their laws have never made us
Their laws could never break us

Contents

Acknowledgments

Books, like most things in this world, are not created by individuals, but by communities. I am honored to have been supported by a cacophonous collective of activists, artists, anarchists, and academics, who have all contributed to the everyday effort of making sense of the worlds we inhabit together. Heartfelt thanks to all who have loved me, sparred with me, mentored me, extended trust to me, forgiven me, kept it moving, and offered grace through this process.

The academic research for this book began as a graduate student at the University of Pennsylvania, where I was supported by incredible faculty and peers at the Annenberg School for Communication and in the Africana Studies Department: Omar Al-Ghazzi, Chris Ali, Doug Allen, Diego Arispe-Bazán, Dan Berger, Sharon Black, Garrett Broad, Chris Cimaglio, David Conrad, Khadijah Costley White, Andrew Daniller, Thadious Davis, Nora Draper, Jasmine Erdener, Kevin Gotkin, Kathleen Hall Jamieson, Elihu Katz, Marwan Kraidy, Emily LaDue, Josslyn Luckett, Deb Lui, Carolyn Marvin, Khwezi Mkhize, Zach Mondesire, Sara Mourad, Emily Plowman, Anthony Pratcher, Monroe Price, Sandra Ristovska, Shantee Rosado, Celina de Sá, Barbara Savage, and Meghan Sullivan.

My deepest gratitude goes to John L. Jackson Jr. who first scooped me under his wing when I was a scrappy undergrad activist at Duke; I have been riding with him ever since. John, your steadfast belief in me, from dumpster diving documentaries to fiery job talks, continues to take me by surprise. Every student should get to write for as generous and patient a reader as John, who embodies what is good and right about the academy. Thank you for being you—you have made my ethnographer's heart possible.

I was fortunate to have a powerhouse dissertation committee guiding me with both their profound scholarship and their kindness. Barbie Zelizer was the first person to believe in this project. When I came back from a conference titled Abolition: Then and Now, I rushed to her office to ask her: "But can you believe that no one discussed the stakes of calling trafficking slavery?!" She told me: "That is the question for a memory scholar." Barbie, your mark is so bright on this work; it wouldn't have been possible without you championing it. Sharrona Pearl has been a reliable sounding board and a helpful navigator of self-doubts and the academy; thank you for always opening your door to me. It was Deborah Thomas, who told our Africana studies class, "If something is bothering you, it means you know something others aren't saying," who first pushed me to start investigating the antitrafficking discourse. Deb, the way that you think about modernity has opened new worlds for me. I endlessly appreciate your mentorship.

Joining the Carter G. Woodson Institute for African-American and African Studies at the University of Virginia as a predoctoral fellow in 2016–18 was an absolute thrill. I am grateful to have had my work engaged so generously by the rock stars there: T. Dionne Bailey, Tiffany Barber, Julius Fleming, Jr., Corey Hunter, Ebony Jones, Lindsey Jones, Talitha LeFlouria, Chinwe Oriji, Kwame Otu, Seth Palmer, Tony Perry, Xavier Pickett, Ashley Rockenbach, Petal Samuel, Ashleigh Wade, and Maurice Wallace. Extra special thanks to our leader, Dr. Deborah McDowell, a visionary of what it means and what it takes to build institutional space for Black studies. Elena Shih and Salamishah Tillet served as commenters on early drafts of chapters while at the Woodson. Thank you all for believing in me.

When I joined Oberlin College as a visiting assistant professor from 2018 to 2019, I was welcomed into a wonderfully supportive community of scholars, friends, and karaoke enthusiasts from near and far who at one time or another called small-town Ohio home: Grace An, KJ Cerankowski, Charmaine Chua, Abbey Chung, Ann Cooper Albright, Meiver de la Cruz, Vange Heiliger, Erika Hoffman-Dilloway, Daphne John, Julie Kleinman, Greggor Mattson, Sabia McCoy-Torres, Gina Pérez, Baron Pineda, Sandy Placido, Danielle Skeehan, Cortney Smith, Danielle Terrazas Williams, and Leah Vonderheide. Extra special thanks to Wendy Kozol for her sagacity and friendship and for her insights and encouragement on an early version of the book's introduction.

This book has been strengthened by the audience feedback I have received from presentations at: USC Annenberg Summer Doctoral Institute on Diversity in Media and Culture; University of California, Irvine Department of African American Studies; Syracuse University Department of Communication and Rhetorical Studies; University of North Carolina Greensboro Department of Communication Studies; Yale's Gilder Lehrman Center for the

Study of Slavery, Resistance, and Abolition; Brown's Center for the Study of Slavery and Justice; Brown's Center for the Study of Race and Ethnicity; the Historians Against Slavery Conference (2015); University of Calgary Department of Communication and Media Studies; University of St. Andrews School of Divinity; William Paterson University; University of Witwatersrand; and Columbia University "On the Possibility and Impossibility of Reparations for Slavery and Colonialism" Workshop. Additional thanks to Sarah Banet-Weiser, Evan Brody, Brittany Farr, Kamala Kempadoo, Greta LaFleur, Julia O'Connell Davidson, Sam Okyere, Joel Quirk, and Allison Schifani. I am deeply grateful to the representatives from antitrafficking organizations who agreed to be interviewed for this study—thank you for sharing your insights into these institutions.

The bulk of this book was written in my first years on the tenure track at McMaster University in Hamilton, Ontario, during a pandemic that shuttered my access to comrades and family across the border in the United States. I am grateful to have landed among the creative and caring gang of feminist media scholars in the department of Communication Studies and Media Arts. Special thanks to my department mentor Sara Bannerman and to my students in International Communication; Public Memory, Media, and African Diaspora Studies; and Theoretical Issues, whose questions and insights have improved the clarity of my argumentation in this book. Much love to new friends in Hamilton and Toronto, without whom surviving COVID-19 restrictions in the land of long winters would not have been possible: David Beisel and Andrew Betzner, Marcelle Constable and Jules McAuley, Bianca Dahl and Philip McKee, Nicole Dalmer and Lucia Cedeira Serantes, Cassandra Hartblay and Sara Schroeder, Linda Hartley, Claudia Manley and Liss Platt, Suzanne Mills, Chris Myhr, Natalie Oswin, Patti Payne and Rita Celotto, Christine Quail and Doug Tewksbury, Yana Stainova, Devon Stride and Kass Byrne, and Andrea Zeffiro.

I am especially grateful for the people who got me through the last push of book revisions amid peak 2021 exhaustion. Petal Samuel graciously workshopped my introduction and her brilliance and kindness restored my confidence. Elena Shih read many drafts, highlighted hidden contributions, and was my landing pad for rants and worries alike. Cherry Henley, whose friendship is always right on time, listened thoughtfully, and said, "Baby, you are just scared. I am betting on you." To my various Zoom happy hour crews and group text lifelines, thank you to: Nadeen Bir, Laxmi Hummel, and Hồng-Ân Trương; Tiffany Barber, T. Dionne Bailey, Tony Perry, and Petal Samuel; Timothy Colman, Egina Manachova, and Beth Patel; Diego Arispe-Bazán and Celina de Sá; Ashley Joyce and Ana Počivavšek; Leigh Freilich, Clare Konizeski, and Sally

Williamson (a.k.a. Loose Cannons); Dilyana Mincheva and Selina Mudavanhu; and Shreena Amin and Jaci Timmons. Thank you to Ebony Jones for keeping things in perspective and Josslyn Luckett for always standing in the light.

Ever since I first slept in a tent for basketball tickets, my blood has run Duke blue, but getting to publish with Duke University Press is a dream come true. Thank you to my editor, the patient and caring Ken Wissoker, who gave me confidence at an early crossroads when he told me, "You should write the book you want to write." Thank you to Ryan Kendall, Ihsan Taylor, and David Martinez. Thank you to the two anonymous readers of this manuscript, whose encouragement and precision has made this a stronger book. Thank you all for seeing the value of my contributions.

The questions about racial justice that animate this book have been nurtured by the many friends, mentors, and coconspirators whom I have learned from in various struggles for migrant farmworker rights, queer liberation, prison abolition, the preservation of free Black historical sites, the destruction of monuments to white nationalism, and the creation of mutual aid projects.

In North Carolina: Nadeen Bir, Dwayne Dixon, Chelsea Earles, Laxmi Hummel, Jillian Johnson, Tony Macias, Libby Manley, Noah Rubin-Blose, Jessica Rutter, Ilda Santiago, Dannette Sharpley-Troung, Charlie Thompson, Hồng-Ân Trươ'ng, Sammy Truong, Denise VanDeCruze, Melinda Wiggins, all my coworkers at Student Action with Farmworkers and IUE-CWA Local 188, and everybody at the House of Mango collective. Across many additional community spaces, there was something in the air in Durham in the early 2000s. Thank you to all the folks who created visionary space for mutual liberation and trained us to keep our eyes on the larger structures: white supremacy and global capitalism.

In New York: Alisa Besher, Penelope Fisher, Radiah Harper, Keonna Hendrick, Monica Mariño, Erin McMonagle, David Rheingold, Madalena Salazar, Andy Stromberg, Maya Valladares, Eleanor Whitney, and all my coworkers at Queens Pride House, the Brooklyn Museum, and Weeksville Heritage Center, especially Pam Green whose vision for centering Black freedom in museum space continues to inspire my work. Special thanks to Scott Loren Moore, for a life of cubbyhole and antiracist strategy.

In Philadelphia: Alex Barrett, Dan Berger, Timothy Colman, Ben Goldstein, Elisabeth Long, Liam Miller, Layne Mullet, Jesse Newcomb, Beth Patel, Annie Re, Reem Rosenhaj, Erika Slaymaker, Hannah Zellman, all my comrades at Decarcerate PA, and all my housemates in the little earthquakes and lil succubi queer and trans collectives. Special thanks to Egina Manachova for teaching me how to write love letters to the universe.

In Charlottesville: Grace Aheron, DeVan Ard, Ben Doherty, Donna Gasapo, Emelye Keyser, Anne-Garland Mahler, Andrew Mahler, Esi Okesanya, Luis Oyola, Jalane Schmidt, Jeannie Sellick, Lisa Woolfork, the team at Charlottesville Low Income Housing Coalition, the team at Southerners on New Ground (especially Jade Brooks, Bia Jackson, and Alan Ramirez), the crew at Showing Up for Racial Justice Charlottesville, and the entire collective that made the Charlottesville Community Resilience Fund, especially Cherry Henley and Carla Harris, without whom none of it would have been possible. Extra special thanks to Pam and Joe Starsia and Sally and Clare, who fed me and kept me safe in Charlottesville.

Finally, families are beautiful, broken, and endlessly unfolding things. My brother, Brice Jamieson Beutin, taught me from a very young age that just because you are right does not mean you will win. His insights about the world have made me a capacious and open-hearted thinker. My father, Brian Wayne Beutin, has been a profound influence on my life. As a kid, he taught me that I could do anything I put my mind to, especially boxing out the boys in the paint and winning arguments. I am grateful for all he sacrificed for me to go to college. My mother, Jenny Mitchell Beutin, is a prolific community builder. She is my biggest supporter and the most generous person I know. She taught me how to find the good in everyone and that anyone is family if you want them to be. Lauren Prost has been my lifelong best friend. Thank you to Vanessa Hamer for our time building a life together and for making many dreams come true. Thank you to Megan McDowell for sharing your heart with me, if for a brief time.

There is no bigger joy than to live life with Cal Biruk. Cal is my playful pup, my researcher for the revolution, who has dealt with every worry, every joy, and every stress cry that writing brings by planning us a zillion beautiful gaycations. Cal, thank you for believing in me with such gusto. You make every future irresistible.

I hope that each of you see your words and thoughts reflected in these pages. You are the hearts that have made my hunches possible.

Introduction

In 2017, CNN released video evidence claiming to show that West African migrants were being sold at slave auctions in Libya. In the video's opening scene, viewers see two Black men standing silently and hear an off-camera voice that seems to be acknowledging bids. CNN's investigative journalist translates the audio from Arabic to English: "Big strong boys for farm work" and then "four hundred, seven hundred, seven hundred, eight hundred." The journalist editorializes: "The numbers roll in, these men are sold for twelve hundred Libyan pounds, four hundred dollars apiece. You are watching an auction of human beings."[1] The video's interpretation evokes the memory of racial chattel slavery and fits seamlessly into antitrafficking campaigns to "end modern slavery." The news story ends by surveying an overcrowded detention center in which the West African migrants are jailed upon being freed from the Libyan slave traders. The migrants will soon be deported back to Nigeria, and, in the framing of the investigation, it is for their own good.[2] In this opportunistic rendering of the causes and solutions to unsafe migration, modern-day slavery is said to be abolished through incarceration and deportation.

In response to the video, the United States, France, European Union, United Nations (UN) Security Council, African Union, and the Libyan Government of National Accord all condemned slavery in Libya and reaffirmed their commitments to antitrafficking legislation in order to ameliorate the problem.[3] Antitrafficking laws and interventions, though, have notoriously prioritized stricter border control and anti-immigration policies.[4] The CNN slave auction video and the responses that it generated elucidate not only the detriments of antitrafficking's solutions, but the racial logics upon which antitrafficking discourse is built. *Trafficking in Antiblackness* unpacks these dynamics with special attention to how the antitrafficking discourse invokes the history and memory of transatlantic slavery and to what political ends. The book does so by read-ing the antitrafficking image economy through Black studies scholarship and alongside racial justice activism. This shift in orientation provokes new ques-tions for critical scholars: Amid so many videos of state violence against Black people, and numerous activist campaigns to abolish policing, prisons, and bor-ders, why is it a video depicting Arab North Africans enslaving Black West Africans that garners widespread condemnation from state and international governance entities? Which state projects, political and moral agendas, and historical imaginaries does this narrative advance?

The imagery and narratives embedded in the CNN Libyan slave auction video are derived from the transnational antitrafficking apparatus, which is the constellation of governments, global philanthropists, the UN, community-based organizations, nongovernmental organizations (NGOs), concerned citizens, churches, corporations, media representations, news organizations (including CNN), and domestic and international policies that design awareness cam-paigns and regulations to end human trafficking.[5] The term *human trafficking* most commonly conjures the dominant media images of sex trafficking—young, des-perate women forced to sell sex on dirty mattresses in dimly lit back rooms.[6] This image has been constructed through decades of antiprostitution advocacy that sought to place "sexual slavery" (i.e., prostitution) on the international political agenda.[7] With the introduction of the US Trafficking Victims Protec-tion Act in 2000, the language of sexual slavery was broadened to encompass forced and bonded labor under the umbrella "a modern form of slavery."[8] In subsequent campaigns mobilized by the antitrafficking apparatus, modern slavery has been made to be visually synonymous with very selective working conditions, including: child laborers in Africa, the Caribbean, and Asia who work in small-scale mining, fishing, farming, brick and carpet making, and do-mestic households; migrant farmworkers in the United States; Asian-owned massage parlors and nail salons in the United States, United Kingdom, and Canada; child soldiers in Africa; non-Muslim captives of war in the Middle East compelled to provide sex and other forms of labor against their will; and all forms of sex work globally. As this book demonstrates, each antitrafficking figure and site articulates to one or more political imperative of the US nation and the US state. Naming these situations "modern-day slavery" places the collective memory of slavery and abolition—and their legacies—at the heart of the political project of antitrafficking.

In the opening scene of the CNN slave auction video, several tropes of an-titrafficking advocacy are repeated: (1) the iconography of eighteenth- and nineteenth-century plantation slavery, particularly the slave auction block,[9] which was one of the most widely used images by abolitionists to draw moral outrage to end the transatlantic and domestic US slave trades; (2) the narrative that Africans have always and continue to enslave their racial or continental kin when left to their own devices and must be intervened upon by more civilized outside forces to stop doing so; and (3) the figure of the Arab slave trader, often positioned within American and British rhetoric as coming before 1619 and after 1807 and as being more barbaric and less caring than plantation owners in the American South.

Each of these representations—the benevolence of nineteenth-century American and British abolition, the pretransatlantic slave trade within Africa, and the brutality and threat of Arab culture—have been used as rhetorical alibis for white historical innocence when the history of transatlantic slavery and its relevance to ongoing racial violence comes up in public conversation. These recurring narratives are framed in specific reference to historical responsibility. For instance, the argument that Africans were already enslaving each other *before* the Europeans joined in, what Ibrahim Sundiata calls "the slavers' canard," was used by defenders of transatlantic slavery in the eighteenth century and continues to be regularly mobilized in arguments against reparations for slavery.[10] Analyzing the relationships among antitrafficking's tropes and narratives about blame, rightful entitlement, and responsibility for slavery is one of the projects of this book.

In the second half of CNN's Libyan auction video, the rescued migrants are asked to recount their experiences being held by traffickers against their will (past tense), while they are still being detained in Tripoli. The video's narrative arc follows a familiar "slavery to freedom" story line, but what constitutes freedom is migrant detention and deportation. One Nigerian migrant named Victory states that he wants to be "taken home" due to the lack of food and water at the detention center. His critique of the detention center, though, is skipped over. Instead, the news coverage emphasizes Victory's desire to go back home, which indicates to viewers that the way to end trafficking is for migrants to stay in place—physically, geopolitically, socially, and economically. The news story frames the African migrants as naive and in so doing helps assuage European anxieties about porous borders and infiltrating Black bodies. It suggests that what is best for African migrants is to stay put at the bottom of political geographies and economic structures.[11] Such narratives offer politically expedient solutions to unsafe migration that do not disrupt the systems that create the conditions for unsafe migration in the first place.

The term *unsafe migration* describes the situation that occurs when individuals and groups are compelled to relocate in search of food, water, security, or wages without access to necessary legal and material means for doing so. The need to migrate, even when it is extremely dangerous, has been created by a host of factors: the centuries-long unjust enrichment of some at the expense of many through colonialism and transatlantic slavery, free trade agreements and corporate globalization, structural adjustment programs and neoliberal policy, environmental degradation, unsustainable mineral extraction, imperialism, the destruction perpetual war reaps, interpersonal violence, and intercontinental violence. In the case of West African migrants to Europe, migration patterns have changed dramatically since the Spanish and Italian states stepped up their off-coast surveillance and return of migrants. This shift in European border policy has pushed migrants to take more dangerous routes through the Sahara and into Libya.[12]

Such migrations are long, taxing, and are not undertaken naively, despite the image of the "naive migrant" being a predominant figure in antitrafficking advocacy.[13] Migrants can face coercion and abuse en route to their destinations, in part because illegalized migration often requires the paid help of migration facilitators or smugglers "who know how to get them across national borders undetected."[14] Increasing the carceral and punitive machinery that makes it more risky and expensive to cross borders only exacerbates, rather than ameliorates, racial and migratory injustice. If these solutions seem paradoxical, they are nevertheless congruent with the antitrafficking apparatus's history of using border control and policing to address its concerns.

Antitrafficking's carceral solutions to migration are an example of what Black diaspora studies scholar Rinaldo Walcott calls "the problems that Black movement poses for nations and citizenship. Once Black people *move*, the limits of freedom and autonomy announce themselves."[15] Notably, the harrowing news photography of Black migration through the Mediterranean Sea has captured the attention of both antitrafficking advocates and Black studies theorists of the *afterlives of slavery* framework. Although both groups invoke the resonances with slave ships and slave auctions of the past, they mobilize them to different political ends. As I will show, afterlives of slavery in Black studies is an analytic based in the ongoing struggle for Black liberation, while antitrafficking's mobilization of transatlantic slavery's aesthetics is based in the desire for white transcendence of historical complicities. *Trafficking in Antiblackness* disentangles the disparate political imperatives that animate the uses of the visual memory of transatlantic slavery in contemporary public and academic conversations, while using media ethnographic methods to name the stakes of the too-easy uptake of slave ship semiotics across all political orientations.[16]

The Libyan slave market story gains widespread legitimacy with CNN's audiences for multiple reasons: it is framed similarly to the visual memory of plantation slavery in the United States, it is congruent with the discursive binary distinction between "the West" and "Africa,"[17] its framing devices advocate for keeping Black people in place, and it leverages the tricky indexical properties of the visual as self-evident truth.[18] The story's tropes repeat and circulate through a robust, well-funded, and self-referential antitrafficking mediascape that this book takes as its object of study. Although the figure of Libyan slave markets was a new issue within the antitrafficking discourse in 2017, the CNN investigation follows a similar pattern to an early documentary about human trafficking, *Slavery: A Global Investigation*, which was released in 2000 when antitrafficking law was first being codified in the United States and at the UN.[19] In that documentary, which was produced with assistance by the antitrafficking NGO Free the Slaves, British journalists go around the world looking for, in their words, "real slaves."[20] One of the places they find them is on cocoa plantations in the Ivory Coast, where the footage of the boys plucking cocoa seeds strongly recalls images of slave labor on sugar plantations in the eighteenth and nineteenth centuries. The Malian migrants are rescued from the Ivorian farms and returned to freedom by being "sent home" to Mali. The antitrafficking narratives about Blackness repeat: references to iconography of nineteenth-century plantation slavery, Black African "slave masters" enslaving other Africans in the present,[21] deportation framed as the abolition of slavery. The antitrafficking narratives about whiteness also repeat: white British people, embodied in the journalists, are heralded as intrepid and concerned citizens in the present, and as having historically progressed from their slaving past. Africans slip back into slavery without white oversight and intervention, and state solutions for safety ("going back home" and "staying in place") restrict Black mobility but call it freedom.[22]

Before the journalists leave the Malian migrants, they ask the teens to re-enact for the camera the physical violence they experienced in the field. Such a ghastly and presumptuous request is legitimated by its assumed efficacy for moving white audiences into action (in this case, to buy fair trade chocolate).[23] The convention of displaying wounds has a long history in humanitarian discourses and has become required "proof" in arbitrating asylum cases.[24] In the context of its repetition across antitrafficking imagery, displaying scars references the nineteenth-century abolitionist photo of the slave Gordon's whip-scarred back. In its twenty-first-century reprise, it also suggests to US and UK audiences that it's no longer white people inflicting pain on slaves, but other

Black Africans. If, following Saidiya Hartman, the spectacle of Black suffering is less likely to incite indignation than to "provide us with the opportunity for self-reflection," then in both the 2000 Ivory Coast video and the 2017 Libya video, the wounded Black body is instrumentalized for American and British audiences to reflect on just how far, compared to African countries, they have come from their slaving pasts.[25]

The antitrafficking apparatus has circulated and recirculated these tropes and visual conventions through a tightly knit set of media and philanthropic institutions that all point back to each other.[26] This is what I term "the anti-trafficking mediascape," which, building on Arjun Appadurai's work, is the repertoire of images and narratives of trafficking that are produced by, and flow through, antitrafficking news coverage, philanthropically funded documentary films and journalism, museum exhibitions, transnational NGO awareness-raising and fundraising materials, and governmental and multilateral policy documents, all of which I analyze in this book.[27] While the circulation of antitrafficking's images and narratives appears unbounded—they pop up in many uncanny places, as I describe in this book's interludes—tracking its tropes and ethnographically following their tentacles through the mediascape reveals how multisector media repetition stabilizes antitrafficking's truth claims. Rhetorically analyzing those truth claims through a memory of slavery framework focuses our attention on the underlying political work that these images and narratives do for former slaving nations.

Tracing the 2017 CNN Libya slave auction video through the antitrafficking mediascape, which reflects this book's method, demonstrates the consistency with which antitrafficking discourse elicits the history and memory of transatlantic slavery, but then minimizes its historical scope and elides the importance of its legacies in the present. Its antecedent documentary *Slavery: A Global Investigation* was based on the research of antitrafficking super-spokesman Kevin Bales, who cofounded the NGO Free the Slaves in 2000 after publishing his much-cited *Disposable People: New Slavery in the Global Economy* in 1999. Since 2011, CNN has collaborated with antitrafficking NGOs to promote news coverage of trafficking and antitrafficking charities through its advocacy site "Freedom Project: Ending Modern-Day Slavery."[28] The programs and facts on the "Freedom Project" site largely recycle the one-liners developed by Bales and promoted by Free the Slaves and many others, such as "there are more slaves today than at any other point in history" and "unlike in the past, slaves are cheaper and more disposable today."[29] Both slogans are cited as facts across the antitrafficking mediascape, including in the National Underground Railroad Freedom Center's permanent antitrafficking exhibition *Invisible: Slavery*

Today, which was sponsored in part by Free the Slaves and the Clinton Global Initiative, and is the topic of chapter 3 of this book. The antitrafficking echo chamber makes trafficking "the new slavery" through aesthetic conflation with nineteenth-century imagery, and then alleges it is "worse" than transatlantic slavery with opportunistic interpretations of transatlantic slavery's economics and numbers, what I refer to in chapter 4 as "deceptive empiricism." In so doing, the world-shaping system of transatlantic slavery is reduced to an instance of labor exploitation,[30] the ongoing legacies of racial injustice are de-emphasized, and the structural racial violence of deportation and policing are renamed as paths to freedom. Whose interests do such uses of the memory of slavery serve?

The Racial Logics of Modernity

Trafficking in Antiblackness argues that the antitrafficking apparatus uses "modern-day slavery" rhetoric and imagery to circumvent historical Western responsibility for racial chattel slavery. I analyze the racial logics of antitrafficking campaigns by drawing on theories of antiblackness, which center the invention of race and the initiation of the transatlantic slave trade in the epistemological and ontological constitution of European liberal modernity.[31] Unlike antitrafficking's "modern slavery," by which advocates mean slavery in the present, this study invokes liberal modernity, following Deborah Thomas, to refer to "how 'the West' and its hegemonic doctrine of modern democratic liberalism has been rooted in the inequalities ordained by capitalism, imperialism, and slavery."[32] European global expansion and conquest, beginning in the fifteenth century, created new political and social hierarchies that taxonomized difference into a hierarchy of rationality and proximity to humanness, which was signified by the invention of race.[33] Economic relations and political arrangements informed each other. Mercantile capitalism fueled the rise of the entity of the state; the systems of settler colonialism and transatlantic slavery fueled capital accumulation and the development of global markets; and the doctrines of race, rights, reason, and rule of law created the political and legal apparatus that justified the violence of slavery, conquest, and colonialism.[34] This set of convergences birthed modernity and its racial logics, which differentiates the transatlantic trade from previous slave systems.

Modernity's new political arrangements were supported by narratives and specters like "slavery in Africa," "Africans enslave each other," "bad Black mothers," and "Black incapacity for freedom and self-governance." Those narratives resurface in contemporary antitrafficking discourse in ways that uphold liberalism's philosophical foundation: the contradistinction between white rationality and Black pathology. For example, when NGOs, philanthropists, and the US Department of State galvanize these antitrafficking narratives in important sites of Black freedom, such as Haiti and Ghana, the longstanding white fear of Black revolution is transformed into proof of Black incapacity for self-governance. When antitrafficking's narratives appear in slavery exhibitions in museums and in US military interventions in the Middle East, the lessons of the nineteenth-century abolitionist struggle *against* the state are channeled into multicultural support for state initiatives of racialized *un*freedom: border patrol, criminalization, and surveillance. In all cases, the nation-building myths that liberalism, capitalism, and US democracy are freedom-granting, benign, and race-neutral systems are affirmed through antitrafficking discourse. Guided by Lisa Lowe's point that "the genealogy of modern liberalism is thus also a genealogy of modern race," I delineate how the racial logics of modernity underpin antitrafficking programs and interventions across the globe.[35]

These insights grow out of my systematic study of four institutional sectors of the antitrafficking apparatus: US and multilateral policy, US-based transnational NGOs, museums, and philanthropic journalism. The bulk of my research took place from 2013 to 2018, and it included rhetorical analysis of documents and media objects, visits to historical sites and museums, and a handful of interviews with antitrafficking advocates. I have situated the antitrafficking mediascape as a Foucauldian discourse, a system of representation that produces knowledge.[36] As such, my analysis is concerned with how the discourse works to persuade its audiences. I consider how the language, facts, and figures that are mobilized within antitrafficking discourse acquire authority through institutional and social contexts, and what truth claims the discourse relies on, advances, and naturalizes.[37] Drawing on visual methods, I pay special attention to the economic, historical, and social relations that constrain, construct, and inform ways of seeing antitrafficking's images.[38] I conceptualize my research method as an ethnographic discourse analysis of the media archives of the present,[39] or as I usually gloss it, a media ethnography. My method departs from most media ethnographies, though, in that it is less interested in what people do with media and technology,[40] and more interested in how ethnographic sensibilities shape what we find in, and how we make sense of, media narratives.

Trafficking in Antiblackness demonstrates that, at its base, antitrafficking is a racial discourse. By staging a conversation among Black studies, media studies, and critical antitrafficking studies, the book focuses on the *political work* that antitrafficking representations do. Rather than adjudicating the inaccuracy of the representations, I explicate the usefulness of the opportunistically framed images for preserving the status quo of racial injustice. In shifting focus from what representations get wrong to what they produce, this book offers an example of how critical scholars can move beyond representational critique and toward assessing the undergirding political projects of image economies.[41] In short, the problems with antitrafficking policy and advocacy have not been sufficiently fixed, despite decades of reforms and critiques, because antitrafficking's narratives and representations are politically useful to state and non-state entities and actors. And, as I will argue, their political utility lies in their ability to recast historical justifications *for* white supremacy as today's abolition of slavery. Doing so discursively absolves state and nonstate actors of historical responsibility for racial wrongs.

In addition to offering sustained racial analysis to existing critiques and genealogies of the antitrafficking apparatus, though, I want to emphasize that this project has come to be through a critical Black studies epistemology. Race, in this mode of knowledge production, is not a variable of demographic difference but a discursive system of power that structures the world as we know it.[42] As such, I account for how the antitrafficking apparatus upholds global white supremacy by reading its narratives through the racial logics that the history of transatlantic slavery and European colonialism instantiated and left in their wake. Antitrafficking discourse is an empirical case that draws out the raciality of international governance and humanitarianism.[43] Antitrafficking is one among many discourses of development and human rights that reproduce European teleology and hierarchies of civilization.[44] But through its use of the phrase "human trafficking is modern-day slavery," antitrafficking discourse uniquely calls our attention to the foundational antiblackness of modernity and its narratives of human freedom. These insights build from a long tradition of Black critique that makes visible how the central terms and assumptions that underpin our studies and our lives—subjectivity, human, rights, reason, empiricism, democracy, representation, citizenship, privacy, property, public sphere—are constituted by race.[45] By naming antiblackness in the book's title, I aim to move beyond pointing out another instance of the instrumentalization, appropriation, and analogizing of Black suffering and toward explicating through media images what it means to say that antiblackness structures how we think about and talk about freedom.[46] My analysis shows how antitrafficking discourse encodes, reclothes, and mobilizes the racial logics of modernity, and in so doing, lays bare why Black studies' insights about the category of the Human are integral to any rhetorical analysis of the present.

Bringing Black studies historiography and theory to bear on antitrafficking discourse reveals underexplored historical and discursive contexts in which antitrafficking discourse has flourished. Scholars have meticulously shown that transnational antitrafficking policy came to be in the late 1990s and early 2000s because of state anxieties about border control, which I further explain below. Reading this era through a Black historical context, though, highlights how the rise of antitrafficking policy was concurrent with transnational organizing for reparations for transatlantic slavery, which I explore in chapter 1. Thinking through the relationship between contemporaneous demands for reparations and states' rhetorical embrace of a new "modern-day slavery" suggests that antitrafficking language and policy coalesce at a time when it is politically useful for former slaving nations to name a new slavery that is not white people's fault.

Similarly, critical antitrafficking scholars have convincingly argued that antitrafficking discourse closely mirrors the historical dynamics of the moral panic about the "white slave trade" in the early 1900s.[47] Reading this era through Black history reminds us that governmental policies to end the so-called white slave trade emerged amid the prominent antilynching campaigns led by Ida B. Wells-Barnett. As such, a new (white) slavery was urgently attended to by the state and progressive reformers with antivice policing while the ongoing white violence against Black people—an immediate legacy in the aftermath of slavery—prospered with the collusion of the police. Antitrafficking campaigns in the past and present have used the language of slavery in ways that directly counterpose campaigns for racial justice.

Throughout the book, I note places where antitrafficking campaigns, which primarily promote state solutions to safety such as policing, police reform, and criminalization, use images and rhetoric of Black freedom and Black suffering to promote their cause in the midst of, and to the detriment of, other social movements that are focused on the racial legacies of slavery.[48] I refer to the latter as "racial justice movements" to emphasize the centrality of structural racial oppression to the intersecting political, economic, and social issues that they address. By "racial justice," I mean justice in its most capacious sense, where people have what they need to live freely as their full selves, have the material and political resources to make self-determined choices, do not face "group-differentiated vulnerability to premature death" (in Ruth Wilson Gilmore's terms),[49] and are supported by systems that recognize, reckon with, and work to meaningfully redress racial injustices in the past and the present.

Invoking the term "racial justice" connotes an expansive vision of freedom, beyond any one juridical or state-based solution or policy. Many different local campaigns exist to achieve immediate and intermediate goals for decreasing racial inequality and moving toward racial equity. These campaigns employ a variety of tactics to achieve goals shaped by local contexts, but when described under the rubric "racial justice," they are anchored in a long-term vision of freedom focused on upending the root causes of unfreedom, the invention of white supremacy chiefly among them.

Although some antitrafficking organizations have adopted the terms "root causes" and "systemic change," their diagnoses of the problems and their solutions do not meet these visions of racial justice. Instead, they name "root causes of slavery" as everything from corrupt or incompetent government officials in African and Asian countries to poor Black Haitian mothers' lack of family planning. If those root causes sound familiar, it's because they piggyback on long-standing antiblack tropes about Africa and about Black mothers, in particular.

In the wake of the June 2020 uprisings for Black freedom, some antitrafficking advocates began to describe their work as "racial justice."[50] Under the banner of "promoting racial justice" to "stop modern slavery," Free the Slaves has emphasized Mauritania as the site where Arab Berbers with "lighter skin" racially discriminate against Black African Haratines by hereditarily enslaving them,[51] which is then used as evidence that ending slavery means ending racial injustice. The figure of Mauritania, though, has long been invoked across the antitrafficking mediascape in ways that produce key narratives analyzed in this book: Africans are behind the times because Mauritania did not outlaw slavery until 1981. Arabs forced Black Africans into hereditary slavery in Mauritania before the transatlantic slave trade and continue to as a result of racist, violent Arab culture. Mauritanian officials are corrupt and only pay "lip service" to enforcing antitrafficking laws, and thus evince African incapacity to govern fairly.[52] To resolve such issues, US-based transnational NGOs, backed by the US Department of State, provide technocratic solutions such as capacity building and human rights training, which models rational and civilized behavior for Mauritanians. Media ethnography of antitrafficking discourse makes plain how media-savvy antitrafficking advocates and conglomerates attach themselves to trending interest in racial justice by reframing sites of long-standing interest but continue to reproduce the same tropes about Africa. Yet, even amid heightened awareness of anti-Black racism through Black Lives Matter protests, the antitrafficking narrative is still framed in ways that downplay white complicity. By emphasizing racial discrimination within Africa, the present-day perpetrators of racial discrimination are multiculturalized and internationalized, leaving white American racial discrimination nonexceptional and less barbaric (it might be bad in the United States, but it's not *slavery*, the reasoning goes).[53]

Critical interpretations of these antitrafficking narratives might point out how they reproduce racial stereotypes, focus opportunistically on "African problems," or unilaterally impose the US criminal legal system transnationally, which itself produces racial injustices by overrepresenting people of color as criminals.[54] All of these conclusions are ways that antitrafficking is bound up with race and racism. Antitrafficking narratives might also be interpreted as producing another iteration of the "white-savior industrial complex" or a reinvigoration of the British colonial "civilizing mission," both of which are indeed drivers of the antitrafficking apparatus.[55] Yet, if we read the tropes in the Mauritania example through European liberal modernity's racial ontologies and racial logics, the depth of the raciality of the discourse becomes apparent.

Antitrafficking's modern-day slavery narratives assert the hierarchy of race and civilization across Africa, Asia, and Europe that white Enlightenment rationality sought to prove. Liberal philosophies that suggest that rights, reason, and the rule of law bring political freedom to the metaphorically enslaved (to sin, irrationality, or self-interest) obscure how those same universals were used to expand empire by positioning imperial subjects as unfit for liberty, incapable of self-governance, and in need of training on how to be civilized, and therefore justifiably exploited, intervened upon, managed, and dispossessed of land, labor, and family.[56] Colonized and enslaved groups were positioned into tiers of proximity to full humanness (European man) through racial discourses of natural, biological, and cultural hierarchy.[57] Drawing on Lowe's elaboration of "the distinct yet connected racial logics" of liberal modernity, this book gives an account of how antitrafficking discourse manifests "the longevity of the colonial divisions of humanity" in the present.[58] For example, colonial discourse about the "natural slave" status of Africans becomes the antitrafficking common sense that makes it believable that Black diasporic mothers would enslave their own children (discussed in chapter 2). The British imperial figure of the "free race" of Asian (exploited) laborers—imagined as docile and incorporable into a racial hierarchy of white ownership and Asian management—becomes antitrafficking's figure of the rural Indian woman brickmaker who is enlightened by cosmopolitan Indian NGO workers about her rights and gratefully and graciously accepts her impoverished place in the global economy (discussed in chapter 4).[59] These different connections, divisions, and distinctions work in concert to uphold global white supremacy. European liberal modernity's racial logics of white supremacy are remade in twenty-first century campaigns to end slavery today.

By white supremacy, I do not mean the most blatant expressions of white people hating and terrorizing nonwhite people, which are typically associated with groups like the KKK. I am referring to structural white supremacy, which is born of the "doctrine that positioned specific racialized groups—'whites'—and the societies they developed—'the West'—as superior to other peoples, nations, or communities."[60] White supremacy justified the enslavement and colonization of people and lands on the grounds that non-Europeans were inferior beings and thus were not "naturally" entitled to rights, property, and freedom. The concepts of rights, property, and freedom—key tenets of liberalism—were simultaneously being worked out in this milieu *through* racial ontologies, which following Charles Mills, helps name why liberalism has actually always been racial liberalism.[61] For instance, in Lockean liberal philosophy, individuals are entitled to rights because they are owners of their own body, which is conceived of as sovereign property that should be protected by political and civil society. Rights follow from property ownership, even if you just own yourself, and rights deter and remedy another person's violation of the body's sovereignty. But if you must own your body in order to be entitled to rights, enslaved people are, by design, not entitled to rights. This is not an unfortunate oversight or exclusion of Black people from liberal humanism's doctrine of rights; this way of thinking about rights and freedom came to be in the context of the transatlantic slave trade to protect white property, with property understood as both social position and the property in slaves.[62] This example is just one way in which justifying the naturalness of white supremacy—which legitimated the range of violent dispossessions that were enacted—required the development of an arsenal of scientific, juridical, religious, and philosophical thought that continues to undergird contemporary society.[63]

Thinking white supremacy's logics in relation to today's antitrafficking discourse helps further articulate white supremacy as a global structure of power in the present. Since "the European domination of the planet . . . has left us with the racialized distributions of economic, political, and cultural power that we have today,"[64] "an analysis of white supremacy must include the historical and current forms of transnational processes that were initiated by European expansion and that are continued through Euro-American cultural and political domination globally."[65] Understanding white supremacy as global shows how racialization and racial formation do not only happen at the level of individual identity negotiation within specific cultures, nor nation-specific societal categorization, nor regional and empire-specific typologies—although all of these sites and registers of race helpfully show how flexible racial power and racial identity can be. Racialization also operates in the register of the global arrangements and constellations of power: international geopolitics, global finance, and the uneven distribution of wealth, safety, and mobility globally. These are all racialized discursive formations.[66]

Antitrafficking's Good Intentions (for Border Control)

When race and racism are invoked in relation to trafficking discourse, it is easy to assume that nefarious characters prey upon racialized subjects or that racialized geographies of global poverty (poor Ghanaian villagers, for instance) are more prone to being exploited by traffickers. It may be a bit harder to grapple with what is at stake in my argument here: that antitrafficking campaigns reproduce the logics of white supremacy in their pursuits to do good.

Global policy and legal consensus names trafficking a violation of human rights. As such, antitrafficking advocacy, even when it produces harm, is often justified by its good intentions. Antitrafficking discourse is, after all, extremely convincing. Advocates depict worker abuse and exploitation in the global South and in racialized migrant communities. Some of the types of exploitation they depict are real manifestations of global capitalism and of the historical dispossessions wrought by transatlantic slavery and European colonialism. Poor and exploited workers are positioned in antitrafficking photography and news coverage in ways that resonate with the visual record of plantation slavery, which connects the systemic and moral horror of slavery to present conditions aesthetically and symbolically. In the United States in particular, sympathetic publics are often acutely aware of, and concerned with rectifying, their complicities in global supply chains and unfair economic development. For antiprison and migrant justice activists interested in making connections between historical and present racialized unfreedom in prison and migration, the connection between historical slavery and contemporary exploitation often doesn't seem like a sensationalizing rhetorical flourish; it just seems true.

Unfortunately, however, multilateral antitrafficking policy was not designed to help people, it was architected to protect states. The current antitrafficking apparatus came to be in the late 1990s and early 2000s in response to states' desire to increase their control over their borders. Critical scholars of antitrafficking refer to these origins of antitrafficking as the border control imperative.[67] Antiprostitution feminists campaigned in the 1990s to make human trafficking a major issue of concern at the UN, in particular by conflating it with all forms of sex work and with women's and children's undocumented migration.[68] Under the banner and discourse of antitrafficking, the state-produced vulnerabilities that migrants face were framed at the UN as an issue of women and children being duped, forced, or coerced to leave home by shadowy criminal agents who secretly wanted to exploit them for sex.[69] This victim-framing created a palatable solution for states: "criminalize those who move people clandestinely and return those who have been moved by traffickers to their 'home' societies as soon as possible."[70]

Antitrafficking's border control and policing agenda is not a secret. The 2000 UN protocol that addresses human trafficking is part of the Convention Against Transnational Organized Crime. By using moral panics about women's mobility, sexuality, and agency as a pretense in the late 1990s and early 2000s, antitrafficking's rhetoric has long "serve[d] to legitimize increasingly regressive state practices of immigration control", which only make migrants' lives more difficult.[71] Feminist scholars who are critical of antitrafficking policy have documented how trafficking has been framed as a security issue for states; as such, state solutions have focused on "enhanced border security and swift deportation of trafficked persons."[72] While many scholars have delineated how a human rights approach would better protect victims and would emphasize people's security (rather than states' security),[73] antitrafficking global agreements come to be at the UN *because* their enforcement would expand crime control, border control, and law enforcement. According to Anne Gallagher, a human rights approach to trafficking was never realistically on the table during UN negotiations, "however, States were prepared to develop an instrument of international cooperation that identified trafficking as a problem of transnational crime requiring a coordinated response and that imposed specific obligations of criminalisation and cross-border collaboration."[74]

Over the past twenty years, protecting victims and centering victims' voices has become a more prominent part of antitrafficking discourse, although this has not significantly shifted the reliance on, and legitimation of, policing and border control. Within the US, antitrafficking policing utilizes surveillance technology to find sex workers and collect information from their phones to build prosecutorial cases against presumed traffickers.[75] These types of "carceral protectionism" surveil, control, and negatively impact the people police assume to be victims in need of help, including, in some cases, by requiring participation in "prostitution-diversion" and other rehabilitation programs.[76] Antitrafficking's carceral protection can also result in deportation if workers are found to be undocumented. In the case of new licensing regulations for Asian massage parlors, for example, even when antitrafficking police interventions turn up no evidence of sex trafficking, undocumented migrant workers can still be put into deportation proceedings.[77] Increased policing and migration control are not the negative implications and outcomes of well-intended antitrafficking policies that can be reformed; antitrafficking policy exists because it aligns with state imperatives for control. Despite claiming to be abolitionists, the larger antitrafficking apparatus "does not challenge the right claimed by states to control and restrict freedom of movement."[78]

The border control imperative of antitrafficking policy is one genealogy of how antitrafficking discourse comes to be, which is entwined with other scholarly genealogies of antitrafficking that place their emphasis on different aspects of transnational politics: the political struggle for sex workers' and migrants' rights, the fraught battles among various feminisms for women's rights, the struggle against "violence against women," post–Cold War discourses about Eastern Europe, and demand for recognition of and apology for the exploitation of Asian women through the Japanese "comfort system."[79] What all these genealogies very helpfully demonstrate is that antitrafficking discourse is nimble and flexible enough to address many state and societal anxieties in ways that preserve, uphold, or extend dominant power structures. What stands out to me, though, is that the racial mnemonic "modern-day slavery"—being slung around by US state and nonstate actors in domestic and transnational politics, in explicit reference to, and contradistinction from, transatlantic slavery—has not merited more attention as *constitutive of* the political work that antitrafficking discourse accomplishes.

Scholars have critiqued the use of the moniker "slavery" as a synonym for trafficking, citing how it moralizes violence into good versus evil binaries and unhelpfully blurs and expands the legal parameters of slavery and trafficking.[80] Most commonly, though, critics simply dismiss the language as sensational, as an imprecise descriptor, or as unnecessary rhetorical device. My work takes the opposite approach by positing the centrality of the phrase "modern-day slavery"—and the racial imaginaries of the past and present it conjures—to how antitrafficking's narratives uphold political projects that advance the interests of state and corporate power. Recognizing slavery to be, on the one hand, an unstable referent, and on the other, always referencing the Black American subject in the dominant US political imagination (even, and especially, when it appears not to be), pushes us to focus on the political work that invoking slavery does for former slaving nations.

A Memory of Slavery Framework for Antitrafficking Discourse

Despite the antitrafficking apparatus's known carceral and otherwise counterrevolutionary origins, its modern slavery rhetoric and haunting imagery circulate within a confounding mix of other invocations of slavery in the present, including the ways in which scholars have articulated racial injustice in present systems of policing, migration, and citizenship as "afterlives of slavery."[81] In order to unpack antitrafficking imagery in this milieu, I utilize a memory of slavery framework that combines historical and structural analyses of Black oppression with a memory studies orientation. In memory studies, representations of history are analyzed as culturally significant in and of themselves.[82] Invocations of history in the present are understood as partial, selective, and mobilized to serve different and competing political purposes.[83] By combining Black studies and memory studies approaches, I center two animating positions: in Black studies "the past is not past,"[84] and in memory studies utterances of the past are shaped by the present. Rather than languish in antitrafficking's definitional debates about slavery and its applicability to various forms of contemporary exploitation, using the memory of slavery framework to read antitrafficking rhetoric allows us to ask: what does invoking slavery *do*—materially, symbolically, politically—and for whom?[85]

Thinking through the politics of the memory of slavery has been a vibrant thread within Black cultural studies since the 1970s. Literary scholars have shown how "the hold of slavery on the national imagination" has significantly shaped American literature and public discourse over the centuries,[86] including in post–civil rights Black American cultural productions that "retur[n] to the site of slavery as a means of overcoming racial conflicts that continue to flourish."[87] Toni Morrison has shown how language is a carrier of memory: narrative structure and strategy, public discourse about the "blessings of freedom,"[88] and central literary themes like "chaos and civilization" are responses to the Black presence, she writes, even when that presence is absented.[89] Whether thinking through how the history and memory of slavery appears in literature, on TV, at museums and historical sites, in diasporic tourism to West Africa and the Caribbean, in reparations discourses and projects, or in DNA and ancestry testing, studies of the collective memory of slavery have analyzed how slavery is included or erased from national histories and myths and how Black people have engaged US and transnational "sites of slavery" to negotiate alienation, belonging, and civic inclusion and exclusion.[90] All grapple with the implications of the past in the present with specific attention to the various ways Black memory works to articulate multiple, diverse, and contradictory visions of Black freedom for the present and future.[91]

Through its use of mnemonic language ("modern-day slavery"), antitrafficking discourse has begun to appear at many of these same sites of memory, including memorials and museums about transatlantic slavery and abolition, diasporic imaginings of Ghana and Haiti, and even reparations discourse. Yet, antitrafficking discourse does not return to these sites in pursuit of global Black self-determination. *Trafficking in Antiblackness* traces these politics of memory in order to analyze what the antitrafficking apparatus gains through its attachment to sites of Black freedom struggle.

Alongside explicit scholarly engagements with the memory of slavery, the afterlives of slavery framework—the phrasing of which originates in Saidiya Hartman's 2007 memoir about her travel through Ghana's memoryscapes of transatlantic slavery[92]—has been a durable and flexible frame for scholarship that engages the question of how histories of political, social, and economic structural antiblack violence are reconfigured post-Emancipation and continue to limit Black self-determination in the present. Scholars' contributions to the afterlives conversation unpack myriad present-day macro and micro practices of controlling and limiting Black freedom with attention to how historical structures underpin ever-new configurations of power. What makes the afterlives of slavery framework more than structural critique, though, is how the term "afterlives" also evokes slavery's ghostly hauntings. Following Avery Gordon, "Paying attention to ghosts can, among other things, radically change how we know and what we know about state terror and about slavery and the legacy of American freedom that derives from it."[93] The afterlives literature has been particularly powerful for how it centers the unquantifiable magnitude of white supremacy's antiblack violence in the banal as well as the spectacular.

Theorizing the long afterlife of slavery has meant asking questions about from whence antiblackness comes. This has led to the popularization of scholarship that interrogates who is Human, what is required to be recognized as Human, and how, if at all, that has changed since Western modernity's inception. Wrestling with the formation of the Human means returning to the origins of liberal humanism, which means engaging Sylvia Wynter's genealogical work that "trace[s] how racial-sexual-economic categories get made, remade, and disrupted through the production of knowledge."[94] Wynter's historical excavation of how ruptures (say, of feudalism, or of colonialism) happen and why categories carry through ruptures only to shapeshift,[95] resonates broadly with theorists of antiblackness because Wynter's work emerged out of similar political questions that continue to face us now: what explains the persistence of antiblackness amid changing governance and economic structures, how can we make a rupture happen, and how can we make sure antiblackness does not carry through into what lies beyond?

By antiblackness, I am referring to ontological antiblackness, which is not simply a synonym for discrimination or racism,[96] but a way to name and grasp the depths of the structuring power of the invention of blackness. On this point, Wynter offers a clarifying distinction between what she calls the "colonial rationale" for representations of Africa and the "ontological rationale" for how "Africa" is discursively produced. The "colonial rationale" created distorted images of Black Africans as primitive and backward in order to justify European civilizing missions. But, she contends that in order to understand the persistence of these narratives in the postcolonial period, we must grapple with the "ontological rationale."[97] The ontological rationale describes the culturally specific governing code of Western bourgeois Man that produced Africa as lack: if over the centuries the West has called Africa primitive, underdeveloped, resource-cursed, unable to self-govern, and unable to master natural scarcity, that is because the West defines itself in opposition to those traits.[98] These are racialized discourses of development that build from the racial logics of modernity that place blackness as the ontological foil to whiteness.[99]

Thinking about antiblackness through the study of being helps us understand race as a discourse of power that creates the genre of the capital *H* Human, who then becomes the (only) liberal rights-bearing subject under European humanism. In other words, the discourse of race brings the category of the Human into existence through who it is contradistinguished from. Because Wynter is attuned to how different group subjugations get justified through various epistemes,[100] I read her work as opening interpretive space within theories of antiblackness to productively bring two lines of thought together: antiblackness is both the anchoring exclusion that coheres white civil society and that elaborates a racial hierarchy which is instrumentalized in different ways to uphold white supremacy. Afterlives of slavery contributors who draw on theories of antiblackness situate its persistence not only in political, economic, and social structures, but also in the ontological order of European liberal modernity's humanism. This is why Rinaldo Walcott says, drawing on Wynter, "our present system of being human . . . is founded on the expulsion of Black people from the definition of what it is to be human."[101]

Thinking with the afterlives literature clarifies how different actors take up the presence of the slave past for different political projects. Despite invoking key terms of Black studies—human, slavery, modernity—and repeatedly referencing the visual memory of transatlantic slavery, the antitrafficking apparatus is not invested in obliterating the systems and structures that reproduce global white supremacy and antiblackness.[102] Antitrafficking's use of the phrase "modern-day slavery" is not an afterlife of slavery, but more precisely, is an afterlife of *white abolition*. This distinction is important because the latter ended racial chattel slavery without regard for sustained enfranchisement of free Black people but with regard for broadcasting white morality. Following W. E. B.

Du Bois, formal abolition left unfinished the project of dismantling the structural and institutional barriers to full Black emancipation in order to reconcile Northern and Southern whites, and their financial interests, with each other. Antitrafficking's brand of abolitionism is the heir of this inheritance, not an abolition that heroically frees Black people but an abolition that redeems white people and slaving nations from the stigma of, and liability of, having been enslavers. In other words, antitrafficking's abolition is antiblack; it is a political project invested in white self-reconciliation and statecraft.[103]

As a white memory project, the antitrafficking apparatus mobilizes the role that the memory of American abolition plays in upholding narratives of American freedom. It evokes a white abolitionist imaginary but feeds it with long-standing white justifications for how Black suffering comes to be: backwardness (slavery in Africa in the twenty-first century), Black violence (Africans enslaving each other), and Black pathological mothering (Black diasporic mothers selling their children to traffickers). The discursive frame of "trafficking is slavery" turns Black people across the diaspora, instead of white Americans or Europeans, into the enslavers in the past and present. In so doing, the antitrafficking industry's use of the metaphor of slavery has gained massive momentum and widespread support from a variety of actors—billionaire philanthropists, media conglomerates, conservative and right-wing governments, and liberal governments, to name a few—who are heavily invested in maintaining the status quo of uneven resource distribution and generational racialized wealth, power, and privilege accumulation.

Black Freedom, Multicultural Slavery, Reparations, and White Indemnity

If white historical responsibility for slavery is diminished through antitrafficking's "modern-day slavery," analyzing antitrafficking discourse as a white memory project also helps clarify its relationship to sites of Black freedom.[104] Unpacking how antitrafficking resignifies Black freedom histories as evidence of Black pathology draws out my ultimate claim: antitrafficking is a racial project that redeems the West *and indemnifies it* against indictments of racial injustice in the past and in the present.

Within antitrafficking discourse, for example, Black mothers in Haiti are said to sell their children into slavery through the restavèk system, which is a process of child fosterage arranged through family and social networks that I explore in chapter 2. Antitrafficking advocates intervene on the situation with parenting classes that educate mothers about the importance of "child freedom" and with family planning education based in population control imperatives geared toward averting Black births.[105] In so doing, Haitian mothers—the descendants of enslaved people who fought for and won their children's freedom—are represented as being incapable of imagining freedom, of needing to be taught what freedom could look like for Haitian children. Following Michel-Rolph Trouillot, "the contention that enslaved Africans and their descendants could not envision freedom" is a result of the racial ontologies that hierarchically organized the world.[106] Lisa Lowe adds that this view remained widespread in the 1930s, when C. L. R. James published *The Black Jacobins* about the Haitian Revolution.[107] By representing Haitian mothers as today's enslavers, Haiti's revolutionary past as the ultimate site of Black self-emancipation from slavery through successful slave revolt beginning in 1791 is rendered as proof that Black freedom leads to chaos. Black mothers are deemed the primary cause, and thus ultimately to blame, for Black children's unequal life chances. If US plantation slavery was once argued to have a "civilizing influence" on Black people,[108] now US-based NGOs and their local partners aim to "civilize" poor Black mothers by teaching them about children's human rights. In both cases, white people are represented as predisposed to care for slaves, and Black unfreedom is represented as the result of Black pathology. These are both alibis of white inculpability.

When antitrafficking discourse constructs contemporary Indians as slaves, exploitation of Indian workers is similarly framed as a problem of education, of Indians not knowing freedom exists, but with a twist. An antitrafficking campaign, seen in figure I.1, proclaims: "How do you reach people enslaved in India to inform them that freedom is possible? Call them!"[109] Such a proposition, that a phone call could free someone from slavery, suggests that the reason people are unfree is because they don't know better. The narrative tells us that a technological fix (the phone call) will end lingering backward practices that relegate even cell-phone-connected India to a not quite "fully modern" status.[110] The figure of the Indian slave, though, also creates a multicultural victim of slavery—which is the subject of chapter 3—that suggests slavery is no longer racial, by which antitrafficking advocates mean not only Black. In so doing, slavery is represented as a victimhood category that is not the exclusive property of the Black diaspora. Black people, in other words, are not exceptionally deserving of redress.

The antitrafficking cell phone is the liberator in India, where it frees Indian women from their culture and welcomes them into the global free market economy, which absolves former colonial powers of wrongdoing while obscuring asymmetries of global economic opportunity. But when antitrafficking discourse

HOW MOBILE PHONES PROVIDE HOPE TO SLAVES IN INDIA

POSTED BY MALIKA MEHTA ON AUGUST 23, 2016

How do you reach people enslaved in India to inform them that freedom is possible? Call them!

FIGURE I.1 Free the Slaves project in India, which sends voice messages about labor rights to people in Uttar Pradesh. Source: Screenshot of Free the Slaves website, https://www .freetheslaves.net/how-mobile-phones-provide-hope-to-slaves-in-india/.

conjures the cell phone in Africa, its magical freedom-granting properties are presented as squandered by Black corruption. In antitrafficking discourse, slavery exists in the Democratic Republic of Congo (DRC) because corrupt Congolese businessmen, militias, and judges exploit and enslave young children and adults to work in unregulated "artisanal" mines that are not overseen by US and UK corporate responsibility regimes and supply chain monitoring.[III] In such a reversal, it is not the plunder of mineral riches by multinational corporations— nor the histories of colonialism and the transatlantic slave trade that have created such structures of economic domination—that exploits workers in either India or the DRC. Rather, it is clean technology that frees Indian slaves with quick techno-utopian fixes, and it is dirty corruption that makes slavery in Africa an intractable feature of Black pathology. In all directions, antitrafficking discourse is constituted by antiblackness, and what it produces is white indemnity for the past and present unjust enrichment of the West by reinvigorating the racial logics and narratives that undergird white supremacy.

In conceptualizing antitrafficking discourse as producing white indemnity, or a rhetorical insurance policy against being blamed for, or having to pay for, slavery's racial dispossessions, I am building on scholarship that theorizes the potential of thinking with and through a reparations lens. Deborah Thomas has shown how employing "reparations as a framework for thinking about contemporary problems" centers the history of structural violence in producing present social inequalities globally.[112] Doing so is especially poignant in postcolonial African and Caribbean national contexts because the reparations framework challenges the durable racialized narrative of "cultures of violence" where (Black) culture is blamed for the problems that economic and political systems produce. Thomas is writing about Jamaica, but these dynamics are apparent in antitrafficking narratives that suggest poverty, inequality, and unfreedom are culturally, rather than structurally, produced. And, in all the geographically diverse contexts and racially diverse figures of "modern-day slavery" that I explore in this book—Haiti, Ghana, India, Iraq, and Black and Latinx Americans—the perpetrators of violence are said to be inflicting slavery on their own communities. How blame is constructed—who is blamed for enslaving who—is a key dimension of antitrafficking discourse.

Analyzing antitrafficking discourse through a reparations lens clarifies how racialized rhetorics of blame, in past and present, underpin antitrafficking representations. Leveraging blame animates its corollary: rightful entitlement. The concept of rightful entitlement references Enlightenment-era discourses that claimed Europeans were rightfully entitled to enslave and colonize other people and places because Europeans were more rational, culturally sophisticated, civilized, and biologically superior. In the aftermath of slavery, rightful entitlement also refers to who is deemed entitled to reparations. Antitrafficking discourse intercedes in both conditions to redirect blame for present and past inequality from European and US states to structurally marginalized individuals and groups. Individuals are blamed for making naive and uneducated choices or for reproducing dysfunctional family structures, which land them or their children in slavery, which, as Kamala Kempadoo notes, "absolv[es] the West from complicity in sustaining contemporary conditions of exploitation, force, and violence in labor markets."[113] With a reparations lens, it becomes clear how this exculpation also extends to the past. For instance, if modern slavery in Africa is the result of ongoing barbaric and continentally inflicted practices that originated before the European transatlantic trade, then Africans have no one to blame but themselves for their present situation. Black people are blamed for enslaving each other in the past and in the present; self-inflicted harm rhetorically renders the West not sufficiently responsible to be liable for reparations.

Reparations for slavery discourse and activism is itself a memory project that thinks through the relationship of the past to the present. Salamishah Tillet reads reparations discourse as "put[ting] forth different claims of both material and mnemonic restitution in order to challenge the purposeful and polite national amnesia around slavery."[114] Scholars have theorized the irreparability of the harm of slavery and of the political limitations of reparations for Black freedom.[115] Reparations is a form a liberal recognition, making it part of "the hegemony of liberalism."[116] Scholars have pointed out that reparations require supplicant petition, fit within liberal narratives of progress and perfectibility, or too easily offer closure and concretize the violence in the past.[117] Despite critiques of the limits that reparations discourse places on the horizons of Black freedom, reparations for slavery remain elusive and controversial among former slaving nations and their racial beneficiaries. Thus, in thinking about antitrafficking through a reparations lens, my analysis is anchored in scholarship that complicates the relationships among memory, redress, and liberalism, but I remain invested in the questions: Why is the state so threatened by the idea of reparations for slavery? In what ways might the perceived threat to state legitimacy be underpinned by a broader white desire to transcend culpability for slavery?

Although former slaving nations have mobilized many different arguments to minimize their responsibility for reparations for slavery, demonstrative of what Jovan Scott Lewis calls "White intransigence,"[118] antitrafficking's frames, figures, and narrative constructions shore up a sense of white proclivity to free slaves in the past and present while purporting to empirically prove with sociological study and statistics the African diasporic inclination to enslave in the past and present. As a seemingly disconnected or adjacent discourse—but one that is nevertheless directly rhetorically counterposed—"human trafficking is modern-day slavery" becomes an avenue for engaging in talk about slavery and its legacies, at state, international, and civic levels, but in ways that "make the world safe for U.S. businesses and political interests."[119] And, I argue, in ways that rhetorically produce alibis of white inculpability for the nation and its citizens. Antitrafficking's slavery talk, then, works to indemnify the West from the charge of historical blame.

Research Design and Overview of the Book

My research design began with an irritation: why do people take the terms of the antitrafficking apparatus seriously? Which turned into a recurring question: what has allowed such bald racial logics to gain so much authority? To address this question, I focused my research on sites that represent themselves to be the most highly respected and the most legitimate institutions that are producing and circulating antitrafficking discourse. There are seemingly endless examples of "trafficking is slavery" in popular culture, in church groups, and in small, local nonprofit organizations. While these locations often provide illuminating examples of the extreme negative implications of the discourse, they are also easily dismissed and sensationalized. Such dismissals have been issued by major antitrafficking players themselves, an act of distancing that shores up their own legitimacy, even as the groups they see as "misguided" mirror the mainstream tactics, facts, and representations closely. This is the performance of critique—demonstrating a group's self-reflexivity and critical sensibility becomes a legitimating factor in and of itself. It also very narrowly circumscribes, and thus controls, the parameters of what can be critiqued within the discourse.[120] My work has investigated and analyzed some of the major players in antitrafficking discourse (the US State Department and Free the Slaves, for instance) in order to uncover the basis of the discursive formation. I have no doubt that many individuals who participate in antitrafficking advocacy do so out of a sense of moral obligation or a desire to do good in the world. In my interactions, I have found many advocates to be earnestly invested in what they are doing. However, analyzing individual motivations and intentions for participating in antitrafficking advocacy is not the subject of this book. Rather, I focus on the *political work* that antitrafficking discourse authorizes, promotes, and accomplishes.

My argument unfolds across several planes. Antitrafficking reproduces the logics and narratives of Enlightenment thought that assert a global hierarchy of race anchored in Black unfitness for freedom. Antitrafficking resignifies sites and histories of Black freedom as evidence of Black inability to self-govern. Antitrafficking multiculturalizes slavery in the past and in the present as evidence that no single nation (especially the United States) is exceptionally to blame for slavery and that no single group (especially Black Americans) are exceptionally entitled to redress for slavery. And finally, antitrafficking uses the discourse and aesthetics of data to make all these claims seem rational and objective. These narratives are rooted in white supremacy's logics and ultimately serve as a white indemnity against claims for reparations for slavery, in particular, and against claims for racial justice more broadly.

Chapter 1, "Reparations and the Rise of Antitrafficking Discourse," shows how the discursive contours of antitrafficking took shape amid widespread international and US-based organizing for reparations for slavery in the 1990s and 2000s. Narrating reparations history as part of the political context in which antitrafficking discourse developed reveals how central the specific language of slavery was to its formation. Nearly one hundred years before the US Trafficking Victims Protection Act was passed in 2000, discourses of "slavery in Africa" and "white slavery" were similarly used by former slaving nations to undermine Black sovereignty and racial justice initiatives, in the case of independent African nations in the League of Nations and antilynching campaigns in the United States, respectively. I show how these discursive defenses reemerge within twenty-first-century antitrafficking advocacy to supersede calls for reparations specifically.

Chapter 2, "Blaming Black Mothers," analyzes how the antitrafficking apparatus promotes the idea that Black mothers cause modern-day slavery. Across news media, policy, and NGO materials, Black mothers in Ghana and Haiti are depicted as selling their own children into slavery. In so doing, sites of Black self-emancipation are resignified as failures of revolution that now need white interventions to teach Black mothers what freedom looks like. I trace the political history of the rhetorical figure of the bad Black mother in US discourse, including during racial chattel slavery, and draw on Tina Campt's invitation to "listen to images" in order to ask why Black mothers' love for their children is not able to be seen by antitrafficking's publics.[121] This chapter is particularly attentive to the place of Haiti in the Black radical tradition. I close the chapter by analyzing the case of #MissingDCGirls to demonstrate what happens when Black mothers in the United States fight for their daughters by galvanizing the language of human trafficking: they get blamed.

The first interlude, "#FreeCyntoiaBrown," thinks through whether, and when, the title "trafficking victim" is available to Black girls and women. I analyze the media discourse around Cyntoia Brown's case—Brown was first denied the title of "trafficking victim" in the press but her eventual release from prison was heralded as an antitrafficking victory—to take seriously a question I have received about my research from interlocutors: "Does it matter what you call it [modern-day slavery] if it helps Black girls get what they need?" The discursive media battles over Cyntoia Brown's case unfolded amid the successful Black

Mamas Bail Out campaigns (which I participated in from 2017 to 2018), which offers an opportunity to disentangle Black feminist prison abolitionist organizing and antitrafficking advocacy in real time.

Chapter 3, "When Slavery's Not Black," analyzes the role of neoliberal multiculturalism within the antitrafficking apparatus to ask: what political work is accomplished when slavery is represented as not Black? The chapter shows how antitrafficking discourse represents enslavers of the past and slaves of the present as multicultural perpetrators and multicultural victims, respectively. I think through the ways in which making slavery not race specific advances the US State Department's interest in representing European and American states as not exceptionally to blame for slavery's pasts and Black and African diasporic subjects as not especially worthy of their claims to redress. But multicultural victims of slavery in the present also do something else for US interests: they legitimate state approaches to safety (war, prisons, security, surveillance, and racial profiling) as paths to ending slavery. For instance, Yazidi women who are captured by ISIS are represented as freed from slavery by US military intervention, and Latinx undocumented farmworkers who are represented as enslaved by Latino middlemen are rescued by Immigration and Customs Enforcement (ICE). In both cases, the public memory of the Underground Railroad is mobilized to render the US state as abolitionist. Throughout, I use the antitrafficking discourse as a case to show how multiculturalism is based in antiblackness, and to argue that neoliberal solutions to trafficking don't just undermine broader social movements, they do so by implicitly and explicitly deploying the figure of the undeserving Black subject.

Chapter 4, "Deceptive Empiricism," explores how antitrafficking uses the rhetoric and aesthetics of data, science, objectivity, and neutrality to make its sensationalist claims about Black enslavers appear substantiated. I analyze antitrafficking's datafication—how the discourse mobilizes infographics, satellite technology, empirically proven models of freedom, and NGO metrics and indicators—by attending to how science has been used to uphold white supremacy as a governing philosophy. In so doing, the depth of antitrafficking's imbrication with antiblackness is laid bare: even in its most self-styled objective claims, antitrafficking discourse repurposes the contradistinction between white rationality and Black pathology in order to liberate cultures said to be prone to self-enslavement. I pay particular attention to how white memory claims of benign paternalism during plantation slavery are repurposed and datafied through antitrafficking's assertion that "slaves are cheaper today than in 1809." Tracing how discourses of data, science, and technology play out in antitrafficking raises the question, following Ruha Benjamin's formulation, who and what does antitrafficking's technoscience fix in place?[122] In addition to shoring up georacialized hierarchies, antitrafficking attempts to hold as historical constant a white predilection to care for Black people.

The second interlude, "#Charlottesville," stages several ethnographic encounters when antitrafficking discourse popped up within the public memory of slavery and Confederate monument activism in Charlottesville, Virginia, from 2016 to 2017. I take these quotidian comings upon of "trafficking is slavery" in sites of memory and the struggle for racial justice as an opportunity to elaborate two points: the congruence of antitrafficking rhetoric with Lost Cause slavery apologia *in practice* and why the research method I call "heart and hunch" is uniquely suited to study how memories of slavery are used in social movements in the present. In both of the book's interludes, antitrafficking discourse appeared within racial justice campaigns I was involved with, a coincidence I use to highlight the lack of attention to racial justice within the antitrafficking apparatus.

Chapter 5, "History Is Antiblackness," serves as the book's conclusion by tying together the antiblack politics of history across three registers: public history and museological spaces, historiography and the politics of the production of history, and the history of the production of racial ontologies. Antitrafficking discourse has made its way into sites of memory of the East African and Indian Ocean slave trade in Zanzibar, but these inclusions, too, are related to continental claims for redress from European slaving nations. This chapter connects the figure of the Arab slave trader in history lessons to the imagery of the Arab slave trader in CNN's coverage of the Libyan migrant auction that opens the book. I offer a meditation on visuality, affect, and afterlives to challenge the too-easy uptake of slave ship semiotics and redirect attention to the political agendas that underpin the circulation of antitrafficking's images in order to disentangle white supremacy's investments in Black migration news photography from Black freedom struggles' investments in it.

Finally, in the summer of 2020, when the bulk of this manuscript was written, several antitrafficking organizations issued statements in support of Black Lives Matter. In particular, they cited antitrafficking's dedication to ending slavery today as proof of their commitment to ending racism. I unpack one organization's statement alongside an email I received from them the same week which touted the effectiveness of policing and incarcerating African families who supposedly sell their children to traffickers as a modern-day abolitionist victory. This final example illustrates, perhaps more clearly than any other, how antitrafficking appropriates Black suffering and Black freedom to racially legitimize projects that uphold global white supremacy.

In total, the book argues that antitrafficking discourse gains traction for two interrelated reasons: it relies on and reproduces antiblackness in the name of ending slavery and it produces a historically inculpable white subjectivity that can be adopted in the face of claims to historical redress and accusations of contemporary racial injustice. *Trafficking in Antiblackness* shows how the racial logics and historical narratives that have been used to justify slavery and white supremacy are remade in the antitrafficking apparatus's campaigns to end slavery today.

White Transcendence

This book is the result of my search to understand more precisely which mechanisms encourage and allow an entire mediascape to mobilize such significant histories and memories of slavery and freedom to contradictory ends, to frame and fight the injustice of unsafe migration so paradoxically. It is born from the belly fire of a centuries-old urgency: global white supremacy remains the most dangerous and pressing threat to life's existence on Earth, white people's included. As a white person who was organized into multiracial struggle for justice in the US South beginning in the early 2000s, I am familiar with the white desire to be free of blame, and of the many futile strategies white people have concocted to transcend culpability, from being the most radical to being the most defensive. It is partially from these experiences that I have come to articulate the immense power of this desire and what white people in the grassroots radical left can do about it: let go of the fantasy of white transcendence and get on with the everyday work that builds toward reciprocity. In so doing, let white shame have the potential to "become a revolutionary emotion," in the generous wisdom of Stokely Carmichael.[123]

This project is anchored in the belief that another world is possible, and that it comes precisely through the hard-won, fragile, and unglamorous work of building cross-racial trust and organizing for mutually interested power from below,[124] while holding central the liberatory truths that lay in the histories and repertoires of those structurally excluded, of those lives lived beyond, and in spite of, liberal recognition.[125] No shortcuts will suffice in this work.

1

Reparations and the Rise of Antitrafficking Discourse

In 1999, "Trillions Demanded in Slavery Reparations" appeared in the BBC headlines. During the first international meeting of the African World Reparations and Repatriation Truth Commission held in Accra, Ghana, delegates issued a demand for $777 trillion to be repaid to African countries from Western Europe and the United States for the lives and mineral wealth stolen from Africa through the slave trade and colonization. The news article explains how the Accra Declaration's figure was calculated and discusses the declaration's additional demands around debt forgiveness. The piece ends, quite jarringly, with the sentence, "Contrary to widespread belief, slavery is still practiced in some parts of Africa, including Sudan and West Africa."[1] The concluding sentence's dramatic departure from the content of the rest of the article raises the question: what is the relevance of this sentence to the demand for reparations?

In the article's adjacent "relevant stories" sidebar, two other news articles report on West Africa's "child slave trade"[2]—which refers to the contemporary trafficking of children for domestic labor—and to "the ancient practice of slavery" said to continue in Sudan.[3] Read together, these August 1999 articles conflate the language of trafficking and slavery in order to suggest: if slavery still exists in Africa, why should the West pay reparations?

In 2015, sixteen years after the Accra Declaration, UK prime minister David Cameron was publicly pressed to address the issue of paying reparations for slavery to Jamaica during a trade relations diplomatic visit. CARICOM, a group of Caribbean states that coordinate foreign policy efforts, had developed a reparations campaign addressed toward the previous colonial and imperial powers of Europe.[4] Cameron dismissed the demands by stating, via spokesperson, that "The [UK] government abhorred slavery and indeed had passed the Modern Slavery Act to tackle human trafficking today."[5]

In the intervening period, the issue of human trafficking gained visibility and traction within international governance structures. Less than a year after the Accra Declaration for reparations, the United States passed paradigm-shifting antitrafficking legislation, the 2000 Trafficking Victims Protection Act (TVPA). The TVPA document introduces its significance by stating, "As the 21st century begins, the degrading institution of slavery continues throughout the world. Trafficking in persons is a modern form of slavery, and it is the largest manifestation of slavery today." The use of the language of slavery in antitrafficking policy documents has stakes for which claims and policies related to historical racial chattel slavery are granted international legitimacy. In a world where the current geopolitical and racial distribution of wealth was unequivocally created by and through the power relations of the transatlantic slave trade, reparations, on the surface, should not be hard to justify.[6] Despite volumes of scholarship and over a century of Black American, Caribbean, pan-African, and African diasporic organizing, demands for reparations for slavery have been persistently dismissed and delegitimized.[7] Schemes to end slavery within Africa, however, continue to gain global recognition.

Trafficking in Antiblackness argues that the antitrafficking apparatus uses modern-day slavery rhetoric and imagery to circumvent Western historical responsibility for slavery. In the process of doing so, it creates a parade of characters and slogans that imply Black demands for redress and racial justice in the present are illegitimate. In this chapter, I show how the discursive contours of antitrafficking took shape amid widespread international and US-based organizing for reparations for slavery in the 1990s and 2000s. Within antitrafficking discourse, the use of the phrase *modern-day slavery* alongside imagery of slavery in Africa developed in contradistinction to calls to redress the slaving pasts of the United States and Europe. In so doing, antitrafficking discourse offered former slaving states a way to talk about the legacies of slavery without taking responsibility for them.

I put this early 2000s history in conversation with early 1900s political contestations over what the legacy and present of slavery meant. Nearly one hundred years before the US Trafficking Victims Protection Act, discourses of "slavery in Africa" and "white slavery" were used by former slaving nations to undermine Black sovereignty and racial justice initiatives in the case of independent African nations in the League of Nations and antilynching campaigns in the United States, respectively. These discursive defenses resurface within twenty-first-century antitrafficking advocacy in ways that contest calls for reparations specifically.

The chapter's argument builds from three discursive spheres. I begin with how the US State Department's contemporary antitrafficking policy redeploys the figure of "slavery within Africa," which operates simultaneously as a justification for intervention and as a rebuttal to demands for redress for slavery. Antitrafficking policy documents use two key avenues of memory work—nineteenth-century abolition and the figure of Africans enslaving their racial or continental kin—to produce an imagined subjectivity of white Euro-American historical inculpability in the midst of calls to recognize the transatlantic slave trade as a historical crime against humanity. In the process, antitrafficking policy reasserts the legitimacy of the governing structures of racial liberalism and racial capitalism that Black reparations organizing often indicts. I then discuss how the antitrafficking apparatus builds from, and adopts, many of the dynamics of the 1910s white slave panic, while suggesting that the concept of "white slaves" in the 1910s was itself mobilized in opposition to Ida B. Wells-Barnett's campaigns for justice for Black women. Numerous contemporary antitrafficking NGOs focus on ending prostitution by rescuing sex slaves or otherwise belittling the agency of migrant sex workers.[8] These organizations, and the rhetoric they employ, also attract supporters who lodge "white slavery" defenses as arguments against Black reparations within the present context of the Movement for Black Lives. The so-called modern abolitionists repeatedly speak of modern slavery but scoff at social movements for racial justice.

The racist rhetorical traditions of "slavery in Africa" and "white slavery" underpin antitrafficking advocacy as it emerges amid pan-African reparations agendas of the late 1990s and early 2000s. Those political, legal, and cultural initiatives, which build from decades of Black American and Black internationalist organizing, put forward a "global anticapitalist and anti-imperialist" framework that would have also addressed the root causes of unsafe migration and exploited labor that antitrafficking discourse says it is concerned with.[9] I close the chapter by discussing these historical contingencies, these untaken forks in the path to full justice, these other futures possible.[10] Renarrating reparations history as part of the political context that antitrafficking initiatives helped neutralize shows how central the specific language of slavery was to its formation. While critical antitrafficking scholars have helpfully named the early twentieth-century white slave panic as the antecedent to contemporary antitrafficking moral panic and have demonstrated how antitrafficking co-opted coemergent international women's rights campaigns into crime and border control measures in the early 2000s, I aim to extend our understanding of the scope of political work that antitrafficking accomplishes by attending to how antiblackness constitutes antitrafficking during a resurgence of Black-led reparations organizing in the 1990s and early 2000s. Racism is not only an implication or outcome of antitrafficking policies, the discourse is shaped through racial anxieties, in particular, the recurrent white fear that Black freedom will lead to Black revenge against white people.

Africa Has Slaves and America Has Abolitionists: Racial Narratives in Trafficking in Persons Reports and at the League of Nations

Across two decades of US antitrafficking policy documents (2001–2021), African countries are consistently represented as being major sites of contemporary slavery. The United States is represented as leveraging its nineteenth-century history of abolition to free Africans from their African enslavers in the present. The US State Department's Trafficking in Persons (TIP) Report is a policy tool that monitors the antitrafficking efforts of other countries by providing narrative "country profiles" and ranking countries into tiers of compliance. The TIP Reports are highly political. Their legitimacy and methodology have been called into question by academics, journalists, and antitrafficking advocates alike.[11] Even a glance at the TIP Report maps of tier ranking distribution by continent reveals how closely Tier 1 countries consistently align with US allies (e.g., Western Europe, Canada, Australia, Israel) and how closely Tier 2 Watch List and Tier 3 countries align with US strategic foreign interests (e.g., Russia, China, Saudi Arabia, Syria, Iran). In her review of a decade of TIP Reports, Anne Gallagher writes, "political and ideological opponents of the USA may never be moved from Tier 3, no matter how much they try to conform to the Trafficking Victims Protection Act minimum standards."[12]

MAP 1.1 Map of tier rankings for countries in Europe. Many European countries consistently rank in Tier 1, indicating highest compliance with US antitrafficking law. Source: US Department of State, Trafficking in Persons (TIP) Report, 2018.

The TIP Report tier maps also demonstrate the overlap between economic development, histories of colonialism, and trafficking rankings, where overly developed nations that are largely responsible for creating the structural conditions that lead to unsafe migration are ranked in Tier 1 (seen in map 1.1) and formerly colonized and underdeveloped nations, who have less money to build the specific types of infrastructure that the United States demands, are ranked lower (seen in map 1.2). On average, only a single sub-Saharan African country is ranked in Tier 1 each year (and many years, zero have been placed in Tier 1).[13] Such representations are built on liberal humanist philosophy about the hierarchy of civilizations. African countries that were made poor by the West's violence are represented as culturally backward and self-enslaving.

MAP 1.2 Map of tier ranking for countries in sub-Saharan Africa. African countries are rarely ranked in Tier 1. Source: US Department of State, Trafficking in Persons (TIP) Report, 2018.

Despite the prevalent use of the language of slavery within antitrafficking public campaigns, the first TIP Report in 2001 accuses only six countries of actually having slavery. Five are countries in sub-Saharan Africa. The sixth country is France, accused of enslaving domestic servants from Africa and other continents. The majority of the accusations say that intra-African rebel armies are turning their victims into sex slaves. In Angola, ranked in Tier 2, "The National Union for the Total Independence of Angola (UNITA) rebel forces are alleged to abduct children, who are used for forced labor and in military service, and women who are used for forced labor, including as sex slaves."[14] In Uganda (Tier 2), "the Lord's Resistance Army (LRA) has kidnapped an estimated 5,100 Ugandan, Congolese, and Sudanese children, taken them to southern Sudan, and forced them to become soldiers, labor and sex slaves."[15] In the Democratic Republic of Congo (Tier 3), "Insurgent groups from neighboring countries have abducted a number of Congolese children to be labor or sex slaves, or to serve in the military."[16] In Sudan (Tier 3), "The militias or raiders abduct women and children as remuneration for their services and keep some of those abducted for domestic servitude, forced labor, or as sex slaves."[17] No citations or additional evidence are provided for the claims. These narratives represent Black Africa in familiar stereotypical tropes: war-torn, vicious, sadistic, barbaric. The narratives suggest that not only are African countries extremely violent to *each other*, they also have no respect for women's rights and are aggressive sexual predators. Such narratives set up the premise for humanitarian military interventions or International Criminal Court (ICC) trials,[18] while casting Black Africa in stereotypes that resonate with those used against Black American men. Although many other country narratives in the 2001 TIP Report accuse non-African countries of "trafficking for sexual exploitation," it is only in Black Africa where "sex slaves" are specifically labeled as such.

Slavery is also used to represent African cultures as inherently backward. In Ghana's 2001 narrative: "The practice of 'Trokosi' is a localized form of slavery or ritual servitude in which girls are forced into slavery for local fetish shrines in repayment for offenses committed by members of the girls' families."[19] This description of Ghanaian life highlights, in order to sensationalize, cultural practices as especially barbarous and insulting to modernity. The 2001 Ghana narrative does not mention any child slavery in Ghanaian mines or fishing industries, two narratives that have become prevalent in the news since philanthropists increased their focus on grant making for antitrafficking media. In more recent TIP Reports, Trokosi has dropped out of the narrative completely and child fishing slaves have gained visual prominence, which suggests the search for slavery in Ghana is more important to antitrafficking's political imperatives than understanding actual conditions.[20] Ghana's modern slavery stands in contrast to its position, following Kwame Nkrumah, as an emblem of anticolonial struggle, pan-African solidarity, and Black freedom in the diasporic historical imagination. Postdecolonization, the TIP Reports recast Black freedom as on the verge of slipping back into its natural state of slavery.

The narrative of ongoing cultural backwardness and slavery within Africa is used as proof that "the problem of trafficking in persons is not new—it is in many ways a modern-day form of slavery, which has persisted into the twenty-first century."[21] The danger of backward cultures is positioned as threatening the rest of the world's progress, which needs to finally be put to an end as the world enters the new millennium. Throughout its antitrafficking documents, the US State Department positions itself as both the most modern state and the most humane and altruistic state (and it was not until the Obama administration that the United States began ranking itself in 2009). The United States will, in this figuration, selflessly take on the burden of ridding the world of such awful African practices.

The idea that slavery in Africa is a threat to civilization has historically been an important rhetorical justification for military and diplomatic intervention. During British imperial expansion into Africa in the 1880s–1920s, ending slavery in Africa was used to justify Britain's civilizing mission and to raise money for Christian missionary expeditions and projects. This imagery did not just affect international policymaking, it aroused European publics as well. Joel Quirk's research on the relationship between colonial antislavery initiatives and contemporary antitrafficking programs describes the phenomenon: "Building on sensational reports by missionaries and explorers, European audiences came to view slavery in Africa as both an emblem of the 'backward' state of the continent and an affliction to be exorcised by paternal intervention by European civilization."[22]

After the 1884 Berlin Conference set in motion the Scramble for Africa, where the continent was carved up and divided among European imperial powers, heads of state reconvened at the 1889–90 Brussels Anti-Slavery Conference to create an international treaty to end the slave trade within Africa. The conference was hosted by the notoriously brutal King Leopold of Belgium, who effectively leveraged slavery abolition sentiment to justify his capture of much of the Congo River Basin.[23] As many scholars have noted, Leopold's Congo Free State, although granted in part on the grounds of Leopold's philanthropic policy to end the East African slave trade, became one of the most gruesome forced labor regimes of the period. Africans were forced to extract rubber and were subject to death or dismemberment for refusing to work or failing to meet quotas.[24] Decades later, in 1935, Italy would invade Ethiopia on the grounds that Ethiopia had not successfully abolished slavery.[25] During the height of European imperialism in Africa, European antislavery rhetoric, mobilized through the image of backward self-enslaving Africans, "proved to be a useful cloak for policies that were chiefly driven by other considerations."[26]

Liberia and Ethiopia, the two countries not annexed by European powers during the Scramble for Africa from 1881 to 1914, also became the only two African state members of the League of Nations. In her pathbreaking work, Adom Getachew demonstrates how their entrance into the league was burdened by an uneven, and racialized, fixation on slavery in Africa.[27] "Within the league . . . European empires were largely absolved of past and present involvement with slavery, and slavery itself was disconnected from colonial labor and cast as an atavistic holdover in backward societies. By framing the slavery problem in this way, the league positioned itself as the agent of emancipation and Liberia and Ethiopia as either culprits of humanitarian harm or incapable of effectively addressing the crisis."[28] Former slaving nations used the figure of slavery in Africa to position themselves as humanitarian abolitionists and to position independent African nations as incapable of self-governance without European imperial presence in the early twentieth century. Abolitionist activists in the period championed the idea that slavery in Africa was a result of Black people's incapacity for self-governance. The British Anti-Slavery Society encouraged the League of Nations to oversee the governance of Ethiopia on the grounds that slavery in Ethiopia was due to the lack of European control,[29] echoing the sentiments that imperial presence could have civilizing effects on races deemed to be less capable of self-rule. That same year, in 1922, Marcus Garvey rallied Black people throughout the world to unite for "political freedom on the continent of Africa" and "to free our motherland from the grasp of the invader."[30] Garvey's pan-African nation building stands in contrast to the contemporaneous white colonial self-interested concern about slavery in Africa. His is a call for Black solidarity for Black freedom across continents: "We should say to the millions who are in Africa to hold the fort, for we are coming 400,000,000 strong."[31] The antiblack abolitionism of the British Anti-Slavery Society, though, leaves its legacy in campaigns to end human trafficking: the British Anti-Slavery Society is now Anti-Slavery International, an NGO that runs antitrafficking programs to end slavery in Africa and is recognized as a global leader in the fight to end human trafficking.[32]

By framing slavery in Africa as endemic to the condition of Black racial inferiority, European officials deflected attention from their concurrent brutal exploitation of labor through colonial and corporate extraction in the 1920s. Forced labor in the colonies was so widespread that Britain and France lobbied to have certain types of forced labor exempted from the 1926 Slavery Convention.[33] The league pressured independent African nations to conform to open-door economic policies and foreign oversight in order to demonstrate their commitment to ending slavery in Africa,[34] which bears a striking resemblance to how antitrafficking policy uses antislavery rhetoric, tied to ending slavery in Africa in the twenty-first century, to implement international governance and economic sanctions. The narrative that Africans have always and continue to enslave their own and need white civilization to save them from themselves has been persistently mobilized by dominant actors to undermine Black sovereignty.

If the first TIP Report echoes these histories by making a stark distinction between slaves in Africa and trafficking in other parts of the world, then the next year's TIP Report applies the term "slave-like conditions" in ways that mirror Enlightenment-era racial hierarchies of civilization. In 2002, eight new countries now had "slave-like conditions"—Nepal, Lebanon, Laos, Haiti, Bahrain, United Arab Emirates, Sri Lanka, and Pakistan—which expands the number of countries explicitly associated with the term "slavery," even if in modified use, and extends the association of slavery beyond Black Africa to include South and Southeast Asia and the Middle East. These rhetorical tiers of slavery position continents into tiers of civilization, recasting old notions of how different racializations rank in proximity to humanness: Africa is the only continent with actual slaves ("sex slaves"), Asia and the Middle East are closer to human with "slave-like conditions," Europe and North America have various types of exploitation, but no explicit slaves. The racial hierarchy of civilization, which at its advent was empirically proven by British imperial scientists, follows a similar pattern.[35] Notably, Haiti's system of restavèk, which will become one of the antitrafficking mediascape's prime examples of child slavery in subsequent years, was significantly less sensationalized in 2002: "Although many restaveks receive adequate care, some are placed in slave-like conditions."[36]

As the TIP Reports have grown longer and more elaborate over the years, the glossy introductions include more and more images of exploitation that are captioned "slavery." Yet, the formula that I lay out remains largely the same in the country narratives through 2016—Black Africans are represented as hurting and enslaving each other, Asians and Middle Easterners face "slave-like conditions" and thus are not quite ready to join modernity (or to be trusted), and the West does not have slaves, only strong states that prosecute the slavery others bring into it swiftly and effectively. The United States further amplifies its highly evolved status, taking a cue from the League of Nations playbook, by juxtaposing nineteenth-century abolitionist imagery with contemporary slavery in Africa in the TIP Reports.

Visual juxtapositions of imagery of iconic American and British nineteenth-century abolitionists and contemporary conditions of exploitation appear frequently in State Department materials, especially in the period 2009–2013 that coincides with Barack Obama's presidency and the lead up to the Emancipation Proclamation sesquicentennial. In the 2009 TIP Report, a quote from Frederick Douglass is emblazoned next to an image of a Black woman from Niger standing with Hillary Clinton and Michelle Obama. The story, as seen in figure 1.1, describes how Hadizatou Mani was born into slavery and sold for $500 when she was twelve to a man who made her work long hours in the field, beat her, raped her, and made her bear three of his children.[37] Her story is structured to elicit the popularized contours of slavery in the American imagination.

The comparison positions West Africa as backward and stuck in the past. By representing a type of exploitation that closely mirrors the experience of enslaved people on Southern US plantations, Niger is rendered as having never evolved from the nineteenth century. America's sins are far in its past; Niger's still remain a problem. The Government of Niger is presented as corrupt and unreliable, pressuring Mani to drop her case but ultimately paying the fine to her for not enforcing its antislavery laws. The saviors of the narrative are the local NGO that is funded by Anti-Slavery International, the successor organization to the British Anti-Slavery Society (which is the same organization that lobbied for European oversight of independent Ethiopia in 1922).

Highlighting how slavery still exists in Africa while reframing American history as a history of abolition casts Black Africans as natural slaves that the United States freed on American soil in the nineteenth century and creates the narrative that the United States must do so again, postdecolonization, in the twenty-first century on the African continent. Africans, it appears to antitrafficking advocates, are always slipping back into slavery without white civilization's oversight.[38] The use of the historical memory of abolition envisions Americans as liberators who are not at fault historically, who are not to blame, or who have successfully overcome their own legacy of enslavement. The

INTERNATIONAL WOMAN
OF COURAGE

Hadizatou Mani, Niger

Hadizatou Mani was born into slavery. When she was 12, she was sold for $500. Her new owner, a man in his 60s, sent her to work long hours in the field, beat her, raped her, and made her bear him three children.

FIGURE 1.1 Hillary Clinton and Michelle Obama present Hadizatou Mani with an award from the US State Department. Mani's narrative elicits the memory of US plantation slavery but places slavery in Africa in the present and slavery in the US in the distant past. Source: US Department of State, Trafficking in Persons (TIP) Report, 2009.

historically innocent white subject is juxtaposed to the ever-enslaving African to reiterate the West's defense in 2001: if Africans continue to enslave each other, how can the West be responsible?

Slavery Is a Crime and It Should Have Always Been So: Organizing for Reparations and the Rise of Antitrafficking Discourse

In May 2001, the US State Department, then led by Colin Powell, stated that it would not support "international compensatory measures" for "slavery and the slave trade of the distant past" in response to reports that reparations for slavery would be on the agenda at the United Nations (UN) World Conference Against Racism (WCAR).[39] A day after the conference ended, Condoleezza Rice told the press, "Given the fact that there's plenty of blame to go around for slavery, plenty of blame to go around among African and Arab states, plenty of blame to go around among Western states—I think we're better to look forward, not point fingers backward."[40] Colin Powell and Condoleezza Rice, serving as the first and second African Americans, respectively, in the role of US secretary of state, were also the heads of global antitrafficking enforcement under Republican president George W. Bush from 2001 to 2009.[41] Less than a year after overseeing the US effort to undermine advocacy for reparations for slavery at the WCAR, Powell released the 2002 Trafficking in Persons (TIP) Report, where he condemned "trafficking as a modern form of slavery" and declared "the resolve of the entire US Government to stop this appalling assault on the dignity of men, women and children."[42] In 2003, Powell expressed his "commitment to end modern day slavery" and support for "US efforts to end trafficking in persons, to protect and help victims, and prosecute those who treat people like commodities or keep them in slave-like conditions."[43] By 2007, Condoleezza Rice, who was then the secretary of state, introduced the TIP Report stating, "Two hundred years ago, the British Parliament outlawed the trans-Atlantic slave trade, culminating a decades-long struggle led by William Wilberforce. Trafficking in persons is a modern-day form of slavery, a new type of global slave trade. . . . As in the 19th century, committed abolitionists around the world have come together in a global movement to confront this repulsive crime."[44] If in 2001 Powell and Rice didn't want the world telling the United States "how to handle its racial past and present" as it related to reparations for slavery,[45] they had since found antitrafficking advocacy to be a politically palatable way to engage in slavery talk; one that could acknowledge the past of slavery by emphasizing triumphant national histories of abolition.

According to Rice, although the United States and the West are not exceptionally to blame for the transatlantic slave trade because African and Arab states also played a role, a single white British man is exceptionally honored for ending the global system. Rice fails to mention how slave uprisings in the Caribbean and the success of the Haitian Revolution hastened the British Empire's decision to end the slave trade. Slavery is in the "distant past" of the West for Powell; abolitionist sentiment is deemed much more representative of the US government's history and present. If, according to the final WCAR declaration language, slavery and the transatlantic slave trade *should* have been a crime against humanity *but were not,* modern slavery is a contemporary "repulsive crime" (in Rice's words) that will be prosecuted to the furthest extent of the law (in Powell's words).

The 2001 WCAR culminated in the Durban Declaration which states:

> We acknowledge that slavery and the slave trade, including the transatlantic slave trade, *were* appalling tragedies in the history of humanity not only because of their abhorrent barbarism but also in terms of their magnitude, organized nature and especially their negation of the essence of the victims, and further acknowledge that slavery and the slave trade *are* a crime against humanity and should always have been so, especially the transatlantic slave trade, and are among the major sources and manifestations of racism, racial discrimination, xenophobia and related intolerance, and that Africans and people of African descent, Asians and people of Asian descent and indigenous peoples were victims of these acts and continue to be victims of their consequences.[46]

According to Hilary Beckles, representatives from the Caribbean nations did not endorse these declarations because of the inclusion of the word "should."[47] Beckles's reparations advocacy is especially notable for this study because it was playing out on the same multilateral policy stages as antitrafficking's transnational discourse. In his extensive recounting and analysis of the negotiations before and during the WCAR, Beckles notes that by including the word "should" Europeans and Americans dodged historical responsibility for the transatlantic slave trade and helped ensure they could not be held liable for crimes against humanity.[48] By including the phrase "and should always have been so," the declaration claims that since the transatlantic slave trade was legal in its time, it cannot be considered a crime against humanity for which reparation is due. Beckles's own body of research demonstrates that this line of reasoning does not "stan[d] up to historical, legal or moral scrutiny."[49] Under pressure from the West, African and Asian delegates endorsed the phrasing of the declaration, in part because of the accusation that African leaders helped enslave their own people, and in part because they were threatened with the specter of being prosecuted for modern-day slavery in international courts. According to Beckles, "tremendous pressure was brought to bear on some African and Asian states when the West and European Union argued that, were such or similar practices to occur today, they would undoubtedly be considered crimes against humanity and prosecuted under international law, and the victims entitled to reparations."[50]

Less than a year earlier, the UN had formalized the definition of trafficking through the Protocol to Prevent, Suppress and Punish Trafficking in Persons Especially Women and Children, which included in its definition of exploitation "slavery or practices similar to slavery."[51] The protocol was a part of the United Nations Convention against Transnational Organized Crime and encouraged member states to pass new laws that criminalized trafficking.[52] In the context of the protocol and its US companion, the 2000 Trafficking Victims Protection Act, the language of slavery, the international legal history of its abolition, and debates over its definition were recirculating. These coinciding discursive contexts helped make the "should" dodge possible. "Slavery and the slave trade *are* a crime against humanity"—those crimes had just been reaffirmed in international and US domestic law with the consolidation of trafficking and modern slavery language. "And *should* always have been so, especially the transatlantic slave trade"—although modern slavery exists and is illegal, its historical form was legal and, while regretful, not criminally sanctionable. Antitrafficking language adds to the temporal confusion of the Durban Declaration. In the passage, slavery and the slave trade simultaneously *were* appalling tragedies, *are* crimes against humanity, but *were not always* crimes against humanity. The rhetorical formations of slavery of the past and slavery of the present—a concept popularized through the fight for antitrafficking legislation at the turn of the twenty-first century—make it possible to merge past and present in politically opportunistic ways that allow former slaving nations to symbolically state regret without sacrificing indemnity.

The 2001 WCAR was a prominent and significant political convergence at the UN amid the surge of organizing for reparations that occurred in the United States and globally from the late 1980s through the early 2000s. Antitrafficking language, policy, and enforcement measures were developed, revised, and refined within this vibrant political context. These co-occurring and competing discourses—antitrafficking and reparations—offered state and nonstate actors two avenues for talking about the legacies of slavery as the new millennium began, yet they were underpinned by different political agendas. Reparations discourse used the history of transatlantic slavery to explain (and address) contemporary uneven accumulation of power and resources. Antitrafficking discourse invoked the history of slavery and abolition to justify the expansion of US global policing in ways that specifically skirted responsibility for redress amid demands for reparations.

The reparations revival in the United States was prompted in large part by the introduction of a bill for the United States to apologize and pay reparations to Japanese American survivors of American internment camps in 1987.[53] That same year, the organization National Coalition of Blacks for Reparations in America (N'COBRA) was founded. In 1989, US representative Bill Conyers introduced H.R. 40, a bill to form a commission to study reparation proposals for African Americans, which N'COBRA supported with lobbying efforts.[54] African Americans filed a lawsuit against the US government, *Cato v. United States*, for damages and an apology for the enslavement of African Americans and subsequent discrimination.[55] The US Ninth Circuit Court acknowledged that the *Cato* plaintiffs may be justified in seeking redress but dismissed the case in 1995.[56] Three months prior, though, Hillary Clinton endorsed antitrafficking initiatives by declaring, "it is a violation of human rights when women and girls are sold into the slavery of prostitution for human greed" at the UN's Fourth World Conference on Women in Beijing.[57] This conference in Beijing is often cited as the beginning of contemporary antitrafficking discourse; such US-led, human-rights-based origins sit uncomfortably next to the dismissal of redress for slavery in US courts only months apart.

Reparations organizing, legislation, and litigation strategies of this era were successful in several cases. Descendants and survivors of the Rosewood massacre won reparations from the Florida legislature in 1994.[58] Black farmers won a discrimination lawsuit against the US Department of Agriculture in 1999.[59] In 2000, lawyer Randall Robinson published his influential national bestseller, *The Debt: What America Owes to Blacks*, and helped organize the Reparations Coordinating Committee (RCC) with Charles Ogletree. That same year, the insurance company Aetna publicly apologized for insuring slaves after Deadria Farmer-Paellmann inquired about the practice.[60] In January 2001, conservative writer David Horowitz published the ad "Ten Reasons Why Reparations for Blacks is a Bad Idea for Blacks—And Racist, Too" in college newspapers, a strategy he thought would expose the liberal bias of college campuses. It had the reverse effect because it generated educational initiatives about racial

injustice and reparations across US college campuses through student organized protests, boycotts, sit-ins against Horowitz and teach-ins about the issue
of reparations.[61]

The pan-African transnational movement for reparations reignited with
the 1993 Abuja Summit, which called for using international law's crimes
against humanity framework to make reparations claims for all Africans and
those in the diaspora.[62] In 1999, the International Reparations and Repatriation Truth Commission Conference was organized by the Afrikan World Reparations and Repatriation Truth Commission, which resulted in the Accra Declaration, referenced in this chapter's opening vignette. The multiyear preparations
for the 2001 WCAR involved several regional reparations meetings, including
the Gorée Initiative that reiterated "the spirit of Abuja" by calling for "just
and fair reparation for the Slave Trade and enslavement of Africans."[63] In this
same period leading up to the WCAR, the United States refused to endorse the
provisional agenda in 2000 because it contained the word "compensatory" and
threatened to boycott the 2001 conference. According to activists at WCAR, the
United States "did everything they possibly could for two years to put pressure
on various governments—particularly African governments—not to discuss
the issue of reparations, not to discuss the issue of the transatlantic slave trade
being a crime against humanity. They put economic and political pressure on
these governments and overtly tried to keep the American people from even
knowing about the WCAR."[64] During this time, the United States also passed
the first Trafficking Victims Protection Act in the name of ending the "evil,"
"abhorrent," and "degrading institution of slavery" in 2000. Reparations and
antitrafficking discourse were both circulating through US and UN policy and
activism.

In March 2002, Deadria Farmer-Paellmann officially filed a federal lawsuit
against corporations who had profited from slavery and the slave trade.[65]
The RCC filed a lawsuit regarding the Tulsa massacre in February 2003, after the
Oklahoma legislature failed to implement the reparations recommended by
the Oklahoma Commission to Study the Tulsa Riot of 1921.[66] Representative
Conyers continued to reintroduce H.R. 40 each session and N'COBRA held the
Year of Black Presence lobbying initiative to support it.[67] The Millions for Reparations rally took place in Washington, DC, on August 17, 2002.[68] The rally
was held on Marcus Garvey's birthday, a symbolic connection to the history
and legacy of pan-Africanism and the decades-long demand and fight for reparations for slavery.[69] A WCAR follow-up conference dedicated to international
organizing for reparations was hosted in 2002 in Barbados and culminated in
the Bridgetown Protocol. The Reparations Working Group segment of that

report cites "white supremacy" as the number one barrier to successfully implementing it recommendations.[70] This brief overview of Black reparations strategies and initiatives of the 1990s and 2000s provides a sense of how far reaching and robust the public visibility and debates about reparations were in the era that coincides with the rise of antitrafficking initiatives.

Although Black reparations are regularly dismissed as impracticable, reading reparations discourse as critique sheds light on why former slaving nations respond to reparations organizing as a threat that needs to be neutralized. Encompassing much more than the recognition of harm done, demands for reparations critique capitalism's basis in the white accumulation of wealth through racialized dispossession. Reparations discourse names the centrality of racial chattel slavery, the transatlantic slave trade, and colonialism to the development of contemporary global capitalism and the uneven accumulation of wealth across the world. The system of white economic and political power in the United States developed through racial violence and justified that violence by producing legal and scientific discourses of racial difference. Demands for reparations forefront critiques of US and European history and liberal modes of racial governance; and some envision anticapitalist Black self-determination based in cooperative and autonomous institutions in its stead.[71] As such, the demand for reparations names the foundational raciality of global capitalism.

The demand for reparations is often framed by organizers and academics as the fight for the righteous and equitable redistribution of wealth to its proper owners: those who generated it. Reparations, in this framing, is not a handout or a gift, but a debt owed. By narrating reparations as a debt owed to African and African diasporic populations, the discourse reorients who constitutes debtor and creditor countries and populations.[72] This framing was particularly poignant in the 1990s which saw the impacts of unfair International Monetary Fund lending practices in the global South, widespread structural adjustment programs, international aid programs, and the aggressive gutting of the American welfare system. All those systems position vulnerable populations as incurring debts, dependent on outside assistance, and owing the global North for its generosity. Flipping the script on who owes who "exposes the history of white privilege and helps us all understand how wealth and poverty are made under capitalism—particularly a capitalism shaped immeasurably by slavery and racism."[73]

Reparations movements confronted and disrupted the discourse of globalization emergent in the 1990s that sought to usher neoliberal racial capitalism into the twenty-first century with moral legitimacy.[74] By neoliberal racial capitalism, I mean the ways that capitalism continues to work through racism—"racism enshrines the inequality that capitalism requires"—under neoliberal governance where the emphasis on individual freedom unburdened by government subsidies and market regulations prioritizes multinational corporations' ability to accumulate more capital while blaming global poverty and exploitation on poor decision-making by racialized individuals or corrupt hoarding by racialized governments in the global South.[75] The global reparations movement was threatening to former slaving nations because it was a social movement built in and through global solidarity that offered anticapitalist and anti-imperialist solutions to problems that corporate globalization was intensifying. For instance, using the reparations movement framework to think about worker exploitation and unsafe migration focused attention on how history and racism operate within the material circumstances of migrants and workers forced to make tough choices under unequal constraints. The Durban Declaration and Programme of Action that resulted from the 2001 WCAR states, "We recognize that interregional and intraregional migration has increased as a result of globalization, in particular from the South to the North, and stress that policies towards migration should not be based on racism, racial discrimination, xenophobia and related intolerance."[76] The declaration notes that the benefits and costs of globalization are "unevenly distributed" and suggests a strategy for rectifying such injustices: "Only through broad and sustained efforts to create a shared future based upon our common humanity, and all its diversity, can globalization be made fully inclusive and equitable."[77] The structural, redistributive approach of reparations advocacy addresses root causes of exploitation by turning over the profits and control gained from the unjust enrichment of slavery and colonialism—which continue to accrue through economic domination of the uneven political geographies they set in motion—in order to support Black self-determination in the present and future. The reparations approach names the centrality of white supremacy and race to global inequality, and more recently has begun to connect decolonization and reparations as joint projects.[78] If, according to Robin Kelley, reparations is "part of a broad strategy to radically transform society—redistributing wealth, creating a democratic and caring public culture, exposing the ways capitalism and slavery produced massive inequality," and if reparations movements of the late 1990s held "enormous promise for revitalizing movements for social justice," then we know why reparations is so threatening to US governance at home and abroad.[79]

We might, then, also know why a corporate and carceral agenda to fight a discursively non-race-specific modern slavery gained so much momentum within transnational governance discourse at the turn of the twenty-first century. Transnational feminist scholarship has carefully documented the rise of antitrafficking discourse and advocacy within the depoliticization and carceralization of women's rights, workers' rights, and immigration justice campaigns.[80] Thinking about antitrafficking's rise within the context of reparations history extends our understanding of the political work that antitrafficking accomplishes for states by revealing how a global racial justice campaign that indicted US global power is rhetorically remedied by the introduction of a new slavery that posits the United States' humanitarian history as the solution for overcoming Africa's enslaving past and present. While it is important to note that I am not suggesting that antitrafficking *caused* reparations campaigns to fail, antitrafficking discourse did offer a rhetorical fix for the state. It became a convenient way to talk about slavery and its legacies and about abolition, while promoting a political agenda that advanced US state and corporate power, in the same transnational political spheres where reparations for slavery was being hotly debated. Antitrafficking's modern slavery stands in direct rhetorical contradistinction to reparations for slavery.

The fervor with which antitrafficking's imagery, language, and constructions are taken up by a wide spectrum of political actors stands in stark contrast to the public controversy reparations talk has historically provoked. This dynamic is evident in law and policy. When the Trafficking Victims Protection Act was reauthorized in 2003, it gave trafficking victims the right to sue for reparations. In the midst of several pending lawsuits for reparations for slavery in the United States, the right to civil remedy for modern slavery victims was added to the Chapter 77 criminal code covering "peonage and slavery." That code derived from statutes penalizing reenslavement and involuntary servitude in the aftermath of nineteenth-century emancipation. Prior to 2003, there was no civil remedy clause for victims of slavery and peonage, which means that the majority-Black victims of those crimes, stretching back to the nineteenth century, had no specific legal recourse to sue their perpetrators. This is notable because Black reparations legal scholars, theorists, and activists in the United States have repeatedly sought to connect reparations claims to post-Emancipation racial violence and injustice and have used creative argumentation to demonstrate the "continuing violation of rights" into the present.[81]

When the legislature added the ability to sue, it was intended only for contemporary trafficking victims and it was specifically limited to the crimes added to the code through antitrafficking legislation in 2000, but it also did not include a statute of limitations.[82] A ten-year statute of limitations was later added in the 2008 TVPA Reauthorization. It is unclear whether this opened a potential legal loophole for Black reparations litigation in the period from 2003 to 2008. Yet, the assumptions embedded in this bait and switch expose the fallacy of antitrafficking's own logics of slavery. Antitrafficking repeatedly claims trafficking is "real slavery" and attempts to make the metaphor definitional by adding trafficking to the criminal codes governing enslavement. At the same time, antitrafficking acknowledges that the two injustices are fundamentally different because it presumes the worthiness of the trafficking victim alongside the unrecognizability of Black injury. Such assumptions reveal the naturalization of the idea that Black Americans do not deserve redress. Black injury becomes unrecognizable even within its own legal context of the criminal codes governing nineteenth-century reenslavement.

Adding the civil remedy for trafficking victims to the "peonage and slavery" chapter of the US code sits in stunning juxtaposition to the dismissal of reparations lawsuits in these same years. A lawsuit against corporations that profited from slavery and a lawsuit against the City of Tulsa for the 1921 massacre were both pending at the time of the antitrafficking civil remedy inclusion into the criminal code about slavery. Both lawsuits were dismissed before the ten-year statute of limitations was added to the civil remedy in 2008. Advocates of antitrafficking in the legislature and in the public bandy the phrase "modern-day slavery" to garner outrage and action for their cause, but the repercussions and responsibilities of actual histories of slavery only elicit denial, defensiveness, and dismissal. The confluence of antitrafficking's slavery talk and the dismissal of claims for reparations for slavery reiterates how antitrafficking is constituted by antiblackness. It is structural antiblackness that creates the situation where antitrafficking's modern-day slavery is magnified *and* remedied while Black American political claims based in the history and legacy of racial slavery are undermined.

White Slaves Never Asked for Reparations: White Nationalist
Memes and Antitrafficking Narratives, Then and Now

As part of the implementation of the 2001 UN Durban Declaration and the Programme of Action, the Working Group of Experts on People of African Descent conducted a January 2016 site visit in the United States to assess the "intolerance faced by people of African descent."[83] The extensive report documents the legal frameworks for protecting Black human rights and the specific types of racism and discrimination present in everyday American life, with particular attention to incarceration and police violence against African Americans. The report makes thirty-five recommendations for how the US government can better support the human rights of African Americans. The recommendations include: immediately halting the demolition of public housing, extending access to affordable health care, reinstating voting rights for people with felony charges, abolishing the death penalty, preventing excessive bail, and abolishing policing in schools. The report recommends passing H.R. 40 and implementing a program similar to CARICOM's Ten-Point Action Plan on Reparations. The report is definitive about the relationship between contemporary anti-Black racism and the transatlantic slave trade: "There is a profound need to acknowledge that the transatlantic trade in Africans, enslavement, colonization and colonialism were a crime against humanity and are among the major sources and manifestations of racism, racial discrimination, Afrophobia, xenophobia and related intolerance. Past injustices and crimes against African Americans need to be addressed with reparatory justice."[84] The UN report makes clear that reparations are justified and due to African Americans.

Mainstream press coverage of the report in the United States focused on, and dismissed, the reparations recommendations. An article in the *Washington Post* notes that the recommendations "are nonbinding and unlikely to influence Washington," and that initiatives such as an apology and health care initiatives "are nowhere in the cards."[85] Although antitrafficking organizations rarely engage with reparations campaigns or broader racial justice movement organizing,[86] the NGO Free the Slaves posted the 2016 *Washington Post* article to its Facebook page. It elicited numerous responses from digital followers who were dismissive of Black reparations.

Respondents tellingly reworked myths of white slavery to justify their defensiveness against Black reparations. In the Facebook comments, the claim to white slavery is positioned as a way to delegitimize claims for Black reparations. One commenter writes, "Descent from white slaves captured in Scotland, shackled below board and sold in New Jersey doesn't count because our ancestry isn't obvious." Another chimes in, "What about the Irish???" A third offers, "How much does Egypt owe me for being Jewish?"[87] The suggestion that reparations are owed specifically to Black people in the United States elicits white claims to unfairness: that white suffering is being unfairly underrecognized and that such underrecognition cannot exist alongside Black oppression; it must supersede it.

The claims about Irish slaves are also a white supremacist meme. In his research on the topic, Liam Hogan argues that although there are "innocent" uses of the Irish slave discourse that simply misunderstand or confuse the relationship among Irish nationalism, indentured servitude, rhetorical uses of slavery for political mobilization, and racial chattel slavery, since 2014, the figure of "Irish slaves" has grown in popularity and circulation by white nationalist groups and their supporters with the specific intent of undermining racial justice.[88]

In response to the Ferguson protests against antiblack police violence, white nationalists used Irish slavery to "mock African-American calls for reparations for slavery, stating 'my Irish ancestors were the first slaves in America, where are my reparations?'" and adding the hashtags #Ferguson and #NoExcuses to their Twitter posts.[89] By tracking the circulation of the meme amid the rise of the Black Lives Matter movement, Hogan uncovered that Google searches for the term "Irish slaves" hit an all-time high in September 2016, the same month that the UN report on reparations to Black Americans was covered by the US press.[90] The myth of white slaves is used as evidence that the idea of white privilege, even structural white supremacy, is unfounded. In this formation, if white people were slaves too but overcame their oppression without government support or reparations, Black people have no one to blame but themselves. Such logic reaffirms long-standing US political and scientific discourse and government initiatives based on the antiblack trope of the biological or cultural inferiority of Black Americans. These sentiments are widely shared nationally and internationally and are not the purview of white nationalists alone. The particular white nationalist logic of Irish slaves minimizes and overlooks many other historical truths, including the numerous government programs that have directly benefited white people but excluded Black people,[91] to say nothing of the system of rewards and wages that white privilege itself accrues its white possessors.[92]

WHITE SLAVERY AND ANTILYNCHING ADVOCACY IN THE PROGRESSIVE ERA

The utility, and centrality, of white slavery within antitrafficking discourse, though, stretches far beyond online white nationalist trolls looking for reparations conversations to muck up for lulz. The concept of "white slavery" was popularized by Progressive Era reformers at the turn of the twentieth century to recast white sex workers as sympathetic, helpless victims worthy of being saved.[93] Critical antitrafficking scholars have traced the roots of contemporary antitrafficking dynamics to the British and US white slave panics of the early 1900s, noting the similarities in how antitrafficking initiatives, both then and now, created moral panics around sex work and women's mobility, used morality to expand state control and policing of sex, staged melodramas of good versus evil, used policing and carceral initiatives in the name of protecting women, attached white slavery to immigration and increased racist xenophobic immigration policies, and used sensationalized media stories to garner support for the cause.[94] All of these themes and implications repeat within contemporary campaigns to end human trafficking. White slavery is also represented in the imagery of contemporary antitrafficking; a simple Google Images search for "human trafficking" returns scores of white hands bound in rope.

Scholars have noted how the white slavery discourse addressed a range of social anxieties present in the early 1900s. The influx of Chinese immigrants and Black Southern migrants into northern US cities had generated a "fear of erosion of racial boundaries."[95] Such fears, cast through the discourse of ending white slavery, prompted stricter border control, increased state surveillance, and expanded federal policing jurisdiction.[96] Urban racial mingling, public health concerns, class mobility, and shifting notions of sex and gender roles in public life stoked fears of the loss of American purity and morality. Although white American women figured prominently as the victims of sexually un-controllable Black and immigrant men within white slavery discourses, some reformers saw immigrant women as "especially vulnerable to exploitation."[97] Concerns about the safety and exploitation of Black women and girls, though, whether domestic workers, sex workers, or otherwise, were largely absent from the white slavery discourse.[98] Tellingly, Progressive Era white slavery narra-tives emerged in the midst of high-profile antilynching and Black women's vot-ing rights campaigns, led by Ida B. Wells-Barnett, to counter the devastating racial and sexual violence perpetuated by whites against Black Americans.[99]

In the period from 1892 to 1922, Wells-Barnett campaigned relentlessly for a federal antilynching law. Despite her many journalistic and state-level leg-islative wins for antilynching protections and awareness, federal antilynching law was not enacted.[100] In that same period, the fever pitch of public discourse about white slavery successfully resulted in the 1910 White Slave Traffic Act. Two years later, the White Slave Traffic Act was used to convict Jack Johnson, the first Black heavyweight boxing champion, of enslaving a white woman with whom he had a consensual relationship.[101] Johnson was seen by many whites as a direct threat to white superiority in his era. His physical success at beating "The Great White Hope" along with his marriages to white women are regu-larly noted by historians and commentators to have threatened and antago-nized white men in a moment rife with white anxieties about Black success, the loss of white control over Black populations, and the deep psychological white fear of Black revenge. Those white anxieties, Wells-Barnett repeatedly exposed, were also the underlying motivations for white lynching of Black men and women. Johnson, the son of parents born into slavery,[102] served jail time for being a convicted enslaver of white women; antilynching law, to help protect Black Americans from extrajudicial murder by white people, justified by the often false rape accusations of white women,[103] was not enacted by the federal government until 2022.

White slavery discourse, then, has consistently undermined organizing for racial justice by replacing the realities of racial violence, the legacies of slavery, and the systems of white supremacy that underpin it with urgent claims to end exploitation of white women. In the case of Samuel Paynter Wilson, a prominent promoter of ending white slavery in Chicago (and a writer at the same time as Wells-Barnett's influential journalism and advocacy in Chicago), white slavery urgently needed to be dealt with because "in the dives and dens of our city's underworld I have heard shrieks and heart cries and groans of agony and remorse that have never been surpassed at any public slave auction America has ever witnessed."[104] White slavery discourse defends the honor of white women by making their exploitation appear worse than racial chattel slavery. In both white slavery reforms and white justifications of lynching, white women must be protected from Black men, but Black women, whose sexual exploitation underpinned the slave system, who continued to face the threat of rape and lynching in the Progressive Era, and who faced increased criminalization under antivice laws,[105] were left unprotected from or by anyone but their own collective efforts and self-defense.[106] The urgency of Wilson's reform plea continues: "Things are being done every day in New York, Philadelphia, Chicago and other large cities of this country in the white slave traffic which would, by contrast, make the Congo slave traders of the old days appear like Good Samaritans."[107] By referencing the Congo, Wilson elicits the narrative that Africans are responsible for their own enslavement. Making white slavery worse than both US plantation slavery and slavery in Africa, white American responsibility is minimized in the context of Black political organizing to protect against slavery's persistent legacy of racial violence.

Wilson and Wells-Barnett, though, shared concern with the African American neighborhood on South State Street in Chicago. Wilson's antivice tract names it as the place where "painted vampires" lure boys into "sexual sin" and get them addicted to drugs.[108] In this example, the racial order of protection is reversed when the neighborhood is coded Black—Black sex working women become the enslavers of innocent young boys.[109] Meanwhile, also in 1910, Wells-Barnett's organization, the Negro Fellowship League, opened a community and housing space on South State Street to help support Black Southern migrants transitioning to Chicago life.[110] These two very different approaches to concerns about migration and mobility unfolded in real time in the same location, demonstrating that such issues can be addressed through racial justice frameworks and need not reproduce cultural myths about Black pathology. Discourses of "white slavery" and "modern slavery" have coincided with racial justice campaigns in both the Progressive Era and the era of corporate globalization.

Under Wells-Barnett's vision, antilynching advocacy sought to expose the anti-Black racism that justified lynching Black men accused of rape by white women alongside the racism and sexism that justified the lack of protection or concern with the sexual exploitation of Black women. She demonstrated that "the rape of black women and the lynching of black men are intricately linked" by connecting white lynch mob violence to the white fear of how Black freedom would impact legal and social white supremacy postslavery.[111] In the 1892 pamphlet *Southern Horrors: Lynch Law in All Its Phases*, Wells-Barnett quotes white Southerners' defenses of lynching that were printed in newspapers at the time. One editorial contends: "The generation of Negroes which have grown up since the war have lost in large measure the traditional and wholesome awe of the white race which kept the Negroes in subjection, even when their masters were in the army, and their families left unprotected except by the slaves themselves. There is no longer a restraint upon the brute passion of the Negro."[112] Through dominating and controlling African Americans in slavery, this Southern white commentator suggests, whites paternalistically civilized Black people by taming the natural instincts of a less evolved race. In this framing, the white example was so awe-inspiring that African Americans enslaved *themselves* by voluntarily remaining in subjection. The logic continues: the racial order has been upended by the North's imposition of Black freedom and therefore lynch law must be enacted to preserve nature's order, for everyone's benefit. The author of the editorial suggests that those concerned with the barbarism of lynching have gotten it confused; it is the Black man's "barbarism which prey upon weak and defenseless women."[113] Defenders of lynching in the South and white antivice reformers in the North both used the rhetoric of protecting "weak and defenseless" white women through lynch mobs or through antiprostitution police raids. For lynching's defenders, slavery was a protective and benign force that lynching restored; for champions of white slavery's abolition, "slavery of black women is abolished in America, but the slavery of white women continues."[114] The narrative justifications of explicit white supremacists and white social reformers' carceral protections to end trafficking once again converge.

By contrast, for Wells-Barnett, herself born into slavery in 1862, it was the history and legacy of the institution of slavery that gave white people extralegal impunity to kill free Black men in the name of saving white women while terrorizing, raping, lynching, demeaning, and otherwise exploiting Black women.[115] In Wells-Barnett's vision, it was winning and protecting voting rights—not antivice police rescue—that would help bring an end to the extreme brutality of lynching and Black women's exploitation. In the context of her multifaceted campaigns against lynching and for Black women's right to vote, the myths of slavery's paternalism and white slavery's horrors persistently rhetorically minimized the wide-ranging assaults of white supremacy on Black life.

REPARATIONS AND ANTITRAFFICKING ADVOCACY IN THE TWENTY-FIRST CENTURY

White slavery discourses have been used by antitrafficking reformers in the 1910s and white nationalists in the 2010s in ways that undermine Black-led campaigns for racial justice. Proponents of such uses and abuses of the history of slavery fit seamlessly into mainstream antitrafficking discourse—across liberal and conservative political orientations—which similarly diminishes racial chattel slavery and its legacies to magnify modern slavery. In both present and past discourse, "white" and "modern" conjunct slavery as oxymorons. The shock embedded in the rhetoric is that slavery cannot be extended to white people by definition and slavery cannot occur under modernity by definition. Both of these strategies figure new slaveries as scary because of old slaveries, not because racial chattel slavery needs to be understood and its legacies redressed, but because it needs to be contained to the past and to Black people.

Within contemporary antitrafficking discourse, slavery is simultaneously over as a racial problem, worse than it's ever been before, and as old as time.[116] Kevin Bales, the original cofounder of Free the Slaves, writes in *Disposable People* that although race-based social issues persisted in the United States after slavery, he sees these as "the vestiges of slavery, as problems that were tough but not intractable."[117] In contradistinction, "real slavery" is what he saw in the Congo. For Bales, within "new slavery race means little," except in Mauritania.[118] (Bales has since backed away from the idea of old versus new slavery, although it is still widely cited by antitrafficking advocates, and the racialized figures of Mauritania persist in Free the Slaves "Stop Racism and Slavery" programs). Bales continues to promote the idea that today's slavery is worse than old slavery because "more people are enslaved today than at any other time in history" and today's slaves are cheaper and more disposable than in 1850.[119] In a more recent line of inquiry, Bales researches how slavery in war-torn areas has existed since "the dawn of time."[120] Together, the ideas that slavery should no longer be associated with racial injustice, is worse than ever before, and has been around forever work to de-emphasize US and Western responsibility for racial chattel slavery and to diminish the urgent need for contemporary campaigns for racial justice, especially ones that trace contemporary anti-Black racism and Black disenfranchisement to slavery and its legacies.

These mainstream antitrafficking constructions and sentiments are echoed in the antireparations responses from the public at large on the Free the Slaves Facebook post about the UN Reparations Report. Three commenters invoke the idea that slavery is an ancient practice that no one group, nor its descendants, is responsible for. "How on earth are we supposed to move forward if we keep blaming people for what their ancestors did?" In this comment, reparations are seen as a punishment to the oppressor, rather than a responsibility, an opportunity, or an invitation to support Black futures. The future is positioned as needing to be protected from the infestation of the past by ignoring, rather than addressing, the past itself. A stern version of this argument followed in the comment, "I owe NOTHING!!! My grandparents didn't even get to this country until slavery was over!" Less concerned about the good of the future, this statement pins evil actions of slaveholders as individual cases of wrongdoing. Such a misunderstanding of the systems of racial slavery and white supremacy is not unlike the logic of the antitrafficking apparatus, where individual bad guys are the problem rather than structural inequity.[121] Another contributor offers, "All countries and even tribal communities have had slavery as an evil practice in their history. No one is exempt—how far back are we going to go in a lineage to tally up reparation." Here, all slave systems are made to be equivalent regardless of their vastly different shapes, practices, and structuring powers. Making everyone complicit in slavery makes no one exceptionally responsible. Such a comment might seem outlandish, but Condoleezza Rice's comments in 2001 put forth this same sentiment as the official US government stance on the WCAR. The trope is so widespread that it pops up in Facebook feeds and government policy discussions alike. Whether the commenters on the Free the Slaves post were trolls, bots, or earnest antitrafficking followers, the sentiments expressed in these public comments echo the talking points of the larger antitrafficking discourse.

Rather than recognizing reparations as a debt owed or a path to other futures possible, antitrafficking discourse authorizes the blatant diminishment of the history and legacy of racial slavery, while its supporters gleefully proclaim themselves to be "modern-day abolitionists." Antitrafficking discourse has given its everyday participants a noncomplicit subjectivity to conjure in the face of massive state violence against Black people and powerful new movements for racial justice and redress. The persistent defensiveness and controversy that reparations for slavery inspires in white people, especially white people drawing on the history of abolition to end modern-day slavery, speaks to just how unimaginable a Black humanity capable of being harmed, hurt, or wronged is to liberal humanism. Following Frank Wilderson, slavery stole "the very semantic field on which one can be imagined to be Human, which is why the price tag on reparations would not merely bankrupt the world economy but would obliterate a global frame of reference," that is, liberal governance and its transnational articulations.[122] Antitrafficking advocates promote ending "slavery in Africa" and "white slavery" in ways that memorialize white benevolence toward natural slaves, escape blame for the past, criminalize Black freedom, and legitimate liberal governance as fair and neutral—redistributive racial justice is written out of the script.

Conclusion: Other Futures Possible

Twenty-first-century campaigns to end human trafficking emerged within an era of widespread Black transnational organizing for reparations for slavery and racial injustice. Antitrafficking's key frames—slavery in Africa, white slavery, and modern-day slavery—are used by advocates to circumvent Western historical responsibility for slavery amid calls to hold former slaving nations to account. These discursive figures are not new; "slavery in Africa" and "white slavery" were also used in the Progressive Era to undermine Black African state sovereignty and antilynching campaigns for racial justice in the United States. Both have been used in the 2000s to dismiss Black claims for reparations, by the US State Department during the WCAR and by self-described white nationalists in the wake of Black Lives Matter protests. Antitrafficking's reliance on, and repurposing of, "slavery in Africa" and "white slave" panics demonstrates how the apparatus is built on and reproduces antiblack logics. Antitrafficking reintroduces these discursive formations within the political context of organizing for reparations, revealing how its specific terms do political work to contest or rhetorically supersede movements for Black freedom and Black futures.

Reparations organizing in the 1990s and early 2000s often framed its work as offering economic and political solutions for ending contemporary exploitation, including many of the same types of exploitative conditions with which antitrafficking advocacy is concerned. Instead of joining forces, antitrafficking advocacy found Black African enslavers to incarcerate and undocumented migrants to deport. By contrast, international reparations organizing offered an alternative vision for the future. In thinking about reparations in relation to other futures, my interest is not with racial reconciliation,[123] but in highlighting historical contingencies of justice—what reparations policy *could have meant* for present and future racial justice organizing as distinguished from what antitrafficking policy has yielded: humanitarian rhetorical cover for increased policing, criminalization, and border control.

If we follow Robin Kelley in thinking about the history of Black reparations movements as social movements, then, although they are often articulated as reconciling the past, demands for reparations come into view as movements, based in structural and historical critique of the causes of contemporary exploitation, that work for economic and racial justice in the present. Reparations organizing and initiatives in the liminal period of the turn of the twenty-first century sought resources to build community-governed sustainable institutions, to connect histories of slavery and colonialism to globalization's inequities, to redistribute resources in ways that could reconfigure uneven development, and to highlight the fundamentally racial character of modernity's accumulation of wealth. In the context of the dawn of the twenty-first century's power struggles over what globalization would look like and who it would work for, the global reparations movement offered a multilayered economic package that would use the history of exploitation to upend the continuities of exploitation moving forward. Reparations in these schemes did not rest on accounting for the past; it put the past to work for the future. Mechanisms like setting up thorough and multigenerational redistribution systems,[124] erasing national debts, and creating alternative paths to citizenship rights beyond the nation-state (such as through diasporic claims) aim to build more just futures by mediating some of the vast material and political power asymmetries that slavery and colonialism fostered and which continue to underlie new formations of exclusion and capital transfer.[125]

While this list suggests some of the varied ideas for logistically implementing redress, reparatory politics, following David Scott, remains rooted in the "demand *now* for what is *owed* for what was taken, morally and materially, symbolically and spiritually, a demand that includes the recognition that the *unforgivable* wrong of generations of enslavement has given rise to a permanent racial debt that, while it can *never* be finally discharged, has necessarily to be honored *before* any common future of freedom can begin."[126] Scott highlights here the irreparability of slavery, the impossibility of providing full restitution that would end the debt, while still demanding redress. Jovan Lewis elaborates further by suggesting that reparations must be taken, not given, and what is deemed reparative "would have to be decided by the people who have the right to make a reparative claim," not through government policies implemented or agreed to by former slaving nations.[127] Such framing helps shift reparations thinking away from important critiques of its reliance on liberal recognition (and congruence with neoliberal policy in some cases) and toward Black self-determination, which is to say, Black freedom on its own terms.[128]

Attending to how histories of slavery and colonialism have created uneven development, extracted material and human resources, skewed the distribution of resources globally, and reorganized and entrenched global centers of power helps us better understand the causes of unsafe migration and extreme labor exploitation. It keeps the history of slavery in the picture of human trafficking at the structural level, rather than at the aesthetic level of opportunistic rhetorical conflation or nineteenth-century abolitionist imagery. Thinking about antitrafficking within the historical context of pan-African reparations activism demonstrates how antitrafficking minimizes the formations that Black reparations discourse centers: race, antiblackness, white complicity, debt, white wrongdoing, racial justice, the past in the present, transnational Black liberation struggles, and the structures of white supremacy that extend from "then" to now.

Instead of naming a highly circumscribed version of exploitation "slavery" and using it to counterpose Black claims for redress, imagine if antitrafficking advocates had envisioned ending unsafe migration and global worker exploitation through reparations for slavery.[129] If that gesture feels laughable, naive, or unrealistic, then it lays bare, as a counterfactual, the political project of antitrafficking. The antitrafficking apparatus, of course, did not come to be to address the historical and structural causes of trafficking. Although the many commentaries about the ineffectiveness of antitrafficking are clarifying, the reality is that antitrafficking is incredibly effective at what it was designed to do: preserve the distribution of wealth and power that was architected through modernity's white supremacy ideologies and governance structures by inventing a new slavery that blames Africans for enslaving each other and popularizes a white subjectivity that is not to blame for injustice. Rather than working to bring about economic and racial justice and redistribution, the "trafficking is slavery" narrative disavows the structural effects of the history of transatlantic slavery in the present in order to rhetorically indemnify US and European states against claims for reparations for slavery.

2

Blaming Black Mothers

Across the antitrafficking mediascape, Black mothers are figured as the enslavers of their own children. This framing builds on antitrafficking's narrative that "Africans enslave each other" by specifically demonizing Black motherhood throughout the diaspora. Black mothers living in Ghana and Haiti, two important historic sites of Black freedom, are featured prominently. Within these depictions, the histories of transatlantic slavery and nineteenth- and twentieth-century Black political revolution are invoked and resignified as evidence of what Black freedom results in: the Black family's inevitable slip back to the premodern state of self-enslavement in the absence of white involvement.

To free Black children from the enslaving choices of their mothers, the antitrafficking apparatus offers mothering pedagogy sessions and family planning interventions in places laden with heavy symbolic meaning for Black freedom struggles. Population control policies, architected through culture of poverty discourses and the pathologization of Black motherhood in the United States, have long circulated transnationally through US imperialism in the Caribbean and other international development projects.[1] Haiti, one of the most important sites of both Black self-emancipation and Enlightenment history, is depicted as needing to be liberated by white outsiders from its *un*enlightened cultural practices and family structures.[2] Ghana, resting as a symbolic, if complicated, site of homecoming for many Black Americans and as an international symbol of postcolonial Black self-determination through Kwame Nkrumah's 1957 inauguration, becomes a symbol of poor, suffering, ungovernable Africa within antitrafficking's narratives.[3] In so doing, the antitrafficking apparatus repurposes two of the most important sites and affective registers of Black self-emancipation and white fear in the American imagination into sites of failures of Black self-governance caused by the improprieties of the Black pathological family.

Within this chapter, I focus on how antitrafficking's white redemptionist project plays out through the imagery and narrative structure of blaming Black mothers in highly significant sites of Black freedom. The figure of the pathological Black mother, built through centuries of racist policy and discourse in the United States, is activated within the antitrafficking apparatus as the rightful locus of blame for global inequities. Blaming Black mothers reinforces the inculpability of white people for racial injustice in the past and present within antitrafficking discourse. To challenge these harmful discursive reproductions, I analyze several of the scenes found in the antitrafficking visual archive of Black mothers to suggest that those capturing the antitrafficking photos and those viewing the photos are assumed to be seeing through the politically expedient frame of unfit Black mothering. Meanwhile, if we "listen to the images," motherly care and refusal of the global humanitarian gaze is immanently captured.[4] Racialization as a way of seeing, and of seeing slavery specifically, constitutes the antitrafficking image economy. Which raises the question: Is it possible for the antitrafficking apparatus to see a poor Black mother's love?

Ghana

A news article in the *Guardian* about child labor in Ghanaian fishing villages reads: "'My Kids Hate Me . . . I Sold Them': Slavery and Child Labour in Ghana— in Pictures."[5] The headline, seen in figure 2.1, is taken from a Ghanaian mother's story that was featured in the photo essay. For several weeks in 2016, the article ran as the main feature on the landing page of the *Guardian*'s "Modern-Day

Slavery in Focus" news platform about human trafficking, which is sponsored by the antitrafficking foundation Humanity United. The article, its images, and its facts, were created by Ubelong, a voluntourism organization that provides international volunteer opportunities in Africa, Asia, Latin America, and Europe for individuals, high school students, and corporate groups from the United States. The organization's motto at the time of the article was "UBELONG is about YOU. You can change the world. We help you get there."[6] The images and the stories in the article are mediated through many layers of the antitrafficking apparatus.

The article features images and stories of several mothers who describe how they made tough choices under challenging conditions to educate and provide for their children, including sending some away to work in order to contribute to the family income. Several photographs depict a lively fishing community engaged in everyday activities and mothers with their children in their homes. One image, seen in figure 2.2, features adolescent boys smiling and playing on the fishing equipment on the beach. Despite the scene of playfulness, the caption sees only misery. It relates the story of a worker "whose family forced him to drop out of school at the age of 14." The legal working age in Ghana is fifteen, but that information is withheld. Such editorial choices demonstrate

Modern-day slavery in focus

'My kids hate me ... I sold them': slavery and child labour in Ghana – in pictures

▲ Children working on a boat on the shore of the fishing village of Nyanyano, Ghana. Photograph: Monica Gumm/Ubelong

FIGURE 2.1 A photograph of daily life in a fishing village in Ghana is used to illustrate the headline's claims about slavery. Source: Screenshot of headline from the *Guardian*'s "Modern-Day Slavery in Focus" column, September 30, 2016. Photograph by Monica Gumm/Ubelong.

the racialized ways of seeing that are produced through the antitrafficking apparatus. Another caption describes a woman, "a mother of seven, [who] is a fishmonger who chose to send her first child to work as a fisherman to provide for the rest of the family. 'We told our eldest son that he is the only one who can assist his father at the boat. He was only 16 but we tried to convince him that he is no longer a child. It's a huge sacrifice and a lot of pressure for him not to disappoint his siblings, but three of my younger children have now completed junior high school.'" Far from "selling" her child, in this example, a mother's teenage son begins working with his father on their family boat once he reaches legal working age, and the additional income allows other children to attend school.

In closely reading the stories, one sees interviewees incisively describe and analyze the complicated circuits that they are caught within: poverty, the need for more familial income, lack of ability to pay school fees, negotiating to have the eldest child work so that the other children can go to school, the recognition that schooling won't pay the bills but that apprenticeship and job training in the fishing industry will, seeing apprenticeship as an investment in a child's future, the stated need for international organizations to bear the burden of funds if children are demanded to go to school instead of to work, and an

Kobina Amoasi, left, with two of his younger brothers at the shore of Nyanyano, a fishing village. Amoasi, 21, is a fisherman whose family forced him to drop out of school at the age of 14. 'I don't like fishing because it is very dangerous. I wanted to be a tailor, but now I am a fisherman. I don't have any idea how or when I can stop. I feel trapped in this life that I have not chosen'

Photograph: Monica Gumm/Ubelong

FIGURE 2.2 Brothers in a fishing village in Ghana play on fishing boats. Despite the scene of fun, the image caption characterizes the brothers' lives as miserable. Source: Screenshot of the *Guardian*'s "Modern-Day Slavery in Focus" column, September 30, 2016. Photograph by Monica Gumm/Ubelong.

implicit critique of such global humanitarian demands. In other words, the participants supply a thoughtful and nuanced analysis of how they are negotiating a complex set of demands on their resources. Yet, rather than thematize these very important textures to better understand why and how children work in subsistence fishing villages in Ghana, or to derive solutions that better solve the economic (rather than cultural) problems that are articulated, one town's struggles and survivals under structural exclusions are reduced to the harmful frame of slavery, deployed as an indictment against Black mothers.[7] Critical antitrafficking scholar Sam Okyere and Ghanaian politician Betty Mensah have critiqued news stories of child fishing slaves because they "reflect a limited understanding of the lived realities" and are "mostly made by Western-based or funded journalists and NGOs with the help of local affiliates" who use the language of slavery to sensationalize uncorroborated claims.[8]

The *Guardian*'s article is notable for how seamlessly the language of slavery adheres to the rhetorical figure of the bad Black mother. The chosen headline uses an interviewee's words as evidence that Black Africans enslave their kin. By emphasizing intrafamilial turmoil and the word "sold," child labor in Ghana is moralized and reduced to an issue that can be solved with education about how to be a better mother. Emphasizing the language of slavery is particularly egregious since most of the interviewees in the article actually refer to "sending"—not selling—children to work. Such a depiction repeats the antiblack tropes that underpin antitrafficking: visual evidence of African self-enslavement, the Black family's unfitness for freedom, and backward African cultural traditions. The word slavery is added into the news version of the story, and that news is featured on a platform funded by an antitrafficking foundation, which elevates the political project of antitrafficking's frames and figures to the level of neutral news content. If it is tempting to dismiss such news headlines as click bait, it still raises the question: what makes it so easy to accept that Ghanaian mothers would sell their children?

Ubelong's photo essay was developed by volunteers who were placed at its field project in Ghana, which focuses on supporting efforts to stop child labor. According to Ubelong's application materials, volunteers assigned to this project work in the offices of a local human rights NGO that is focused on getting children in fishing villages back to school. One of the local partners is the Cheerful Hearts Foundation, a local Ghanaian-led organization that uses international volunteers to interview children and "individuals who have forced children into child labour" about their experiences, to conduct research to attract new investment in the project, and to tutor rescued children.[9] According to research conducted by Cheerful Hearts, the main factors contributing to child trafficking are "limited knowledge on the long-term importance of education, little knowledge on children's rights, lack of alternative livelihood, teenage pregnancy (early motherhood), weak law enforcement and poverty." In one of the organization's collaborations that was funded by the Danish Youth Council, volunteers went house to house to educate community members about the need to send children to school and to use contraceptives and abstinence to reduce "children being traffic[ked] by young mothers due to poverty."[10] According to a report by the organization, during a community event to celebrate the project, the executive director encouraged "parents especially mothers to overlook 'poverty' and see education as an investment into their children who are going to be the future leaders of the community, the nation and hence a big asset to their families."

At the end of the event, a mother reportedly asked the Ghanaian government officials and NGO guests that had spoken at the event: "I am a mother with 4 children, I have the love to send my kids to school but due to poverty I am sending to 2 of them to school while 2 are sold to traffickers to work and help me support the education of the other 2 in school. Is this child trafficking or a bad act?"[11] The report was written by the executive director of Cheerful Hearts himself, and as such, must be read with an attention to the various audiences it might be for, including potential international volunteers, foreign humanitarian investors, and funders of the antitrafficking apparatus who have created the terms and solutions of the apparatus. Still, the emphasis on blaming rural African mothers and figuring education and birth control as the solution speaks to the easy demonization of Black motherhood and the history of developing policies of social control to regulate Black women's reproduction in response. In the mother's question reported above, it is possible to read against her implied naivete (the implied viewer for this report might have his worldviews confirmed by learning that supposedly these mothers don't know that selling their own kids is bad) to see a clear articulation of love in the midst of duress and a clear analysis of the cause of such vexed choices: not poor mothering but poor economic realities. These stories, even though circumscribed through layers of global aid economies, humanitarianism, and journalism, portray anything but naivete. They evince negotiation, love, and mothering for Black futures against all odds. Why is such mothering not seeable by antitrafficking's publics?

In *Revolutionary Mothering*, Malkia A. Cyril suggests why Black mothers are such an important locus of blame in US political discourse: "mothers are a key vehicle for social change and critical to the fight for democratic rights.

Perhaps this is why the conservative Right has so viciously and aggressively targeted their communications at mothers and motherhood within communities of color, poor communities, and young communities. Without the voices and visions of mothers, and their leadership at multiple levels, 21st-century progressive movements cannot win."[12] Mothers of color, in other words, are understood as posing a direct threat to white supremacy. White violence against Black self-determination has produced a whole set of myths and narratives that figure Black women as the problem that must be overcome, subdued, or controlled in order to advance racial and societal progress. Within antitrafficking discourse, such barriers to progress are visualized and narrated as the global Black mother, who, directly or indirectly, is responsible for the modern enslavement of children.

In the 2010 Free the Slaves video about Ghanaian children working in the fishing industry, viewers encounter a scene in a village where a Ghanaian child rescuer negotiates with the village elders to release a boy. An agitated Ghanaian woman, whose words are not translated, is referred to by the film's white female narrator as "the slaveholder." The representation suggests to the viewer that African children are enslaved because of outdated rural African practices; the family, and notably a Black woman, is demonized as the sole, cruel culprit of the problem. Such a depiction uses evidence of African self-enslavement to pathologize Black women as, quite literally, the progenitor of the problem. The scene is presented as a self-contained community, inured and isolated from the market forces and power asymmetries in the world around it. In such a rendering, the free market forces of capitalism and the freedom loving forces of liberalism *would* save Black children from their Black women enslavers if only it could reach them.

In the Free the Slaves video, the Ghanaian child rescuer convinces the Black woman to turn over the child. The rescuer is James Kofi Annan, director of the Ghanaian nonprofit Challenging Heights, a local partner organization to Free the Slaves and a collaborator with Cheerful Hearts Foundation. Annan has become a well-known antitrafficking crusader who has helped the antitrafficking apparatus make its narratives of freeing child slaves and blaming mothers appear more authentic. Annan, who is often described in media profiles as working on fishing boats as a child before escaping and eventually becoming a Barclays Bank manager in Ghana, has received numerous awards for his antitrafficking rescue missions, including the Free the Slaves 2008 Frederick Douglass Freedom Award and the 2013 Swedish World's Children's Prize. His profile for the World's Children's Prize reads, "Child slavery is very common in

Ghana. Children are sold by their parents or relatives. Often by single mothers with many children, who can't afford food for everyone."[13] Here, the single mother is especially villainized for her irresponsible reproduction.

After the child leaves with Annan in the video, he is pictured on a speed-boat, traveling to other places, with upbeat music playing. In other words, the child is free. The intended messages of the video are: Freedom is being in the world. Slavery is being in the isolated African village. Slavery is an antiquated practice that has no relevance to a global economy. Unfree laboring conditions are produced by African cultural practices, not by neoliberal policies that exacerbate historically produced precarity globally.

This stunning rhetorical reversal of the history of racial capitalism repurposes antiblack tropes of bad Black women to insulate capitalism from critique. It depicts capitalism as the hero—the freedom *grantor*—rather than as the historical system of enslaving Black children. Such antitrafficking narratives obscure the actually existing history of slavery and its intimate relationship to discourses that blame Black mothers in order to uphold white supremacy. It was, after all, not Black women who enslaved their kids, but the seventeenth-century white British colonial law of *partus sequitur ventrem* that made children born to Black enslaved mothers legally enslaved. Black women's manual labor and reproductive labor ("labor and laboring" in Jennifer Morgan's terms) fueled the white accumulation of wealth by dispossessing enslaved Black people of labor, autonomy, wages, and kin. It allowed white slaveowners and their heirs to produce and inherit future laborers *for free*, despite antitrafficking's present-day claims that slaves are cheaper today than in the nineteenth century. Such a system preserved white property interests, it racialized social control, and it secured the social hierarchy of race in the New World.[14]

Even while not being legally allowed to protect their children's freedom or safety, Black enslaved women were blamed, and punished, for being unfit mothers, "devious reproducers,"[15] or otherwise unruly. For instance, Black enslaved women were blamed for getting pregnant to get out of work and for not getting pregnant to intentionally undermine the slave owner's profits.[16] Black enslaved mothers were blamed by white physicians for the poor nutrition of their babies or were accused of forcing their children to eat dirt.[17] Black enslaved women were blamed for being raped because "they were naturally lascivious."[18] Black enslaved women were blamed by white women for their husbands' "unfaithfulness" when Black women were raped by white slave owners.[19] Black enslaved mothers who ran away were blamed by white slave owners for "inhumanely" abandoning their children in fugitive slave ads.[20] Enslaved Black women experienced extreme structural and interpersonal violence on the plantation and were told they only had themselves to blame for it. Antitrafficking discourse inverts these histories by representing Black women as the present-day enslavers, and thereby distancing slavery from white ownership, while simultaneously drawing on and propagating the historical narratives that blame Black women for the structural inequities that Black children face. The antitrafficking media figure of the Black African mother who enslaves children is believable to antitrafficking's publics because the bad Black mother is a constitutive feature of American political discourse.

During Black History Month in 2019, the antitrafficking philanthropic journalism site CNN "Freedom Project" released an investigation into the fishing industry in Ghana. The investigation, "Child Slaves Risk Their Lives on Ghana's Lake Volta," begins by stating the children are "sold by their parents."[21] As depicted in figures 2.3 and 2.4, a striking photograph of adolescent boys marching in a single file line firmly positions the scene as a site of slavery by visually recalling nineteenth-century drawings of slave coffles (figure 2.4). Perhaps the most widely circulated of these nineteenth-century images was the European missionary David Livingstone's scene of African guards marching African slaves to be sold in the East African trade, after the British had abolished the trade.[22] The Ghanaian boys' brightly colored clothing indicates the present-day continuity of the slave trade within Africa. Reading against the grain, though, the image also indicates the continuity of using the trope of "slavery in Africa" to uphold a white subjectivity of benevolence.

The 2019 investigation follows the narrative structure of the Free the Slaves 2010 video about Ghana fishing, which repeats across the antitrafficking mediascape. Young boys disappear under murky water to untie fishing nets, a local Black male NGO worker leads the rescue, local people are confronted about their practices or negotiated with to release the children, children are freed to orphanages funded by global philanthropists (who make their money through capitalist exploitation of workers), the rescued children are depicted on a fast-moving boat headed away from the village and toward the future. The Ghanaian NGO featured in the CNN investigation is PACODEP (Parners in Community Development Programme), which runs an "aftercare shelter," and collaborates with both Free the Slaves and Challenging Heights on the Growing Up Free project, which has also been supported by the US State Department.[23]

The CNN investigation asserts that the children need to be freed because they are "sold by their desperately poor parents to human traffickers, sometimes for as little as $250." The film does not address what has caused the parents to have so little income, but does emphasize the parents' lack of care: "Achibra says, in their experience, it's nearly impossible to reunite the children with their

FIGURE 2.3 Boys in Ghana walk in a line. The photograph recalls the imagery of nineteenth-century slave coffles. Source: CNN, "Child Slaves Risk Their Lives on Ghana's Lake Volta," 2019. Photograph by Michal Przedlacki.

FIGURE 2.4 Livingstone's drawing of captives being marched to the East African slave trade, published in 1865. Source: "Gang of Captives Met at Mbame's on Their Way to Tette," *Slavery Images: A Visual Record of the African Slave Trade and Slave Life in the Early African Diaspora*.

families, because the parents are the ones who sold them in the first place. Extreme poverty often forced parents into a ghastly choice: whether to sell one child to traffickers, to provide money for their other children to eat. 'We've realized that when we rescue these children and give them back to their family, they don't really take care of them, but end up re-trafficking them,' he says." The economic reality of needing children to contribute to family income is ultimately rendered as the result of uncaring parents, who are construed as having not learned their lesson even after they have been saved by NGOs. The NGO and the orphanage it funds are rendered as better parents to the children than their actually existing parents. The children are taken away from their families, often in collaboration with local police, and sent to live in orphanages that operate outside the bounds of their parents' prearranged networks. Critical antitrafficking scholar Sam Okyere and collaborators recently interviewed families directly impacted by this style of NGO rescue; one father described being violently arrested while his children were taken from him off his fishing boat in the name of rescuing them from slavery. The father was eventually released with no charge.[24]

In a telling visual reverberation of the problems with such NGO rescues, one young boy depicted in the CNN story looks distraught while he sits on the lap of a white woman during the boat ride to the orphanage. When another rescued boy reaches out to playfully tease or comfort him, the white woman pulls the boy close to give him a hug. The boy recoils uncomfortably from her, asserting his bodily autonomy, and she mimes to him that she is trying to care for him. The white woman is Dominika Kulczyk, the Polish billionaire who is the president of the Kulczyk Foundation that funds the organization PACODEP that is being promoted in the CNN coverage. Below the visual scene, the text describes the rescued boys' situation: "It may not be the last time these two boys board a boat on Lake Volta, but it's the first time they've done so in freedom." The story tells its reader: the boys have been freed from work and freed from the family structures that would sell them into slavery. The palpable discomfort and unease of the boy sitting on a stranger's lap is not worried over by the editor, perhaps not even noticed by the reader amid the sea of Black pain. White women's philanthropic laps are assumed to be the gentle caring balm that undoes the Black mothering that is assumed to be harsh, overly practical, and unloving.[25]

Despite the imagery and narrative structure of fishing in Ghana stories that suggest the forever nature of slavery within Africa, the CNN interactive feature states that slavery in Ghana's fishing industry is a relatively new problem. "While slavery may be as old as recorded history, the problem of children being used in the fishing industry of Lake Volta is not. The lake was only created in 1965." Slavery within Africa narratives collide with resignification of Black freedom histories: the article asserts it is not until postcolonial independence that Ghana begins enslaving its own children. Antitrafficking's frequent assertion that slavery is as old as time works to rhetorically de-exceptionalize any one system of slavery (and thus any one group of enslavers); making slavery new to Ghana in this rendition, though, makes Ghanaians appear to be unmistakably to blame. Even histories of colonial rule and the structures that they set in motion are rendered blameless. In CNN's telling, it is only after independence from the British that child enslavement comes to be.

Lake Volta, where child slavery is said to be rampant, was created by the Volta River Project, which was a signature project of Kwame Nkrumah's plan for Ghana's postcolonial economic independence in the 1960s.[26] In order to build the project, the newly independent nation needed foreign investment and was coerced into agreeing to an unfair and exploitative economic arrangement to receive it. Jemima Pierre has called this agreement "the clearest example yet of how the complex mix of options available to the newly independent state . . . inevitably led to an intractable neocolonial predicament."[27] An economic development and independence project was undermined by US corporate influence that jury-rigged the contract to enrich itself in the 1960s, and the lake that was created from damming the river is now rendered a site of child slavery in Ghana, where Black mothers need white volunteers to teach them how to keep their kids free. The damming of the river also displaced thousands of farmers in the region.[28] This point is not noted in the antitrafficking coverage, even though the antitrafficking organization featured in CNN's interactive claims to train fishermen to be farmers in order to reduce child trafficking. CNN's story is underpinned by longstanding antiblack logics; it reinforces nineteenth-century social scientific thought that Black freedom leads to Black ruin, and that without white intervention, Black people are prone to enslaving their kin.

The narrative that Ghana's child slavery begins after decolonization becomes a rhetorical resource that opportunistically papers over President Nkrumah's powerful address to the Organization of African Unity in 1963. Nkrumah named the relationship between the past of colonialism in Africa and the economic status of African nations in independence: "On this continent it has not taken long to discover that the struggle against colonialism does not end with the attainment of national independence. Independence is only the prelude to a new and more involved struggle for the right to conduct our own economic and social affairs; to construct our society according to our aspirations, unhampered by crushing and humiliating neo-colonialist controls and interference."[29] Colonial structures subtend the uneven distribution of economic power and postcolonial economic arrangements, which have, in Nkrumah's figuration, neocolonial effects that limit the self-determination of sovereign African states. The disproportionate economic power that former slaving and colonizing states maintain postemancipation and postindependence—an economic advantage that they gained by dispossessing Africa and the Caribbean of its resources—is too easily invisibilized through the naturalization of white supremacy's logics. In the aftermath of colonization, Ghana's problems become Ghana's fault in media and policy narratives; Ghana's problems in freedom appear to evince Black inability to self-govern and Black incapacity for freedom. In other words, such narratives make it appear that white supremacy is, indeed, natural. Antitrafficking discourse in the present contributes to this naturalization of white supremacy's logics. Antitrafficking discourse actively minimizes the role of the history of the transatlantic slave trade in shaping modernity. Antitrafficking discourse actively blames Black mothers for structural inequalities. Antitrafficking discourse repeatedly resignifies important sites of Black independence as sites where Black mothers *cause* Black unfreedom. Across advocacy and news representations of fishing in Ghana, slavery within Africa is either a timeless problem of cultural isolation and backwardness or a brand-new problem that begins under Black rule. In either temporality, white enslavers and European colonists are free of blame, and privileged global capitalists are rescuers who escape scrutiny. Choosing to demonize Black mothers in highly symbolic places of Black freedom manifests, once again, white common sense about Black freedom: today's modern-day slaves have no one to blame but their Black mothers.

Blaming Black Mothers in Political Discourse

Blaming Black women has done a tremendous amount of political work to support the governance imperatives of states that are structured by white supremacy. This is at least part of what Hortense Spillers means when she writes, "My country needs me, and if I were not here, I would have to be invented."[30] The figures of the bad, undeserving, unfit, unloving, immoral, devious, culturally impoverished, incompetent, and race-genocidal Black mother are useful political tools. The histories, structures, and conditions that create social inequities are obscured by shifting the blame onto Black mothers themselves. The political usefulness of this rhetorical trick has inhered across decades of US history since Emancipation and through a variety of political environments. To contextualize antitrafficking's use of the imagery, I briefly summarize how at various discursive and political turns—post-Emancipation statistics on Black fitness for freedom, Black domestic migration and Progressive Era reforms, the Moynihan Report, post–civil rights backlash, the figure of the welfare queen and the affirmative action Black lady, and the Ghanaian mother who sells her child to a trafficker—Black mothers have been blamed for their own oppression. The trope of the bad Black mother, constructed through US racial logics and histories, travels transnationally through US foreign policy, of which antitrafficking policy and programs have been an enduring feature across every administration, regardless of political orientation, since 2000. It also travels through the larger global aid economy, which US billionaires and NGOs play an outsized role in shaping. Antitrafficking campaigns seamlessly adopt these taken-for-granted ideas about poor Black women to fundraise and gain popular public interest in their cause. The demonized Black mother—discursively naturalized as the root cause of Black inferiority—is now named within the antitrafficking apparatus as one of the root causes of modern-day slavery.

The figure of bad Black mothers has been created through centuries of US policy, media narratives, and scientific thought. In the aftermath of formal Emancipation in the United States, a burgeoning nineteenth-century race science turned its attention to proving that Black inferiority was a naturally inherited racial trait. The biological inferiority of Black people had long been asserted and assumed by white scientists and slaveholders as a convenient justification for Black enslavement. In the build-up to the American Civil War, proslavery advocates claimed that the natural state of Black people was enslavement. In order to assuage the massive white anxiety that four million free Black people presented to the racial ordering of society, scientists set out to prove that the formerly enslaved would die out in freedom because they were an inferior race who had been protected by slavery. Writing about this period, Khalil G. Muhammad comments, "Now in freedom, many of the experts reasoned, blacks would have to rise or fall on their own virtues or vices, no longer benefiting from slavery," which a leading white Harvard scientist, Nathaniel Shaler, claimed was "the mildest and most decent system of slavery that ever existed."[31] The notion that American slavery was mild and decent is directly counterposed to the prevalent idea that Africans brutally enslaved their own on the continent. Contemporaneous liberal philosophical theorists had asserted that Africans were "still" in a state of nature compared to civilized societies. A proslavery pamphlet declared, "The doom that has made the African in all ages and countries, a slave—is the natural consequence of the inferiority of his character."[32] Haiti was also used as evidence of Black unfitness for freedom.

In his 1884 article entitled "The Negro Problem," Shaler wrote, "Every experiment of freeing blacks on this continent has in the end resulted in even worse conditions than slavery brought them," claiming that Haiti had once been a great industrial and cultural society that has since the revolution descended into "a corrupt government and a failed economy."[33] Never mind that Haiti freed itself, Shaler codified in academic research the widely held slavery apologist narrative that Haiti was *the* "proof that black people were incapable of freedom and self-government."[34]

The massive inequalities faced by the formerly enslaved in the United States were explained as a result of their own inherent weaknesses.[35] Black reproduction in freedom was seen as a threat to white civilization and thus needed to be controlled. Whereas Black enslaved women were commodified for their potential "future increase," now it was white society's duty to save civilization from Black survival.[36] Fields like demography and actuarial science employed census data, statistics, and moratory reports to prove what white scientists already assumed to be true: Black people were inferior to white people, they needed to be controlled for their own good, and they would naturally die out in freedom. This is what Khalil G. Muhammad has called "the standard repackaging of proslavery beliefs for a postbellum audience."[37] Sylvia Wynter has described it as the value division that orders society through recourse to extrahuman justifications, in this case, the scientific discourse of biological racial hierarchy.[38]

As Black extinction hypotheses gave way to the rise of the use of statistics to prove that Black people were inherently criminal, blame was more directly pinned to Black people's actions. Although statisticians like Frederick L. Hoffman continued to publish studies that "fram[ed] black criminality as a key measure of black [biological] inferiority,"[39] criminality became associated with Black behavior and pathology. Black mothers were subsequently blamed for instilling or not controlling such behaviors in their children and in themselves.

In her book on the relationship between young Black women's freedom practices and the role of crime and pathology in the early twentieth-century, Saidiya Hartman elaborates how Black mothers were blamed for their daughters' behavior. In the case of a young Black woman arrested on a neighbor's accusation of prostitution, the court decided against probation, preferring instead to place her in an institution that would be a better parent to her than her mother, for her own good. Her mother, it was said, was responsible for passing down her immoral character to her daughter, which was made apparent to the court by the mother not being visibly ashamed of her daughter. The state "believed the prison a better and more nurturing environment than the average Negro home."[40] The state could only see her mother as pathological and immoral, the original source of the problem of the young girl's deviance. The state could not see the love extended in the lack of shame, the instilling of the example of autonomy and dignity in her daughter's refusal to express regret, the persistent care practiced in long journeys for prison visitation, or the clear-eyed appraisal of which freedoms would be granted by the city and which would need to be taken. Progressive Era reformers mobilized the idea that unlike new immigrants from Europe, Black migrant women from the American South were not as easily redeemable because they were from cultures that lacked refinement due to the history of slavery.[41] The history of slavery was used to explain Black cultural pathology, but not structural inequities.

The theory that Black cultural pathology was inherited from slavery and explained differences in social outcomes among racial groups was codified with the 1965 Moynihan Report, which built on previous studies from the 1930s and 1940s that asserted the pathological structure of Black families, both in the United States and the British Caribbean.[42] Officially titled *The Negro Family: The Case for National Action*, sociologist Daniel Patrick Moynihan argued that Black matriarchal family structures, which grew out of the disruption of the Black nuclear family unit in slavery, set off a chain reaction that ultimately destroyed Black futures. In this "tangle of pathology," Black families have "reversed roles of husband and wife," women's employment emasculates, humiliates, and drives away Black men, "broken families" leave Black children undisciplined by patriarchy, unmoored by solid family structure, "with little knowledge of their . . . fathers' occupations," and ultimately set adrift into vice, delinquency, and impropriety with no respect with the social order of things.[43] While the Moynihan Report blames slavery as the root evil of such destruction, referring to American slavery as "the most awful the world has ever known,"[44] it converts the violence of white slaveowners who separated families on the auction block and prevented or controlled slave marriages into an internalized cultural pathology of Black mothering.[45]

Black cultural pathology discourse gained robust and damaging political expression in the rhetorical figure of the welfare queen, which continues to shape policy and white American common sense about poor Black women. The welfare queen, popularized by Ronald Reagan, is the figure of the dysfunctional Black matriarch, whose poverty is her own fault and was brought on by her own self-indulgence, irresponsibility, and selfish and unloving attitudes toward her children.[46] If the controlling image of the Black matriarch's strength indicted Black women, the welfare queen image grafted greed, and importantly, the willingness to *sacrifice her own children's wellbeing* for her indulgences, onto her rhetorical, even magical, strength.[47] Grace K. Hong demonstrates how the rhetorical figures produced through the Moynihan Report and the welfare queen also bifurcate liberal inclusion of Black women. Images of Black women who conform to normative family and middle-class values become social proof that poor Black women have only themselves to blame for their situation, and thus, they require social oversight.[48]

Even Black American women seemingly deemed to be "deserving" of social inclusion are not freed of the rhetorical bind of the pathological Black mother, though. As Wahneema Lubiano's work on the media reception of Anita Hill during the Clarence Thomas Supreme Court confirmation hearings demonstrates, overachieving Black women are also perceived as threats that need to be controlled because they scare off and emasculate Black men and reproduce autonomous Black female subjects in their children. Lubiano writes: "Whether by virtue of *not achieving* and thus passing on bad culture as welfare mothers, or by virtue of *managing to achieve* middle-class success via education, career, and/or economic success (and thus, I suppose, passing on genes for autonomous female success?), black women are responsible for the disadvantaged status of African Americans."[49] Both the underachieving and the overachieving Black woman are said to be unfairly thriving because of their dependency on state programs, whether welfare or affirmative action. The dismantling of social welfare distributive programs and affirmative action readjustment programs is then rendered appropriate and ethical because both are argued to enhance Black women's pathology.

Unfit Black mothering has been endowed with the power to justify both the expansion and the contraction of the state as it suits political imperatives. Welfare programs must be restricted and more tightly regulated because of conniving low-income mothers; carceral infrastructures and penal systems must be expanded to protect society from the criminals that Black mothers are destined to raise. Ultimately, blaming Black women and controlling their reproduction and life chances in response "perpetuates the view that racial inequality is caused by Black people themselves and not by an unjust social order."[50] Across centuries and changing political imperatives, the Black mother who impoverishes her children (biologically, culturally, morally, economically) is a political resource that can be deployed to alleviate state fears and white fears of Black freedom, Black rule, Black migration, Black class mobility, Black political power, Black demands for redress, and Black radical organizing for racial justice.

Within contemporary antitrafficking, the Black mother who enslaves her children by selling them to traffickers upholds dominant worldviews: poor Black mothers lack discernment, morality, and decency; they are the true culprits of intergenerational dependency; they are the true enslavers. In such narratives, poor Black mothers' desperation may be pitiable, but if they choose to procreate in poverty, they only have themselves to blame for the situation they create. Antitrafficking's use of the figure of the enslaving Black mother, then, redirects blame for the racial histories that create vast unevenness of life chances globally onto the too-naturalized villain of the Black mother. Such uses uphold US state projects transnationally in multiple directions: they circumvent and redirect responsibility for historical slavery and its legacies, they justify US-led population and reproduction control initiatives in countries underdeveloped by the histories and legacies of slavery and colonialism, and they preserve and advance racial logics amid postracial or antislavery rhetorics. Importantly for US-led transnational antitrafficking regimes, they also bolster US narratives of gifting freedom, first to the formerly enslaved at home through the abolition of slavery, which then qualifies the state to gift freedom to the rest of the world's unfree, comprised of subjects and figures who are nevertheless bound to US liberal empire in myriad ways.[51]

Haiti

The United States invaded Haiti in 1915 in the name of benevolently civilizing and paternalistically aiding the country's development, and established a brutal military occupation there until 1934.[52] During that period, the United States conscripted Haitians into forced labor regimes to build national infrastructure and violently repressed dissent against the occupation.[53] The US occupation reshaped Haiti's financial sector and rewrote its constitution; US involvement in the region through trade policy and international financial institutions continues to disadvantage Haitians.[54] In the 1970s, for instance, US-backed development strategies "turned Haiti into the supplier of the region's cheapest labor for the garment industry."[55] When the antitrafficking apparatus invokes child slavery in Haiti, though, it does not refer to such exploitative labor conditions or histories of extraction. Rather, it refers to a system of child fosterage known as restavèk, where poor mothers in rural areas of Haiti are said to sell their children into domestic servitude because they have too many mouths to feed. Anthropological understandings of restavèk tend to figure it as an informal, extended network of rural-urban kin and social relationships that families may utilize to make ends meet when raising children. Restavèk involves sending children elsewhere to stay with other families but is rarely characterized by extreme interpersonal violence and is certainly not a result of the much stereotyped Haitian "culture of violence."[56] Antitrafficking advocates and organizations, on the other hand, tend to figure the problem as resulting from outdated cultural practices and naive and poor decision-making by rural Black mothers who end up enslaving their own children because they don't know better. It is clear, by now, that such antitrafficking narratives reaffirm foreign intervention in Haiti as benevolent while invisibilizing its violences and histories, so what I wish to dwell on is how through the use of the phrase "modern-day slavery," the antitrafficking apparatus, backed by the US State Department, has refigured the ultimate site of Black self-determination through successful slave uprising as the site of Black Haitians who reenslave their own children. Black self-liberation is rewritten as a cautionary tale in Black inability for self-governance and, perhaps most astoundingly, Black incapacity to imagine freedom.

It would be hard to overstate the importance of Haiti to the Black radical tradition and to the historical memory of Black freedom more generally.[57] In 1791, the enslaved people of the French colony of Saint-Domingue revolted against the brutal conditions of the imperial plantation economy that made France rich, and after twelve years of self-organized struggle, they won. In C. L. R. James's heroic retelling, "The slaves defeated in turn the local whites and the soldiers of the French monarchy, a Spanish invasion, a British expedition of some 60,000 men, and a French expedition of similar size under Bonaparte's brother-in-law. The defeat of Bonaparte's expedition in 1803 resulted in the establishment of the Negro state of Haiti which has lasted to this day."[58] The Haitian Revolution was a stunning victory, and it has been said to be "unthinkable" in its own time for the ways in which it "required that the foundational ideas of civilization be recast."[59]

The impact of the Haitian Revolution reverberated throughout the Atlantic world. Large and small slave uprisings in the United States were inspired by the revolution; in particular, the 1811 German Coast uprising near New Orleans saw over three hundred enslaved people take up arms and burn down plantations.[60] White fear of Black revolt spread like wildfire and white suspicion and repression was violent and gruesome, notable under the already violent and gruesome regime of racial chattel slavery. The fear of successful slave revolutions contributed to the British decision to outlaw the slave trade within the British Empire in 1807.[61] Under Thomas Jefferson's leadership, the United States imposed a trade embargo on Haiti in 1806 and refused to recognize Haitian independence because of the fear that its revolution would spread to the United States.[62] The United States did not restore diplomatic relations with Haiti until 1862. In the aftermath of revolution, and under the threat of war, France coerced Haiti to pay reparations for the loss of property endured by French subjects when enslaved Haitians emancipated themselves.[63]

In exchange for paying back France for freeing themselves, France offered state recognition of Haiti, which it needed due to the "refusal of any nation to recognize Haitian independence."[64] The debt, which Haiti repaid in full, was estimated by Haitian president Aristide in 2004 to be worth nearly $22 billion, which is greater than Haiti's current gross domestic product of $18 billion.[65] The first independent Black nation in the Western Hemisphere was saddled with drastic debt and forced to navigate international affairs without formal recognition at its inception in an attempt to contain the threat it posed to Europe's wealth and power, the Atlantic slave economy, and the entire ideological underpinnings of racial capitalism and racial liberalism.[66] The threat to white supremacy that Haitian independence posed resulted in the swift narratological reconfiguration of Black freedom into tropes of racial degradation, barbarism, and political instability, which, as Marlene Daut has argued, were constructed through scientific discourses, and social anxieties, about racial mixing.[67] And, in US political discourse during Reconstruction, "maligning Haiti" was a way to "undermine black civil and political rights" in the United States by making Haiti the "racist shorthand for the looming evils of social equality" and the symbol of the threat Black rule posed to white progress.[68]

In 1938, C. L. R. James published *The Black Jacobins*, which told the story of Black agency in "the only successful slave revolt in history" and appeared in public just after the end of the brutal US occupation of Haiti.[69] James's account corrected the white-washed historical record that had erased the centrality of the Haitian Revolution to the modern world.[70] Since its original publication, *The Black Jacobins* has influenced generations of Black freedom fighters, including militant pan-Africanism in the 1930s, African independence movements and anticolonial struggle, US civil rights, Black Power movements in North America and Britain, and the antiapartheid struggle in South Africa.[71] Through James, the history of the Haitian Revolution has played a pivotal role in the Black radical imagination, in the countermemory of slavery and freedom, and has "come to be rendered as a crucial site of black inheritance and the claim of black self-determination."[72] That particular imagination of Haiti comes in direct response to white historians, policymakers, scientists, and imperial governors who had figured, and often continue to figure, Haiti as "the paradigmatic instance of the horror and failure of black self-determination."[73] To this day, when conditions of extreme poverty in Haiti are discussed in the news, they are generally narrated as naturally occurring, apolitical, or a product of political corruption, rather than resulting from various forms of structural and international exploitation. When the eighteenth-century revolutionary history of Haiti is invoked, it is often to dramatize the seeming contradiction—the first free Black nation in the Western Hemisphere is now the poorest. Underlying this conjunction is its antiblack logic: Black self-determination results in Black people returning to their natural state of chaos.

The conditions of poverty that many Haitians experience has been the justification for missionary, humanitarian, and NGO interventions in the country. Following Bill Clinton's 2009 assertion, it has been frequently noted in news and political commentary that Haiti hosts the second highest number of NGOs per capita in the world.[74] Considering the massive aid geographies and economies operative in Haiti, which continue to give actors from the global North an outsized role in determining social and political outcomes for Haitians while accruing their own social and material capital, it would make sense to analyze antitrafficking's programs in Haiti amid these problematics and constellations of power. Yet, given Haiti's place in the memoryscape of slavery and freedom, and with particular attention to how Haiti has loomed large in the imagination of white slaveowners and their descendants and in the imagination of Black revolutionaries, it is imperative to understand the political work that US State Department–funded antitrafficking programs do for upholding white supremacy in the space of successful slave revolt. By mobilizing the figure of the pathological Black mother who enslaves her kin, the antitrafficking narrative of modern slavery in Haiti safely reconciles the insurrectionary past of Black freedom into white supremacy's logics: left to their own devices, free Black people cannot govern themselves and are prone to selling their own children into slavery. Such framing affirms white historical inculpability and implies the benevolence and civilizing effects of enslavement and colonization. Antitrafficking advocates, in other words, turn Black Haitian mothers—the descendants of the first successful slave revolt—into modernity's slavers.

The figure of the Haitian restavèk gained visibility within the international humanitarian sector upon the publication of Jean-Robert Cadet's *Restavec: From Haitian Slave Child to Middle-Class American* in 1998. In the opening to his book, Cadet lays out the parameters of antitrafficking's narrative of child slavery in Haiti that recur across contemporary NGO, policy, and museum representations:

> Restavecs are slave children who belong to well-to-do families. They receive no pay and are kept out of school. Since the emancipation and independence of 1804, affluent blacks and mulattoes have reintroduced slavery by using children of the very poor as house servants. They promise poor families in faraway villages who have too many mouths to feed a better life for their children. Once acquired, these children lose all contact with

their families and, like the slaves of the past, are sometimes given new names for the sake of convenience . . . they are often seen in the streets running errands barefoot and dressed in dirty rags. Restavecs are treated worse than slaves, because they don't cost anything and their supply seems inexhaustible.[75]

In his description, Cadet invokes the revolutionary abolitionist history of Haiti in order to evince how African diasporic subjects enslave their own racial kin. His narrative of class maps onto two different enslavement stories, both of which deexceptionalize white slaving of African and African diasporic people. The first naturalizes the idea that upper-class exploitation of lower classes is rational and universal. By extending ruling-class status to affluent Black people, the story suggests to its US audience that affluent Black people are no better or worse than affluent whites, they enslave and exploit because that is a rational economic choice. Framing affluent Black people as enslavers works to make affluence the culprit, not racial identity, which suggests white enslavers were rational actors who are not exceptionally to blame for slavery. This formulation, ironically, blames greed while also relying on an internalized capitalistic logic that makes greed seem rational. Most importantly, it blames Black Haitians—and, in a reprise of the earliest narratives about the Haitian Revolution, "mulattoes"—for Haitian problems.[76]

Cadet's story reconstitutes former US president John Adams's nineteenth-century claims about Black incapacity for full freedom in the immediate aftermath of the Haitian Revolution: "Did they not immediately fall into the Power of Aristocrats of their own Colour?"[77] Cadet's use of slavery comparisons also echoes colloquial narratives of the internal African trade, where African royalty is said to have "sold out" poorer Africans by capturing and selling them to European slave traders. These echoes reiterate the narrative that Africans have always, and continue to, enslave their own. They are accented within the antitrafficking rhetoric with the recurring sentiment that contemporary slavery is "worse than" historical slavery. This insertion of antitrafficking rhetoric is particularly notable given the history of slavery in Haiti, where "planters deliberately worked [slaves] to death rather than wait for children to grow up."[78] Cadet's rhetorical maneuvers make historical slavery seem to be more benign in comparison to the present. Such framings do little to explain the impoverished conditions in Haiti that factor into restavèk, but do significant political work to assert a historically inculpable white subject amid late 1990s pan-African demands for redress for histories of transatlantic racial chattel slavery. The pro-US politics of the book are not obscured. Cadet's epigraph positions the US presence in Haiti as a positive force of democracy: "In 1994, the United States sent in troops to restore democracy in Haiti and to give hope to a people who are accustomed to living under the iron fist of dictators. Yet, there are over 250,000 restavecs in Haiti—slave children who have no hope of ever becoming educated participants in the restored democracy."[79]

As Cadet's autobiography develops, the reader learns that his white affluent father paid a Haitian woman named Florence to take care of Cadet after his biological Haitian mother died. It is not the absentee white father who is the enslaver or the unloving party who abandons or enslaves his own kin in this story, rather it is Florence, the Black woman who legally adopts Cadet, and who is said to have enslaved him. Florence is rendered as unloving and abusive. Cadet describes her as taking him in for the money; in essence she scams the rich white father by taking his money but not caring for his son, a narrative made familiar in the US imagination of Black mothers accused of birthing or claiming children for additional welfare benefits. Cadet claims that Florence whipped him depending on her mood, made him sleep under the kitchen table, ostracized him, and denied him any form of mother-son intimacy.

The contours of Cadet's story—wearing rags, being whipped, not going to school, being ostracized from family—repeat across the subsequent uptake of the Haitian restavèk figure in antitrafficking discourse. The reported causes of the restavèk system similarly repeat: poverty and cultural backwardness. Less commented upon, although just as repetitive, is the figure of the unloving Black mother figure who tortures the restavèk in her home or the naive and overly fertile poor Black mother who enslaves her own child, first by birthing her, and second, by sending her away because she cannot care for her. Cadet's upbringing is contrasted with that of his own son, birthed by his white American wife, who is well cared for by his white mother and white grandmother, unlike the Black American children Cadet teaches at a public school in Cincinnati who he characterizes as "lazy," prone to fighting with each other, and uninterested in education.[80] Cadet concludes his autobiography with the following indictment: "Restavec slavery is wrong. It is the worst crime imaginable, because the victims are incapable of resisting their adult predators. It is a crime against nature as well, because the child's very rights to life—to belong, to grow, to smile, to love, to feel, to learn, and to be a child—are denied, by those whose ancestors were slaves themselves."[81] The text is written in explicit reference to the history of slavery and abolition in Haiti and is punctuated with racialized logics of care and mothering. Despite what may seem to many to be Cadet's outlandish claims and characterizations, Cadet's narrative and the figure of restavèk slavery that it popularizes has been taken up by the UN,

UNICEF, ILO, antitrafficking NGOs, international journalism, and the US Department of State.

In the Free the Slaves video *Haiti's Model Communities Fight Restavek Child Slavery*, which was funded in part by the US State Department, the narrator opens by saying "Haiti was the first nation on Earth to outlaw slavery, but today it has one of the world's highest concentrations of children working as household servants."[82] Never mind that Haitian law was the result of slave revolt and Black revolution; in this rendering, Black people are not able to govern themselves and are only "beginning to recognize" the children's hardships.[83] Focusing on child servitude, and framing it as modern slavery, in the space of one of the most important sites of Black freedom replaces histories of revolutionary Black freedom with an image of poor Black children who need to be saved. The film narrates the problem of restavèk in Haiti: poor parents send away their children to receive schooling in return for domestic labor but are naive to the conditions their children face upon arrival. The narrator in the film describes the problem as originating in poverty and cultural practices. The film proceeds to showcase Free the Slaves' solutions for the problem, which say nothing about ending poverty and solely address cultural practices. Such figuration draws upon a grammar of long-standing stereotypes of Black family pathology.

One mother and her daughter, now reunited, explain their circumstance on camera. The daughter agreed to be sent to the city in exchange for the chance to go to school, but when she arrived, she was saddled with babysitting responsibilities. Her mother explains, through translated subtitles, "It was very hard for me. I did not want to do it. But I realized I could not take care of her." Later in the film, the mother describes how she retrieved her daughter from restavèk after attending the community sessions on children's human rights. She says, through translation, "So when I was attending those sessions I got to understand that I had to bring her back and they would help me take care of her." In this representation, the Washington, DC–funded but locally led NGO project trains Black rural mothers to care for their children by enlightening them to discourses of human rights. The women are constructed as pitiable but irresponsible mothers because they cannot provide for the children that they have brought into the world.

The NGO encodes its way of seeing Black motherhood through the video's shots. What it frames as visual evidence of the success of their programs to train poor Black mothers to keep their children tells a different story when those images are listened to. The mother herself expresses deep care for her child amid constrained choices to ensure her daughter's survival. The educational lesson that the woman reports could be read as less about human rights and more about global aid economies: here was a way for mother and daughter to be reunited, a daughter whom she never *wanted* to send away, because the organization would help pay for the costs of the child. Recognizing the mother's struggle and knowing the history of the figure of the bad Black mother makes new insights possible. What is represented here is not the mother's conversion into a governable liberal subject, but antitrafficking's racial logics: what is assumed to be visually self-evident by depicting a poor Black mother?

These antitrafficking images were never "intended to figure black subjects, but to delineate instead differential or degraded forms of personhood or subjection."[84] Yet, the images are full of visual and sonic evidence of "the everyday practice of refusal": refusal to be rendered unloving, refusal to be reduced to a cultural pathology in the face of centuries of racial dispossession, refusal to be willingly enlisted into an NGO morality campaign, while still deftly maneuvering aid economies.[85] For instance, in a scene depicting how local Haitian NGO fieldworkers conduct community education workshops, the participants sit outside in a circle and the educator points enthusiastically to images within the NGO's picture book that model appropriate child treatment and family planning. The group of women appear to listen patiently. Some look down with arms crossed. One looks directly at the male educator with suspicion. In another scene, the narrator explains that the next step in the process is to form a Child Protection Committee. The same peer educator is shown explaining to a different group of assembled community members, "You are the people of the community who had difficulties meeting the needs of your children and had sent them away." As he speaks to the group, the Haitian woman immediately to his left avoids all eye contact with him and the camera. She looks displeased and uncomfortable. She fixes her gaze directly upward, refusing to be fully compliant or interpellated as a mother-enslaver. Her body language "appears to hold back, hold in, or keep something in reserve . . . an effortful balancing of compulsion, constraint, and refusal that vibrates unvisibly yet resoundingly."[86] Another woman anxiously avoids looking at the camera or the peer educator. She keeps the camera in her peripheral vision but avoids its gaze, suggesting discomfort and resistance to the filming, to the premise of the committee, or both. Despite what appears to be unease with the process, the white American narrator triumphantly proclaims over the images, "Community dialogue works!" The narrator's interjection is so jarring that it provokes the questions: What exactly is working? What was this scene visual evidence of? The video's gaze filters the existence of Black women in a global aid geography of poverty through the common sense of blaming Black women and thereby renders them to be, self-evidentially, a problem that must be solved with pedagogical intervention. Riffing on Tina Campt, what appears in the video is not simply community support for the program, despite the narrator's declaration, but is also embodied responses to the global aid gaze and the histories of racialized dispossession it is built upon.[87]

The video ends with the narrator asserting, "Village by village, a wave of activism has begun. A wave that says no child deserves to be sent away as a restavèk. A wave that says children deserve freedom." Here, the revolutionary history of successful armed slave uprising in Haiti is erased and forgotten, replaced with the conflation of global development projects as activism. In this fantasy of historical reversal, US organizations are represented as educating Haitians into understanding what freedom is and how it should be achieved.

Within Free the Slaves' monitoring and evaluation report about Haiti's Model Communities project, a clearer picture develops regarding community expectations and NGO models of freedom. Free the Slaves' program was a partnership with a local Haitian NGO and was titled: "Freedom for Haiti's Children: Community Action to End Slavery Locally and Nationally." It was funded by the US State Department to Monitor and Combat Trafficking in Persons (J/TIP). According to the report of the project, the program was "designed through an analysis of the risk factors that underlie the sending of children into *restavèk*."[88] The intervention focused on educating parents about children's rights, educating Haitians about reproductive health and family planning, and a year of "nearly free" education for at-risk and retrieved children. According to the report's results and findings, "returned children reported overwhelmingly that they feel happier to be home with their families," but that "parents are facing difficulty in providing for returned children as a result of underproductive farmland and little to no work opportunities."[89] In fact, participants in the intervention often cited wanting their children to get an education but not being able to afford it as one of the reasons why they sent away or did not retrieve a child.[90] Such findings point to the real underlying risk factors: not a lack of knowledge, love, or desire to protect and educate their children, but a calculated choice under unfair economic conditions to care for and educate their children by mobilizing resources in extended social networks.[91] In the Haiti report, parents of retrieved children expressed a conflicted position: they are happy to be reunited with children and grateful that the NGO is paying for their schooling temporarily, but they still sometimes cannot afford to feed or clothe their children. Thus, although it is not thematized as such, the report's findings present participants who clearly articulate their love of their children and the barriers they face. To see the love in such responses, to assume that people do their best with what they have, excuses neither interpersonal nor structural violence; it is a frame that makes evident the antitrafficking discourse's restaging of opportunistic tropes that support white supremacy's distribution of resources and pain.

Within the report, sending and receiving families articulate poverty as the root cause of the restavèk system. Among participants, the report finds that there is also an expectation that if the parents retrieve the children, the NGO will pay to support them, which is not the case. In fact, when funding goals were not met for the NGO intervention, the aspect of the program that was eliminated was "livelihoods."[92] The report concludes that the major threat to the sustainability of the NGO intervention is the economic challenges faced by families. Poverty is acknowledged to be the root cause of family separation and the biggest threat to the success of the NGO program, but the interventions are not focused on addressing economic issues. Instead, they are they focused on education and family planning.

When poverty is invoked within antitrafficking discourse, it is not done so as a structural critique of capitalism; it is a code that primes viewers to indict Black women for their choices. Free the Slaves' Haiti report does not frame the lack of resources as the problem but instead focuses on the number of children that families have that they cannot take care of because they are poor. Receiving families are also figured through family size: "Receiving families cited the need for inexpensive domestic labor to manage the household of relatively large families, as well as their intention to offer a goodwill gesture to provide children with a much needed home."[93] In both cases, the cause of enslavement is figured as overpopulation in underdeveloped countries.

Family planning initiatives have been a part of US-led international development funding since the 1960s and 1970s. In *The Economization of Life*, Michelle Murphy traces the racial history of population control initiatives. She shows how population economics links birth rates to GDP, a continuation of the racial and racist logic that impoverished conditions led to higher birth rates and thus birth rates in poor populations needed to be controlled in order to secure positive economic futures for the wealthy. Murphy's research highlights the calculations of US economist Stephen Enke, who argued that, in developing countries, "averting a birth contributed more to GDP than the average labor of a living adult."[94] Based on Enke's findings, US president Lyndon B. Johnson incorporated family planning initiatives into both domestic welfare programs and international aid. The 1974 Kissinger Report also classified population growth in developing countries as a severe threat "to world economic, political, and ecological systems."[95] Poor women's fertility and reproduction needed to be controlled in order to prevent them from imposing an undue economic burden on developed countries (or social welfare programs). Suggesting that Black and third world women's reproductive choices posed a threat to world political systems, specifically, also invokes the white fear of the specter of revolution, mass uprisings, democratically elected socialist policymakers, and Black political power more generally. As a causal relationship between population and civilization was naturalized, its harmful effects extended: "the figure of the averted birth did more than devalue future life; it cast a shadow over living people, who were also better-not-born."[96] Maintaining political and economic power through policies and programs that attempt to control the reproduction of poor women of color at home and abroad is, quite simply, racist. Antitrafficking interventions recapitulate these logics of white supremacy in the name of ending slavery today. Antitrafficking imagery, narratives, and programs that blame Black mothers for enslaving their own kids construct the problems that histories and presents of global white supremacy create as problems born of irresponsible Black mothers. Such narratives graft smoothly onto the solutions, such as population control initiatives, that are preexisting funding priorities of the US state. The problem, in other words, is not unloving Black mothers; the problem is the enduring white fear of Black revolution, which suggests that perhaps the problem for the United States in maintaining its transnational power is just how much Black mothers might love, and fight for, Black futures.

Figuring Ghanaian and Haitian mothers as enslavers of their own children, and noting how widespread and convincing such representations are for antitrafficking's publics, demonstrates how thoroughly antitrafficking discourse is a white memory project built upon reproducing antiblack logics. Blaming Black mothers in Haiti and Ghana resignifies two key locations of Black freedom in the African diasporic imagination and two key locations of fear in the white imagination into places that, since (Haitian) revolution or (Ghanaian) independence, have slipped "back" into slavery. The antitrafficking apparatus, then, does double duty in sites of Black freedom: it confirms white civilizational and racial superiority theories, and it exculpates the white imagination from responsibility for histories and structures of violence and from fear of Black revenge. Blaming Black mothers accomplishes many political imperatives.

Black Mothers Respond

During the 2010 Haitian earthquake recovery, several high-profile NGO-based scandals unfolded.[97] One of those cases involved Idaho missionaries attempting to transport presumably orphaned children across the border to the Dominican Republic for the international adoption market. Although the missionaries were arrested and their actions legally met the threshold for child trafficking, none of them were found guilty of trafficking.[98] Bill Clinton's diplomacy on behalf of the missionaries helped diffuse the case which reduced the charges,[99] which is notable since the Clintons have been key figures in placing antitrafficking on the domestic and international political agenda. Bill Clinton, in fact, signed the US Trafficking Victims Protection Act into law, which greatly enhanced criminal sentences for those found guilty of trafficking. Despite their actions, the white missionaries were not featured in NGO publicity materials as modern-day enslavers nor were they trained on how to be better parents with picture books about children's human rights. Rather, they were assumed to be well intentioned, if overzealous and misguided, despite evidence that they were not well intentioned at all.[100] Which tells us: Haitian mothers who labor under extreme conditions to provide for their children are enslavers and white missionaries who steal children from poor families are well intentioned. "Trafficking is slavery" works as a narrative when it is attached to Black women as culprits. It falls apart when it is attached to white women as culprits. Antitrafficking discourse gains traction through the ways in which it does political work to uphold racial projects.

Back in the United States, the problem of human trafficking in Washington, DC, has been widely publicized through police and public awareness initiatives since 2004 but was disavowed when Black American mothers accused DC police of not taking seriously the cases of missing Black girls who may have been trafficked. In March 2017, the chronic issue of missing Black girls rose to public prominence when several celebrities retweeted a mistaken post that fourteen Black girls had gone missing in twenty-four hours. There was outrage over the lack of media and police attention given to Black girls compared to when white girls go missing. The DC police quickly intervened on the social media conversation to explain that fourteen Black girls had not gone missing within twenty-four hours. The police clarified that this situation was definitely not an issue of human trafficking: "There's no evidence to suggest that D.C. has a human trafficking problem, the police spokeswoman said."[101] The police attempted to reassure the Black mothers who were troubled that there were no Amber alerts for the missing Black girls by explaining that Amber alerts cannot be used for runaways.

The police's insistence that the missing girls were runaways did not sit well with many parents within Black communities, especially families who had experienced the lack of attention to their children's cases by the police. It is quite jarring to hear that DC does not have a human trafficking problem considering the volume of resources directed to the issue and the number of awareness-raising campaigns the city has sponsored. For instance, the DC Human Trafficking Task Force, started in 2004, receives federal funding to increase police capacity and services to victims. The task force consists of twenty-four DC-area nonprofit organizations, including Stop Modern Slavery-DC,[102] and sixteen DC-area law enforcement agencies, including the Human Trafficking Unit of the DC Metropolitan Police Department.[103] Organizations within the task force conduct community outreach and trainings for government agencies, businesses, and churches to identify warning signs of a trafficked person and report them. After years of trying to legitimize the problem of human trafficking, train police to fight it, and bulk up the criminal legal system to prevent it, officials were now backing away from trafficking being a problem *at all*. Such a position either admits the discourse of human trafficking and the apparatus built up around it is a scam or that the police do not see Black girls as innocent enough to be legible within the discursive parameters of trafficking victims—or both. The accusation that these children were runaways once again recasts Black girlhood as deviant and delinquent and Black families as unsupportive and unloving. In Haiti, Black children are trafficking victims of their own families; in the United States, Black girls are not trafficking victims, just deviant offspring of deviant homes who prefer to run away than reside with their unloving mothers. In both cases, trafficking victim labels apply or don't apply in ways that blame Black mothers.

Despite police intervention to try to calm public outrage, some Black leaders and activists took action to raise the profile of the problem of missing Black girls. The Congressional Black Caucus sent a letter to the attorney general and the director of the Federal Bureau of Investigation on March 21, 2017, demanding they "devote the resources necessary to determine whether these developments are an anomaly or whether they are indicative of an underlying trend that must be addressed."[104] On March 29, 2017, there was a Protect Black Kids vigil at the African American Civil War Memorial in DC.[105] The Black feminist podcast, *The Black Joy Mixtape*, amplified the issue that same week, offering a nuanced analysis of why Black girls might run away, their entitlement to childhood, and calling for effective and non-police-based support services for them. On April 9, 2017, Black Lives Matter Greater New York held a 140-block march in Manhattan to raise awareness about the sixty-four thousand missing Black girls and women nationwide, a number that was generated by the Black and Missing Foundation and has circulated widely in the press.[106]

Discourses of antitrafficking are deployed by the police and government agencies partially and when they suit their needs, for instance, to garner new sources of funding from the federal government, to pilot new neighborhood surveillance systems, or to villainize and criminalize people of color. The same resources, however, were perhaps not ever intended to be used to help Black American girls and women, which is why the conflation of the discourses of human trafficking and missing Black girls can be immediately dismissed by the police. The act of adopting a dominant discourse to serve Black interests often reveals the discourse's limits; in this case, the problem of human trafficking suddenly disappears from DC when it is raised by Black mothers and community members. The sudden evaporation of a decades-long national moral panic when it is not being mobilized in the interests of the state and in the interest of white supremacy demonstrates just how dependent on reproducing those systems the issue is.

A notable outcome of the #MissingDCGirls case for this study is how the issue was taken up by some Black activists and with it, the antitrafficking discourse. For instance, Black Lives Matter Greater New York, under the banner #FindOurGirls, announced that it would begin confronting human trafficking, precisely because the police disengagement with the missing Black women reiterated once again that Black lives do not matter to the state. The group also expressed caution by referring supporters to "trusted partners" on the topic and described it as "new territory" for Black activists.[107] The antitrafficking apparatus, however, did not use #MissingDCGirls as an opportunity to further broadcast their campaigns. It did not take up the Black-led concern about missing Black girls, nor the concern about over- and underpolicing Black communities, even as it has helped reproduce a plethora of suffering Black victims of trafficking in need of help.

When antitrafficking organizations accuse Black mothers of selling their own children, they elicit funding from US government agencies and billionaire philanthropists alike. That funding is used to create trainings that teach Black women either how to love their children or how to stop having children. When Black mothers publicly display their love of their children by raising their concerns about Black girls who have gone missing, state agencies and NGOs alike dismiss or ignore them. The loving and concerned Black mother is blamed for creating the home conditions in which a child would rather be trafficked than be with her mother. Antitrafficking discourse, like the figure of the bad Black mother it deploys, operates flexibly to rhetorically address political problems in ways that uphold the legitimacy of white supremacy by discursively erasing white culpability.

Interlude   #FreeCyntoiaBrown

When activist Mariame Kaba talks about Black women who survive cycles of violence only to be criminalized by the state for defending themselves, she asks: "Can Black women ever be victims?"[1] In the case of Cyntoia Brown, a Black woman who was convicted of murder for killing a man in self-defense during an underage commercial sex exchange, the antitrafficking media's answer was no, then yes, but still not really.

Kaba's framing of the question of Black women's social worth indicts carceral systems, media narratives, and public policy as perpetrators of violence against Black women. Beth Richie describes how Black women's experiences with sexual and interpersonal violence "are made more dangerous by communities that tolerate or dismiss the degradation that Black women experience." She continues: "Furthering this effect are state institutions built on racist stereotypes that profoundly misunderstand and misrepresent Black women's experience of male violence, and public policies characteristic of a prison nation that create a hostile social environment for many poor Black women."[2] Black feminist antiviolence organizing and theorizing understands state, community, and intimate violence as interrelated and compounding harms faced by Black women.[3] Because Black women are often not seen by dominant institutions as possessing the quality of innocence, nor as victims deserving of protection from violence, they are often criminalized for being victimized.

Carceral solutions to interpersonal and state violence introduce additional sites through which individuals and state actors can enact violence in people's lives. Women in prison face the threat of sexual violence at the hands of prison guards, separation from family and community, loss of children to child protective services, and limited job and housing opportunities upon release.[4] Because carceral systems do not ameliorate violence, Black and women of color feminist antiviolence and prison abolitionist activists and organizations such as Critical Resistance and INCITE! have fought against the use of prison as a solution to violence against women and other social harms. They have advocated for material resources to be invested in the systems that do make communities safer, such as affordable housing and health care, robust and well-financed schools, food security, public spaces, and community centers.[5] When Cyntoia Brown's case garnered widespread public attention in late 2017, the injustices of her story and the thousands of other women like her who have been imprisoned for defending themselves against violence had long been central to the analysis and struggle for Black women's freedom. These organizing traditions form the backdrop to the media representations of Cyntoia Brown's struggle, although their methods were largely glossed over in antitrafficking's narrative of sexual slavery.

#FreeCyntoiaBrown began trending after pop artist and entrepreneur Rihanna posted to Instagram some of the details of Brown's case in November 2017. The post described Brown as a sex trafficking victim who had been "purchased" and then unjustly punished for it by the criminal legal system in the United States. At the time of Rihanna's post, Cyntoia had been in prison for thirteen years; she was convicted and sentenced to life in prison as a juvenile in 2006. When Rihanna's post popped up in my feed, I was still celebrating the recent release of a friend from jail that resulted from months-long grassroots organizing and participatory defense strategies that I was involved with in conjunction with SONG's 2017 Black Mamas Bail Out.[6] I was a bit taken aback by Rihanna's framing of Cyntoia's case, noting her critique of incarceration alongside her invocation of antitrafficking discourse. Antiprison and antitrafficking campaigns seldom coincide, although they sometimes share competing metaphors of "modern-day slavery," and they both invoke abolition (prison abolition versus "modern-day abolitionists" of trafficking).[7] I began following the news of Cyntoia's case on outlets that generally cover trafficking, wondering if this case would address the question some interlocutors had asked of my work, "Does it matter what you call it ["modern-day slavery"] if it helps Black girls get what they need?" Would the publicity of Cyntoia's struggle be a case where antitrafficking's narratives helped advance Black women's freedom?

The initial response from mainstream media outlets was no. Although Cyntoia's situation now meets the legal definition of sex trafficking victim—under US law any person under age eighteen engaged in sex work, regardless of consent, is considered a sex trafficking victim—when her case began recirculating, she was still cast in the media as a murderer and a thief who was pretending to be a victim in light of recent celebrity attention. In 2017, *Newsweek* used the headline "Cyntoia Brown Wasn't a Victim, Stole Money after Killing Johnny Allen: Prosecutors" to grab readers' attention by opportunistically leading with the inflammatory language of the prosecutor who tried her.[8] Other articles about Cyntoia's case in *Newsweek* use quotation marks around the phrase sex trafficking victim: "Who Is Cyntoia Brown? 'Sex Trafficking Victim' Gets Support from Celebs on Instagram."[9] The quotation marks distance Cyntoia from being rightfully labeled a victim; the quotation marks cast doubt on Brown's status as a victim. A CNN headline read: "Why Cyntoia Brown, Who Is Spending Life in Prison for Murder, Is All Over Social Media."[10] The *New York Times* headline read: "Why Celebrities Have Rallied behind Cyntoia Brown, a Woman Spending Life in Prison."[11] CBS News reported via Associated Press: "Cyntoia Brown Case: Celebrities Support Teen Killer, Highlight Sex Trafficking Abuse."[12] In each case, Cyntoia is predominately represented as a criminal and a murderer.[13] Both *Newsweek* and CNN regularly report on sex slavery cases and sex trafficking victims, with an emphasis on sensationalized, individualized victimhood and without the use of qualifying quotation marks. In fact, in 2015, *Newsweek* ran the salacious feature "Sex Slaves in America: Trafficking Down on the Farm" on the cover of its magazine—no quotation marks needed there.[14] Both news outlets have benefited from the unqualified expansion of the term *modern-day slavery* in their coverage to get clicks, yet don't apply the same label or victim status to a Black woman in prison who meets the legal definition of trafficking victim.

Across much of the 2017 coverage of Cyntoia's situation, tropes that indict Black families and Black culture were reproduced: Brown was born with fetal alcohol syndrome from her (white biological) mother, she experienced a "childhood marked by abuse and drugs," she ran away from her (Black adoptive) home, was abused by a pimp, and then became a thief, a prostitute, and murderer.[15] Although the multiracial dynamics of Cyntoia's life are complex,[16] her experiences of violence were often reduced within news coverage to racially unspecified but racially coded tropes that have historically been used to stereotype Black families and Black culture (despite her adopted Black mother being the stable and loving presence in her life). Through these tropes, the innocent victim status of "trafficked" becomes unavailable to Cyntoia. The naturalized criminalization of Blackness takes precedence in the coverage.

The #FreeCyntoiaBrown case mirrors the dynamics of how Black girls' exploitation is fit into, and distanced from, mainstream antitrafficking campaigns. These dynamics generally unfold as such: sexually exploited Black girls are framed as sex slaves when the narratives are used to accuse Black families and Black cultures of being the new enslavers, but when Black counterpublics invoke antitrafficking language to gain justice for Black girls, as in #FreeCyntoiaBrown and #MissingDCGirls, institutions like CNN and police departments that generally advance antitrafficking narratives without hesitation, delegitimize Black women's experiences of violence as not meeting the threshold of victim status. Representations of sexual violation of Black girls within antitrafficking discourse, then, become objects to advance the cause of predominantly white trafficking abolitionists and place blame for the new slavery on Black families, but fall short of garnering mainstream antitrafficking advocates' support of Black women's self-defense and self-determination. This dual reality exposes the underlying antiblack ideologies operative within antitrafficking discourse. Black people are figured as enslaved within antitrafficking when it serves white humanitarian self-making and reinforces stereotypes; they are framed as criminal, controversial, undeserving, or suspect when their exploitation calls into question the legitimacy of the state, the police, or the criminal legal system.

As #FreeCyntoiaBrown gained momentum in November 2017, it generated several online petitions and a direct email campaign from the racial justice advocacy organization Color of Change. In contrast to the criminalizing narratives of mainstream press, Color of Change presented Cyntoia Brown's case to its supporters as "another devastating example of how the criminal legal system time and time again fails Black people, especially young Black girls and survivors of sexual violence." The organization denounced the criminalization of Black girls and women who "us[e] their agency to fight back against abusers." In making their case, Color of Change also embraced the slavery frame by likening Cyntoia Brown to Nat Turner for being a modern-day slave who killed her slave owner in an act of self-emancipation. An email to their LISTSERV of supporters on December 14, 2017, reads: "Cyntoia is a survivor of sex trafficking, which is apart [sic] of the modern-day institution of slavery. She is now in prison for essentially killing her slave owner. This is something Black folks have historically been celebrated for—Cyntoia is no different than Nat Turner."

Rather than using slavery to repopularize imagery of heroic white abolitionists or a freedom-loving nation-state (as antitrafficking discourse does), Color of Change invokes Nat Turner, a beloved image of righteous Black self-liberation and a haunting symbol of fear in the white imagination. Invoking Nat Turner, an important historical figure and symbol of armed and educated Black masculinity, positions US history as one of Black resistance, not cultural backwardness; of Black agency, not passivity; of histories of oppression overcome in ways deemed illegal by the state precisely because the state is structurally responsible for the oppression.[17] These are stark differences of political vision, of past and of future, from the logics that underpin antitrafficking discourse. The two uses mobilize histories and images of slavery and freedom to very different political ends. Color of Change mobilizes around Cyntoia's case as part of their larger campaign to end mass incarceration and as part of an organizing strategy to put pressure on district attorneys to review juvenile sentences for life without parole. The antitrafficking apparatus uses abolition language to advocate for harsher sentences for traffickers domestically and internationally and to rhetorically position carceral mechanisms as paths to freedom from slavery. In some cases, antitrafficking legislation's harsher sentences have resulted in Black women sex workers being convicted of enslaving other women under the Mann Act (the still-existing law known as the White-Slave Traffic Act of 1910) and then being forced to register as sex offenders, which drastically limits housing and job options and freedom of mobility and privacy.[18]

While Color of Change's use of the historical memory of slave revolt for social justice issues contests antitrafficking's carceral agenda, it raises additional questions about the visibility of Black women's freedom struggles, and the affordance of vulnerability and strength, within sex trafficking discourse. What changes if Cyntoia was no different from *Celia, a Slave?*[19] What would it mean to think about Cyntoia's case through the historic case of an enslaved Black woman named Celia, who killed her white slave owner after repeated rapes and then was sentenced to death by an all-white male jury?[20] In this historical example, the structural relationship between the history of sexual violence under slavery and the contemporary "matrix of violence" that Black women experience as a result of sexual violence is made apparent.[21] Rather than connect the two discursively through "modern-day slavery" rhetoric, invoking Celia emphasizes the centrality of Black women's sexual exploitation and physical and reproductive labor to the functioning of racial chattel slavery and racial capitalism in the United States.[22] It highlights the role of white state repression against Black women when they take their liberation in their own hands. This historical comparison opens a conversation about the relationships among histories of Black women's oppression at the hands of the white owning class and contemporary Black women's oppression at the hands of criminal legal systems. And, as Mariame Kaba notes, it highlights how Black women remain unprotected from state violence, and their citizenship rights to self-defense against interpersonal violence remain unprotected by the state. Cyntoia's case, in fact, could be read alongside myriad figures in a long line of Black women who have experienced intersectional violence, who knew their worth despite all external threats to it, who fought back, and who, like Harriet Jacobs, bravely told complex stories about their own vulnerability, agency, exploitation, and survival, despite the threat of being publicly shamed.[23] Black women and girls should not have to be endlessly powerful and heroic, nor agentless victims, to be rallying calls for social justice. There are many histories and models that can help publics navigate, understand, and see vulnerability, bravery, and agency under constrained and limited choices.

Mainstream media narratives around Cyntoia's victimhood changed dramatically over the course of her case. In 2012, Cyntoia Brown's lawyer filed for a new trial after a new antitrafficking law was enacted in Tennessee that would have given Cyntoia a stronger defense. Yet, coverage of the hearing continued to refer to her as a "teenage killer."[24] The tag "teen killer" persisted in much of the coverage from 2006 to 2017, despite lawyers, advocates, documentarians, and loved ones bringing public attention to her case.[25] The criminalizing language was mostly replaced with more sympathetic language in the wake of the trending hashtag and grassroots support from Color of Change, Black Lives Matter Nashville, and the antitrafficking organization End Slavery Tennessee. Each organization galvanized various publics concerned with the different political issues her case raised—ending juvenile life sentencing, ending child prostitution, ending the criminal legal system, and validating Black women's right to self-defense and safety from sexual harm—to pressure Tennessee officials to hold a parole hearing. In the lead up to her parole hearing in May 2018, her eventual granting of clemency by Republican governor William Haslam in January 2019, and her release from prison into supervised parole in August 2019, news frames were much more likely to identify her, without qualifier, as a trafficking victim. On May 3, 2018, the *New York Times* reports, "Cyntoia Brown, Trafficking Victim Serving Life Sentence for Murder, Will Get Clemency Hearing."[26] That same month, CNN reports, "Parole Board Splits on Clemency for Trafficking Victim for Killing a Man Who Picked Her Up for Sex."[27] Associated Press in Nashville reports, "Cyntoia Brown: Sex Trafficking Victim in Prison for Murder Granted Full Clemency."[28] No qualifying quotation marks; no "teen killer." And, although the *Guardian*'s antitrafficking column, "Modern-Day Slavery in Focus," did not initially cover Cyntoia's case, upon her release from prison it framed her story as: "Cyntoia Brown: Trafficked, Enslaved, Jailed for Life at 16—and Fighting Back."[29] Across much of the news coverage that represents her as a victim, Cyntoia is named a "model prisoner" because she has expressed deep remorse for her actions, attained a degree inside prison from the Christian university Lipscomb (which has ties to antitrafficking programs), and works "side by side with the courts and Juvenile Justice system as an unpaid consultant."[30] Tennessee Republican governor Haslam's justification for Cyntoia's clemency rested on his belief that her sentence was too harsh because of the "extraordinary steps Ms. Brown has taken to rebuild her life."[31]

Cyntoia went from not being legible as a victim in the press to mattering because she was a total victim who completed a perfect conversion from dysfunctional family and out-of-line Black girlhood to a selfless, upstanding, moral Christian, and heteronormative woman citizen. In the words of the *Guardian* antitrafficking coverage, a decade in prison allowed Cyntoia to "obtain two university degrees, find God and get married."[32] Prison is heralded as a corrective device that reformed unruly Cyntoia, who has now proven that she "deserves" to be free.[33] All of these narratives conform to the status quo; none challenge dominant arrangements of power. Such narratives reinforce carceral solutions, rather than undermine them, even though undermining carceral solutions by showing their racist inhumanity was one of the political goals of many participants in the #FreeCyntoiaBrown campaigns.

Not being legible as a victim and only being legible as a victim aren't opposites. They are two sides of white supremacy that work together to undermine Black women's self-determination. Legibility as a victim that is predicated on being legible as a deserving subject in the eyes of a white male Republican governor is hardly a win for ending structural violence and societal discrimination against Black women. Still, Cyntoia is no longer in prison, and while she must navigate the merciless constraints of state supervision for ten years while on parole, there is immeasurable, unnamable relief, joy, and reunification in release. Considering how the media narrative changed around Cyntoia Brown—from prostitute and murderer to child sex slave and trafficking victim—and considering the role that antitrafficking-based law and advocacy played in the governor's clemency reasoning, how should we understand the power of antitrafficking rhetoric for getting Black women and girls who face sexual violence more resources? What is gained and what is lost in these approaches?

The antitrafficking industry's defense of Cyntoia circa 2018 regularly invoked the talking point that since "there is no such thing as a teen prostitute," Cyntoia is innocent. The "no such thing" framing is a way of saying that regardless of consent, any underage commercial sex work is considered trafficking, and thus all underage sex workers are victims.[34] Through the antitrafficking lens, Cyntoia was a tragic victim of interpersonal circumstance, not a survivor of many intersecting and compounding systems of violence and oppression. Naming pathological families and an abusive Black boyfriend as the forces that drove Cyntoia into trouble—that *enslaved* Cyntoia—fit neatly into antitrafficking's tropes. Naming childhood trauma and men who force prostitution as the root causes of harm intends to portray victims as agentless in the commission of crime, but it also repeats the narrative that Black culture is the agent of enslavement.

If the sex trafficking victim label made Cyntoia a more sympathetic victim to some, it came at the cost of understanding many details and dynamics about prison and violence. Those details are important to engage in order to organize for freedom at the nexus of interlocking oppressions. It came at the cost of understanding how Cyntoia was subjected to the school-to-prison pipeline through overdiscipline for acting out at an early age, which had a cascading effect on her life chances.[35] It came at the cost of understanding the dynamics of survival sex economies and how the compounding harms are intimately related to the criminalization of sex work and lack of other social service supports.[36] It came at the cost of understanding the long history of sex workers' organizing against antitrafficking laws because they often result in further criminalization and unsafe conditions.[37] It came at the cost of understanding how the rhetoric of "good" or "deserving" prisoners further entrenches and condones violence against those to whom the title is unavailable.[38] And most importantly, the trafficking victim framing of Cyntoia deprioritized the narrative that Black women's lives are worthy of defense and self-defense *without condition*.[39] None of these dynamics are captured in antitrafficking narratives; many of antitrafficking's narratives directly oppose them.

When trafficking language gets tagged onto racial justice issues, and when antitrafficking organizations attach themselves to racial justice campaigns, what is lost is exactly that: racial justice. Antitrafficking's labels, narratives, and spokeswomanship obscure the long-standing Black-woman-led, Black feminist antiviolence and prison abolition organizing that keeps its focus on the layered matrix of violence that Black women face. Such theorizing and organizing continues to name and enact solutions to violence beyond police, prisons, and perfect victims.[40] In contrast, antitrafficking narratives are built on, and gain traction through, reworking the racial logics of white supremacy. Such genealogies make it hard to use antitrafficking language and frames for racial justice. So, while getting any individual out of prison by any means possible should not be taken lightly, it still runs the risk of tightening the state's grip on others. Understanding these dynamics is paramount to building long-term change. Antitrafficking's frames offer too few options and too narrow paths to freedom, none of which are based in an intersectional racial justice framework and none of which have the capaciousness to work toward freedom from all violence, the prison and racism included.

3

When Slavery's Not Black

The Ark of Return is the United Nations memorial to the victims of the transatlantic slave trade. Located in New York City, the stunning white marble structure evokes a slave ship pointing eastward toward the west coast of Africa. The memorial solemnly conjures both the transatlantic trade and the Door of No Return through its abstract use of triangles and passageways. Pointing eastward activates the rich memoryscape of Black diasporic speculative returns to Africa.[1] Such imagined returns attend to the diasporic dispossessions experienced through the transatlantic slave trade and its legacies, where "freedom remains elusive as racism is persistently renovated."[2] The ship pointing eastward draws upon Black political analysis of, and creative responses to, alienation through making home and making kin, while simultaneously referencing the complex and conflicting relationships among Black diaspora, mobility, and freedom. The memorial was first authorized by the 2007 United Nations (UN) Resolution in response to the 2001 World Conference Against Racism (WCAR) Durban Declaration. The original justification for the memorial was framed as a way to honor the memory of the victims of the transatlantic slave trade, to increase attention to and awareness of the trade's history and "its lasting consequences," and to take a stand against racism in the present.[3]

At the sculpture's public unveiling on March 25, 2015, the UN secretary-general invoked the memory of the victims of the transatlantic slave trade to highlight the need to fight the injustice of modern slavery across the globe. In a press release for the event, Secretary-General Ban Ki-Moon called for "a renewal of our commitment to end modern slavery."[4] The commissioning documents, which built upon the antiracism work of the hotly contested WCAR in Durban in 2001, centered racism as the legacy of the transatlantic slave trade. By the 2015 unveiling, international human trafficking became the human rights issue that legitimated the need to remember slavery.[5] Anti-Black racism and Black global disparities are replaced with trafficking victims of every race and from every country.

After spending time observing the Ark of Return, I went inside the UN building to see what contextual information the organization provided for the memorial. The bookshop contained academic and public scholarship related to each of the key areas of the UN's sustainable development goals, including ending human trafficking and modern slavery, which is a target indicator of achieving "decent work and economic growth." Among the related titles, I found Siddharth Kara's *Modern Slavery: A Global Perspective*, Nadia Murad's *The Last Girl: My Story of Captivity and My Fight Against the Islamic State*, and Nicholas Kristof and Cheryl WuDunn's *Half the Sky*. Each book draws on the imagery and language of transatlantic slavery and nineteenth-century abolition to discuss contemporary sex and labor trafficking, primarily in South and Southeast Asia and the Middle East. Kara and Kristof are especially notorious for their sensationalized depictions and reproduction of colonialist stereotypes.[6] The victim types represented in these three selections are paradigmatic multicultural representations of the global present of slavery within the antitrafficking apparatus.

Next to the multicultural global present of slavery were titles representing the multicivilizational global past of slavery: *Byzantine Slavery and the Mediterranean World* and the textbook *Five Thousand Years of Slavery*.[7] I was especially struck by the cover image on *Five Thousand Years of Slavery*; the exact same unidentified color photograph of a South Asian adolescent peering through a wire cage is also the front matter of the 2009 State Department Trafficking in Persons (TIP) Report. Thinking through this multicultural context at the UN memorial to transatlantic slavery raises the question: what political work is accomplished when slavery is represented as not Black within antitrafficking discourse?

The UN assemblage of slavery past and slavery present manifests two of the antitrafficking discourse's refrains: slavery is as old as time and it is still happening today. In other words, a global history of slavery preceded the transatlantic trade and a global present of slavery succeeded the transatlantic trade.[8] In such a frame, white Europeans and Americans are not exceptionally to blame for slavery and Black and African diasporic subjects are not exceptionally righteous, nor especially worthy of, their claims to redress. The logic implies: if other groups have had and *gotten over* slavery, those who haven't financially succeeded or moved on from the past evince their own deficiencies. Slavery's legacies of racial injustice and structural inequity, in this logic, are not the contemporary focus, but real living slaves, who innocently suffer at the hands of evil individuals. Innocent suffering—those deemed worthy of care who passively, patiently, and gratefully await it—is contradistinguished from perceived Black diasporic cultural deviance, ungratefulness, and too-aggressive demands for justice.

Bookending racial chattel slavery with multicivilizational pasts and multicultural presents assists in manifesting neoliberalism's cultural and political project: to "cannibalize the histories of antiracist movements"[9] through the simultaneous "disavowal of racialized injustice as a figment of the past" and the public and private investment in systems of regulation and punishment framed as help and care.[10] If "under contemporary neoliberalism, the negative effects of continued disenfranchisement are framed as signs of Black pathology," then multiculturalism is used as visual proof that societies and states are no longer racist.[11]

Antitrafficking discourse and policy is, in many ways, the quintessential example of neoliberal multiculturalism. It projects a narrative that US capitalism and democracy are the drivers that have propelled a culturally and racially diverse American public into prosperity. Because some members of every racial and cultural group have prospered, those who have not are deemed in need of help or training, but not seen as victims of state-based or market-based racial oppression.[12] Antitrafficking discourse acknowledges global precarity but attempts to rectify it by welcoming culturally and economically isolated groups into the free market and rational, civil, global society. The ways that "race has continued to permeate capitalism's economic and social processes" is made to disappear.[13]

This chapter analyzes how multicultural pasts of slavery and abolition are employed to endorse neoliberal state agendas specifically through the figure of the non-Black multicultural victim of slavery today. Representations of multicultural global slavery, past and present, delegitimize claims to race-specific harms and state-specific accountability for that harm. Neoliberal multiculturalism within antitrafficking discourse helps contain contestatory social movements aimed at holding states and systems responsible for uneven safety in working, living, and mobility globally.[14] Antitrafficking's multicultural victims are then saved by neoliberal solutions: state investment in militarized humanitarianism abroad and carceral care at home are legitimated through various instantiations of the global slavery victim. In two examples that I explore below, the Yazidi woman enslaved by ISIS for sex is freed by US military intervention and the Latinx undocumented farmworker, who is depicted as enslaved by Latino middlemen, is rescued by Immigration and Customs Enforcement (ICE). The state agencies responsible for destruction are redeemed as benevolent abolitionists. In both cases, memories of interracial cooperation on the Underground Railroad are invoked to depict citizen surveillance initiatives that assist the state in enacting racial violence as antiracist action. Across historical memory in textbooks, public memory in museums, and media campaigns in airports, antitrafficking's narratives of multicultural slavery and multicultural abolition consolidate state approaches to safety—war, prisons, security, surveillance, and racial profiling—as paths to ending slavery. A variety of paradigmatic trafficking victim types are used to work through a range of geopolitical anxieties and US complicities in global injustice and unrest in the present, from war in the Middle East to immigration policy on the US-Mexico border. If neoliberal multiculturalism has worked in ways that displace social movements, and antitrafficking is a transparently neoliberal project,[15] then analyzing the uses to which multiculturalized pasts and presents of slavery and abolition are put reveals not only how antitrafficking discourse undermines specific social movements against corporate globalization, workers' rights, sex workers' rights, and immigrant justice,[16] but also how such containment of struggle is anchored in liberal modernity's discursive projects to prove Black criminality and Black incapacity for freedom and self-governance, and therefore to deem Black subjects undeserving of redress.

Five Thousand Years of Slavery

Before leaving the UN bookshop, I purchased the award-winning textbook *Five Thousand Years of Slavery*.[17] Its narrativization of slavery's multicultural past and present is instructive for thinking through the relationships among neoliberal multiculturalism, the antitrafficking apparatus, and antiblackness. The book aims to provide middle school students with a history of global slavery in order to inspire them to take action to free today's slaves. In the book's opening vignette, the authors write, "Much has been written about the abolition of slavery in the Americas, but we know a lot less about slavery in the world we live in today." Although they don't mention their motivation for conducting research on global slavery within the text itself, on their web page, they link it directly to living through pre–civil rights America in the past and hearing about slavery in Africa in the present:

> Marjorie and Janet, who are sisters, grew up in an America where "Whites Only" signs could still be seen. They remember how a powerful civil rights movement fought off the legacy of slavery to gain equality under the law for all Americans. When they learned about slave raids in modern Sudan and about children sold into slavery in modern Ghana, they decided that the story of world slavery had to be told. *Five Thousand Years of Slavery* was the result.[18]

The authors depict racial injustice in the United States as finished, while seeing slavery within Africa as aesthetically resonant with the US past. In order to better understand how slavery could still exist in Africa when slavery in the United States—*and its legacies*—had long been abolished, they went in search of the history of slaveries around the world. What they found was, among other things depicted in the text, Arab travelers' stories of "slave raids in Africa before the Europeans arrived there."[19]

In the textbook, the authors anchor the global history of slavery in the origins of the written record of history itself to demonstrate that "slavery has been woven into our history since the earliest times."[20] Slavery, in the text, begins in Sumer, an ancient civilization in the region of present-day Iraq. The sweeping history describes slavery within ancient Egypt, Israel, Greece, and Rome. It discusses Viking slavery within Europe and slavery under Islam during the Middle Ages. The book describes slavery within Africa existing before the Europeans and continuing after the British abolition of slavery. Slavery in the Americas is claimed to have been practiced within Indigenous communities before Columbus arrived. In other words, the textbook argues, slavery has been everywhere; if one looks back far enough, all races have enslaved, all have been enslaved. Who, then, could realistically be blamed? Representing global histories of enslavement practices lends multicultural equivalence to slavery and obscures the world-shaping role of the transatlantic slave trade in particular.

Within the textbook, every cultural group has had slavery, but Europeans are repeatedly represented as reluctant enslavers. After describing the pre-European history of slavery in Africa, the authors assert, "Since slave trading and slave raiding were already in place in Africa, the Europeans could get all the human merchandise they wanted."[21] In the discussion of slavery in Africa during European colonization after abolition, the authors state, "Though their country-folk back in Europe were against slavery, many colonists were afraid to upset local people by tampering with their traditional way of life, which relied on slaves and slave trading."[22] Europeans were, it is made to seem, too culturally sensitive to impose their abolitionist ways on the ever-self-enslaving African. King Ferdinand and Queen Isabella of Spain are valorized as not wanting Columbus to enslave Indigenous people, and even though he still did, the authors emphasize, "for hundreds of years before and after Columbus's arrival, they captured one another for use as slaves."[23] Although the chapter describes in detail cultural practices of Indigenous groups and slavery, it dedicates the section on European enslavement of Indigenous groups to Bartolomé de Las Casas's denouncements of Indigenous enslavement.[24] The argumentation suggests: while every culture has had slavery, Europeans also have a strong abolitionist tradition.

Additional chapters in the textbook cover the transatlantic triangle trade, with an emphasis on British abolition, and slavery in the United States, with an emphasis on white and Black abolitionists. A startling sidebar claims: "abolitionist movements happened only in Western cultures—in Britain, the United States, and Europe. Asia, Africa, and the Middle East have never produced mass movements to end slavery."[25] The authors' geography of abolition conveniently overlooks well-organized slave revolts across the Caribbean, most notably the successful Haitian Revolution. The Western cultural trait of being abolitionist is attributed to two uniquely Western institutions: religion and Enlightenment philosophy. John Locke gets credit for the idea that all people "share the same basic human rights."[26] Such received histories of Western liberal philosophy fail to mention Locke's financial investment in African slave trading through the Royal African Company and his exclusion of Black enslaved people from the category of the human.

Throughout the textbook's narrative of the multicivilizational pasts of slavery, the drastically different scales of slavery, and the drastically different effects of slave economies, are flattened into diverse cultural representations of instances of slavery. The multicultural slave past narratively deexceptionalizes the Black experience of slavery in the United States. European traditions of abolition are overrepresented; practices of slavery among Indigenous groups of the Americas and within Africa pre-European contact are overrepresented in relation to the vast amount of devastation and violence that European systems and practices of settler colonialism, Indigenous genocide, and African enslavement wreaked upon multiple continents. African, Arab, and Asian cultures are defined by their proclivity to slavery; European cultures are defined by their proclivities toward abolition and freedom. Only the chapters on the history of slavery in Africa, the Middle East, and Asia and the Southern Pacific make explicit connection to ongoing practices of slavery today. By contrast, the chapter on the American Civil War ends with a description of how the civil rights movement eliminated "the obstacles that black Americans faced" (past tense), as further evidenced by Barack Obama's triumphant election.[27] In other words, the United States has overcome its racism and any racist legacies of slavery; other countries, though, need US support to end slavery today. The textbook's historical narrative justifies the claims of the antitrafficking apparatus by using a multicultural past of slavery to discursively construct a multicultural victim of slavery today who will be freed by the freedom-loving US neoliberal agenda.

The textbook ends by discussing several examples of people who have been enslaved since Emancipation. All of these cases correspond to US state discourses of freedom or otherwise address, and rework, a range of geopolitical anxieties and US complicities. The US government exploited indigenous Alaskans, but it eventually paid them reparation, and thus is represented as having learned from mistakes of the past. The Communist Soviet Union, however, used forced labor in prisons; Nazi Germany enslaved the Russians; the present-day Chinese government imprisons political dissidents into slavery; North Korea and Cuba also repress dissent. All of these global enslavers map easily onto US foreign adversaries. All of these global enslavers are used to highlight US democratic freedoms.

Additional examples of contemporary slavery directly reproduce the paradigmatic figures within antitrafficking narratives: child soldiers in Africa, hereditary slavery in Mauritania, farmworkers in the United States, cocoa slaves in the Ivory Coast, and, of course, a Ghanaian child fishing slave who was sold by his parents. The caption next to the Ghanaian child baling water out of a fishing boat reads: "Mark Kwadwo was five when his parents sold him to this fisherman. He was rescued by a woman from Missouri who read about him in a newspaper in the United States."[28] In Ghana, the antitrafficking narrative repeats: Black parents sell their children into slavery and need white ladies to rescue them. In choosing these examples, the causes of modern slavery are narrated through the antitrafficking frame: they are the result of backward cultural practices (hereditary slavery in Mauritania, poor parents selling children in Ghana, Latinx-on-Latinx crime in the United States) or the result of weak or nonexistent law or corrupt disregard of international law (child soldiers in

Africa, exploitation of migrant workers in other countries due to lack of adopting the US-led antitrafficking law protocols). The textbook sets up a past that feeds directly into the antitrafficking apparatus's vision for ending exploitation. Indeed, Kevin Bales is credited with giving the authors "an expert's insight into the complexity of modern slavery" in the book's acknowledgments.

In the case of slavery within the United States, the textbook narrates the story of Latinx farmworkers who are smuggled into the country and held captive by Mexican and Guatemalan middlemen. The workers were freed by reporting their situation to US government officials who arrested and incarcerated the bosses. The story ends: "Many farm workers still face intimidation, mistreatment, and terror, but the Federal Bureau of Investigation (FBI) now actively enforces the law against human trafficking. When slave owners are behind bars, they cannot hurt honest workers."[29] Of course, it is very risky for undocumented workers to interact with the state, and imprisoned bosses don't change working conditions in the field. The distinction of "honest" workers also reinforces the binary of "good migrant" versus "bad migrant." In all of these cases, the US government frees today's multicultural victims of slavery through its laws and its example. Multiculturalism is employed to depoliticize slavery's legacy of antiblack structural racism; multiculturalism makes slavery in the present *not* Black American slavery in ways that redeem and maintain the legitimacy of US global governance.[30] Universalizing slavery in the past as having happened forever and everywhere rhetorically renders no specific nation, culture, or race exceptionally to blame, nor exceptionally financially liable.

Critical ethnic studies scholars have convincingly shown how neoliberal discourse and policy arose in ways that thwarted the multiracial solidarity of social movements in the 1960s and 1970s and that continues to reconsolidate the power of the capitalist class by disempowering and delegitimizing labor power through free trade, deregulation, and privatization.[31] Multiculturalism assists the enterprise by "manag[ing] racial contradictions on a national and international scale for U.S.-led neoliberalism."[32] Representations of multiculturalism become the proof that racial inequality has been overcome and thus legitimize US moral authority for global leadership. Making slavery multicultural, specifically, accomplishes this political task while also producing an efficacious antireparations rhetorical dodge. Narrativizing multicivilizational slavery and European abolition set up a past that maximizes white historical innocence. It creates a past usable for promoting neoliberal solutions to the problems facing today's victims: pass harsher punitive antitrafficking laws, imprison traffickers, regulate mobility and borders, deport migrants for their own good, encourage would-be migrants to stay in place, call the police if you see someone who looks suspicious.[33] Such solutions justify state violence in the name of abolishing slavery. And, central to my point here, these US state-based techniques and discourses about controlling mobility—promoting "stay[ing] in their designated, subordinated places" for their own good—were codified through racial segregation practices in the aftermath of slavery.[34] US histories of Black containment and US heroic memories of emancipation undergird antitrafficking's multiculturalism.

The Underground Railroad

Alongside the usefulness of slavery's multicultural pasts and presents for advancing antitrafficking's neoliberal solutions, antitrafficking campaigns render *abolition* in a multicultural past and present frame by centering the Underground Railroad. The Underground Railroad's narrative of interracial cooperation for freedom has been especially productive for legitimating the US Department of State's carceral approach to ending trafficking.[35] In order to reconfigure nineteenth-century abolitionist collaboration against the US government into twenty-first-century endorsement of arrest as global humanitarianism, the State Department has attached itself to history museums that utilize liberal multicultural interpretive frames for understanding the history of abolition through the Underground Railroad. In so doing, the Underground Railroad's narrative of diverse people coming together for freedom provides a past adaptable to a multicultural US public galvanizing itself to free today's multicultural victims of slavery. If white Europeans were the primary architects of abolition, as the textbook *Five Thousand Years of Slavery* suggests, now, according to Julietta Hua, "the fact that Latina/os, blacks, and Asian Americans are able to rescue the non-national Latina/o, black, and Asian trafficked subject demonstrates the exceptional ability of the U.S." to include those it previously excluded in the project of freedom.[36] By channeling the abolitionist past multiculturally, diverse US publics are called upon to carry out state projects of control, regulation, and punishment in the name of freedom. There are many ways to use the memory of the Underground Railroad for political projects in the present, but antitrafficking discourse allows the US state to transcend its racist past by globally expanding its institutions of control.

Perhaps no US State Department collaboration better exemplifies these dynamics than its relationship with the National Underground Railroad Freedom Center (NURFC) in Cincinnati, Ohio. The NURFC is a museum aimed at preserving the history of the abolition of slavery in the United States for diverse publics. In 2010, it began incorporating antitrafficking discourse into its permanent exhibitions and public programs. In order to tell the history of abolition, the museum offers a richly contextualized history of the transatlantic slave trade, the internal US slave trade, and the sites and communities of Black resistance to slavery, replete with rich scholarly detail and interactive features. The museum's primary exhibition *From Slavery to Freedom*, named for John Hope Franklin's classic study of the history of African America, does important work to name how liberalism founded the United States and its prosperity: individual freedom for some based on the exclusion and exploitation of others.

The NURFC explicitly uses a liberal multiculturalist lens to achieve its vision of promoting "inclusive freedom."[37] The museum is a transparently corporate-funded and state-sanctioned memory project that names the state violence of racial chattel slavery while amplifying memories of abolition to promote liberal narratives of national progress and racial inclusion. The museum was envisioned as a racial reconciliation project, first proposed in the early 1990s, to ease racial tensions and shake Cincinnati's reputation as a racist city.[38] The museum emphasizes the Underground Railroad narrative to promote a message that, as in the past, interracial cooperation will overcome racial injustice in the present. Like multiculturalism, cooperation suggests that racial injustice results from interpersonal conflict or prejudice, rather than structural racism, and it emphasizes "the goodwill of tolerant whites," while "affirm[ing] a positive cultural pluralism . . . to describe the United States as an internalized model of global diversity."[39] Neoliberal multiculturalism and racial reconciliation share compatible logics—discursively transcending racism without redressing power and material asymmetries—and both slip easily into dominant narratives of the Underground Railroad.

Cincinnati, the local context of the NURFC, has a long history of racism to overcome. Mob violence against Black communities has plagued Cincinnati's history. Violent white mobs in 1829, 1836, and 1841 drove Black residents out of the town in response to fears that the growing free Black population would increase competition for jobs and upset social order.[40] Such racial violence was also a product of the racial anxieties stirred up by Cincinnati's geographical location as the first free state point on the North side of the Ohio River, a location central to the NURFC's narrative of the Underground Railroad. The museum's telling of that narrative largely erases Cincinnati's ambivalence about Black freedom, though. Although Ohio drafted its 1802 constitution as an antislavery state, it rescinded African American male suffrage, restricted Black immigration from other states and territories, and enacted Black codes to disenfranchise, segregate, and limit Black movement and political participation.[41]

Since the 1990s, Cincinnati has been the site of many police murders of Black residents, including two high-profile cases in 2001 and 2015 that each sparked mass protests. When the NURFC opened in August 2004, the aftermath of the 2001 Cincinnati uprising against police brutality was still in full swing. Hundreds of activists had been arrested for participation in the protests; ongoing and new multi-issue social justice campaigns, boycotts, and lawsuits were galvanized by the uprising. Several of these activists saw the museum's project as in direct opposition to their own work for Black freedom in the present.[42]

Like many popular uses of the mythology of the Underground Railroad, the museum's emphasis on interracial cooperation tends toward smoothing over tensions—in Martin Luther King Jr.'s words "a negative peace"—rather than robustly addressing structural racial inequities that would lead to a "positive peace."[43] The Underground Railroad is a politically useful frame because it emphasizes cross-racial collaboration for freedom. It exists as the "great healing metaphor for the American psyche."[44] The story of the Underground Railroad does, indeed, give white and Black people across a wide spectrum of political orientations and affiliations a historical lesson with which they can agree. Depending on how one tells and remembers the Underground Railroad, many different narratives about self and country can be affirmed and upheld. The Underground Railroad could symbolize: a people united across difference in patriotic duty, the rugged individualism of the American spirit, the primacy of personal agency in the unquenchable American thirst for freedom, a quintessentially American entrepreneurial spirit, the centrality of white saviors to social movements, a past we have moved on from, a ray of hope in a sad chapter of American history, a biblical reminder to "help the less fortunate," a secular mode of apolitically "helping each other," or even, a historical model of what it will take to disrupt the ongoing white supremacy of the United States.[45] In order for each of these lessons to be gleaned from the history of the Underground Railroad, particular imagery, figures, and registers must be elicited and others elided.[46] According to Eric Foner, "The popular appeal of the underground railroad is not difficult to understand, even apart from the inherent drama of escaping from bondage. At the time of renewed attention to the history of slavery, the Civil War, and Reconstruction, subjects that remain in many ways contentious, the underground railroad represents a moment in our history when black and white Americans worked together in a just cause."[47] The Underground Railroad mythology helps Americans deal with an unpleasant past, although the lessons drawn from it vary widely.[48]

In 2010, the NURFC opened a permanent exhibition on human trafficking called *Invisible: Slavery Today*. In so doing, the museum used the Underground

Railroad's lesson of interracial cooperation to end nineteenth-century racial chattel slavery in the United States to endorse global cooperation for international human rights through supporting carceral agendas. *Invisible* is arranged to follow the life stories of five contemporary victims of slavery: Brazilian charcoal miners, Indian children working in brick kilns, Eastern European women who migrate for sex work, Central American agricultural workers on US farms, and Haitian children in restavèk. These paradigmatic victims of antitrafficking's multicultural slavery in the present repeat within *Invisible: Slavery Today* because the exhibition was designed in collaboration with several well-known antitrafficking NGOs: Free the Slaves, International Justice Mission, Polaris Project, and GoodWeave. The language and aesthetics that these organizations use shapes the exhibition.[49] In mounting the exhibition, the museum names the contemporary struggle for freedom resulting from the history of slavery and abolition as injustices that are beyond racial. The interracial cooperative past of abolition calls upon the multicultural US publics of the present to band together to free today's multicultural victims of slavery. The exhibition describes how visitors can bring that freedom to today's slaves: consume ethically, collaborate with the police, train the police, join a social media group, learn how to see the signs of slavery and trafficking, and involve the police when you suspect someone is enslaved. The aesthetic of racial unity symbolized through the Underground Railroad is repurposed through its attachment to antitrafficking to move beyond perceived racial tensions while bypassing, and providing a more palatable alternative to, solidarity-based social movement work for racial justice. The adoption of antitrafficking narratives within the NURFC troublingly offers up the history of slavery and abolition to be put to use as an endorsement of the benign heroism of the US government and Immigration and Customs Enforcement (ICE) in the midst of ongoing local and national campaigns against racist policing, carcerality, and immigrant detention.[50]

One of the five victim stories included in *Invisible: Slavery Today* is a Florida tomato picker named Mariano. His profile is the only one of the five that acknowledges trafficking into the United States. His character is drawn from the work of the Coalition of Immokalee Workers (CIW), a farmworker-led grassroots organization that has assisted in prosecuting employers on enslavement charges in the fields.[51]

Mariano is introduced to museumgoers as a migrant agricultural laborer who works long hours in poor conditions. According to the panel, Mariano is in this situation because of the lack of jobs in his home country: "Migrant laborers, like Mariano, are especially vulnerable to becoming enslaved. Desperate for work, they pay to be smuggled into countries where jobs are available. Employers can exploit these laborers by stealing their pay, coercing long hours of work, and keeping them in squalid conditions." This introduction to the plight of migrant farmworkers has the potential to very accurately unpack the structural conditions that make these sentences true. Agriculturalists in Mexico and Central America have been particularly desperate for jobs since the 1994 passage of the North American Free Trade Act (NAFTA) gutted national seed and fertilizer subsidies to small, cooperative, and subsistence farmers in Mexico.[52] That same law made an exception for American growers to continue to receive domestic subsidies, allowing them to sell their product on the so-called free market supracompetitively at below the cost of production. Mexican farmers who were not able to compete crossed borders in search of jobs. The United States facilitates this border crossing through its H-2A program, a temporary guest worker visa for agricultural workers that requires workers to remain with their sponsoring farm, requires those farmers to provide housing for the guest workers, and offers limited protections.[53] Many workers also choose to cross the border without temporary status. Because there are few, if any, legal ways for low-income Mexicans and Central Americans to obtain a pathway to permanent residence and citizenship in the United States, many workers are compelled to cross without documentation. What the museum's narrative sets up, then, is the individual manifestation of the structures engineered by the United States government that keep migrants vulnerable: free trade laws and tiered immigration laws.

Rather than address these underlying causes of precarious labor conditions in the United States, the exhibition represents Mariano's experience as the result of individual Latinx smugglers acting violently toward individual Latinx workers. In magnifying interpersonal violence as evil and irrational, the state violence of immigration control and economic policy is downplayed and invisibilized. The exhibition then resolves Mariano's unfreedom through figuring the US government as his hero-protector. The panel (seen in figure 3.1) reads: "Mariano told his story to investigators. Cesar was arrested, convicted, and sentenced to 12 years in prison. Mariano received a temporary visa for his testimony against Cesar. He still picks tomatoes but he is no longer a SLAVE." The state investigators are figured as benevolent protectors of migrants, even though in reality, undocumented workers are extremely vulnerable to police coercion and intimidation due to their status. The crime of smuggling is represented as an evil choice by bad people that will be eradicated through punitive measures. Through the figure of the victimized migrant worker, whose vulnerability is produced by state policies, the state erases its own complicity by refiguring

FIGURE 3.1 Exhibition panel in the National Underground Railroad Freedom Center's *Invisible: Slavery Today* exhibition. Photograph by the author, 2015.

itself as the protector of migrants. State-based punitive solutions are held up as effective resolutions to the exploitation built into the structure of migrant labor. Cesar was sentenced to serve twelve years in prison, to pay $239,882 in restitution to the victims, and to be deported after time served.[54] The deportation of Mexican-born criminals is thus normalized as righteous and just, and as *abolitionist*.

Cesar's arrest does nothing to keep Mariano safe in the fields or more financially secure in his home country. This panel suggests that the state cares for Mariano by providing him with a legal status, which ideally, would prevent him from being exploited by employers. However, the *legal* working conditions for H-2A workers are abysmal and even the low standards often go unenforced. How, then, does a temporary visa and an incarcerated perpetrator free Mariano from his enslavement? He is still subject to the structures that create his conditions. As a US tomato picker, he remains vulnerable to the terrible working conditions and low pay of work in the fields. By suggesting that only the most extreme forms of smuggling are the problem, the everyday exploitation of migrant farmworkers is naturalized.

Emphasizing the violence of smuggling as perpetrated by individuals obscures state-sanctioned and state-inflicted violence. A panel describes Mariano's "escape":

> Mariano arranged to be smuggled into the US so he could find work and help his family in Guatemala. He met Cesar who promised room, board, and loans to help cover the off-season. The work was brutal and exhausting. Anything that prevented Mariano from working resulted in beatings, knife slashing, or chain shackles. Worst of all was the isolation: no family or friends knew where he was. One day in 2007, Mariano was locked inside his home, a truck. Seeing a hole in the roof, he punched until it was big enough to wriggle through and then escaped.

Aesthetic similarities to the visual memory of racial chattel slavery are accentuated: beatings, chains, shackles. Aesthetic similarities to the visual memory of the Underground Railroad are also emphasized: dramatic escape, crawling through small spaces. In this rendering, physical confinement is the problem, the evil acts of the smuggler are the barriers to freedom, and freedom is represented as freedom of movement, but not freedom to migrate safely. Structural freedom remains unaddressed: the freedom to cross borders safely and legally or the freedom to be safe after "escape" are not problematized. Even though the state creates the conditions of, and for, precarious and exploitable migrant labor, the discourse of enslavement by individuals allows the state to figure incarceration as abolition and its border patrol agencies as abolitionist. Not only is state violence against migrants invisibilized in this narrative, but state violence is also called abolitionist.

The state-sanctioned approach to ending trafficking does nothing to protect laborers, but does legitimize the carceral logic of the United States. Justifying the positive outcomes of incarceration within NURFC's exhibitions is particularly striking in the context of contemporary organizing against mass incarceration that disproportionately, negatively, and unjustly affects Black American families. Justifying the positive role of ICE to free Latinx migrant workers is striking in the context of contemporary organizing for immigrant justice, including to abolish ICE, expand protections for undocumented students, and to end immigrant detention at the border. Using the gallery space to promote public buy-in and miseducation about immigration policy, undocumented Latinx immigrants, and border control is disturbing in light of the high-profile ICE raid near Cincinnati which resulted in the detainment of over a hundred undocumented workers in 2007, just months before exhibition planning for *Invisible: Slavery Today* began. Such raids continue throughout Ohio; in 2018, at least 260 migrant workers were arrested during ICE raids of major corporations.[55] In legitimating carceral and deportation mechanisms, antitrafficking discourse obscures the realities of present labor exploitation and undermines social movements for justice. The museum's endorsement of the antitrafficking agenda misses a compelling opportunity to link shared struggles for Black and Latinx freedom, as well as to link histories of the criminalization of Black movement (i.e., fugitive slaves) to the present criminalization of Black mobility.[56]

Mariano's story is an example of how antitrafficking discourse winds neoliberal multiculturalism through abolition rhetoric: the state agencies that produce the unfreedoms faced by migrant workers are deemed the new abolitionists. The logics of carceral care and deportation as care are produced through neoliberal policy and are now popularized as mechanisms of abolition, as instruments of freedom, through antitrafficking's naming of highly circumscribed instances of exploitation as modern-day slavery. In Grace K. Hong's work on neoliberalism, she traces the seeds of neoliberal logics of care, regulation, and punishment to the 1965 Moynihan Report, which legitimated the regulation of working-class Black women in the name of helping them achieve the respectability that made Black middle-class families secure. Hong describes neoliberalism as "a change in the distribution of respectability in response to the crises in racial capital as marked by the social movements of the mid-twentieth century."[57] US "official antiracism" is, then, evinced by inclusion and celebration of normative Black middle-class families into the harmonious multicultural present, while Black families struggling with precarity are deemed to have their shortcomings produced through their own immorality.[58] As such, the state authorizes itself to invite working-class Black families into respectability through regulating their behavior in the name of caring for them. Those regulations quickly enact state violence through punitive welfare restrictions, lack of access to affordable childcare and housing, and excessive policing of low-income Black neighborhoods. In other words, the broader logics of carceral care, of state regulation as care, and, thus, of deportation as care were architected through policies to control poor Black mothers. These neoliberal logics of differential inclusion and punitive care also extend to nation-states postdecolonization through international debt and its mandated structural adjustment policies.[59]

Neoliberalism functions in ways that splits intraracial solidarity within social movements by inviting some members of the group into greater capital comforts and social freedoms, while other members of the group are punished for not achieving normative success. Neoliberalism is built on liberalism's racial hierarchies to confound solidarity within and between social movements by substituting political critique of the structural roots of racial violence that tie various group oppressions together for market-based solutions to racism.[60] Narratives of individual success of some Black people plus discursive success of the entirety of certain groups (the Asian "model minority" rhetoric for instance) are used as evidence that states are no longer racist and that people are free, if they choose to be. Following Melamed, "multiculturalism has coded the wealth, mobility, and political power of neoliberalism's beneficiaries as the just desserts of multicultural global citizens while representing those neoliberalism has dispossessed as handicapped by their own . . . historico-cultural deficiencies."[61]

As deregulation and privatization shift more social care work from the state to nongovernmental organizations, NGOs become more involved in determining which groups or populations are deemed worthy of care. In the case of antitrafficking organizations and rhetoric, innocent, passive victims that have slavery inflicted upon them by individual bad guys are contradistinguished from the criminal, lazy, riotous, looting, immoral—in other words, completely undeserving—poor Black American descendants of slavery. Multicultural neoliberalism is architected in response to solidarity movements for racial and social justice, its logics of punishment as care were developed to solve the "problem" of poor Black women, and now the multiculturalized victims that are made visible as worthy of freedom from slavery are constructed in contradistinction to undeserving Black women. Antitrafficking's neoliberal project accomplishes all this through the language of slavery and abolition and by making slavery and abolition multicultural, which not only demonizes Black mothers (across the United States, Haiti, and Ghana), but also valorizes carceral solutions and restrictive border policies as the new abolitionism. In other words, antitrafficking advocacy uses the language of slavery and abolition to promote carceral-care-based solutions that undermine migrant social justice movements, and that containment strategy was architected through oppressing Black women.

Antitrafficking discourse centers representations of multicultural, international slaves who are victims of violence that their own cultures inflict upon them and who will be freed through strategies that were created to contain and control Black people in the first place. At the NURFC, then, the antitrafficking exhibition does a lot of political work to displace connections between the history of fighting against slavery in the United States and the ongoing struggle against antiblack violence in the United States. Through antitrafficking's neoliberal multiculturalism, the history and present of antiblackness is replaced with stories of other slaveries in other places not caused by the United

States nor by white people. Combining the mythology of the Underground Railroad with the multicultural slave of today racially legitimizes the antitrafficking project and valorizes solutions that neither provide safety nor liberation for precarious workers of any race, culture, or region. The Underground Railroad mythology can be instrumentalized for many political agendas, but antitrafficking's multicultural victim of modern slavery is particularly adept at offering former slaving states a narrative of transcending racial injustice in the present while figuring its domestic and international agents of terror and racial violence as the instruments of liberation.

Freeing ISIS Slaves on the Underground Railroad

The NURFC's relationship to the antitrafficking apparatus extends beyond its exhibition *Invisible: Slavery Today*. The museum houses its own antitrafficking nonprofit, End Slavery Now, which it acquired in 2013 to support antitrafficking efforts with learning resources and action tips. The museum has partnered with the US Department of State on several additional antitrafficking projects, including producing the film *Journey to Freedom* in 2012, which compares nineteenth-century Underground Railroad conductors with recipients of the State Department's Trafficking in Persons (TIP) Hero award. The film, which features TIP Heroes touring the NURFC, has been shown at US embassies across the world. In conjunction with their work with TIP Heroes, NURFC was contracted by the State Department to develop the Trafficking in Persons Hero Global Network to publicize the work of the honorees. According to the website, "The *TIP Report Heroes* often include NGO staff and government officials, from lawmakers to police officers, who are committed to ending modern slavery. They are recognized for their tireless efforts—despite resistance, opposition, and threats—to protect victims, punish offenders, and raise awareness of ongoing criminal practices in their countries and abroad."[62] As part of the TIP Award annual celebration, the TIP Heroes tour the NURFC before heading to Washington, DC, to be honored by the US secretary of state.

The TIP Heroes program is an important aspect of US-mandated antitrafficking enforcement abroad, which focuses primarily on punitive and rule-of-law solutions to end labor and sexual exploitation. By designating individuals and NGOs across the globe as the "heroes" of antitrafficking enforcement, the US government affirms a national imaginary of the uniquely American rugged individualist everyman quest for freedom that is central to its national myth-making and international reputation. Such antitrafficking individual heroes are, through connection to the National Underground Railroad Freedom Center, imagined as modern-day abolitionists and conductors of today's Underground Railroad. This figuration also frames the coordinated efforts of nineteenth-century abolitionists as individual people who acted alone in the name of what was right. In other words, freedom is simply a part of the human spirit, and no nation has exemplified that more than the United States. It completely erases the fact that nineteenth-century abolitionist actions, big and small, were being taken against the US government. In this sense, the modern-day equivalent would be more like smuggling people across the border or busting people out of jail—neither of which is condoned by antitrafficking. That is, unless the people being smuggled are Yazidi women escaping sexual enslavement at the hands of ISIS.

In 2015, Ameena Hasan, a former member of the Iraqi Council of Representatives, was awarded the TIP Hero for her efforts to free Yazidi women who were being enslaved by ISIS fighters for sex. Several days before receiving her award, PBS Frontline aired the documentary Escaping ISIS, which tells the story of how Ameena and her husband Khalil run a hotline to receive information about kidnapped Yazidis and then conduct a series of risky maneuvers to find and free individuals. The documentary "presents the gripping, first-hand accounts of women who escaped the brutal reign of ISIS—and follows an underground network that's helping them escape." [63] Ameena Hasan's efforts to free Yazidi women from sex slavery are framed within the drama and suspense of planned escape, aided by mobile phone technology. The antitrafficking philanthropic news website CNN "Freedom Project" aired Yazidi: Strength and Survival several months later. The narrator of that film describes Ameena Hasan's approach: she utilizes "a network to smuggle the women out" and her "weapon against ISIS is her phone."[64] The Hasans are represented as blending the methods of the Underground Railroad with the modern technology of cell phones to fight off the anachronistic evil of Arab slave traders that ISIS threatens to reintroduce to modern society.

The figure of the ISIS sex slave was integrated into antitrafficking discourse shortly after ISIS attacked Mount Sinjar in northern Iraq in August 2014 and killed and kidnapped many Yazidi people. News reports suggest that the attack was motivated by religious persecution; US secretary of state John Kerry declared ISIS's actions against the Yazidi a genocide, noting that ISIS "captured and enslaved thousands of Yazidi women and girls, selling them at auction, raping them at will."[65] The figure of the enslaved Yazidi woman is backed by reports from Human Rights Watch, Amnesty International, and ISIS itself. Through its English-language magazine Dabiq, which is widely held as propaganda, ISIS claims that slavery and sex slavery are allowable. Footage of ISIS fighters discussing the price of women or circulating images of Yazidi women captives further advance the image of the Yazidi woman being sold for sex and traded among ISIS men.[66] Public and political outrage against Arab terrorist persecution of religious minorities combined with the specter of sexual slavery provoked cross-partisan support for the United States to more directly intervene in the region militarily in the name of humanitarianism.[67]

The case of Yazidi sex slaves demonstrates how the figure of the sex slave—a well-worn template designed and deployed for moral panicking and generating support for militarized humanitarian intervention—is mobilized around a new political anxiety: ISIS. The US public's lack of knowledge about ISIS combined with the gruesomeness of its media spectacle, make the case ripe for the insertion of a clear-cut figure for moral panic.[68] To work out the anxieties of perceived loss of control and rise of evilness, the figure of the sex slave soothes the panic by inserting a familiar figure that clearly separates good from evil. It provides a simplified way for readers to enter the political conversation about ISIS because it marks a clear perpetrator and a clear victim (a victim who is depicted as a red-headed, blue-green-eyed religious minority that is constructed by news agencies to "metonymically stand in for Christians").[69] This simplicity covers over the very complicated political landscape of domestic Syrian and Iraqi politics and US complicity in the region.

The figure of Yazidi women enslaved to ISIS fighters follows the imagery first used in the US State Department TIP Reports of barbarous insurgent forces taking sex slaves in sub-Saharan Africa, now extended to the Middle East. But instead of framing the practice as modern or timeless, Yazidi enslavement for sex is framed as an ancient practice that ISIS seeks to reintroduce anachronistically to the modern world. This change in temporality positions ISIS as reintroducing a new strand of an old sickness that the United States has long since cured. Reintroduction as a theme imagines a purposeful pull backward, with sinister agency and force, rather than a sorry, static state of uncivilization as portrayed in sub-Saharan Africa. Julietta Hua describes how antitrafficking tropes that mobilize "the resurrection of an 'old evil'" figure transatlantic slavery as "an aberration—a lapse and error of judgment that, like terrorism, threatened moral principles by introducing evil."[70] In such a frame, the United States' past of racial violence is overcome through the uniquely American drive to fight for liberty, which is also what makes the United States morally qualified to fight terrorism and free Yazidi women from slavery under ISIS. The frame of old(er) evil exculpates US pasts; it also maps onto antitrafficking's use of the imaginary of the Arab slave trader, said to have come before Europeans began enslaving people and to have persisted after Europeans had abolished the practice. Remember that, according to *Five Thousand Years of Slavery*, slavery itself began with the ancient civilizations in the region of present-day Iraq. Islamophobic justifications for antiterrorism militarism extend into antitrafficking discourse[71] and, in the case of sex slavery specifically, offer contemporary evidence that Arabs are truly *the* brutal enslavers and have *always* been so. Visual evidence of the Arab slave trader in the present lends veracity to antiblack and antireparations slavery apologist narratives that rely on the figure of the Arab slave trader in the past.

Media narratives suggest ISIS fighters enslave Yazidi women for sex and a Yazidi Kurdish couple sets up an underground railroad to smuggle them to safety. In this media economy, antitrafficking discourse and logic are employed to work out geopolitical anxieties resulting from the war on terror.[72] Ameena Hasan's work is acknowledged by the State Department, which simultaneously downplays US complicity in the rise of ISIS and highlights the US abolitionist past through the imagery of the Underground Railroad. The American people and government, then, are imagined as model abolitionists who invented the methods of the Underground Railroad, and who now help lead the Middle East to freedom by supporting individual efforts to emulate the Underground Railroad with militarized humanitarian aid. The Underground Railroad mythology proves to be a flexible tool for soothing national anxieties about complicity at home and abroad. The State Department ties its antitrafficking agenda—promoting safety through policing, militarism, and counterterrorism surveillance—to the Underground Railroad through its discursive relationship to modern-day slavery and, in part, through its institutional relationship with the National Underground Railroad Freedom Center. The US government casts itself as the ultimate conductor of the Underground Railroad by intervening in modern-day slavery scenarios to "sav[e] brown women from brown men."[73]

Antitrafficking depictions of multicultural pasts and presents of slavery and abolition soothe contemporary political anxieties of former slaving nations. In the case of demands for Black reparations on the US government, the existence of many slaveries among many regions, cultures, and racial groups in the past renders the United States not exceptionally to blame. In the case of Mariano's story, political anxieties about migration, people moving across borders, and the US complicity in creating these situations is eased with a US state-based hero narrative that resolves unsafe migrant mobility through the very institutions that create the precarity: immigration laws, borders, and policing. In the case of the depictions of Yazidi women, the moral clarity of the figure of the sex slave is used to "clear up" any public confusion about the role of the United States in the region—the United States is supporting local leaders like the Hasans to (finally) lead their own people out of slavery through an Underground Railroad–like infrastructure that US heroes engineered over 150 years ago. Examples of non-Black, multiculturalized contemporary slavery victims are inserted into the discourse of slavery and its aftermath to steer the narrative away from Black demands for justice that indict the US government in favor of narratives of slavery and abolition that uplift the US government as a benevolent geopolitical entity that solves, but bears no responsibility for creating, the global issues of insecurity faced by Latinx farmworkers and Yazidi women alike.

Take Flight

Borders, mobility, security, racial profiling, antiterrorism, and surveillance: all the concerns and techniques of state approaches to safety manifest in antitrafficking awareness raising campaigns in airports. Antitrafficking advocates have focused on raising awareness within air travel because of the assumption that traffickers transport people by airplane, and therefore airports become key sites for public pedagogical and state agency-based antitrafficking interventions. The campaigns specifically draw upon the antiterrorism citizen surveillance discourse of "if you see something, say something." Positioned within the highly securitized scrutiny of airport travel, such antitrafficking campaigns and slogans are smoothly and readily incorporated into the state security apparatus. The antitrafficking industry's focus on airports as a hot spot of trafficking can also be tied to the popularization of Anti-Slavery International's image of the slave ship turned airplane. In that image, the nineteenth-century abolitionist image of the slave ship *Brooks* is superimposed onto an airplane. The poster reads: "Trafficking Is Modern Slavery. The Methods Have Changed but People Are Still Suffering." The poster tells its viewer to be aware of trafficking in airports and airplanes but leaves it to the viewer's imagination to determine what such trafficking might look like. It invokes the history of slavery to endorse heightened citizen surveillance in airports and racial profiling of air travelers. By contrast, Simone Browne's study of the history and development of surveillance practices analyzes the same abolitionist print of the *Brooks* slave ship to demonstrate "how racism and antiblackness undergird and sustain the intersecting surveillances of our present order."[74]

The antitrafficking organization A21 airs its "Can you see me?" awareness raising videos in airports across the United States and the United Kingdom. The organization's mission is to "abolish slavery everywhere, forever," and it proclaims that its staff and supporters are "the abolitionists of the 21st century."[75] The organization works closely with the FBI, Homeland Security, the US

Department of Justice, and the UK Border Force.[76] The "Can you see me?" campaign "helps the public identify a victim" and trains them to make reports to law enforcement, government officials, and NGOs.[77] I first encountered a "Can you see me?" video while sitting in the international boarding area for a plane; in it, an ambiguously raced Latina teenager was drugged and trafficked by an ambiguously raced Latino young man. In the video, the white classroom teacher, from whose classroom the teenager was trafficked, saves the girl in the end. Another poster from the campaign hangs in the Washington Dulles airport. As seen in figure 3.2, it depicts a young Asian woman working in a nail salon under the harsh eye of an older Asian woman. The young woman looks slyly toward to the white woman customer, longing to be saved.[78] All A21's "Can you see me?" public service announcements alert airport passengers that "Slavery still exists. If you suspect it, report it." But all that travelers are being trained to do through these awareness raising materials is suspect racialized people of being dangerous. At Atlanta's Hartsfield-Jackson airport, there are standing banners throughout busy walkways that depict ambiguously light-skinned hands wrapped in rope, with the slogans "Human trafficking is not welcomed" and "Human trafficking is a form of modern day slavery. . . . If you see something, say something." These antitrafficking campaigns utilize securitization strategies of citizen surveillance and racial profiling to be able to "spot the signs" of trafficking and call on police and other agencies to intervene. What constitutes the signs of trafficking, though, is highly ambiguous. Racialized suspicion becomes the key mode of public engagement.

The violence of racialized suspicion is escalated when antitrafficking organizations "empower" citizens to involve the authorities based on these ambiguous racial markers.[79] Reporting racialized travelers to the police or to border enforcement is condoned as the best way to free people from slavery. Calling the cops is rendered as twenty-first-century abolition. Racial profiling, as an antitrafficking method, is reframed from its status as an unintended but necessary consequence of antiterrorism practices into an antiracist technology for the abolition of slavery. Such uses of racial profiling soothe generalized anxieties about racial mobilities and racial liminalities while reinforcing airport racial profiling as legitimate. In the larger social context, antitrafficking advocacy legitimates racial profiling as an abolitionist strategy, amid high-profile police violence against and public profiling of Black people, including as Simone Browne notes, the disproportionate surveillance faced by Black women with US passports in airports.[80]

Delta Airlines, whose hub is in Atlanta's Hartsfield-Jackson airport, posts the following indicators of human trafficking on signs throughout its terminals:

FIGURE 3.2 Ad for A21's antitrafficking "Can you see me?" campaign.

A21.ORG/CANYOUSEEME

08000 121 700
NATIONAL MODERN SLAVERY HELPLINE

"Be alert for human trafficking. They hide in plain sight. Signs of asking for help, avoids eye contact, heavily guarded, physical signs of distress, high level of nervousness, *something is just off*. Report any signs by contacting law enforcement or the National Human Trafficking Hotline."[81] Such descriptors, as seen in figure 3.3, are strikingly ambiguous, cuing civilian surveillers to fill in the blanks with the dominant imagery that has been associated with trafficking and slavery. Paired with A21's scenarios from the "Can you see me?" campaign videos, which endorsers have described as "provid[ing] the public with real life examples," airport travelers would visualize young Asian girls accompanied by older Asian women, young Latina teenagers accompanied by older Latino men, or white girls and women accompanied by anyone of color.[82]

In 2017, a Mexican man traveling to the United States by airplane was accused of human trafficking by another passenger on the plane. The flight attendant alerted Customs and Border Patrol ahead of the plane's arrival and the man and his biracial daughter (the presumed trafficking victim) were immediately taken into custody and questioned until the man's white American wife vouched for them.[83] The figures of the Mexican man and the ambiguously white female child reference paradigmatic victim figures in the antitrafficking discourse: the Latinx pimp who traffics Latina women for sex, the Latina victim of trafficking, the white underage female victim of sex trafficking. Although the family was eventually released, they were harassed and racially profiled. It is not hard

FIGURE 3.3 A Delta airlines antitrafficking campaign banner describes indicators for identifying victims of human trafficking in airports, including "Something is just off." Photograph by the author, 2018.

to imagine this incident ending with more dire consequences, if the father was a single parent, if the two had different last names, or if an unpaid parking ticket turned up in the background check.

It is not a coincidence that this seemingly bizarre antitrafficking intervention took place. Antitrafficking materials train airline passengers and employees alike to report trafficking based on these exact indicators. Beginning in 2009, the organization Airline Ambassadors International (AAI), comprised of airline employees, has included ending human trafficking in its mission. The group trains flight attendants to identify and rescue human trafficking victims. According to the group's website, "AAI worked closely with Customs Border Protection to develop an industry specific training consistent with the Department of Homeland Security's 'Blue Campaign.'" In 2018 alone, the group conducted thirty-three human trafficking trainings to 2,328 employees, which it claims has "enabled the effective monitoring of 65 million travelers."[84] The organization has expanded its relationship with the US State Department, which has supported AAI trainings in the Caribbean and Asia, and has developed a "TIP Line" reporting phone app for trainees to report suspected trafficking cases directly to law enforcement.[85]

In the slides that accompany AAI's antitrafficking training, the majority of the images of trafficking victims are young white women or girls. One slide pictures small white hands bound together with a baggage tag marked from Mexico. The training materials list the visible indicators for trafficking victims as "afraid of uniformed security, unsure of destination, frightened, ashamed or nervous." Another slide suggests ways to spot a trafficker including: "may answer questions for the victim," "observe[s] victim persistently," and "poses as a relative." That slide concludes with the statement, "Flight attendants have correctly assessed trafficking situations with each of these indicators."[86] If a flight attendant observes these indicators, they are instructed to radio the upcoming airport, call the Department of Homeland Security tip line, and call the National Human Trafficking Hotline. By the standards of the AAI, then, the airline passenger had correctly identified the Mexican dad as a trafficker, his daughter as a trafficking victim, and the flight attendant had acted appropriately to free a slave. Except that she had not.

Racialized depictions that trade in stereotypes are used to appease generalized fears of insecurity. Antiterrorism airport practices that gained intensity through post-9/11 Islamophobia connect to fears about migration to call for further surveillance efforts that are doled out by the populace against each other.[87] Antiterrorism's tactics, now naturalized and widespread, are made more benevolent through the antitrafficking apparatus. Antitrafficking surveillance, it is made to seem, is not to justify war or national safety, but to free individual slaves. Antitrafficking discourse encourages neighborly collaborations with the state that increase interventions into public and private spaces for state surveillance. Those interventions in airports double down on populations that are already more at risk for surveillance and state-imposed violence. Antitrafficking indicators and campaigns promote racial profiling in ways that assist other state security projects of surveillance, especially in airports, "where enactments of surveillance reify boundaries and borders, and weigh down some bodies more than others, where the outcome is often discriminatory treatment."[88] By framing antitrafficking's racial profiling as the abolition of slavery, citizens can feel good about both their racist suspicions of bodies out of place and their actions to alert authorities to regulate such bodies. By calling these actions abolitionist, individuals become antiracist for participating in state racial violence. Such uses of the ideas of slavery and abolition are particularly disturbing because of how practices of racial profiling were architected through a long history of patrolling and policing Black people.[89] If a multicultural slavery of the present is, following Jared Sexton, an example of the "consistent analo-gizing to abstract black suffering that actually displaces black struggles," then racial-profiling-as-abolition analogizes Black freedom struggles of the past (the abolition of slavery) to displace Black freedom struggles in the present (to abol-ish the police) by legitimating state racial violence.[90]

Employees of Homeland Security and the Transportation Security Admin-istration (TSA) are also trained in trafficking identification methods and enact racial profiling to screen for potential cases of trafficking. While waiting to cross the US border from Toronto, Canada, I coincidentally witnessed an an-titrafficking intervention between a US border agent and an Asian father and daughter who did not have US passports. The border agent asked the father the standard questions: how long they were staying in the United States and if they had return tickets. The agent asked the daughter, who looked to be about twelve years old, what day they were coming back to Canada. She looked nervously at her dad, who was observing her intently and seriously and lovingly, and who then answered for her, "Monday." This nondescript, subtle family in-teraction had just ticked five of the indicators of human trafficking (victim is afraid of uniformed security, acts nervous, trafficker poses as relative, answers for victim, observes victim). As if on script, the border agent then immediately asked the girl, "Who is this man?" She looked surprised and said "my dad." Both the dad and daughter laughed nervously and the girl asked "Why?" The agent did not respond and passed them through. As I approached the same agent, next in line, he muttered to me: "Kids just don't get it." I laughed nervously and re-sponded, "Oh?" He told me: "She asked why I asked if that was her dad. They don't get it. People steal people." I nodded silently as he looked over my US pass-port and Canadian temporary work permit and asked me: "What do you teach?"[91]

Near the exit that I passed as I cleared, a poster from the Department of Homeland Security's Blue Campaign depicted a young Latino man looking forlorn while working at a sewing machine. The poster instructed passersby to "recognize human trafficking" and "to report suspected trafficking" by call-ing US Immigration and Customs Enforcement. Human trafficking, then, is recognizable as Latinx workers and young Asian girls with older Asian men or women. In both of these cases, the need for an antitrafficking screening was correctly identified by the reporters through the indicators taught to them by NGO and government antitrafficking campaigns. In neither case was the young girl a trafficking victim. In neither case was her father a trafficker. In both cases, racial profiling in order to free slaves enacted racial harm.

Airline Ambassadors International developed its antitrafficking training based on the indicators determined by the US Department of Homeland

Security's Blue Campaign. The Blue Campaign promotes a variety of aware-ness raising materials to educate citizens as well as government agency em-ployees on how to detect and report human trafficking to Homeland Security. The Blue Campaign's trafficking victim indicators are:

Does the person appear disconnected from family, friends, community organizations, or houses of worship?

Has a child stopped attending school?

Has the person had a sudden or dramatic change in behavior?

Is a juvenile engaged in commercial sex acts?

Is the person disoriented or confused, or showing signs of mental or physical abuse?

Does the person have bruises in various stages of healing?

Is the person fearful, timid, or submissive?

Does the person show signs of having been denied food, water, sleep, or medical care?

Is the person often in the company of someone to whom he or she defers? Or someone who seems to be in control of the situation, e.g., where they go or who they talk to?

Does the person appear to be coached on what to say?

Is the person living in unsuitable conditions?

Does the person lack personal possessions and appear not to have a stable living situation?

Does the person have freedom of movement? Can the person freely leave where they live? Are there unreasonable security measures?

The Blue Campaign instructs civilians to "report suspected human traffick-ing to federal law enforcement."[92] There is also a wallet card available with several trafficking indicators listed and the direct line to report suspicious ac-tivity to ICE.

In the summer of 2019, new reports emerged that Latinx migrants were get-ting stranded in airports because of family separation and the migrant detention crisis along the US-Mexico border. Juan González, a journalist for the activist media outlet *DemocracyNow!*, reported witnessing migrant distress in airports:

But right on our flight, we noticed that there were several other passengers who appeared to be Central Americans, obviously couldn't speak English, didn't know what was going on. And so we sort of tried to help them try to figure out where to go to try to rebook their flights. It turns out they were all Central American refugees who had just been released from detention centers and were being basically shipped by the federal government to relatives somewhere in other parts of the United States. . . . But then we discovered that there were—the American Airlines people were of no help whatsoever in terms of trying to assist these people, because the lines were so long. But we discovered that there were several employees of—not of the airlines, but who worked in the airport . . . maintenance people and others, who have been now for months trying to assist these stranded Central American refugees, trying to provide them food, blankets, whatever they could. They were doing it all on their own time and pulling money out of their own pocket to try to assist these folks. The airlines wanted to ship them to Minneapolis or to Miami or to Greensboro to stay overnight in those areas, to get new flights to go wherever they were trying to head to. And as the employees started telling me this, they said this is happening every single day, and especially in the hub airports, like Denver and Dallas and Chicago. When storms, these summer storms come and there are outages and plane cancellations, these migrants are completely lost. And no one is assisting them. No one is helping them. . . . And I just think if anyone who speaks Spanish who's in one of these airports and sees someone who's completely lost, any help you can give them, I think, would be appreciated.[93]

In this situation, the stranded migrants meet many of the "key indicators of trafficking" as laid out by the US Department of Homeland Security's Blue Campaign. The airport-stranded migrants are, indeed, disconnected from family; the children have stopped attending school; they appear disoriented, confused, fearful; they show signs of being denied water, food, sleep, and medical care; they lack personal possessions and have not had a stable living situation; and they are, most clearly, being denied freedom of movement and subjected to "unreasonable security measures." Despite meeting all of these criteria, the migrants are not being assisted by flight attendants; no pilots are calling the police to report that Homeland Security and ICE are trafficking victims from Central America. There are no well-funded awareness raising campaigns pasted throughout the airports explaining how to help stranded migrants. There are no TV commercials encouraging civilians to get involved. There are no PSAs warning of the criminal activity of ICE and its agents and the need for civilian surveillers to report on the illegal activity of ICE. Flight attendants trained to help trafficking victims don't see stranded migrants as meeting the criteria. Corporate airlines tout their own social responsibility for the role they play in freeing modern slaves while actually existing people in need languish in their terminals. The airport workers themselves, far from calling ICE to save the day, pool their individual resources to support the migrants, in acts of community-based care for community safety. Thinking though this counterfactual reveals the absurdity of antitrafficking indicators and airport messaging: they are invested in monitoring and controlling the movement of racialized populations. They do so through multicultural narratives of neoliberal freedom.

Antitrafficking airport campaigns construct slavery as an intraracial phenomenon. The enslavers in these campaigns are Asian or Latinx; they enslave members of their own race and culture. The abolitionists are the agents of US government agencies and the compliant US multicultural public who collaborates with them. The multicultural enslaver and the multicultural slave are freed by the no longer racist US government agencies that continue to be responsible for committing racial violence against migrant populations, including Black migrant populations. Members of the public mobilize their own racialized suspicions and hone their racial profiling skills in the name of being abolitionists. The former slaving nation of the United States and the current racially violent nation of the United States are exculpated of responsibility in multiple directions. Slavery is no longer Black; slavery is enacted primarily by Latinx and Asian figures; Homeland Security frees people from being enslaved by their own cultures; racial profiling and harassment result in freedom for the people profiled. Racial profiling's origins in US policing and antiblack violence is renamed an abolitionist technology.

Several months prior to González's report, Donald Trump justified his administration's violent policies toward refugees and immigrants in the name of protecting women and children from human traffickers. During the 2019 State of the Union address, he states:

> Tolerance for illegal immigration is not compassionate—it is cruel. One in three women is sexually assaulted on the long journey north. Smugglers use migrant children as human pawns to exploit our laws and gain access to our country. Human traffickers and sex traffickers take advantage of the wide open areas between our ports of entry to smuggle thousands of young girls and women into the United States and to sell them into prostitution and modern-day slavery.[94]

In this rhetoric, building a border wall, which increases the precarity of migrants, who are already vulnerable to extreme exploitation by middlemen, is justified in the name of ending modern-day slavery. Trump, whose politics are built on white nationalism and racist and anti-immigrant sentiment, refashions himself as a modern-day abolitionist who uses the tools of ICE and border walls to set migrants free. Trump's speech was informed by his meeting a few days prior with Timothy Ballard, founder of the antitrafficking organization Operation Underground Railroad.[95] Operation Underground Railroad uses paramilitary vigilantism to free children in Haiti and Thailand from sexual predators.[96] Ballard chose to name his antitrafficking organization after the Underground Railroad because it gave an example of "a group that acted and infiltrated."[97] He uses the stories and likenesses of Harriet Tubman and Harriet Jacobs, two formerly enslaved Black American women who freed themselves, to endorse posthumously, and to racially legitimize, his organization's paramilitary, carceral approach to ending trafficking.[98] Slavery and abolition, then, are multiculturalized to evince US racial transcendence even amid the resurgence of explicit racial hatred and transparently and boldly racist state policy.

Antitrafficking rhetoric, and its paradigmatic victims and enslavers, has demonstrated a remarkable flexibility for addressing a diverse array of political issues and political anxieties for leaders and residents of former slaving nations across the political spectrum. Across all political uses, though, antitrafficking discourse renders state-imposed racist violence, in the past and in the present, as proof of national progress and promotes regulation and surveillance as care for racialized groups. The parade of multicultural slaves from other times and other civilizations in world history establish the history of US racial chattel slavery as just one instance in a long line of humans enslaving one another, leaving white Americans not exceptionally to blame, nor Black Americans deserving of special protected status or redress for histories of injustice. The multicultural slavery victim of the global present, often constructed as enslaved by members of their own racial, cultural, or geographic community, is freed by the US government through the exact state agencies that enact structural violence, whether border enforcement, the police, or the military. The antitrafficking apparatus's multiculturalism draws on narratives of the Underground Railroad, and of abolition more generally, to make state approaches to safety—racial profiling, surveillance, border control, militarism—seem antiracist. They are rendered antiracist because the racialized language of slavery elicits abstract Black suffering, but the struggle to ameliorate anti-Black racism is then elided through the multiculturalization of slavery.[99] Employing neoliberal solutions to end modern slavery further obscures the antiblack origins of such neoliberal solutions, whether punishment as care or profiling as abolition, while fortifying, and affirming as antiracist, the ongoing racial violence that such solutions inflict across many racialized groups.

The subsection title with which I close this chapter—"Take Flight"—is a reference to Meshell Ndegeocello's song "Nova," which is the theme song for Ava DuVernay's TV show *Queen Sugar*. The lyric, "keep the colors in the lines / take flight / dreams never die," and the rapid urgency with which the phrase "take flight" punctuates the song's various lyrical configurations, calls to mind the political possibilities and freedom dreams that lay in Black speculative flights for freedom, which extend and proliferate amid, despite, and in stark contrast to highly securitized air travel and antiterrorism practices of racial profiling.[100] Those state security practices have been refined and normalized through the everyday racial profiling of Black people in US domestic life. Taking flight, here, might offer a path, following Simone Browne's idea that "dark sousveillance . . . speaks to black epistemologies of contending with antiblack surveillance,"[101] to read antitrafficking imagery against itself. The imagery of the slave ship turned airplane antitrafficking poster (from Anti-Slavery International) does, indeed, offer a historical archive of continuities and antecedents in surveillance, containment, and regulation practices that racialize, from the slave ship *Brooks* to racial profiling and airport security post-9/11. The instrumental schematics of the diagram of the slave ship *Brooks* attest to the bureaucratization of the business (and violence) of slavery, but they also flatten and conceal the insurrectionary contestations for freedom that such harsh measures were put in place to control.[102] The Black fight for freedom, Black flights for freedom, to Africa, from Africa, and circumnavigating the globe, far exceed the antitrafficking apparatus's vision for freedom. Perhaps Black flight is exactly what antitrafficking aims to control.

4

Deceptive
Empiricism

A popular antitrafficking infographic compares the average price of a slave in 1809 to the average price of a slave in 2009. The 1809 slave, represented with the black bathroom logo for the men's room, is equated with fifty bags of money. The 2009 slave, represented with the same black logo for man, is equated with four single dollars. The infographic claims that "adjusted to today's value," a single slave cost $40,000 USD in 1809, but two hundred years later, a single slave costs only $90 USD. The source of this data is attributed to "Kevin Bales, Freetheslaves.net." Bales introduced the claim in 1999 in his book *Disposable People*.[1] The infographic, represented in figure 4.1, has been stationed on CNN's "Freedom Project: Ending Modern-Day Slavery" website, on a sidebar titled "The Numbers . . . a glance at the data behind the problem," since 2011.[2]

The infographic uses datafied aesthetics to make a highly politicized claim about care toward slaves in the past and present appear neutral and objective. The infographic is built upon the assumption that if slaves are worth less today, they are more easily disposed of, and thus, less well protected by slave owners than in the past. Such a claim mirrors Lost Cause paternalistic ideologies and proslavery narratives that suggested plantation slavery in the United States was benign and that Southern race relations on the plantation were peaceful, harmonious, and importantly, the *natural order* of the hierarchy of the races. The claim, reconfigured through antitrafficking discourse, deploys economic reasoning that presumes plantation slaveowners' motivations were economically rational. It implies: why would a slaveowner undermine his own financial investment by hurting one of his slaves? This logic casts slaveowners as sympathetic, rational men of their time and suggests that they took care of the people they owned. These assumptions are made explicit on Free the Slaves' website, which states "modern slaves are not considered investments worth maintaining."[3] Such historical projections about slaveowners' financial incentives are shaky at best,[4] and derive from liberal notions of the productivity of free labor, that, based in Adam Smith's philosophies, were also used to argue that "slave labor was the more expensive form of labor" during the age of abolition.[5] Yet, even if antitrafficking discourse's slave economics are accepted at face value, such reasoning opportunistically emphasizes one assumption about economic rationality and the profit motive for slavery while obscuring many others: how much more might it be worth to assert white dominance, supremacy, and power at all costs?[6]

The idea that slaves are cheaper now than ever before, and its underpinning erroneous assumption about historical white care for Black people, circulates widely as an empirical fact throughout the antitrafficking mediascape. An exhibition panel at the National Underground Railroad Freedom Center explains the "economics of slavery" by quoting the difference in cost of slaves, stating, "As modern day slavery expert Kevin Bales wrote in *Disposable People*, slaves today 'are treated like cheap plastic ballpoint pens . . . no one worries about the care and maintenance of these pens.'" An online course at the University of Nottingham has introduced over ten thousand students globally to Bales's concept that slaves are cheaper today, claiming that unlike in the past where slaves were "major capital purchases like a car or a tractor," (which implies they would be taken care of), today slaves are more like "a tool that you could use, crumple up, and throw away" (which implies they are more exploited).[7] In 2017, the Freedom Fund, an antitrafficking fund invested in research, data, and

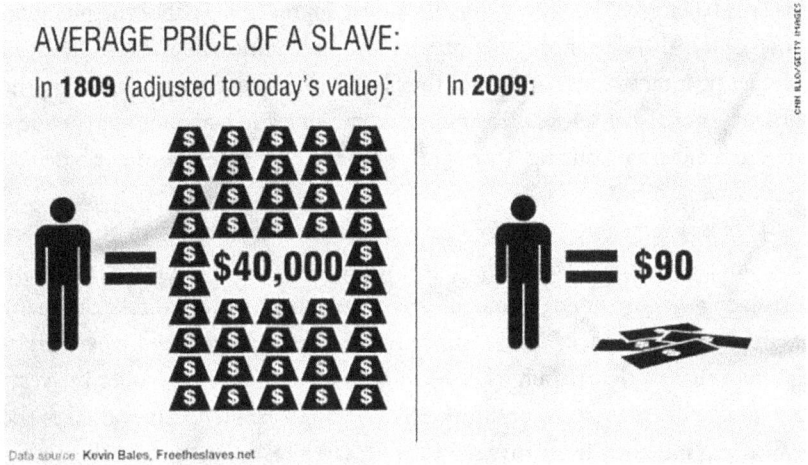

AVERAGE PRICE OF A SLAVE:

In **1809** (adjusted to today's value): | In **2009**:

$40,000

$90

Data source Kevin Bales, Freetheslaves.net

FIGURE 4.1 This infographic, attributed to CNN/Getty Images, is based on the research of Kevin Bales. It implies that since slaves were more expensive in the past, they were better cared for by slave owners. Source: CNN "Freedom Project" website, 2011.

measuring impact, tweeted "The average modern-day slave is sold for $90–100 compared to the equivalent of $40,000 some 200 years ago, says @kevin_bales via @TR_Foundation" as part of its promotion of Bales's speech at the Trust Conference.[8] The Trust Conference is an annual human rights event hosted by the Thomson Reuters Foundation. The foundation has heavily invested in news reporting on human trafficking and in training journalists to "report on this issue accurately and effectively."[9] What is it, exactly, that makes the "cheaper now" claim so compelling, and so convincing, that it has been repeated vociferously across a variety of institutions for over twenty years?

Antitrafficking numbers circulate through a tightly knit web of institutions that use discourses of data in ways that reframe the industry's underlying anti-black logics as rational, neutral observations and impartial scientific findings. Antitrafficking advocacy has used the rhetoric and aesthetics of a scientific approach to slavery to justify modern slavery's existence since 1999. The hallmarks of this approach include: quantification (of people, of degrees of exploitation, of NGO project outputs), data visualizations, devising and promoting replicable models, and performing neutrality. Since their introduction within antitrafficking advocacy, discourses of data have only gained traction as legitimating tools, from NGO metrics and indicator culture to the increasing faith in, and reliance upon, technological fixes to structural problems.[10] An excerpt from Free the Slaves' organizational approach describes the phenomenon aptly: "It takes more than passion and indignation to eradicate the evil of slavery. It takes science . . . Free the Slaves spreads freedom by applying the principles of social science, economics, community organizing, rights education and effective policing. Our approach has freed more than 10,000 people from slavery."[11]

The antitrafficking industry's investment in using science to end slavery is connected to the ways in which science has been used to uphold white supremacy as a governing, colonizing, and enslaving project. Across the many examples that I unpack in this chapter, antitrafficking advocates invoke empiricism to suggest that reason will overcome the irrationality of modern slavery: a scientifically proven nonprofit model of freeing slaves is counterposed to the efficacy of nineteenth-century slave revolt; satellites are used to finally put an end to African self-enslavement and backward Indian traditions; and antitrafficking metrics and indicators are cited as proof that antitrafficking logics are not racist and that its advocates are not white saviors. Within each example, antitrafficking discourse reiterates Enlightenment philosophy: white rationality can see Black pathology and fix it. Antitrafficking advocates advance claims about using science to end slavery alongside their repeated use of racially charged imagery to prove that slavery still exists. In such a context, science's affect of neutrality is used rhetorically and performatively to counterbalance critiques of antitrafficking's sensationalism, white saviorism, and racism.

Using a scientific approach as an alibi, though, only further reveals the depths of the antitrafficking apparatus's imbrication with antiblackness. Discourses of science historically came to be through the codification of racial difference. Race, science, and data have been effective epistemologies for securing white supremacy and making it appear natural. In Denise Ferreira da Silva's terms, this is the post-Enlightenment Subject's "knowledge arsenal": the tools and discourses of science and history that were invented and used to prove that white people had the exclusive right to self-determination. Such a knowledge arsenal "now governs the global (juridic, economic, and moral) configuration" upon which the antitrafficking apparatus deftly relies to free today's slaves without disrupting modernity's racial order.[12] It is the combination of science and history—of data and of memory—that naturalizes white supremacy's assumptions within antitrafficking discourse. Thinking through the political work that discourses of science do within antitrafficking raises the questions around which this chapter circles: What does antitrafficking's data convince us of? And, following Ruha Benjamin's formulation, who and what does antitrafficking's technoscience fix in place?[13]

In 2018, Yale's Gilder Lehrman Center for the Study of Slavery, Resistance, and Abolition hosted a conference called "Fighting Modern Slavery: What Works?" The conference was organized by Yale's Working Group on Modern Slavery, which primarily consists of critical scholars of antitrafficking who connect trafficking to structural issues of global capitalism, labor organizing, and sex workers' rights. The last panel of the conference featured Kevin Bales, who is also a member of Yale's Working Group, although he does not share these critical approaches. Much of the discourse about modern-day slavery's facts and figures, and the institutional responses they have triggered, can be traced to Bales.[14] He was scheduled to give a talk at the conference entitled "The Most Resistant Slavery: Slavery in War." In this line of research, Bales sets out to show that slavery is as ancient as civilization and has been fueled by both technological innovation and tactics of war. In one of the recorded versions of the talk, he explains that the idea for the investigation arose while spending time in the Congo in the early 2000s for his work with Free the Slaves. While he and his team were taking a "dispassionate and scholarly" approach to investigating what was then being called slave-like conditions in the Congo (although he "felt fairly certain that we would find some types of enslavement going on"— one wonders where the certainty comes from), the researchers uncovered six distinct types of enslavement being practiced at the same time. This insight led Bales to better understand that "there has been a fair bit of slavery within conflict and has been since the dawn of time."[15]

By the time it was Bales's turn to present "The Most Resistant Slavery: Slavery in War" at the Yale conference, conference attendees had been exposed to two days of scholars critiquing the antitrafficking apparatus's claims, imagery, and overreliance on market-based and punitive systems, including my own argument that antitrafficking's narratives that "Africans enslave each other" and that "slavery has always existed" operate to circumvent historical Western responsibility for slavery and reproduce antiblack tropes. Bales began his presentation by saying:

> My goal this afternoon is to do the most boring of all presentations about what really works. There is going to be a lot of numbers on the screen and so forth. Why boring? Because sometimes methodologies are boring. If you get things right and you begin to get things to work along in a process, a process that you refine over time, it almost becomes, like, mechanical work. And that's exactly what is going on in this situation.[16]

Without acknowledging his change in presentation topic, Bales focused his talk on one of Free the Slaves' community organizing projects in India instead of discussing how slavery is as old as war in Africa. Throughout the talk, Bales emphasized two key aspects of the project: it was run by the local community and its success was supported by data. To distance himself from the critiques of sensationalism and white saviorism, he showed no pictures. He showed lots of charts and wordy slides. In so doing, he used the *aesthetics* of numbers, data, and technoscience to lend credibility to his cause. Bales responded to general critiques of anti-Black racism by switching from humanitarian imagery and "slavery as old as time" narratives to employing discourses of data, methods, and models. He suggested that the model of liberation he was presenting is a *scientifically proven* method for freedom. His talk also implied: How could this be antiblack if it's taking place in India?

The project Bales discussed was started by a local group in northern India with which Free the Slaves has partnered and has featured in several of its promotional videos. The local organization, Manav Sansadhan Evam Mahila Vikas Sansthan (MSEMVS), has a methodology of liberation which Bales explained to the Yale audience by showing slides of a baseline survey of 174 households. He claimed the households improved after the intervention. He never told the audience what the intervention was. He did, however, mention that all the numbers were verified by an independent outside assessment team from Harvard. Bales continues: "I could have put up here a whole series of emotional and beautiful images taken on the scene, but I thought, no, I think it's time to stop with that. We don't need those. We are actually here to talk about what works and we don't necessarily need pretty pictures to do so."[17] Aesthetics of numbers and social scientific methods alongside discourses of data and indicators legitimize antitrafficking interventions amid critiques of paternalism, white saviorism, and racism within a community of scholars.

Bales ended his presentation with a comment about community organizing. He refers to the work of Free the Slaves and MSEMVS as the "Fannie Lou Hamer method," a metaphor he also included in his 2007 book, *Ending Slavery: How We Free Today's Slaves*. By invoking Hamer, Bales refers to her legacy as an influential Black community organizer in the American South during the civil rights movement. Bales states: "It's fundamentally a community organizing model. It works with community organizers. It doesn't work with white saviors parachuting in. In fact, we never see those folk. It is all about people on the ground and many of them have in fact been enslaved in these villages themselves."[18] Bales appropriates an iconic Black freedom fighter in order to prove to an audience critical of his work that he is not a white savior. Bales fails to recognize the irony of appropriating Black freedom struggle and symbols to legitimate the broader antitrafficking apparatus's political investment in solutions that preserve the status quo, including, in the words of the organization he cofounded, "effective policing." He invokes Fannie Lou Hamer to distance himself from critique while grafting the power of historical memory of Black freedom struggle—and Black endorsement—onto his project.

Of the many asymmetries in such a metaphor, one striking aspect is the relationship between Fannie Lou Hamer's activism and her experience as a survivor of forced sterilization in 1961. Forced sterilization was an accepted medical practice in the United States that was backed by science in the twentieth century. After eugenics was repudiated as bad science in the 1940s, Black women were still subjected to sterilization abuse, which was justified by scientists, biologists, doctors, and policymakers as a way to limit poor Black women's reproduction, and with it, the problem of poor Black mothering. Reformers and policymakers named poor Black mothering as the cause of racial inequalities, Black poverty, social disorder, and inflated government spending on social programs.[19] These logics continue to inhere in antitrafficking interventions. Blaming poor Black women for enslaving their children by selling them to traffickers and funding community interventions that educate poor Black mothers abroad about reproductive health and family planning are two projects that the antitrafficking apparatus, Kevin Bales and Free the Slaves among it, continue to promote. Fannie Lou Hamer's community organizing prowess is employed as a flattened symbol for antitrafficking's valor while antitrafficking interventions build upon legacies of social control of Black women's bodies. Fannie Lou Hamer's effectiveness as a community organizer is reduced to a folksy instantiation of the potential of everyday people while the antitrafficking industry's corporate and carceral solutions are institutionally, discursively, and materially positioned as more effective than contemporaneous grassroots social movements for racial justice and workers' rights. India's poor laborers, in Bales's presentation example, have not yet modernized through a civil rights movement like that which Black Americans created decades before. Black American freedom struggle becomes a universalized symbol of American progress. But situating it in the past signifies the completion of the Black freedom struggle, even while it rages on.

In his talk, Bales uses numbers and social science methods to convince the critical audience that his brand of antitrafficking is not sensationalist nor antiblack but based in truth and science. He demonstrates that the antitrafficking intervention in India works because it is backed by data that proves it works. The data that proves its efficacy is more important to his presentation than the intervention itself—which he never describes to the audience. Bales appropriates Black freedom iconography to prove antitrafficking is based in community organizing in India, even as antitrafficking initiatives in India have undermined grassroots community organizing among sex workers in India,[20] and antitrafficking talk and solutions have provided a palatable alternative for governments and corporations to address social injustice outside of a racial justice framework. He does all this while extolling the virtues of using science to free slaves. How is it that discourses of science—including scientific practices, methodologies, and technologies that have been shown by historians to have produced empirical knowledge of Black inferiority and to inflict, in the name of science, medicine, and progress, extreme violence on Black women's bodies—have now become a central hinge in the project to free today's slaves?[21]

We Can't Call This Science

Scientific American's April 2002 editorial dedicated itself to worrying over whether or not Kevin Bales's research on human trafficking counted as real science. The editors write: "We worry that the study of contemporary slavery is more of a protoscience than a science. Its data are uncorroborated, its methodology unsystematic. Few researchers work in the area, so the field lacks the give and take that would filter out subjectivity."[22] The magazine, though, still chose to publish Bales's sociological article because they found it in line with their aims to "offer insight into an important and little-understood aspect of our world." Next to those words, a thumbnail photograph is captioned, "Indentured Call Girl in Bangkok says her parents sold her into prostitution."[23] Antitrafficking's science might be called into question, but the plausibility of poor mothers of color selling their kids into harm is, for the editors, self-evident.

The nine-page magazine spread, "The Social Psychology of Modern Slavery," announces itself with the heading: "Contrary to conventional wisdom, slavery has not disappeared from the world. Social scientists are trying to explain its persistence."[24] It begins with the story of a woman who lives in an "unmapped village in the hills of Uttar Pradesh" where "the entire population was in hereditary debt bondage."[25] In this opening, slavery never ended in areas where coded language such as "untouched" or "remote" index these regions' spatial and temporal backwardness alike. To emphasize the point, Bales notes, "In parts of South Asia and North Africa, slavery is a millennia-old tradition that has never truly ended."[26] Framed as the persistence of slavery, India retains its status as backward in the US public imagination, despite its rising middle class and global prominence in the early 2000s. Slavery, in backward India, becomes simultaneously not-Black and not-American, which offers readers in 2002 a new, but old, slavery to concern themselves with amid the vibrant public debate about reparations for Black Americans in the same period.

Antitrafficking's connection, here, to Black American suffering, past and present, is not implied; Bales explicitly invokes it and then uses data to justify its rhetorical minimization. In his murky definition of slavery within the piece, he distinguishes it from prison and domestic violence (by suggesting slavery is worse) even as he universalizes it: "throughout history, slavery has meant a loss of free will and choice backed up by violence, sometimes exercised by the slaveholder, sometimes by elements of the state."[27] Bales describes his research findings on the universal features of slavery as grounded in the historic price of slaves: "Foremost among these commonalities is the basic economic equation. In 1850 an agricultural slave cost $1,500 in Alabama (around $30,000 in today's dollars). The equivalent laborer can be had for around $100 today. . . . The expensive slave of the past was a protected investment; today's slave is a cheap and disposable input to low-level production. The slaveholder has little incentive to provide health care or to take care of slaves who are past their prime."[28] The economic rationale and figure of the paternalistic slaveowner in the American South returns to remake racial chattel slavery as not as bad as contemporary debt bondage in India, which then becomes a way to talk about slavery today amid concurrent struggles against racism or for Black reparations. The language of economics, and the use of numbers, empiricizes Bales's claim. Slavery in India is as old as time and more exploitative than it was in the American South. Racial chattel slavery is deexceptionalized, its structuring power as part of imperial world systems is minimized, its ongoing legacies are deprioritized, and its perpetrators are portrayed as simply rational actors of their time. The historical and structural relationships among British Empire, slavery, colonialism, racial capitalism, and global dispossession and today's poverty in parts of India are concealed. Discourses of data and science are used to uphold as neutral the damaging civilizationalist narratives that they reinforce. Black pain is minimized and confined to the completed past (which suggests reparations are unjustified); culturally self-inflicted Indian pain is maximized as evidence of the need for intervention by rational actors (which suggests empire is justified). White people's persistent predilection to reason, care, and freedom is held as the corollary constant of history and the present.

The *Scientific American* article features a two-page map of the world with each country shaded to represent its prevalence of slavery. The darkest countries are located in the west coast of Africa, North Africa, South Asia, and Brazil. The United States, Canada, and most of Europe are the lightest countries. A sidebar written by the editor explains Bales's methodology for generating the map, which he reiterates is based on statistics that are "extremely unreliable." To justify its inclusion amid such unreliability, the editor repeats the antitrafficking claim, "the subject matter is hard to detect, let alone quantify."[29] And yet, here we have a datafied infographic of the globe that is divided into regions with the highest incidence of slavery, which correspond directly to hierarchical categories of civilization and race that Enlightenment-era scientific innovation proved to be true. Science returns to externally validate racialized assumptions. If such uses of data aim to convince the reader that modern slavery is really real, what else—and who else—does antitrafficking's data fix in place?[30]

Antitrafficking's science of slavery upholds a Western worldview that other cultures are backward and are waiting to be enlightened by the West's freedom-inventing folks; that slavery is worse now and therefore the West is not solely to blame; that social problems and injustices are "there" not "here"; and that science is an objective way to see what is real and true about the world. For all the editors' misgivings about Bales's inability to validate his empirical findings, their concerns also rest on the seduction of science's objectivity, and importantly, of science's presumed racial neutrality. In their editorial, they distinguish what they consider to be Bales's protoscience from real science which is also distinguished from social science: "the social sciences lack the precision of the physical or biological sciences, and they are more likely to have political implications."[31] Such an assertion is precisely the rhetorical political work that discourses of science and empiricism have been, and continue to be, employed to work out.

In Sylvia Wynter's analysis of the rise of the physical and then biological sciences, she argues it is precisely the degodding of society, the turn toward secularism, that necessitates the creation of a new racialized Other, one that is then scientifically proven to exist in an inferior position. For Wynter, religious hierarchies of the spirit and flesh are projected into secular humanism as hierarchies of people and places. The theocentric Christian self is reinvented as the Rational Self of Man who is defined against his irrational Others. Being freed from theocentricism enabled the rise of the physical sciences and then the biological sciences, but the figure of the Other was not abandoned in these transformations; it was reworked to fit the governing modes of reason, what Wynter calls "a newly projected human/subhuman distinction instead."[32] Indigenous groups in the Americas who were dispossessed of their land and Africans who were kidnapped, transported, and enslaved were made to become "the physical referent of the idea of the irrational/subrational Human Other."[33]

The development of the sciences not only coincided with this shift in thinking, it was constituted by it. The rise of the sciences, "were to be processes made possible only on the basis of the dynamics of a colonizer/colonized relation that the West was to discursively constitute and empirically institutionalize on the islands of the Caribbean and, later, on the mainlands of the Americas."[34] New scientific understandings of the Earth and the skies came through, and enabled, Europe's expansionist voyages.[35] New scientific understandings of taxonomy came through, and enabled, racial hierarchical ordering.[36] New scientific understandings of human biological processes came through, and enabled, medical experimentation on Indigenous and enslaved African populations.[37] The rise of actuary science and the legitimation of early statistics came through, and enabled, the search for proof that formerly enslaved Black Americans were dying out in freedom due to their biological inferiority.[38] Statistics and social science were used to prove Black criminality; the presumed neutrality of those methods "concealed the racist thinking that guided the strategies federal policymakers developed for the War on Crime, first in the 1960s, then through the 1970s and beyond."[39] Secularism's empiricism had been built through dispossession; that same empiricism justified dispossession and its violences as the natural order of things. As Dorothy Roberts's work shows, the interrelated history of race and science is not safely in the past, nor can it be consigned to the notion of "scientific racism" or "pseudo-science" or even racist applications of otherwise pure scientific methods.[40] The interrelated workings of science and race are remade in each new era of scientific innovation, including contemporary genomic science, surveillance technologies, and predictive policing.[41] To promote the natural sciences as less likely to "have political implications," as the *Scientific American* editors do, is to manifest the self-concealing logics of white supremacy. Aligning with, and mobilizing, discourses of science in order to legitimize and justify the impartiality of modern-day slavery's culturalist, civilizationalist, and racist narratives is the naturalization of white supremacy's logics in action.

In response to the critiques of *Scientific American*'s editors, Bales states, "There is a part of me that looks forward to being attacked by other researchers for my interpretations, because then a viable field of inquiry will have developed."[42] Bales recounts and reiterates this sentiment nearly twenty years later on Yale's podcast, *Slavery and Its Legacies*.[43] In the intervening years, Bales has helped publicize, populate, and in some cases create a set of institutions, research centers, academic journals, conferences, and academic collaborations that largely legitimate his findings and his approach to antitrafficking as scientific. Janie Chuang has extensively documented the echo chamber of the antitrafficking apparatus, including the web of philanthrocapitalists implicated in the datafication of antitrafficking through their emphasis on the idea that "resources should be used in a targeted and rational way based on data in order to identify and scale successful social programs."[44] Humanity United, Walk Free Foundation, and Freedom Fund, three prominent producers of data, media stories, indicators about human trafficking and discourse about the number of slaves freed, are all funded primarily by billionaires. Walk Free Foundation created the Global Slavery Index in response to Bill Gates's advice that "if you can't measure it, it doesn't exist."[45] Kevin Bales was the principal investigator for the Global Slavery Index in 2013, 2014, and 2016 and remained part of the "expert working group" in 2018.[46] Grave concerns have been raised about the methodology and reliability of the index, including by influential antitrafficking advocates, legal scholars, and journalists. Such concerns have not affected the ubiquity with which its estimates are cited.[47]

Antitrafficking's datafication has been supported by several academic institutions. At the University of Hull, where Bales used to teach, students can earn a PhD at the Wilberforce Institute for the Study of Slavery and Emancipation (WISE) with a concentration in "Modern Slavery, Human Rights and Social Justice." The University of Nottingham offers an MA in Slavery and Liberation that focuses on human trafficking and uses the Global Slavery Index and Free the Slaves videos as course content. Yale's Gilder Lehrman Center for the Study of Slavery and Abolition created a postdoctoral fellowship in Human Trafficking and Modern Day Slavery in 2012 and hosted the Working Group on Modern Day Slavery and Human Trafficking (2016–19), of which Kevin Bales and Zoe Trodd are members. Trodd, close colleague and coauthor with Bales, has helped institute modern slavery discourse within the academy through coediting the *Slaveries Since Emancipation* book series at Cambridge University Press. Trodd is the Director of the University of Nottingham's Rights Lab, which considers itself "home to the world's leading modern slavery experts" and has "built a large-scale research platform for ending slavery," which they intend to achieve by 2030.[48] In December 2020, the Rights Lab virtually hosted all of the Universitas twenty-one-member institutions for the annual early career researcher workshop, which trained faculty members at research intensive universities across the world how to end slavery by 2030 through "new data on prevalence, geospatial mapping of slavery sites" among other legal and narrative analysis strategies.[49] The Rights Lab also houses the Slavery from Space initiative, that I unpack below, which attempts to use geospatial science to end slavery.[50]

The 2014 inaugural issue of the peer-reviewed journal *Slavery Today* featured Bales's article, "Unlocking the Science of Slavery," wherein he describes the debate over definitions of contemporary slavery through a taxonomic analogy: "there is a *Genus* made up of categories such as 'human trafficking,' debt bondage, and slavery, and there are a large number of specific *Species* of slavery that are expressed in ways that reflect local 'ecosystems' of culture, economics, discrimination, and so forth. What is also very clear is that we are nowhere near an exhaustive description of the variant *Species* of contemporary slavery around the world."[51] Such an analogy uses the aesthetics of the language of the natural sciences to legitimize the study of contemporary slavery as a scientific exercise, while erasing the politics that underpin these definitional disagreements.[52] Such analogy work problematically recalls the biologization of the idea that slavery was the natural status of Black people. In order to support his argument, Bales then includes a scatterplot diagram developed from the data in the Global Slavery Index 2013, of which he was the lead author. Antitrafficking's data aesthetics and production reverberate through institutional echo chambers, which proliferates its own legitimation. These examples, even in instances that seem hard to take seriously, are institutionally legitimated through funder-driven initiatives and academic credentialing. In this sense, Bales has helped create the field of inquiry that *Scientific American* said he needed in order to validate his findings as real science. But the question remains: what is being validated by the science of ending slavery?

The year 2018 marked the inauguration of a new list, derived from an algorithm, that identifies the one hundred top modern slavery influencers. According to the founders, influence is measured by a "combination of influence on social media, as measured by Kred scores, and advocacy—policy input, speaking and media engagement—in public life, which is evaluated by desktop research. The two metrics are then aggregated via a proprietary algorithm and evenly weighted to produce the final rankings. An independent panel has verified the index's transparency, impartiality and robustness."[53] Kevin Bales is ranked number one; Monique Villa from the Thomson Reuters Foundation is ranked number four; Nick Grono from the Freedom Fund is ranked number six; Zoe Trodd from University of Nottingham's Rights Lab is ranked number thirteen. Algorithms, then, spit back out—now further coded as impartial, empirical proof of efficacy—the exact players and parameters of antitrafficking's narrowly constructed echo chamber. Technoscience's affect of neutrality is used to invisibilize antitrafficking's racial logics and white redemptionist project.

"I could tell a story about being in a CIA safe house with government officials where they all said it was a great idea, but they would never do it, something like fifteen years ago. Finally it has come into the open, finally we are going to have shared data," Bales states triumphantly during his keynote address on how to use science to end slavery at the 2018 Trust Conference.[54] After being introduced as a "pioneer" of the "very recent science on modern slavery," Bales tells the audience about how the Rights Lab at the University of Nottingham has combined satellites and citizen science to abolish slavery. He describes how the research team has trained citizen scientists to "look at satellite images and learn how to detect sites, particularly brick kilns, that have a high preva-lence of slavery." How such identifications of slavery from space are possible is not discussed. It turns out that citizen scientists were training an algorithm through machine learning techniques to be able to identify *all* the brick kilns in South Asia. The quick slippage from slavery to brick kiln is by design. It is based on the assumption that brick kilns are exceptional sites of enslavement, so spotting brick kilns from space will help locate, and thus, help end, slavery. Of course, the existence of a brick kiln tells neither researchers nor the public anything about the labor practices inside it. By Bales and Free the Slaves' own terms and accounting, many of the slaves they have freed continue to work in brick kilns postslavery. The discourse of science and the political agenda of modern slavery combine to conceal the racial logics that make publics suscep-tible to believing that India is riddled with slavery while also confounding the dynamics of global capitalism's georacialized pasts and racializing effects in the present. India is said to have slaves because its "unmapped" regions are backward (a reiteration of civilizational and colonial narratives); white aboli-tionists in the West are said to have highly advanced technology to free people. Where that technology comes from—historical scientific experimentation on Black and brown bodies globally, the present of the tech industry's global re-source extraction and associated labor and environmental exploitations, and the ongoing present of surveillance practices being incubated in military and carceral geographies—is neutralized and depoliticized.[55] If, according to the director of the satellite project Doreen Boyd, "You can't see slavery directly, but you can infer it"[56] through satellite imagery, then upon what assumptions, logics, and epistemologies are such inferences scaffolded? What—and who—is fixed in place by such technological solutions?

Bales plans to adapt satellite technology to the context of gold mining in Ghana, where satellite images are purported to be able to tell the difference between legal and illegal mines. For Bales, it is not the presence of the past of colonial extraction nor the contemporary multinational corporate extractive economies that are endangering Ghanaians.[57] Rather, it is the illegal mines, the ones owned and operated by local Ghanaians—who supposedly enslave their own countrymen—that are the problem to be solved with technology. In Bales's description, satellite technology allows antitrafficking advocates to

> see the difference between legal mines (that look like this from space, and if you look closely you can see heavy equipment, you can see bulldozers, you can see diggers) and illegal mines, which are in some ways marked by the fact that there are no machines. It is all being done with hand labor, like ancient Egypt. People digging with their hands, with shovels, digging with picks. . . . We can identify these illegal mines, which are horrific, saturated with mercury, saturated with brutality, long term slavery.[58]

In such a formulation, West Africans without access to heavy machinery are still stuck in the past of slavery, like their Egyptian enslaving and enslaved ancestors; but now they enslave their own, which is evidenced by the lack of technological tools, and thus the lack of markers of moral progress. The multinational corporation, in this formulation, is inferred to be providing protections for the workers and paying its fair share of remediation costs. What makes such an inverted narrative believable? Antitrafficking's discourse of technoscience repackages naturalized antiblack logics in fanciful geospatial technology, which becomes its own self-evident proof of progress. Progress, within the narratives of modern slavery, stands as technological and civilizational progress and as racial and moral progress. Technology for antitrafficking, then, simultaneously reasserts the natural order of white superiority and redeems the West as progressing beyond its racist past.

What the satellite images miss are the histories that have produced Ghana as a place to be mined. Small-scale miners fight for subsistence wages in the shadows of corporate entities getting rich off Ghana's natural resources. Small-scale local mining operations, in fact, sprung up after local farmers lost their land to multinational corporate investment in mining in the region.[59] International Monetary Fund structural adjustment required Ghana to open its mining sector to private investment; local residents were then dispossessed of their land so that one of the world's largest gold mining corporations could open and operate a mine there.[60] In the aftermath of such destitution, small-scale mining operations have set up communities of mutual care within them, as Sam Okyere's research shows, in ways not perceptible by global elites, let alone by satellites. In his ethnographic study of children working at a small-scale gold mining site in Ghana, Okyere describes: "The site was populated by adults and children collaborating in an attempt to scrape out a living on the margins of society in the face of mutual hardships arising locally from the loss of lands and nationally from decades of enforced austere socio-economic reforms. Social relations at the site were therefore characterised primarily by mutual dependence in recognition of their limited or non-existent opportunities and livelihood alternatives."[61] Antitrafficking discourse and intervention continue to unsee modes of Black mutual aid and lifemaking, which persist even under extreme duress from global capitalism's uneven and georacialized effects. In its stead, antitrafficking discourse maximizes white rational science to end the self-enslaving tendencies of Ghanaians.

The use of satellites puts a safe distance between the dirty problem of slavery and the clean technologies that might save Africans from themselves while reaffirming the advanced rationality of Western civilization. For antitrafficking advocates, it is not the violence of colonialism, transatlantic slavery, and capitalism that has created unsafe and uneven working conditions around the world; it is the pathological Others that European modernity created to exploit in order to save its own (white) morality. Such tech distancing abstracts the geographies of displacement from the histories and presents that produce and profit off them. It also pumps more racialized assumptions into algorithmic neutrality—the mere existence of brick kilns in India or the lack of tools in Ghana mines is now the black box from which "site of modern slavery" is printed on its ticker-tape output. Racial assumptions about cultural traditions, interpersonal violence, fitness for freedom, and parenting are the database upon which antitrafficking's algorithm churns.[62]

Antitrafficking's discourse of science uses technochauvinism to find politically palatable solutions to problems that were created through dispossession and structural violence. Technochauvinism, in Meredith Broussard's terms, is "an unwavering faith that if the world just used more computers, and used them properly, social problems would disappear and we'd create a digitally enabled utopia."[63] In so doing, technical fixes also position structural inequality as a technical problem to be solved, rather than a problem produced through past and current governing modes of racial liberalism and racial capitalism.[64] Within antitrafficking, tech solutions oversimplify and obscure complex situations, but, in the process, they endow the antitrafficking apparatus with sophistication and legitimacy. Pankhuri Agarwal's critique of the Slavery from Space project demonstrates how even though it is based in a basic flaw—satellites can't detect violence in enclosed spaces—the allure of an easy and technofantastical approach diverts resources and energy away from supporting and engaging in long-term solidarity work to "learn from the struggles and innovative strategies of informal workers' movements in India and other global south contexts."[65] Instead of revolutionary solidarity, the use of satellite surveillance technology in antitrafficking programs is expanding. International Justice Mission (IJM) announced in 2020 that it "struck a revolutionary new partnership with Maxar, a satellite imaging company" to map Lake Volta and rescue "children from enslavement" despite the pandemic.[66] Social distancing justifies aerial surveillance which sees slavery through modernity's racial logics and the antitrafficking mediascape's racial figures.

According to Bales, "Through science, we can move from the simplistic, emotive and disorganized response of 20 years ago, and towards a more complex, logical, unified approach."[67] Recourse to technology as a bias-free, more efficient, and more precise way to deal with social issues actually does nothing to move antitrafficking advocates away from the discourse's underpinning racial logics. For all of Bales's talk of affectively neutral science, data, and empiricism, he continues to opportunistically invoke Black struggle alongside proslavery rhetoric: it's the Fannie Lou Hamer method; the price of slaves keeps getting cheaper; Africans have always and continue to enslave each other. By making the study of contemporary slavery a science that produces and is justified by data, which is then solved with technologies like satellites, the antitrafficking apparatus generates a hall of mirrors of legitimacy that does more to reassert the logics of white supremacy than resolve worker precarity. The visual surveillance technology of satellites fix in place the white gaze as neutral empiricism. It fixes in place racialized geographies and communities as inferable slaves. It fixes in place racial logics that support modernity: some communities are not naturally fit for freedom, some are not naturally fit for self-governance; all need white rationality to overcome the persisting state of slavery in their communities. This is not solely a case of implicit bias being built into the machine. As the following case shows, antitrafficking's science of slavery is mobilized to convince global publics that technological fixes are more rational, more sophisticated, and *more effective*, than grassroots uprisings for racial justice and Black self-determination.

A Scientifically Proven Model of Freedom

In an online course called "Ending Slavery," instructors Kevin Bales and Zoe Trodd juxtapose the history of slave revolt in the Caribbean—rendered as inspiring but brutally violent—with what is deemed a more rational, systematic, empirically based community-based NGO model for freedom. The course was created in 2016 as a massive open online course, or MOOC, sponsored by the University of Nottingham, where Bales and Trodd are both professors. It is based on Bales's book *Ending Slavery* and incorporates materials from many government initiatives, NGOs, researchers, and philanthropies with which he has collaborated. Each of the lesson plans, which span four weeks, puts content about eighteenth- and nineteenth-century history of slavery and abolition into the service of helping students end contemporary slavery. The comparative structure is based on the Antislavery Usable Past humanities initiative at the Rights Lab at Nottingham, which seeks to adapt "examples of past antislavery movements for NGO strategies, international law, and government policy" to end contemporary slavery by 2030.[68]

The course was promoted on the FutureLearn web hosting site as "the world's first ever massive open online course about contemporary slavery." I participated in the course in its initial iteration, from October 17, 2016, to November 15, 2016.[69] The course was retired from the platform on April 29, 2020, but in the intervening years, learners were still able to sign up for and take the course. An Arts and Humanities Research Council grantee profile reported that "more than 10,000 learners from 150 countries" took the course and that "aspects of the course were embedded in at least five undergraduate courses in the UK, United States, and Australia, and used as professional development by numerous antislavery NGOs. The MOOC was shortlisted for the Learning on Screen Awards 2017."[70]

The first week's lesson emphasizes "the reliable facts and figures around contemporary slavery."[71] In the introductory video, "Slavery Today," Bales orients the class with facts about modern slavery: "There are about 45, 46 million people in the world today in slavery. That's a recent, reliable, social scientifically sound measurement, one of the first that we have."[72] Bales goes on to explain that what is new about modern slavery is that, unlike in the past, slaves today are cheap and disposable, repeating the numerical comparisons of cost. He asserts that the main cause of modern slavery is "population explosion" followed by other causes such as "conflict, corruption, poverty, environmental, and climactic change and disaster." Choosing to name population as the cause naturalizes worker exploitation as an inevitable outcome of rational supply and demand economics. It cues long-standing racialized narratives and scientific discourses about the need to control birth rates of poor women in the global South and Black American and Puerto Rican women in the United States to maintain social control, upend social pathologies of poor mothering, and ultimately, prevent widespread global uprisings.[73] Naming population explosion as the cause—and not historical dispossession, ongoing structural violence, and global capitalism—also suggests that control of women's reproduction in the "hot spots" of slavery is a logical, appropriate, and scientifically sound solution.

The MOOC anchors its learners firmly in the scientific basis of ending slavery to situate all the information and solutions that follow as credible. Additional materials for the first week focus on measuring contemporary slavery by making inferences based on statistics. Bales interviews his coauthor Monti Datta, a professor of political science at University of Richmond, about how the Global Slavery Index generates its annual estimates of slavery. Datta explains the networked set of inferences that the Global Slavery Index uses as its methodology: "working with Walk Free, we developed questions with Gallup. We had them tested in the field. And using those questions, we were able to ask in such a way so as *to infer slavery from the person's network*, who was approached by Gallup. And then infer, with statistical significance, that those persons were representative of that country. And then taking that country estimate, then use that as a data point to extrapolate for other nations."[74] As Janie Chuang notes, such extrapolations make for some odd assumptions that get called reliable science: "the number of slaves in Singapore is based on it being half like Sweden and half like Japan, with Japan's figure based on it being just like South Korea, whose figure is based on it being somewhere between Cyprus and Western Europe."[75] These statistical inferences and extrapolations are anchored in the data collector's task to "infer slavery from the person's network." The inferences are concretized and codified abstractions of entire international aid geographies, where networks of field workers collect data and skillfully maneuver through donor demands, local community expectations, mutual aid networks, and economies of abandonment. The demographic and methodological training local field workers often receive is itself based in logics of racialized suspicion, which speaks to the fundamental role that racialization plays in international data collection.[76]

Sometimes, though, country level extrapolations are bluntly based in racial logics, as in when "the number of slaves in South Africa is calculated on the basis that this country is 70% like western Europe (because 'historically, South Africa has been culturally similar to western, democratic nations') and 30% like Africa."[77] Racialized and spatialized assumptions, built through centuries of the embedded white gaze in science's objective methods, are mixed into inferential reasoning, which is then produced as a single, abstracted, authoritative number: forty-six million enslaved today. Each country is assigned its own extrapolated number of slaves, which then affects foreign policy, aid, and NGO and domestic initiatives. To eradicate such extrapolated prevalences of slavery, the course emphasizes corporate solutions such as supply chain monitoring and ethical consumption, technological solutions such as locating slavery from space, legislative solutions such as the UK Modern Slavery Act and the US Trafficking Victims Protection Act, and museological solutions such as incorporating antitrafficking discourse into museums of slavery and abolition. Antitrafficking's circumscribed slices of problems and solutions repeat and proliferate across the mediascape, making it appear to be the whole universe of possibility for ending trafficking.

Antitrafficking's discourses of data do important political work to convince publics that antitrafficking's status quo–preserving solutions are the most effective and efficient way to achieve freedom. In the final week of the course, students explore the history and present of slave self-emancipation. What begins as a history lesson in Black self-liberation and slave revolt, quickly converts failed revolts into a teachable lesson about the need for models for freedom that are empirically proven to work. Such a model, the course suggests, is to be found in Free the Slaves' community-based Model for Freedom, which uses NGO indicators and outcomes to assess effectiveness and has spawned several monitoring and evaluation reports.

The unit begins with a video of historian Arthur Torrington describing his African and Caribbean British public history organization's exhibition *Making Freedom*. The exhibition portrays how Africans throughout the Caribbean were inspired by the Haitian Revolution and took freedom into their own hands through organizing an orchestrated set of revolts. Throughout the video, Torrington explains that this history is important because it demonstrates Black agency, gives Africans voice, and shows how massive resistance leads to, and is the crucial precursor to, top-down legislative changes. In his discussion of the historical events in Barbados, Guyana, and Jamaica, the narrator also discusses the limitations of the slave rebellions—the enslaved did not have enough weapons, communication was extremely difficult, and British Army response, marked by mass murdering of enslaved people, was swift and decisive. He mentions that peaceful protest of the enslaved did not convince the British government to decree emancipation. Rather, it was armed protest, rioting, and mass disruption that finally forced the British to concede to the demands of the enslaved. The video concludes with the sentiment, "Making Freedom makes a point. It makes a point about the agency of Africans in their own liberation."[78]

The revolts in the Caribbean are used as an inspiring example and as a cautionary tale about what *won't* work to end slavery today. The slave revolt module is immediately followed by the next course segment that offers a more civil(ized) and more rational means of achieving freedom: Free the Slaves' "community-based model." The segment begins by stating, "The antislavery movement needs evidence-based models that yield significant, sustained declines in the prevalence of slavery."[79] It goes on to explain Free the Slaves' four-step model for ending slavery through research, organizational capacity building, police protection, and accessing social services. In so doing, Black uprising against a violent system is juxtaposed against a representation of empirically sound liberation that is proven to work. Black freedom struggle of armed slave revolt is invoked and then channeled into politically palatable advocacy, such as passing laws and working with NGOs. Well-organized collective action against a violent system is minimized in favor of an empirically sound model for freedom.

In order to convince learners that Free the Slaves' model works on the ground, students watch a series of promotional videos made by the organization. NGO fundraising materials, here, become both visual evidence of the model's effectiveness and accredited curricular tools. From the view of the course administrators, this juxtaposition strategy worked. The week's email summary stated, "We began the week looking at historical slave revolts and comparing their approaches to contemporary ones, including the Free the Slaves 4 step community-based model. Learners had an overwhelmingly positive response to this approach, which they saw applied in a video made by Free the Slaves about villagers in the Indian village of Sakdouri."[80]

The video about Sakdouri, titled *What Freedom Looks Like*, begins with the South Asia director for Free the Slaves saying, "people in slavery have to be rescued." It tells the story of a group of brick kiln workers who were abused on the job and then rescued by the police and the local Indian NGO MSEMVS (the same group Bales discussed at the Yale conference). Three years after the rescue, the Free the Slaves director revisits the site and finds that "they have fully matured and have accessed all of their rights." The mechanism of freedom that is portrayed is humanitarian rescue with local police, community-based meetings to educate each other about their rights, and then, magically, freedom. How does a rescue followed by a rights training free a slave? What does slavery and freedom mean here? Two community members mention on screen that they are earning decent wages now, but it is not clear what new job opportunities or government entitlements became available after the rescue. The video tells an uplifting tale by depicting a community that cares for and supports one another through community meetings, riding bikes, and doing basic life tasks like pumping water while smiling. The energetic music makes it feel like liberation is possible, and it is possible through civil conversations with one another. The model of freedom presented here is comforting because it depicts a state that is already available to help its citizens be free once they are enlightened. Slavery is ended, then, with the rule of law. In this narrative, individual Indians might be cruel and backward slaveholders, but local Indian leaders and well-trained Indian police give the outsider-viewer-funder confidence that racialized Others can become modernized. Local human rights NGO workers and volunteers are positioned as "the enlightened few leading the way out of darkness."[81] India as an imaginary, here, is simultaneously beholden to its backward cultural traditions, corrupt or negligent at governing, but reformable and redeemable. The video is an ode to the narrative of modern liberalism: "liberal ideas of political emancipation, ethical individualism, historical progress, and free market economy" that simultaneously include, exclude, pathologize, and racialize.[82]

The MOOC shows "how liberation actually works in practice" by watching four additional promotional films from Free the Slaves. *Building Freedom Brick by Brick* returns to exploited brick kiln workers to explain how they sustain their freedom after being rescued with two mechanisms: the Community Vigilance Committee and starting their own brick kiln. Freedom, in this video, is represented as the freedom to enter the free market. The video's narrative follows the familiar antitrafficking arc from naivete to enlightenment. It begins by identifying the workers as beaten, confined, and forced to work long hours, over images of workers wearing few clothes and engaged in dirty manual labor. The South Asia director for Free the Slaves describes the problem: the workers "do not have the courage to come out of it until MSEMVS fieldworkers reach to them and that is the time they start realizing how they can change their situation." As the tempo of the musical score quickens, the same workers are depicted sitting in a circle and talking, not engaged in work, and smiling. Once the villagers have been trained by Free the Slaves and MSEMVS to set up their Community Vigilance Committee, they engage in clean civil conversation, which is represented as alleviating the burden of doing dirty manual labor. The problem here is described as one of personal courage and lack of information, and thus lack of capacity to imagine freedom. The solution is figured as empowerment, education, and processes whereby people are "trained in order to become civil" and transformed into enlightened subjects.[83] Such programs have been common initiatives of international NGOs, in part because they are relatively easy to quantify and nonthreatening to states and global order.

From these community discussions, the participants developed a plan to start their own brick kiln business. The same villagers are then shown engaged in the same work of brickmaking but this time with smiles on their faces and with breaks to play with their children. While self-determination through autonomous production can be dramatically different from other forms of wage labor, the video presents this harmonious group of happy people outside of the market forces that their entrepreneurial project still depends on. It insulates industry, and more generally, neoliberal geographical and racial division of labor from complicity in creating the conditions that drive down wages and increase unsafe migration. It instead welcomes the global poor into the marketplace, but assures them (and the West) of their continued place near the bottom of those structures. Such figuration safely welcomes new producers into the marketplace without threatening global capitalism's asymmetrical power relations. The video adheres to Randall Williams's critique of human rights discourse wherein Western NGOs figure poor non-Western subjects as "exemplary models of domesticated postcolonial otherness, demanding nothing and dutifully accepting their subordinate place in the structures of capitalist globalization."[84] The video and the empirical basis work together: willing, able, and incorporable Indian subjects reject models of Black-led violent uprising in favor of rational models of small business ownership that simply need to be cleaned up of holdover, backward cultural practices of violence. Free the Slaves' videos use humanitarian affect and imagery as visual proof that its evidence-based model works.

Visual proof of the model's efficacy is then substantiated by a program evaluation report that the Freedom Fund financed and researchers at Harvard's Center for Health and Human Rights conducted. The repeated citation of the Harvard report's endorsement of the effectiveness of MSEMVS has gone a long way to discursively legitimize the empirically proven nature of the community model to free slaves. The Harvard report analyzed the MSEMVS's Community Vigilance Committee interventions in Uttar Pradesh. Community Vigilance Committees (CVCs) are at the heart of Free the Slaves' model to build resilient communities across all six countries it works in. The name is derived from nineteenth-century US slavery abolition societies that set up vigilance committees to protect self-emancipated, formerly enslaved people from being legally recaptured by citizens and government agents, to provide escapees with material aid, and to help them on their migration journeys. The CVC model is now used widely in antitrafficking interventions throughout the world to differing effects. It is particularly troublingly that such important historical models are instituted in name to assist carceral antitrafficking projects that aim to dissuade people from migrating for work and that widely coordinate with the police to orchestrate so-called slave rescues. In a different context in Benin, for instance, Neil Howard's ethnographic research with migrating youth found that CVCs created additional barriers that youth have to negotiate around, including increased police presence. [85] Mike Dottridge discusses a similar situation in Mali, where vigilance committees increased the risks posed to children willfully migrating for work. Even after such failings were brought to the attention of the international NGOs who had implemented them, the organizations were "reluctant to recognize their failings."[86]

In the case of MSEMVS, CVCs are the vehicle for "raising public awareness of labor issues, educating their community about civil rights and building local leaders."[87] In Harvard's assessment, this model was not found to eradicate forced and bonded labor, but did have "a dramatic impact on improving the lives of individuals and households in these communities, for example in reducing indebtedness, improving participation in government job programs and increasing community empowerment."[88] Although the Harvard report is used discursively by Free the Slaves and Kevin Bales as empirical proof of its model's effectiveness at ending slavery, the report only mentions the word "slave" or "slavery" three times. Despite the report's 108 pages of analysis of change in family circumstances between baseline and endline surveys, the description of the intervention that is being tested for effectiveness is not substantially discussed. It is only mentioned once—in the parenthetical elaboration of what the "mature" CVC does: raise awareness about labor issues and help community members access their rights and government entitlements.[89] While it is certainly wonderful that more people are now accessing their government entitlements, let's be clear: the intervention that Harvard is testing for effectiveness in freeing slaves is awareness raising and rights education workshops. Educating exploited workers about the rights and entitlements that their government *already affords them* is made synonymous with freeing slaves.

While facilitating rural access and organizing for collective power to access rights is important work, it is hardly surprising that a program that connects people to government benefits succeeds at doing just that: connecting people to government benefits. This is the circular nature of indicators, which I discuss below. More important to my point here is understanding the *rhetorical work* that the report accomplishes for Free the Slaves. The report is inserted discursively within academic presentations and media appearances to legitimize the proven rationality and effectiveness of Free the Slaves' approach. But what the report analyzes and concludes is far more humble than, and greatly outpaced by, the mediascape echo chamber through which the deceptive empiricism of antitrafficking's claims reverberate. In this sense, it is "the genre of the 'study'—its existence in tangible form as a report—more than its content that allows it to play a supporting role in validating a link that everyone assumes is already there."[90] As its claims are repeated and Ivy League university names are invoked, they are "elevated as 'evidence' that travel through citational webs with little critical analysis."[91]

Consider the political work such empirically backed rhetorical slippages between accessing rights and freeing slaves does: instead of India being represented as a robust state with many government entitlement programs, "the presence of 'slavery' [in India] appears as an indicator of how far the country has left to travel in order to become a truly modern nation."[92] The structures that support labor exploitation in India are replaced with apolitical understandings of slavery as a natural evil, benignly, if remorsefully, a part of the order of things, that white Enlightenment principles of liberal humanism—themselves constructed through Black enslavement and European colonialism—can overcome. The discourse of antitrafficking is constructed in relation to racial chattel slavery through its claims, data, affective imagery, and argumentation; but, in rendering economic exploitation in India as slavery, the histories and structures of colonialism, capitalism, and racial ordering are reduced to an economic relation. Much to the contrary, such structures encompass a constellation of policies, sentiments, ideologies, laws, investments, divestments, violence, land theft, social control, and feelings that those systems required, endorsed, and proliferated.[93] Antiblackness and white supremacy, and the hierarchy of race that they structure, are at the center of how the history of slavery creates our current conditions—profound antiblack violence at home and abroad, continued dependence on underpaid and unsafe labor at home and abroad, and the uneven global development and distribution of wealth and resources throughout the world.

Let me be clear that the point I am making is not that Free the Slaves or the Harvard researchers are doing program evaluation poorly. I have no doubt that, as the organization states on its web page, "the Free the Slaves Monitoring, Learning & Evaluation Department adheres to the American Evaluation Association Guiding Principles." My point is that the racial logics and politics that underpin antitrafficking's language of slavery are neutralized through empiricism. The Harvard report and Free the Slaves' focus on indicators is not exceptional—indicators have become an integral part of resource distribution networks that enlist NGOs as key nodes in their infrastructure.[94] Yet, they also contribute to the deceptive empiricism about (anti)trafficking and how widely it circulates. Discourses of data are used to make highly circumscribed renderings of exploitation and their solutions appear to be objective, technical, and effective. They are also used to make antitrafficking's solutions appear to be more successful at ending slavery *than Black self-emancipation*. NGO models of freedom highlight civility in contradistinction to slave uprisings, which suggests liberal humanism has moved the world beyond the need for violence.

Violence becomes irrational in this configuration. Liberalism's narrative of civility obscures the structural violence that states and global economies impose on communities.

The proposition that Free the Slaves' model of freedom can quantify and measure incremental progress toward ending slavery is a result of what Sally Engle Merry calls "indicator culture." Indicator culture uses numerical data to "persuade publics and influence governance decisions" and "assumes that all things can be measured and that those measures provide an ideal guide to decision making."[95] Within indicator culture, NGOs seek to quantify their impact on social problems by defining indicators (determining or naming that which they deem to be indicative of a problem) and then designing programmatic responses (called outputs, these are the activities the organization will carry out) which will lead to better outcomes. Indicators and outputs must be measurable to show that the outcome has been reached, but the theory of the relationship between the indicator and outcome is exactly that: a theory. Since organizations define for themselves what is indicative of the problem and what will solve the problem, when NGO programs are tested for effectiveness through monitoring and evaluation reports, like the Harvard study, what is being analyzed is the program's ability to carry out its programs and its effectiveness, but what is often not being analyzed is the theoretical relationship between the indicator and the outcome.[96]

For instance, in the monitoring and evaluation report that Free the Slaves undertook to test its model's effectiveness across six countries (Ghana, Haiti, Democratic Republic of Congo, India, Nepal, and Brazil), the indicator "more local NGOs integrating anti-slavery approaches in their work" is listed as evidence that, if achieved, the community-based model would be succeeding.[97] Whether or not that leads to more people being free is a different question. Yet, once complex phenomena are quantified and abstracted, "these numbers convey an aura of objective truth and scientific authority despite the extensive interpretive work that goes into their construction."[98] Another success indicator for Free the Slaves' model is "lower incidence and prevalence of slavery in communities," which seems like more straightforward criteria for determining success. However, the monitoring and evaluation report for the model notes that "the evaluation is missing information on slavery prevalence, due to the challenges in accurately measuring this indicator."[99] Nevertheless, the report concludes that "4,494 slaves were freed" (83 percent of them were in India) and combined with awareness raising activities and arrests, "the evidence is strongly indicative that the community-based approach reduces slavery, though more research is needed."[100] The number of slaves freed is determined by the indicator that Free the Slaves developed to measure the phenomena: indicator 2.II "number of slaves freed" is calculated by the number of people "now living in freedom as a result of: rights education, rescue efforts, and other [Free the Slaves] and civil society partner organization efforts."[101] In order to be now living in freedom, the individuals had to previously meet all three conditions of the organization's definition of slavery: "forced, coerced, or deceived to provide labor or sexual service, under the threat of physical or psychological violence or other serious harm, and unable to walk away."[102] Once again, participating in rights training is datafied as one way slaves are freed.[103] It is the circularity of indicators that are essential to their rhetorical power. The nitty gritty details of how things are defined and counted is obscured by tautological statements such as, "When people in slavery are coming into freedom, you have a pretty sure indicator that you've reached the people most in need."[104]

What this example shows is how indicator culture itself creates circular empiricism that makes particular definitions, assumptions, or theories of change appear to be scientifically proven to be effective. Following Sally Engle Merry, "indicators risk producing knowledge that is partial, distorted, misleading. Since indicators are often used for policy formation and governance, it is important to examine how they produce knowledge."[105] In this example, a community-based model to end slavery, which, by its own report, does not have evidence on slavery's prevalence, is suggested as the way to "yield significant, sustained declines in the prevalence of slavery,"[106] and therefore offer a more effective, more sophisticated, and more civil path to freedom than riotous, righteous rebellion for Black freedom and racial justice. By the MOOC's own accounting, we already know that those revolutionary methods *did work* to end slavery in the Caribbean. The history and present of social movements tell us that riotous protest methods continue to change material realities, legislation, and national conversations. What other political goals, then, is the scientific model of freedom achieving?

We Need a Slavery Lens

In the final segment of the University of Nottingham's online course, co-instructors Kevin Bales and Zoe Trodd describe the way forward for the antislavery movement. They explain it will be easier than ever to eradicate slavery now because unlike for the abolitionists of the past, the moral, economic, and legal arguments have now been won. "So in that sense, our struggle [as trafficking abolitionists] is easier than the one facing the nineteenth-century abolitionists. We don't have to break laws to help enslaved people."[107] The statement is a testament to the utility of the memory and language of slavery: if the term was not slavery then these abolitionist victories would not be available to them. If, for instance, the problem of trafficking and coerced labor was understood through the proliferation of antiunion sentiment and policy, anti-immigrant sentiment and policy, mandated privatization of public resources in developing countries, mass incarceration, corporate globalization, and global climate change (all factors that contribute to labor coercion and unsafe migration), then, we would not have won the moral, economic, nor legal arguments. In fact, we would be steadily losing ground on all three.

For Bales and Trodd, "Ending slavery will be humanity's watershed" and the only major obstacles left are "lack of awareness and lack of resources." The specific suggestions they pose invoke the discourse of data: "a commitment to data collection and analysis" and "an independent structured program of monitoring and regular evaluation."[108] These goals have begun to be realized. In December 2016, the End Modern Slavery Initiative was passed under the FY17 National Defense Authorization Act to develop a US-based global philanthropy on a matching fund basis from foreign governments and private investors. Antitrafficking projects that receive such funds will be monitored and evaluated based on "outcomes that can be empirically measured."[109] According to the press release from the Senate Foreign Relations Committee, programs that fail to achieve a 50 percent reduction in slavery will be terminated. Since 2018, Free the Slaves has scaled up its Community Liberation Initiative, which integrates the community-based model discussed herein into a "wide range of other international development initiatives in communities where slavery is worst" and will "measure impact by implementing Free the Slaves techniques to assess a community's ability to avoid enslavement of residents in the future."[110] It bears noting that according to its own evaluation report, Free the Slaves "cannot say whether the overall incidence and prevalence of slavery has been reduced in the countries where we worked," yet such claims about "where slavery is worst" are easily asserted and believed when they graft onto racialized assumptions about Africa, the Caribbean, and South Asia.[111]

In the vision of Trodd and Bales, there is no limit to how far their approach could travel:

> For example, the next Peace Corps appropriation bill in the US Congress could include a line announcing that in the next intake, there will be a call for volunteers who want to work on the liberation and the reintegration of enslaved people. . . . World Health Organization strategies need to be refocused through a slavery lens, as do government policies on debt

relief, law enforcement, military cooperation with other countries. Foreign aid should be thought through with an antislavery focus, some of it targeting the underlying economic desperation that engenders slavery. Trade policies should reflect the idea that slave-made goods are taboo on the world market.[112]

The slavery lens that the broader antitrafficking movement wants to expand asserts police, border patrol, detention centers, corporations, and the rule of law as the mechanisms of abolition. Antitrafficking discourse's slavery lens renders freedom as capitalist inclusion, sees ending slavery as good for business, and suggests that we "do not have to end global poverty to end slavery,"[113] even while acknowledging ex-slaves need financial support to stay free. Proposing such an orientation's expansion is a sobering prospect. The antitrafficking apparatus is not simply another white savior project. Its tentacles continue to reach further and wider because it is compatible with dominant logics and white common sense: science is once again used to externally validate ingrained assumptions about race, poverty, geography, and civilization.

The appeal of antitrafficking discourse's slavery lens to dominant institutions is directly related to the discourse's ability to galvanize the language and aesthetics of data and empiricism. Antitrafficking's data make its racial logics appear neutral. Antitrafficking's data make its approaches appear effective. Antitrafficking's data make the enterprise appear sophisticated, civil, and orderly. Antitrafficking's narratives, now presented as scientifically proven, reproduce the rhetorical sleight of hand that liberalism is based in: Western discourses of freedom and science will eradicate the lingering backwardness of people and places where slavery still exists, proving Western rationality, all the while obscuring the historical violence that liberal modernity is based on and the contemporary violence it fuels. Antitrafficking's slavery lens combines two very powerful discourses to gain credibility: the image of the suffering, racialized Other in need of enlightenment and the discourse of data-driven, sophisticated, rational, and technocratic solutions. Those two discourses are mutually reinforcing; they are both underpinned by the contradistinction between white rationality and Black pathology. Antitrafficking discourse offers a white subjectivity that is not historically responsible for slavery; antitrafficking's slavery lens symbolically extols Black self-emancipation but fixes it in the past in favor of more scientific and rational models of freedom that are disconnected from the ongoing Black freedom struggles in the United States in its midst.

There are, of course, many other slavery lenses that might be productively utilized to end global oppression: pan-African lenses, reparations lenses, repair

lenses, afterlives lenses, antiprison and prison abolitionist lenses, racial justice lenses, Black internationalism lenses, Black radical tradition lenses, antiblackness theories lenses, Black feminist antiviolence lenses.[114] These are all
slavery lenses insofar as they use historical analysis of racial power to drive political action, and while each has different emphases, factions, politics, and tactical
orientations, what they all hold in common is precisely what is obscured by
antitrafficking's slavery lens: more capacious visions of Black freedom that
"would necessitate the destruction of all the systems of oppression"; visions
that are born through histories of resistance to unfreedom, that fix their
gazes on the nimble reconfigurations and new manifestations of enduring
structures of power.[115] These slavery lenses have ushered in, undergirded,
supported, and grown out of various social movements for racial justice.

That antitrafficking's slavery lens exists alongside such a constellation for
freedom returns to the central point of this book: antitrafficking is a racial discourse that, at its base, addresses white racial anxieties about Black freedom,
Black freedom movements, and demands for redress for white violence by usurp-
ing central terms of those struggles—slavery, history, abolition, freedom—and
reworking them through palatable political projects that reaffirm white supremacy's rationality amid organized movements to eradicate it. Antitrafficking's datafication is used to legitimize its racialized sensationalism, claims, and
proposed solutions. Antitrafficking's data concretizes and fixes in place vast
and complex histories and presents of unfreedom into manageable bits that
can be counted as "freed." Antitrafficking discourse uses capital S Science and
capital H History in ways that obscure how the racial logics and narratives that
have been used to justify slavery and white supremacy are remade in its campaigns. Antitrafficking is a racial project that calls itself a neutral project. It is a
political project that promotes white historical inculpability through utilizing
the obfuscating lenses of science, liberalism, and history.

After over a century of Black organizing and theorizing about the legacies of
slavery and racial injustice in the present, the untenable contradictions of racial liberalism and racial capitalism are once again being felt on a massive scale
in the United States. Sustained protest against police violence in 2020 liberated
streets and provoked state repression, the concepts of prison and police abolition are gaining wider recognition, local mutual aid initiatives and collectives are
being recognized as mainstream strategies for dealing with crises that the state
produces and exacerbates, statuesque symbols of white supremacy are falling all
around us. What, then, have the racial justice slavery lenses allowed us to see?
What have these slavery lenses blueprinted and built? What methodologies

have these slavery lenses utilized to annotate history and reconstruct historical memory?[116] Far from reproducing antitrafficking's narratives of unenlightened racialized subjects' inability to imagine freedom until it is paternalistically bestowed upon them, racial justice slavery lenses continue to imagine, and then create, new ways to be free.

Interlude   #Charlottesville

"Would you like a T-shirt? We have all sizes." A crowd is forming outside of the Walker School in Charlottesville on November 10, 2016. "Do you stand with the 52 percent? If so, grab a T-shirt here!" Concerned community members have been testifying in city meetings for months about why the Lost Cause era Confederate statues must be removed from the city's parks. The hearings are the result of student activist Zyahna Bryant's letter to the editor and petition to Charlottesville City Council, which described why the Robert E. Lee statue is "offensive to all people" and that the statue stands for "anti-black terrorism."[1] Tonight is the final community forum where the Blue Ribbon Commission on Race, Memorials, and Public Spaces will reveal its preliminary report regarding what the city should do with the monuments.

The meetings have brought out a range of opinions, most notably a relatively small, but visually striking and persistent group of Confederate sympathizers. They testify to keeping the statues because they don't want to erase history, because the Confederacy was not about white supremacy, because Robert E. Lee freed his slaves and was nice to Black children in church, because their ancestors fought for the Confederacy, because their families still live on the same land in Albemarle County that they did during the war. Several sympathizers have come in historical costumes. Others wave Confederate flags during their testimonies, or let them fly conspicuously out of their back pockets, while saying this has nothing to do with racism. Many liberal and progressive types of this town have avoided engaging in such civic participation opportunities. Some urge action on more immediate racial disparities in town; others think that it is so obvious that the statues need to be removed that the commission must just be a cover for the city to make it appear that they are carrying out the people's mandate when they decide to remove them.

That is not how the meetings are going.

In a straw poll on November 1, 2016, the commissioners voted, 6–3, to keep the monuments in place. The exasperated chair of the commission wants the monuments gone—melted down and sold, preferably. Two antiracist commissioners insist that the most meaningful way to change the narrative of history in this town is to confront the statues in place.[2] The proposal to "transform the statues in place," though, was consistently interpreted by slavery's apologists as a vote for keeping the statues. Pro-Confederate testimony that indicated as such became further evidence for many antimonument protesters that recontextualization would never go far enough; the monuments had to be removed.

"You're saying it will cost nearly $300,000 to remove them, then? I think that is a very important aspect to consider in our decision." I was sitting in a school auditorium listening to Blue Ribbon commissioners discuss the removal of the statues in late September 2016. I came late, this was my first meeting, I did not know anyone in the room, but during my walk to my new post at the University of Virginia, a banner advertising gay pride in Lee Park hung near the Robert E. Lee statue. "No to Pinkwashing the Confederacy!" I posted on social media. At the end of the Blue Ribbon Commission meeting, there was time for public comment. It was eerily civil and noncontentious; almost all comments were from Confederate sympathizers. Without thinking much about it, I told the commissioners it was outrage to debate the relatively small cost of moving the statues, when the entire wealth of this city and state was built upon what those statues stood for: protecting white supremacy. Afterward, a sympathetic resident activist slipped me her card. Welcome to Charlottesville, she smiled, in that Southern "there's more to know" way.

"When Union troops invaded Charlottesville, that was Liberation Day for the majority of residents. At that time, 52 percent of the town's population were enslaved African Americans, another 2 percent were free Black people. We stand with the 52 percent and demand the statues be removed immediately." This was Jalane Schmidt's talking point in the early days of the antimonuments work. (She later cofounded Black Lives Matter Charlottesville.) It became a rallying slogan. The Blue Ribbon commissioners included it in their recommendations to name March 3 "Liberation Day" to commemorate Charlottesville's surrender to Union forces in 1865.[3] In the final public forum, resident after resident, about sixty-seven in total, stood before the commissioners and repeated the demand: "We stand with the 52 percent and demand the statues be removed immediately." One after another, wearing identical hand drawn T-shirts, we filed through the final meeting. It was a well-orchestrated civic performance. The commissioners began referring to us as "the T-shirt people." This (what we thought at the time to be) last push to remove the statues, to intervene on the too-compromising recommendations to the city council, took place two days after Donald Trump was elected president of the United States. We thought, I guess naively, that would be the final nail in the coffin. Who could now defend huge monuments to white supremacy as benign parts of long-gone history? Who could now defend "both sides" as civility? Who could now dare suggest that it would be possible to sufficiently recontextualize the sheer scale of Lee towering over Charlottesville's central park, his heft laden with prescient political weight?

We outnumbered the Confederate sympathizers in that final community forum by a lot: 82 to 10. But ten white people boldly and baldly defending white supremacy without repercussion, with the aura of respectability, with their sincere confusion when they point to the predominately white antimonuments crowd at the meeting and say, "You are white, why do you care?"—those ten people still had an effect, their voices ominously strong in the wake of the election. One of the ten, though, took a different approach: "There are twenty million slaves alive today. I do not understand why we are going on and on discussing and worrying about slavery that's over when we should be putting our energy to end slavery that still exists. In India. In Africa. Women are even trafficked here, into Charlottesville." Two of my comrades, eyes wide and mouths agape, turned to me. "Your project!" one silently mouthed. We had just been discussing my research, casually getting to know each other better, while hand drawing the T-shirts earlier that week.

This incident falls far outside the mediascape that I designated for my study. But this is clearly also part of the antitrafficking mediascape: how "trafficking is slavery" pops up in unexpected places as a way to redirect attention away from the present implications of slave pasts that are not past and as a way to redirect attention toward white supremacy's investments. The comment manifested one of my project's early hunches: antitrafficking's slavery talk could be used for antiblack ends, explicit and implicit.

#Charlottesville, though, did not trend on Twitter in August 2017 because of publicly permitted agitation at community meetings a year earlier. #Charlottesville became a social media spectacle after local and nonresident white nationalists gathered in Charlottesville for a city-sanctioned and permitted protest to contest the city council's decision to sell one of its Confederate monuments. The protest was met with fierce and well-organized antiracist counterprotests. The city and state police stood down; their lack of interference meant street fights between white nationalists and antiracist activists ensued unabated. A white woman, Heather Heyer, was murdered when a white nationalist drove his car into a crowd of counterprotesters. Scores of additional activists were injured. The trauma of the summer extended into nearly all branches of community organizing in Charlottesville for months to come.

Of the many news stories and aftermaths of the protests, one of the least recognized is how the events emboldened and bolstered the already existing community-based infrastructure for self-defense. From mutual aid programs, local bail funds, participatory defense programs, economic redistribution collectives, and an on-call network of community members ensuring one another's security, to the prolonged fight against urban renewal plans led by the organized residents of public housing, and across a multiracial left with many different political orientations and tactical inclinations, Charlottesville's broad-based movement for racial justice proved to itself that we were and are the ones we've been waiting for. The state did not protect us. For some politicized whites, this perhaps newly felt embodiment of the lack of state protection offered a terrifying clarity about the white stake in struggle, about the mutuality of our collective safety, about just how protected by the state white people are, about just how threatening to the state we are perceived to be when we withdraw our consent to white supremacy.

There are many stories to tell about #Charlottesville and even more ways to tell them. The convergence of pro-Confederate monument testimony with antitrafficking rhetoric, while strikingly exemplary of my argument about antiblackness, probably doesn't rank highly among them for most. There are also many secrets to keep about Charlottesville, but how the memory of slavery is used to promote vastly different political agendas in the present is not one of them. When the City of Charlottesville initially announced it was going to remove the Lee statue and was looking for recommendations for where to move it in February 2017—before the deadly Unite the Right rally, before the lawsuit that kept the statues in place for over four more years, and before their eventual removal in July 2021—there was only one party that was rumored to be seriously interested. The city set parameters around who would be allowed to purchase the Lee statue so that it would not end up in white nationalist hands and serve as a fetish on private property. The story goes that the potential steward was a white Virginian whose ancestors had owned slaves and whose partner was an antitrafficking advocate from Ghana. The couple was considering opening a new museum about the relationship between slavery pasts and slavery presents on their private land. This initiative, clearly distinct from white nationalist worship of Confederate general Robert E. Lee, was tentatively deemed to be an appropriate recontextualization for a statue that was unveiled in 1924 with a Ku Klux Klan parade.[4]

Unfortunately, it turns out that antitrafficking discourse doesn't do much to recontextualize these histories at all. The Robert E. Lee statue was commissioned in the Progressive Era to reclaim the honor of slaveholders, to remember slavery as a benign institution. The statue was placed on the edge of the Black community of Vinegar Hill to terrorize Black residents, to claim that white presence had civilized Black people out of their natural underdeveloped state during slavery, and to suggest that Black citizenship had failed.[5] The statue was erected in an era that saw academic research at the University of Virginia work to enshrine "fictions of racial difference through writings, science, and law."[6] Antitrafficking's most common slogans, figures, and empirical measures are rooted in similar antiblack logics that resurface the Lost Cause claims about white paternalism and Black cultural inferiority. For instance, old slavery was more benign than new slavery because old slave owners protected their investments; slavery exists today because of Black pathology and poor parenting choices; free Black communities slip back into slavery without white outside forces.

In July 2021, the statues were finally removed, but their ultimate museum placement still remained to be determined. The city received at least ten responses from its request for statements of interest for "any museum, historical society, government or military battlefield interested in acquiring the Statues . . . for relocation and placement."[7] Several of the responses were made public, including the very compelling proposal from the Jefferson School African American Heritage Center to melt down the statues and commission new public art from the bronze.[8] The plan for the antitrafficking exhibition did not appear among the proposals.

Academic nomadism has since moved me from Charlottesville to Ontario (with its own burgeoning battle over monuments to white supremacy and settler colonialism), but my love of public history and my belief in its power to help foster political consciousness about racial injustice and multiracial struggle for collective freedom remains. That love brought me to that first monument meeting in Charlottesville. It continues to bring me to sites of conscience, marked and unmarked, all over the world. It has also brought to my attention the alarming number of historical sites of slavery, abolition, and civil rights that have incorporated antitrafficking narratives into their work, some of which I analyze in the following chapter. This constitutes another early hunch that continues to fuel my investigations into antitrafficking discourse: too much is at stake to cede the public pedagogical space of antiblack pasts and radical freedom fights to contemporary political projects not based in racial justice.

I have come to think of these quotidian comings upon of "trafficking is slavery" in sites of memory and the struggle for racial justice as an everyday research method. A few years ago, I started calling my research method #ethnographers-heart, which was a nod to bringing ethnographic sensibilities to bear on media archives and rhetorical analysis. I have thematized these ethnographic sensibilities toward the study of metaphor and memory as "heart and hunch."[9] D. Soyini Madison suggests that ethnographers approach language from the understanding that "words are indeed performative and do have material effects . . . they do something in the world; and that something is to reiterate (in terms of Derrida) speech, meaning, intent, and customs that have been repeated through time and that are communicative and comprehensible because they are recognizable in their repetition."[10] In Madison's words, we can "think of ethnography as critical theory in action" where theory helps to "articulate and identify hidden forces and ambiguities that operate beneath appearances" and allows us "to name and analyze what is intuitively felt."[11] Intuition, hunch; ethics, heart; #ethnographersheart.

Madison is part of "the decolonizing generation" of anthropologists who seek to use knowledge and the methods of producing it toward liberation.[12] This influential group of Black and allied scholars has transformed anthropology's approach to race, culture, and the nation-state in part by situating racism as a key constituent of capitalism and liberalism, locating global capitalism in longer histories of forced and voluntary migrations and movement, and theorizing diaspora as political mobilization.[13] An ethnographer's heart shaped by this "unruly brood of intellectual projects" might sense tricks of power and write poetry back to it.[14] Still, conceptualizing an ethnographer's heart carries the discipline's complicities in the global system of white supremacy (and all disciplines have complicities). White ethnographer hearts have, after all, helped colonize, fetishize, and invent Africa. Since my project here is not to erase nor transcend complicity, #ethnographersheart might also remind us that complicity need not manifest as, nor retreat as, guilt. Following Audre Lorde, "Guilt . . . is a response to one's own actions or lack of action. If it leads to change then it can be useful, since it is then no longer guilt but the beginning of knowledge."[15]

My work to articulate the role of the heart and the hunch in rhetorical research has brought me to the following proposition: ethnographic sensibilities are specifically needed for, and suited to, engaging the archives of the present, in part because of how the mutability of collective memory mediates the discourses found there. The present takes shape from and makes meaning with the past. The past is constructed and reworked in relation to the present, as the field of memory studies has astutely shown. We need ethnography to study a discourse of memory, because memory is not stable. It is uncanny, partial; it pops up in unexpected places. It is not reducible to the a priori cues and patterns demanded by sociological methods because its uses are for a variety of social, collective, familial, and personal purposes. Following around those memories like an ethnographer—memories codified in language and image, but not relegated to those forms alone—allows the researcher to embrace the unpredictable, to roam with the words and memories, and to ruminate on their appearances, disappearances, and uses. Because for all of memory's instability, the memory of slavery, in particular, does have a subject, an imagery, in the American imaginary: the Black American subject. Instantiating slavery as ancient and always, as multicultural, and as *subjectless* amid and within a context marked by unrelenting antiblack violence, through the historically specific imagery of the Black mother, is one key to the antitrafficking apparatus's discursive power. Recognizing this wink of white supremacy is an example of what an ethnographer's heart can bring to a rhetorical analysis of media archives.

Accounting for our methods is important because methods delimit what we allow ourselves to see and what we say can be included in the frame of our research. We use data gathering and analysis techniques, we use conceptual frameworks for interpretation, we have theoretical orientations. And then, we have our hearts: our lived experiences, the circuitous paths that bring us our insights, our political lives, our burdened and unburdened citizenships, our personal and collective wounds, our freedom dreams. The heart harbors the archival collection from whence rhetorical analysis builds. The heart's collection is the personal archive of practiced and embodied intuition that results from a life lived in John Jackson's everyday ethnographic mode of being in the world.[16]

5

History Is Antiblackness

At the former slave market site in Zanzibar, there is an open-air statue of five African figures, standing chained together, and placed in a five-foot-deep cut in the ground. The heads of the figures peer out, just above ground level. When it rains, the monument fills with water and the statues appear to be barely keeping their heads above water. In some seasons, the ground around the base of the statues is rocky, in others, it looks more like a pillowy bed of wildflowers. The artist, Clara Sörnäs, designed the bodies of the figures to appear as if they are crumbling away from erosion from the chest down. The memorial attempts to visualize the unknowable cruelty of the conditions faced by enslaved Africans along slave trading routes. The sculpture evokes, through its dynamism in relation to the weather, the resistance of the enslaved in all conditions. The water-filled tomb elicits the hold of the slave ship and the history of throwing captives overboard to skirt British abolitionist patrols of the East African slave trade. The pillowy bed offers comfort in the afterlife and calls to mind the fruits of Black freedom that spring forth from the seeds of ancestral Black resistance. The crumbling away connotes loss of life, but also the erosion of such monumental acts of violence from public memory.

Near the statue, the slave market site has an expansive historical exhibition called *East African Slave Trade, 1800-1909*. The interpretive panels discuss the home cultures enslaved people came from, the overland and overwater journey to the port of Zanzibar, and the many groups of people who participated in the trade at the Zanzibar slave market including "Arabs from the Gulf," Somalis, Baluchi mercenaries, and French Catholic Spiritans who described slave purchasing as saving and civilizing, "a way to uproot heathen Africans from hell." The exhibition explains how Zanzibar became the world's largest supplier of cloves from 1840 to 1870, which were cultivated on plantations run by slave labor. In discussing the eradication of slavery, the interpretive text states, "The movement for the abolition of slavery in the Indian Ocean was led, ironically, by Britain—the very nation that initiated the Atlantic slave-trading system 250 years before. Britain dominated the international slave trade from the mid-16th century for 200 years." This section displays abolitionist imagery from Britain, portraits of William Wilberforce and Olaudah Equiano, and photographs of British soldiers capturing and imprisoning East African slave traders. The museum connects the legacy of the East African trade to "the stigma of slavery," describing that "to be descended from a slave still holds a sense of shame" but such a mixing of people "created the kaleidoscope of diversity that makes Zanzibar so unique." The final segment of the exhibition, entitled *Slavery Today*, proclaims, "The abolishment of slavery in the 19th century only made slavery illegal, yet it still continues to this day. Slavery exists in every country of the world and has dramatically increased in the 21st century. There are more slaves today than were seized during the entire African slave trade." The statistics for the panel are credited to the Global Slavery Index 2014.

What explains the incorporation of the antitrafficking narrative into the public history of the Indian Ocean slave trade? What political project does it serve here? The *East African Slave Trade, 1800-1909* exhibition explains the brutal history of Arab and African slaving of Africans. The British are recognized for their abolitionist pursuits in the region. There's an explicit jab to unjust British enrichment through its history of slaving but no reference to Britain's brand of antiblack abolitionism, invested as it was in colonial and missionary projects. The legacies of these histories are named, by way of the exhibit, as Black shame, festive multiculturalism, and the US- and British-led transnational governance project to prosecute and punish human traffickers in Africa and elsewhere.

Throughout this book, I have shown how antitrafficking discourse opportunistically employs the tropes of slavery in Africa and of Africans enslaving their continental kin to intervene on Black sovereignty and to belittle Black claims for redress for histories of transatlantic slavery. The actually existing history of slavery in Africa does not change this point. The ways history is remembered, interpreted, and used is always political. Antitrafficking advocacy and antireparations arguments both find shelter in histories and memories of the Indian Ocean trade because they both use Arab and African complicities to offset and circumvent Western historical responsibility for slavery.

I close out the book's investigations with this chapter by touring select outposts of the antitrafficking mediascape—sites of history I visited for other reasons but where antitrafficking discourse nevertheless unexpectedly arose—to demonstrate how #ethnographersheart works as a method for rhetorical and visual analysis of the archive of the memory of slavery in the present. The goal of this chapter is to show how language, history, and racial ontology are connected through the politics of the production of knowledge, and ultimately, how these registers inform the racial semiotics of antitrafficking images. Historic sites are places where public memory meets mnemonic language ("modern-day slavery"). The inclusion of antitrafficking discourse at these sites moves in two directions. At historic sites with what I consider to be underlying political congruence, antitrafficking's insertion works to undermine racial claims for justice. At historic sites with narrative incongruence—if not complete political incongruence—antitrafficking's attachments work to racially legitimize antitrafficking's antiblack project. The image of the Arab slaver, the specter of slavery in Africa, and the narrative that Black people are incapable of sustaining freedom recur. Taken together, they are politically powerful historical narratives that traverse historiography, historical sites, and the history of the production of reason through racial ontologies—three registers of history that produce antiblackness. Each layer of knowledge production sediments in antitrafficking's ways of seeing, and imaging, modern slavery. From CNN's Libyan auction video to Ghanaian children playing in fishing communities and everyday life on the beaches of Zanzibar, I conclude the book by reflecting on how the gravity of slavery's afterlives requires us to annotate antitrafficking images with care.[1]

A photograph of the slave market's sculpture described in the chapter's open-ing is featured in Precision Air's in-flight magazine.[2] Rather than discuss the historic site, the corresponding article attempts to explain to readers what it glosses as "East Africa's Little Known Dark Past."[3] The author's stated aim is to recover the historical significance of the Arab slave trade and the central-ity of Zanzibar to it. The article juxtaposes this "forgotten past" to the Af-rican continental claims for reparations publicized through the 2001 United Nations (UN) World Conference Against Racism (WCAR) in Durban and the 2006 Pan-African Reparations Forum (PANREF) in Ghana. Directly quoting PANREF's goals to use reparations and pan-African unity to overcome conti-nental problems imposed by what PANREF named "imperialist globalization," the author opines, "The implication is that despite the abolition of slavery in the 19th century, many contemporary Africans blame the slave trade for today's problems. And yet, neither PANREF or the UN delegations in Durban alluded to the East African slave trade and those responsible for it."[4] Despite the United Nations African delegations at the 2001 WCAR ultimately aligning with the West's antireparations angling on the grounds of African complicity, remembering the slave trade in Africa is framed in the article as important *because* it undermines claims for redress. Africans, it is suggested, should take personal responsibility for the present, which resonates with the political uses of the rhetoric of Black personal responsibility throughout the diaspora.

The article concludes by connecting the trope of uncivilized Africans willing to sell their kin to justifications for upending the fight for reparations from the West:

> The most infamous of all slave traders was Tippu Tip (Hamed bin Moham-med). In spite of his Arab name, his grandfather was an African slave. Yet with a flagrant disregard for this familial tie to the commerce of flesh and blood, he operated trade in an area that stretched over 160 kilometres—from inland regions to his birthplace in Zanzibar. What this means in modern days: This should really be at the heart of any serious discussion on the East African slave trade, bearing in mind that it was British gun-ships, which put an end to the slave trade between East Africa and the Arabian Gulf in the late 19th and 20th centuries. How is it possible that demands for reparations from this region tend to look towards the West but not East towards the Arab world, or inwards at Africa itself?[5]

In this account, the Arab slave trader is revealed to be an African who de-scended from enslaved people. The figure of both the Arab slave trader, who came after the European slaver, and the African who enslaves his continental kin, work together to lessen the blame on the European. Those nonwhite figures combine with the memory of British abolition in the eastern trade to redirect responsibility for the massive dispossession caused by British slave trading and European colonialization of Africa back onto Africans themselves.

Such narrativization of history parallels antitrafficking's discursive investments. Antitrafficking advocacy, like slavery in Africa narratological opportunism, minimizes the world shaping effects of the transatlantic slave trade and European colonialism in order to maximize African complicity in slave trading, whether in the nineteenth century or in twenty-first-century migrant exploitation. Recentering attention on the Arab slaver resonates with, and naturalizes, stereotypes of evil Arab warmongers that uphold the political imperatives of the US-led war on terror and fit seamlessly into antitrafficking's narratives. When antitrafficking infographics attach themselves to historic exhibitions of the Arab trade in Africa, the Arab figure's natural state as an enslaver of women, through hijab, sex, or otherwise, is heightened to give the United States and its allies a twenty-first-century opportunity to abolish slavery in the "axis of evil." In this narration, the Arabs are the masterminding villains, the Africans are the corrupt middle men willing to sell their racial kin, and the Europeans are the civilized, selfless evangelists of freedom and emancipation.

In W. E. B. Du Bois's account of the role of Arab slave traders in African history, he writes, "In this whole story of the so-called 'Arab slave trade' the truth has been strangely twisted. Arab slave raiding was in the beginning, and largely to the end, a secondary result of the British and American slavery and slave trade and specifically was based on American demand for ivory."[6] Du Bois makes this point, not to deny the trade within Africa, but to note its structural relation to white accumulation and to reveal its historiographic narrative function. Writing in 1946, Du Bois continues, "Although author and chief supporter of modern slavery, Great Britain could hold up her head and, by suppressing a slavery now becoming unprofitable, lead world philanthropy as the great emancipator of the slave."[7] Du Bois highlights the historical function of the narrative: rebranding empire as emancipatory, while shifting the types of labor exploitation to continue to maximize profits and influence under changing discursive conditions postabolition.[8] Du Bois's invocation of the term "modern slavery" pricks. He is referring to the modernity of the transatlantic trade—the trade that brings modernity into being. Yet his sentence resonates so startlingly with critiques of contemporary British state-led antitrafficking efforts to introduce the Modern Slavery Act of 2015, which similarly used Britain's history of abolition to promote supply-chain-based reforms and carceral approaches to immigration in the name of ending modern slavery.[9]

Within historical narrative, "Some facts are recalled more often than others; some strings of facts are recalled with more empirical richness than others."[10] Walter Rodney, echoing Du Bois, writes "The slave trade on the Indian Ocean has been called the 'East African Slave Trade' and the 'Arab Slave Trade' for so long that it hides the extent to which it was also a European trade."[11] He goes on to explain that at the height of its trade, the major destination of enslaved captives was European-owned plantation economies off the east coast of Africa, and that even enslaved Africans in Arab countries were "ultimately serving the European capitalist system which set up demand for slave-grown products, such as cloves grown in Zanzibar under the supervision of Arab masters."[12] By reconnecting the Arab trade to its larger context of European markets and accumulation, Rodney demonstrates the political utility of historical narratives that overremember Arab and African slavers and underremember European beneficiaries.

The figure of the Arab slave trader has been used in US and British political and popular discourse to make the transatlantic trade nonexceptional, suggesting that the Arab trade was longer, more widespread, and more brutal than the European trade. After the British outlawed slave trading in its empire, British imperial forces used the specter of Arab slave traders to construct central Africa as needing Western humanitarian intervention to save it from itself. Arab slavers in Africa are said to have come before and after the Europeans, which has been used by European colonial powers to justify both European enslavement of Africans and European imperialism in Africa in the name of ending slavery. Antitrafficking advocacy opportunistically attaches itself to public histories of slavery in Africa because they elicit narratives that lessen the blame on whites for slavery, which rhetorically serves to weaken pan-African claims for redress while refiguring the white enslaver as the white emancipator.

Forget about White Saviors: Antitrafficking Discourse in Black Histories of Struggle

If antitrafficking's insertion into public histories of the East African trade can be explained through its congruence with the political work of the antitrafficking apparatus, what explains the presence of antitrafficking discourse in public history institutions dedicated to preserving the history of Black struggle for rights and civic freedoms? The National Civil Rights Museum (NCRM) at the Lorraine Motel in Memphis, Tennessee, preserves the historic site where

Dr. Martin Luther King Jr. was assassinated. The museum houses an impressive and expansive interpretive center that contextualizes King's death within the complex and multifaceted civil rights struggle and the history of slavery in the United States. The exhibition room on slavery includes the important sentence, "Slavery made America one of the wealthiest nations in the world." There are extensive exhibitions on many civil rights actions and groups, including the Greensboro sit-ins, the Montgomery bus boycott, the Freedom Rides, March on Washington, Student Nonviolent Coordinating Committee (SNCC), grassroots organizing in the South by the Council of Federated Organizations (COFO), Black Power, and the Memphis sanitation workers' strike. Each section paints a nuanced picture of lesser-known participants, the different perspectives and tactics used within the movements, Black women's leadership and contributions, and how people worked through political differences within movement spaces.

There are no white saviors here. On a wall dedicated to abolitionists of slavery, only Black abolitionists are represented. Belinda Royall's successful 1783 lawsuit for reparations for unpaid labor during her fifty years of enslavement is highlighted. The Emancipation Proclamation is referred to as a "strategic military decision," not a heroic white leader's gift of freedom. President John F. Kennedy's moves toward passing civil rights legislation are recontextualized as directly tied to the bad press he was receiving abroad during the Cold War. There is a brief mention of SNCC's White Folks Project, where Southern white organizers tried to educate and organize poor whites into the Civil Rights Movement in hopes of building an "interracial movement of the poor" and upending white violence against Black people.[13] It was short-lived and dangerous work, although the SNCC digital archive mentions that a canvassing arm of the project "convinced twenty local whites to register with the [Mississippi Freedom Democratic Party] after just two weeks of canvassing."[14] Including this history of organizing, as opposed to common valorizations of white abolitionists that obscure white divestment from Black enfranchisement, offers a more honest historical precedent for antiracist whites who want to be engaged in racial justice struggles.

In 2018, the rotating exhibition in the orientation room, *MLK50: A Legacy Remembered*, focused on making connections to the present and the continued impact of King's legacy on social movements. The exhibition "compar[ed] contemporary events like the Occupy Movement and the Living Wage Campaign with the Poor People's Campaign and Sanitation Strike."[15] The temporary exhibition devoted a large section to Black Lives Matter, including a replica of Trayvon Martin's hoodie and enlarged reproductions of Patrisse Cullors's tweets. Toward the end of the exhibition, there was an interactive element where visitors could give their thoughts on the prompt, "Where do you go from here?" The exhibition offered six potential issues to further explore: Justice, Peacemaking, Living Wage, End Poverty, Fair Housing, Education. Ending human trafficking was not suggested; there was no mention of antitrafficking's modern-day slavery in the exhibition. Upon exiting the orientation exhibition, visitors wind their way through the expansive museum complex, leading up to a single file line where visitors pass through the motel room where Dr. King was assassinated. It is a chilling, sobering, and galvanizing experience. It leaves you humbly in awe of the power and the sacrifice of lives lived in struggle.

As I exited the viewing area during my visit, I funneled into an amphitheater seating area where I looked up to see a video of Bradley Myles, the executive director of the antitrafficking organization Polaris Project, explaining to me how important it is to correct the misconception that slavery ended with the Civil War. He mentioned several groups of people who are still enslaved: farmworkers, factory workers, and "children sold for sex and prostitution by pimps." When he discusses child sex slavery, the video cuts to an image of a young white girl huddled in a corner. Myles describes the work his organization does: they run a hotline that trafficking victims can call to get help. He doesn't mention that hotline collaborates extensively with local police nor the organization's history of supporting carceral initiatives to end commercial sex. He then says, "we are fighting the same fight that the historical abolitionists were fighting." In addition to the slippage between civil rights and Civil War, Myles's insertion into the space felt incongruent with what I had just experienced in the museum's interpretation. I had, after all, come to the museum out of my interest in how Black struggle is remembered in America, not for my research on the antitrafficking mediascape.

The Polaris Project, named after the North Star in reference to the Underground Railroad, was cofounded by Brown University alum Katherine Chon. Through her advocacy and support, Chon has tied her antitrafficking work to Brown University's Center for the Study of Slavery and Justice (CSSJ). CSSJ is a Black history research institute and racial justice project that was created out of the recommendations from Brown's pathbreaking Slavery and Justice Report. The report, completed in 2006, investigated the role of Brown in the transatlantic slave trade and recommended a variety of reparations-based proposals. CSSJ opened in 2012 as a reparative response to Brown University's unjust enrichment. In 2015, it created the Human Trafficking Research Cluster. Chon's project against "modern-day slavery" inserts antitrafficking's roots in paternalistic and criminalizing carceral protection strategies into a space that was designed to challenge the antiblack legacies of slavery. To CSSJ's credit, the trafficking cluster, under the leadership of critical antitrafficking scholar Elena Shih, has actively resisted the harmful frames and solutions of the antitrafficking apparatus by collaborating on community research with activist organizations dedicated to sex worker and migrant rights.[16] In the aftermath of the murder of Asian massage parlor workers in Atlanta in March 2021, several people and organizations involved in this cluster's work organized vigils, raised awareness in the media about Asian migrant workers' rights, and, crucially, pointed out how antitrafficking advocacy, like Polaris's program, which is aimed at shutting down illicit massage parlors in the name of ending trafficking, contributes to the violence that Asian massage workers experience.[17] My interest in Polaris at CSSJ is less about CSSJ, though, and more about the antitrafficking apparatus's persistent attachment to Black history. Polaris's inclusion at CSSJ, as its inclusion at NCRM, demonstrates an investment in linking antitrafficking discourse to sites of Black history, freedom struggle, and repair. Those investments suggest that the antitrafficking industry needs, and benefits from, Black endorsement. Such legitimating institutional relationships reiterate how much political work the racial mnemonic "modern-day slavery" does for the antitrafficking apparatus.

The inclusion of the Polaris Project promotional video at NCRM is a departure from the narrative and the power of the museum. Myles's appearance is barely more than a blip on the screen. Many visitors do not stop in the amphitheater; others who do might only see one or two of the other organizational promotional videos that loop in the space.[18] Yet, this antitrafficking blip on the screen, this insertion of rhetoric and policy based in antiblack logics organized in opposition to the Black freedom struggle and racial justice more broadly, is one blip among patterned insertions of antitrafficking discourse throughout Black memoryscapes globally. It is another example of the antitrafficking apparatus's repeated and sustained cannibalization of the histories and symbols of Black freedom and Black self-determination, whether Haiti, Ghana, or the civil rights movement.[19]

The Antiblackness of History

Du Bois concludes his magisterial intervention in the historiography of Reconstruction by demonstrating how "the facts of American history have in the last half century been falsified because the nation was ashamed."[20] (Walter Rodney, in delineating how European history has opportunistically misrepresented Europe's role in economically devastating Africa, offers a related aside: "Many guilty consciences have been created by the slave trade . . . To ease their guilty consciences, Europeans try to throw the major responsibility for the slave trade on to the Africans").[21] Citing a review of the ways that Reconstruction was taught in textbooks, Du Bois discusses three recurring narratives about the Black capacity for freedom: African Americans were "ignorant and unfit to govern themselves"; they were thieves and dependent on the state to take care of them; and they were corrupt and incompetent rulers when elected to legislatures in the US South.[22] Such historical narratives, Du Bois argues, are fueled by the white fear of Black rule. Black rule threatens not only white control, but the historical narratives and ontological ordering that white supremacy is based in. Black freedom and Black governance are perceived as so threatening to historical narratives and to present social order that they must be renarrated to conform to white supremacy's logics: Black unfitness for freedom, Black natural status as slaves, Black inferiority, Black passivity ("the only people to achieve emancipation with no effort on their part"[23]), the Black need for white civilizing instruction, the Black need for white people to free them from themselves.

White supremacy's antiblack logics accumulate and circulate through historical narrative. They recur, are recombined, and are reconstituted in antitrafficking's narratives about the present of Black unfreedom and the past and present of white benevolence.[24] Black mothers in Haiti are ignorant to the dangers their daughters face in restavèk; Black parents naively and ignorantly sell their children in Ghana and must be educated (or jailed) to stop doing it; Haitian courts are corrupt and liable to take bribes from convicted traffickers; Black African countries are unable to prevent slavery because of weak rule of law; Haiti, Democratic Republic of Congo, and Ghana need US-based NGOs to end slavery in their countries. US-led transnational antitrafficking enforcement policies help other countries rid themselves of slavery and join modernity. British and American pasts of abolition intervene on Black presents of slavery to enlighten and educate.

Antitrafficking's narratives, then, illustrate a contemporary example of Michel-Rolph Trouillot's insight: "The narrative structures of Western historiography have not broken with the ontological order of the Renaissance."[25] Writing about the historiography of the Haitian Revolution, Trouillot is referring to the ontological order that developed in response to the question "What is Man?" during Europe's quest to colonize other lands and enslave other people.[26] Such philosophies elaborated a hierarchy of humanness, where European men were overrepresented as the only fully human beings, and Chinese, Persian, and Egyptian people were lesser humans because they were suspiciously evil but still advanced through their ties "to strong state structures."[27] Indigenous groups in the Americas could be *legitimately* dispossessed of their lands through state, imperial, and Christian theological reasoning; and Black Africans were deemed "destined to slavery" and thus "*legitimately enslavable.*"[28]

Sylvia Wynter describes how European knowledge systems blended theological and juridical explanations of subhumanness to advance state projects of expropriating land and labor. Those lines of reasoning changed as dominant modes of knowledge production changed, but they continued to legitimate the hierarchy of who counted as human. In so doing, Wynter elaborates how unjust systems are produced through *enlightened* thought. She writes: "What is of specific interest here is not only that it was this initial, large-scale, one-sided accumulation of lands, wealth, power, and unpaid labor by the West that was to provide the basis for today's 20/80 wealth and power ratio between the world's peoples but also that this primary accumulation had been effected on the basis of a truth-for, or system of ethno-knowledge."[29]

Theft for the West's accumulation was justified by reason. Reason was articulated in explicitly racial terms. Following Wynter, the True Christian Self that sought to self-liberate from his enslavement to sin transitioned into the Rational Self of Man who could self-liberate from the enslavement of irrationality. Black Africans were enslaved by brute force but then their enslavement was used as evidence of their irrationality (and thus inferiority). Phenotypical and cultural difference became the visual proof that ordered the hierarchy of rationality and humanness.[30] Wynter calls this a "sustained rhetorical strategy," where Indigenous and Black people were made into the Human Others of the West's self-conception as rational man.[31] Wynter and Trouillot both discuss the subsequent religious and cultural forces that consolidated the color of blackness into the position of badness as the transatlantic slave trade flourished. Ultimately, "the practice of slavery in the Americas secured blacks' position at the bottom of the human world."[32]

Excavating these historical discourses is crucial for understanding how power is discursively legitimized and specifically how the West's violent power is discursively legitimated through racial logics. If, following Mignolo's reading of Wynter, "domination precedes accumulation," then "domination needs a cultural model . . . that legitimizes and naturalizes exploitation."[33] The cultural model is created through the production of knowledge, the production of history, and the memory of the past in the present. For Du Bois, historiography made this evident: "In propaganda against the Negro since emancipation in this land, we face one of the most stupendous efforts the world ever saw to discredit human beings, an effort involving universities, history, science, social life and religion."³⁴ The politics of the history of the production of knowledge about modernity, its Humans, and its Others underscore the centrality of antiblackness to language, logic, and historical narrative. The invention of the category *Human*, inaugurated in and through European liberal modernity, is a sustained rhetorical project that legitimates unjust accumulation of material and symbolic capital by the West through the creation of racial order of being and knowing. The elaboration of humanism that follows from it rests on the West's basis of self-conception in intervening in Black irrationality.

Antitrafficking discourse reproduces such antiblack humanism every time it educates a Haitian mother about the dangers of selling her children or circulates images of the scarred bodies of young Ghanaian boys brutalized by the fishermen that are said to enslave them. Examples of antiblack humanism abound in studies of humanitarianism, global development, human rights, and philanthropy (even as, Jemima Pierre points out, they aren't often discussed by scholars as racial projects).³⁵ Social scientists reproduce antiblack humanism when they imagine race as only pertinent to analysis when studying racialized subjects. Communication scholars should especially take heed: rhetorical projects are central to the history of modernity's raciality. Modernity's language is constituted to support white supremacy; the Human is a project of narrativization; language and history are constituted by antiblackness. Understanding how is imperative to be able to conduct a rhetorical analysis of anything. Racial ordering to justify racial violence subtends Western historical narratives. Those historical narratives surface in political speech, social movements, journalism, policy negotiations, museums, research questions, and more. "If a specific history produced *man*, then this same history produced its ontological lack—the figure of the Black."³⁶

Antitrafficking discourse's investment in Black history sites is, thus, related to the antiblackness of history across all three registers summarized above: the history of how the West produced modernity through racial ontologies, the history of academic knowledge production, and public history sites. These different realms of history are all connected through enduring narratives about Blackness that resurface in antitrafficking campaigns.

Although I often experience antitrafficking's inclusion in public history sites as bizarre and out-of-place comings upon—that's why I started calling my method #ethnographersheart—if you trace the underpinning logics of the sites, as I have tried to do throughout this book, you often find them to be invested in compatible logics. When the logics don't seem to line up, there are generally additional considerations at play. Museums, in particular, rely on public interest and curricular alignment to attract school groups and visitors; they also rely on funding from individual donors, philanthropies, and government grants to keep their doors open. Museum exhibitions reflect a variety of complex negotiations among individual staff expertise, board member interests and agendas, and budgets. Depending on the museum's political orientation to Black history or the history of slavery and abolition, antitrafficking narratives can offer a lot of resolution for uncomfortable pasts: the racially specific injuries of the past give way to antitrafficking's multicultural victims and heroes of the present, antitrafficking's racial redemption narratives ease white psychic tension in spaces where white complicity with antiblack pasts cannot be ignored, the US nation is redeemed as freedom loving and the just protector of other nations and people, visitors of all racial identities can be like abolitionists of the past without having to engage in confrontational tactics of racial justice movements. In other words, antitrafficking narratives in museums about slavery, in particular, give many people many ways to resolve the past and move forward with their subjectivities intact.

When antitrafficking discourse is attached to sites that commemorate Black liberation and Black self-determination, though, the antitrafficking apparatus's investment in modernity's racial logics is laid bare. By inserting a new slavery that has either always existed in Africa or has suddenly arisen through globalization's new markets, antitrafficking campaigns do not address the ongoing structural legacies of the history of slavery nor the ongoing struggle for racial justice. Rather, they intervene on the powerful spaces of Black freedom struggle to reestablish the centrality of modernity's legitimating lie: Black people are not capable of freedom, if granted, they will slip back into their natural state of enslavement, chaos, or ignorance, and then the West's "civic-humanist" Self will intervene, thereby reaffirming its own humanity. Trouillot's insights return: "The contention that enslaved Africans and their descendants could not envision freedom—let alone formulate strategies for gaining and securing freedom—was based not so much on *empirical evidence* as on an *ontology*, an implicit organization of the world and its inhabitants."[37] Antitrafficking discourse offers no break from this ontological order, and it relies on these historical narratives to inform the racial semiotics of antitrafficking photography, which purport to finally offer empirical evidence in the present of the self-enslaving nature of Black diasporic subjects.

In the morning on the beaches of Zanzibar, women tend their seaweed farms in the low ocean tide. In the late afternoon, men on fishing boats come back to shore. If photographed from a distance, the scene could be inserted into the visual economy of the antitrafficking apparatus without much suspicion. Black women standing in shallow water, bent over and picking seaweed, heads wrapped in bright cloth, balance large rice bags filled with the morning's harvest. Several Black men crowded on a relatively small, sturdy but humble fishing boat pull blue fishing nets onto the boat. As the water gets shallow, some men reach their arms out to grab ropes or anchors or other docking devices. Lush green palms frame the scene. At dusk, the ocean is bright blue, teen boys do pushups on the side of overturned fishing boats to show off for each other, tourists sipping cocktails at (Freddie) Mercury's Bar take in the ocean view, beach boys dressed up as Maasai titillate white imaginations. Some people are laughing, others, selling or shouting across the way. When I took in this scene during my visit to Zanzibar's slave market site, it occurred to me how easily each of these snapshots of unspectacular daily life could become (erroneous) visual proof of modern slavery on an antitrafficking organization's website.

What are pictures of modern-day slavery in Africa pictures of? What do antitrafficking sympathizers see in these images? In too many antitrafficking images, the only content is Black people, engaged in some aspect of everyday life, sometimes while playing and smiling, many times in places that look like what Africa is imagined by the West to be, often with a blue fishing net, often on a blue ocean, often with some visual symbol that cues poverty for the enriched viewer, often with some visual symbol that cues US plantation slavery in the viewer's imagination. Seaweed becomes cotton; fishing boats become slave ships. The visual economy of antitrafficking relies on the apparent self-evidential indexicality of the Black body to slavery. It relies on the naturalization of poverty in Africa in the white mind's eye to communicate exploitation or desperation. It relies on "the self-evident defilement besmirching black geographies and corporalities."[38] It also relies on a set of symbols within antitrafficking photography that have come to signify modern-day slavery. Simple daily tools, like the presence of a blue fishing net in a fishing village, have become proof that children are enslaved because of how they repeat throughout the antitrafficking mediascape. The visual economy of antitrafficking assumes that Black everydayness, Black joy, and Black self-making are not seeable by antitrafficking supporters, perhaps because they are not seeable by antitrafficking photographers. After all, "audiences draw on a host of historical associations, cultural narratives, structures of feeling and belief, and rhetorical expectations in their engagement with images."[39]

In April 2019, the Black transnational cultural tastemaker organization Afropunk posted an image of a young Black boy with a smile on his face splashing in waist-deep water. A follower on Instagram wrote "love this"; the next one wrote "heartstrings"; the next posted three broken heart emojis in a row; the next wrote "What a contagious mood—PURE JOY!" The next, an angry emoji face; the next, "black boy joy. I love it!!!" Then comes, "The world breaks my heart," followed by a sad face icon, and then another "wow so so sad!" For some readers, the image depicted pure joy, for others, child fishing slavery in Africa.

What could have caused so much confusion over the image? How can a kid playing in water be "so so sad"? The image, seen in figure 5.1, was taken by Jeremy Snell as part of his series on child slavery on Lake Volta in Ghana, which also features many blue nets. The post quotes the artist's description, "Thousands of kids are forced to fish and work on Lake Volta in Ghana. Many are convinced they are being taken to go to school, but instead are enslaved in forced labor on the lake that threatens their life and childhood." Clearly, some of the post's followers read the caption and some did not. More importantly, how does a smiling kid playing in water indicate he is enslaved? It doesn't, but water, plus Black child, plus West Africa operates as a metonym for slavery by invoking a transatlantic slavery past and filtering it through antitrafficking's antiblackness as a way of seeing. As critical antitrafficking scholar Sam Okyere and his colleagues have written about Lake Volta fishing in Ghana, "Outsiders . . . can wrongly translate the sight of a child in a boat with an adult as a child being exploited or forced to work."[40] It is obviously possible to see beyond Black suffering in these images.[41] It is possible to see Black joy in an image of a child splashing in water; several of the followers name it as such. But, that is not what antitrafficking photography thinks it is seeing, thinks it is showing, thinks it is proving.

When I taught this social media case study in my Media Ethnography class, I only showed the screenshot of the Afropunk post, without the caption. I asked the students what it was an image of. The consensus was "a child playing in water." (Race was conspicuously left unnamed.) I asked them how they knew. They gave details drawing on visual analysis strategies that we had been learning about for conducting research. I then showed them the same image with the caption, and asked: What is this a picture of? They said, "Slavery in Africa." I asked: How do you know? They weren't sure. I moved on to a discussion of the various followers' comments to explain the openness of images, the complexities and pay-offs of using media ethnography as a method, the need to understand liberalism's constitution with antiblackness to be able

FIGURE 5.1 An Afropunk Instagram post depicts a smiling Black boy splashing in water, but the caption characterizes the boy as enslaved. The photograph in the post is attributed to Jeremy Snell.

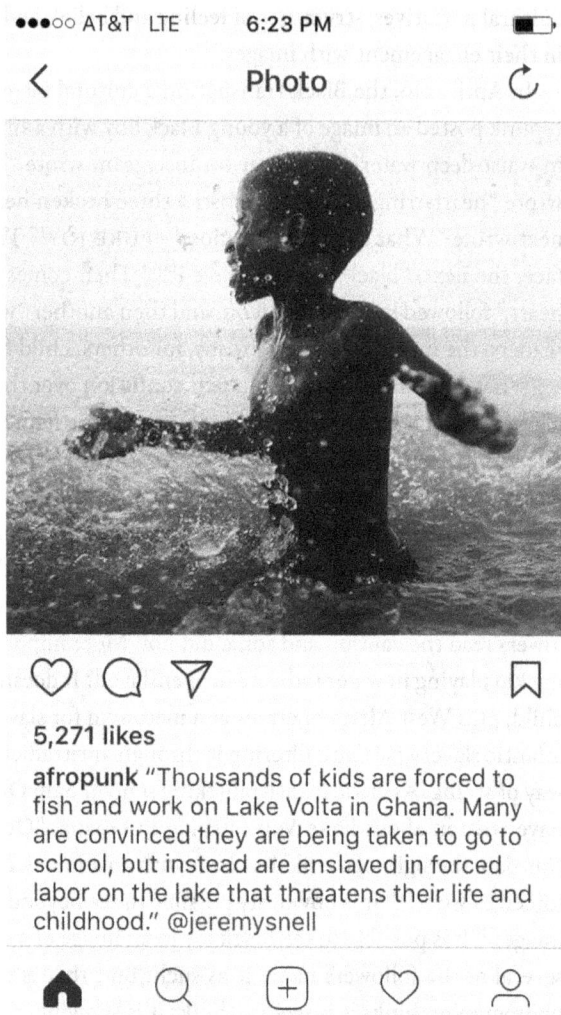

●●●○○ AT&T LTE   6:23 PM

‹   **Photo**   ↻

♡ ♡ ⎘   ⊓

5,271 likes

afropunk "Thousands of kids are forced to fish and work on Lake Volta in Ghana. Many are convinced they are being taken to go to school, but instead are enslaved in forced labor on the lake that threatens their life and childhood." @jeremysnell

to interpret news images, the need to know Black history to conduct rhetorical analysis.

When I teach the CNN video of the migrant auction in Libya that opened this book, I reverse the line of questioning: Did the video convince you that there are slave auctions in Libya? The unanimous answer has always been yes. When I ask how it did so, the discussion revolves around the fact that the journalist was actually there, that we are seeing what really happened, it's visual proof. Students then make a list of what they actually see in the video:

men, dark alley, spotlight, car, detention center, road, outside of a warehouse, parking lot, streetscape. The clips of the "auction" scenes are short, shaky, and either too tightly framed or too far away to decipher. The clips of the detention center, however, are more robust. The proverbial wheels start turning. We return to the question again: what, exactly, is this visual proof of?

When Rinaldo Walcott grapples with images of Africans crossing the Mediterranean Sea to Lampedusa, Italy, he writes: "In the long emancipation such crossings are an extension of the Middle Passage and are not a new Middle Passage."[42] In so doing, he emphasizes two things: (1) the transatlantic slave trade cannot be analogized because it inaugurated modernity's racial logics, racial hierarchy, and social relations,[43] and (2) Black unfreedom of movement continues in the present because of those logics and relations. In explicating what he terms "slave ship logics," he writes, "This slave past produced the contemporary Black body [which is] now violently policed globally."[44] Striking visual resonances with the past unfold onto structural analyses of how Black unfreedoms in the present come to be.

Walcott builds on Christina Sharpe's work that invokes the slave past when meditating on the haunting repetition of the violences faced by enslaved Africans on the Zong in 1781 and undocumented African migrants drowned off the coast of Lampedusa in 2013. Sharpe is clear to connect the spectacularized violence to the everyday violence of policy: laws that prohibit safe immigration, laws that criminalize and deport African migrants who survive the journey, laws that prioritize surveillance over rescues at sea, and trade agreements and military interventions that shape the geopolitical conditions for the urgency of migration. The migrants will face criminal investigation, she writes, the multinational corporations will not.[45] Both antitrafficking advocates and Black studies scholars connect news images of Black suffering in the Mediterranean to the history and collective memory of slavery, but to different political ends. One is invested in white transcendence, the other in Black freedom of movement.

The image economy of Black Mediterranean migration, mobilized by and refracted through two different interpretive frames and political projects, makes it imperative to attend to Walcott and Idil Abdillahi's "contention that the politics and logics of contemporary immigration have embedded in them anti-Black logics."[46] Such logics shape the differences in migration conditions across forced, coerced, and voluntary Black migration experiences, while offering a way to think about how they are nevertheless interconnected through systems of violence that morph and traverse geographies of time, departure, arrival, and home.[47]

Black unsafe migration through Africa and the Mediterranean can be understood through slavery's structural and affective afterlives, but, within the antitrafficking apparatus, Black life in Black geographies that has been shaped by logics of dispossession is rendered seeable through coloniality's lexicon of the suffering Black African who is desperate for and dependent on European help, who cannot self-govern, who has been hurt by his continental kin, who is ignorant of or naive to the dangers that await him, who is childlike in his impatient refusal to find a legal path to migration (one doesn't exist), who has a greater capacity to withstand the pain of the harrowing journey. This is a discourse that was repeated until naturalized by an entire modern world history of antiblack logics, upheld by science's visual regimes of truth, first designed in the rupture of the Renaissance, and first mobilized to empirically see Black inferiority.

Despite these substantial and critical political differences, afterlives of slavery racial justice frames and antitrafficking discourse's white transcendence frames come dangerously close to slipping into one another, in part because of how the images circulate through the antitrafficking mediascape, and in part because of the antitrafficking apparatus's vested interest in inserting itself into Black memoryscapes in order to racially legitimize its antiblack political project. I offer, then, a moment to pause and, drawing on Sharpe, annotate the continuities of the "semiotics of the slave ship" with care.[48] Too easily galvanizing contemporary news photography that invokes slavery's memory can lead to importing antitrafficking's imagery and narratives, which are constituted by antiblackness, into the struggle for racial justice and the scholarship about the afterlives of slavery.

Less than two weeks after the 2017 CNN investigation into Libyan slave auctions was published, images of Black-led European protests against slavery in Libya circulated in the news. In the news images of a protest in Sweden, which also populated social media platforms, Black, Black Arab, and non-Black Arab protesters held signs that read "Black Lives Matter," "#NOTFORSALE," "We are not slaves," and "Slavery never ended."[49] The images lent racial legitimacy to CNN's investigation and, perhaps inadvertently, connected movements for racial justice to antitrafficking campaign slogans and the antitrafficking image economy. "Slavery never ended" and "slavery still exists" are two of the most common slogans of the antitrafficking apparatus. In the protest's invocation, they meld into the ways that afterlives of slavery frameworks have been taken up sometimes too reductively in popular discourse, which can confuse rather than clarify what changes and what stays the same in slavery's afterlives. Perhaps the most noticeable antitrafficking convergence is the #NOTFORSALE sign, which is also the name of a very popular evangelical global antitrafficking organization that was started by US investment banker David Batstone. Not for Sale upholds the racial narratives and corporate solutions of the larger antitrafficking apparatus, including collaborating with local police in the United States and leveraging racial narratives about Africa by suggesting that the presence of "slaveholders in the Ivory Coast" is "not surpris[ing]."[50]

Antitrafficking images of Black migrants in Libya, which circulated through antitrafficking philanthropic news sites, provoke protests where protesters connect ongoing anti-Black racism to contemporary unsafe migration, but in mediated form, their presence and signage is also used to legitimize the antitrafficking apparatus. The organizer of the Swedish protest has since used her platform to amplify the mandates of antitrafficking policy in her birth country of Gambia. Her advocacy demands were later incorporated, anonymously and without citation, into the 2021 US State Department Trafficking in Persons Report as evidence of the Gambian government's slow pace of progress in protecting victims of human trafficking.[51] Without careful annotation, invocations of slavery's resonances can mistake important past-present connections for antitrafficking's opportunistic agenda, which operates in effect as a politically palatable alternative to demands for redress by reconstituting antiblack historical narratives (Arab slavers, slavery in Africa, corrupt African governments) to endorse solutions to trafficking (staying in place, deportation) that ultimately uphold global white supremacy.

"In the wake, the semiotics of the slave ship continue: from the forced movements of the enslaved to the forced movements of the migrant and the refugee, to the regulation of Black people in North American streets and neighborhoods, to those ongoing crossings of and drownings in the Mediterranean Sea, to the brutal colonial reimaginings of the slave ship and the ark; to the reappearances of the slave ship in everyday life in the form of the prison, the camp, and the school."[52] Christina Sharpe offers the powerful analytic of the wake to recognize the simultaneity of both "antiblackness as total climate" and "Black visualsonic resistance to that imposition of non/being."[53] Through extended meditations on several images, Sharpe offers a method for producing knowledge about the presence of the past ethically through annotation and redaction. Annotating news photography of contemporary structural conditions that resonate with slavery's aesthetics opens space to think beyond structural connections, to reach beyond too easy breaks with the past and too easy linear connections.[54] Such annotations and reflections activate the capacity to know something more, even when—especially when—there are no words to name the nimble, if uninterrupted, gratuitous violence of antiblackness, nor the persistent, vigilant, undying "insistence on existing,"[55] the everyday work of maintaining the self-conception of being human despite all external threats.[56] There is an immense amount of potential, of transformation, in adopting Sharpe's ethics of seeing as a way of remembering and doing.[57]

Antitrafficking discourse, however, obscures such possibilities by opportunistically conflating discourses of slavery and its afterlives with political agendas that uphold the racial logics, material distribution, and symbolic violence of the governing structures of modernity. This is both the power, and the stakes, of language. It is the specific language of modern-day slavery coupled with the specific status-quo-preserving agenda of antitrafficking that has garnered its efficacy at recruiting advocates, philanthropists, governments, international law, and social scientists to its cause. Such assemblages have recognized the power of the memory of slavery and the power of redirecting it to politically palatable agendas. My hope is that this study helps us see the difference, so that we may be able to name not the power of a visual metaphor, but the power of the political agenda for which that metaphor is mobilized.

Understanding how historical structures have brought slavery resonances into being requires attending to what has changed and what has not. To do so ethically would require the antitrafficking apparatus to be honest about what is known. It requires "honesty vis-à-vis the present as it re-presents the past."[58] Ethical engagement with visual resonances must recognize modernity's foundation in antiblackness, must recognize the political context of the present struggle for Black freedom and racial justice in its midst. Each time recognition of the present struggle and movement for racial justice is ignored, downplayed, or co-opted by antitrafficking's modern-day abolitionists, slavery's past and present is invoked for white transcendence.

Let us accept that there is no white transcendence amid modernity's ontologies and get on with the work of building the world anew.

Afterword

Throughout this book, I have been pointing to how the political project of the antitrafficking apparatus arises in contradistinction to movements for racial justice. Whether by drawing on historical narratives built to undermine Black self-determination or by inserting itself into sites of mobilization for social justice, antitrafficking discourse has persistently offered a political alternative for publics and nations to engage with the history of slavery and its legacies outside of the realities of racial violence and the frameworks of racial justice. The irony of self-proclaimed abolitionists calling for carceral solutions to end trafficking, especially amid a robust prison abolition movement, has been noted by some critical antitrafficking authors. The simple fact that the antitrafficking apparatus rarely supports projects based in racial justice has been noted by others. Consider my surprise, then, when flagship antitrafficking organization Free the Slaves (FTS) released the following solidarity statement with Black Lives Matter during the summer 2020 uprisings for racial justice:

> On behalf of Free the Slaves, we stand in solidarity with the growing global outcry against racial violence and for racial justice in the United States. Free the Slaves is appalled by the ongoing systemic injustices directed at Black people and other people of color in the United States. Though the protests we have seen in recent weeks are powerful responses to the vigilante killing of Ahmaud Arbery and the police killings of Breonna Taylor and George Floyd, these are just the latest, and most visible, manifestations of longstanding anti-Black violence, racist policing, and institutionalized white supremacy—all of which are legacies of slavery in the United States. Since its founding in 2000, Free the Slaves has been a leader in the fight to eradicate all forms of modern slavery

throughout the globe. This work necessarily involves a shared commitment to dismantling slavery's root causes, which include racism and white supremacy, poverty and prejudice, and all forms of discrimination and exploitation that both perpetuate slavery and persist after its abolition. As a human rights organization, we understand the urgent need for brave and intentional moral leadership in this moment. We also understand that freedom work is a long-term struggle. It always has been and always will be. As we continue to stand for the values of social justice, equal rights, and human dignity, we will work in solidarity with other individuals and institutions of conscience to move freedom forward in the United States and everywhere in the world. And that can only happen if we demand—clearly and emphatically—that Black Lives Matter.[1]

On Free the Slaves' website, the Black Lives Matter banner announcement is followed by a banner promoting FTS's "Formula for Freedom" and then another citing the organization's twenty-year success at "how we've awakened the world & freed more than 14,000 people." Both the formula for freedom and the twenty years of accomplishment use white liberal enlightenment logics to obscure the structural racism of liberalism and capitalism's unfreedoms. This is a Black Lives Matter solidarity statement tacked in front of the organization's business as usual without reckoning with its complicities. In the solidarity statement, FTS states its outrage at racist policing and institutionalized white supremacy before heralding its own efforts at "dismantling slavery's root causes," of which it elsewhere considers "overpopulation" one. The organization fails to mention its endorsement of carceral collaborations and police raids. It fails to acknowledge how antitrafficking has undermined struggles for racial justice by inventing "new slaveries" that minimize the antiblack legacies of transatlantic slavery. It fails to take responsibility for recirculating long-standing antiblack logics to bolster claims about Black women selling their children into slavery, the cultural backwardness of Africans, and paternalistic notions of plantation slavery. It once again co-opts Black liberation struggles and their language to boast its own leadership, while obscuring how its investments in policing and juridical approaches to justice, underpinned by myths of Black cultural pathology, do the centuries-long freedom struggle a grave injustice.

A week after the release of the solidarity statement, FTS released another statement in commemoration of the World Day Against Child Labor. The statement begins, "Many are forced to work by their families or by traffickers. Many are beaten and whipped into submission." The post proceeds to tell the story of a Ghanaian child working in the fishing industry by including two photographs of the child's back filled with scars. The whip-scarred back image once again recalls nineteenth-century abolitionist imagery and recirculates the Black body in pain. The letter describes, in graphic detail, the torture the child endured. The story ends with freedom: "Kofi was quickly rescued by police. His stepfather was arrested and sentenced to pay a heavy fine or serve time in jail. Thanks to your contributions to Free the Slaves, Kofi is now safe."[2] Carceral humanitarianism relies on antiblack logics and historical narratives (parents selling children, Black people harming each other, the NGO is more caring than the child's parents, Black people commit crimes irrationally, punishment will educate them) to gain legitimacy for naming systems that keep Black people unfree—policing, jails, global capitalism, humanitarian imagery of Black suffering—as the path to Black freedom. A solidarity statement with Black Lives Matter has not changed the organization's priorities, imagery, or narratives.

If antitrafficking organizations want to fight for Black lives, let them publicly renounce and end all police training contracts, policing-based programs, carceral collaborations, and criminal legal approaches to justice. Let them disband their organizations and redistribute all their funds to existing grassroots movements for workers' rights, sex workers' rights, migrants' rights, border justice, and prison abolition. Let them withdraw from grant applications geared toward decriminalization, instead of incorporating the new palatability of decriminalization into their agendas.[3] Let them pay back their tax breaks as reparations for slavery and colonialism and their legacies. Let them stop leveraging racial justice discourse for their own ends. Let them acknowledge their role in naturalizing the antiblackness of world order through the racial logics that underpin antitrafficking discourse. Anything less is simply the next instantiation of the antitrafficking apparatus invoking the history and memory of transatlantic slavery to produce white indemnity.

Notes

INTRODUCTION

Throughout the book, I use the spelling "anti-Black" when referring to a specific type of racism (racism against Black people). The spelling "antiblack" is used for all other structural and ontological meanings.

1 "Migrants Being Sold as Slaves," CNN, November 13, 2017, video, https://www.cnn .com/videos/world/2017/11/13/libya-migrant-slave-auction-lon-orig-md-ejk.cnn.

2 See, for example, Stephanie Busari, "Nigerians Return Home with a Warning to Others: Don't Go to Libya," CNN, December 6, 2017, https://www.cnn.com/2017/12 /06/africa/nigeria-libya-refugees-intl/index.html.

3 Strongly Condemning Slave Auctions and the Exploitation of Migrants and Refugees as Forced Laborers in Libya, and for Other Purposes, H. R. Res. 644., 115th Cong. (2017–18), https://www.congress.gov/bill/115th-congress/house -resolution/644/text; United Nations, "Security Council Presidential Statement Condemns Slave Trade of Migrants in Libya, Calls upon State Authorities to Comply with International Human Rights Law," press release, December 7, 2017, https://www.un.org/press/en/2017/sc13105.doc.htm; Patrick Wintour, "Macron Vis-its Africa amid Anger over Human Trafficking and Slavery," *Guardian*, November 26, 2017, https://www.theguardian.com/world/2017/nov/26/emmanuel-macron-visits -africa-human-trafficking-slavery.

4 Ticktin, *Casualties of Care*, 181; Chapkis, "Trafficking, Migration, and the Law"; Kempadoo, "Introduction: Abolitionism, Criminal Justice, and Transnational Feminism," xiv; Shih, "Trafficking Deportation Pipeline," 57, 60.

5 My use of the term "antitrafficking apparatus" expands upon Jennifer Suchland's definition in *Economies of Violence*, 5–6.

6 Vance, "Innocence and Experience," 208.

7 Kang, *Traffic in Asian Women*, 83–116. Kang writes, "feminist activists worked from several angles to install 'sexual slavery' and 'female sexual slavery' in the United Nations through a series of publications, workshops, offshore consultations, and fortuitous UN certification procedures in the 1980s," 87.

8 Victims of Trafficking and Violence Protection Act of 2000, Pub. L. No. 106-386, 114 Stat. 1464 (2000).

9 Trodd, "Am I Still Not a Man and a Brother?"; Beutin, "Black Suffering for/from Anti-trafficking Advocacy."

10   Sundiata, *Brothers and Strangers*, 4; Darity and Mullen, *From Here to Equality*, 244; Ransby, "Henry Louis Gates' Dangerously Wrong Slave History." See also Rodney, *How Europe Underdeveloped Africa*, 94. Tryon Woods makes a similar point about antitrafficking when he writes, "[the] position that Africans were as culpable for the transatlantic slave trade . . . as were Europeans and Americans . . . aims to diffuse the reparations movement," in Woods, "Surrogate Selves," 124.

11   Woods, "Surrogate Selves," 131.

12   Maher, "Historicizing 'Irregular' Migration from Senegal to Europe," 88; Kleinman, *Adventure Capital*, 3; Perkowski, "Deaths, Interventions, Humanitarianism." On race, antiblackness, and the spectacle of African migration and death in the Mediterranean, see Danewid, "White Innocence in the Black Mediterranean"; Saucier and Woods, "Ex Aqua"; De Genova, "'Migrant Crisis' as Racial Crisis."

13   Parreñas, *Illicit Flirtations*, 12; Sharma, "Anti-trafficking Rhetoric."

14   Sharma, "Anti-Trafficking Rhetoric," 89.

15   Walcott, *Long Emancipation*, 14 (emphasis in original).

16   Sharpe, *In the Wake*, 21.

17   Wynter, "Africa, the West, and the Analogy of Culture," 25. See also Hall, "West and the Rest."

18   Zelizer, *Remembering to Forget*, 8–9; Tagg, *Burden of Representation*, 3.

19   Woods and Blewett, *Slavery*.

20   The film distinguishes "real slaves" from "exploitation and child labor," and proclaims to find "real slaves" in India (child carpet makers), Ivory Coast (young men working on cocoa farms), and the United States and United Kingdom (temporary migrant domestic workers).

21   I have thematized this as "Africans enslaving Africans" rather than the more specific Malians versus Ivorians to emphasize the homogenizing representational payoff of this video, which was created for audiences in the United States and United Kingdom. The journalists refer to the Black Ivorian farmer as "a slave master" throughout the segment.

22   In the scene of the Malian teens departing in 2000, one pledges to tell people back home "Don't go to Cote d'Ivoire." In the aftermath of the CNN Libya slave auction exposé in 2017, the same framing was applied in CNN's article headline: "Nigerians Return to Home with a Warning to Others: Don't Go to Libya."

23   Bama Athreya explains that the corporate accountability solutions that this film advocates for have largely resulted in organizations like Free the Slaves and the International Cocoa Initiative "convincing chocolate companies to offer greater sums of money to northern-based development NGOs to implement corporate-friendly programs. In no cases have those at the table suggested any fundamental reform of the commodity trade toward greater wealth distribution for farmers." See Athreya, "White Man's Burden," 55.

24   Didier Fassin calls this phenomenon a new regime of truth for evidence in asylum cases. Fassin, *Humanitarian Reason*, 111. This is also an old phenomenon that Black people have been subjected to in order to have their stories believed by white audiences in the United States and United Kingdom.

25 Hartman, *Scenes of Subjection*, 4. See also Morrison, *Playing in the Dark*, 5; Saucier and Woods, "Ex Aqua," 67; Tryon Woods and P. Khalil Saucier, "The Sadism of Anti-trafficking and the Erasure of Racial Slavery," *openDemocracy*, March 27, 2017, https://www.opendemocracy.net/en/beyond-trafficking-and-slavery/sadism-of-anti -trafficking-and-erasure-of-racial-slaver/.

26 See also Chuang, "Giving as Governance?" 1550–51.

27 Appadurai, *Modernity at Large*, 35.

28 Tony Maddox, "Modern-Day Slavery: A Problem That Can't be Ignored," CNN "Freedom Project," March 4, 2011, https://thecnnfreedomproject.blogs.cnn.com /2011/03/04/modern-day-slavery-a-problem-that-cant-be-ignored/.

29 See "Our Model for Freedom: Slavery Today," Free the Slaves, accessed May 21, 2020, https://www.freetheslaves.net/our-model-for-freedom/slavery-today/. The *Guardian* also promotes these facts on its antitrafficking advocacy section called "Modern-Day Slavery in Focus." See Kate Hodal, "One in 200 People Is a Slave: Why?" *Guardian*, February 25, 2019, https://www.theguardian.com/news/2019/feb /25/modern-slavery-trafficking-persons-one-in-200.

30 King, *Black Shoals*, 118–21, 135; Wilderson, *Red, White, and Black*, 14–15, 50–53.

31 Savannah Shange introduces the term "antiblackness theory" when engaging with what is "glossed more or less controversially as Afropessimism." Shange, *Progressive Dystopia*, 7. Frank Wilderson describes that Afropessimists make the ontological claim "that Blackness is that outside which makes it possible for White and non-White (i.e., Asians and Latinos) positions to exist." Wilderson, *Red, White, and Black*, 65.

32 Thomas, "End of the West," 125.

33 Wynter, "1492: A New World View," 10–12; Lowe, *Intimacies of Four Continents*, 7; Mills, "Illumination of Blackness," 20; Hua, *Trafficking Women's Human Rights*, 17–20.

34 Clarke and Thomas, *Globalization and Race*, 11–12.

35 Lowe, *Intimacies of Four Continents*, 7.

36 Hall, "West and the Rest," 155.

37 Rose, *Visual Methodologies*, 13, 144, 161.

38 Tagg, *Burden of Representation*, 4, 12, 21; Hall, "Work of Representation," 44; Rose, *Visual Methodologies*.

39 Elizabeth Bernstein describes her research on sex trafficking as "an ethnography of a discourse," where "there is no 'thing in itself' beyond its discursive construction, because the discourse produces the issue under consideration in the first place—shaping how the problem is defined, how it can be perceived, and the possible moral and political responses that emerge." Bernstein, *Brokered Subjects*, 28.

40 Classic examples of this approach are Miller and Slater, *The Internet: An Ethnographic Approach*; Boellstorff, *Coming of Age in Second Life*.

41 Gray, "Race, Media, and the Cultivation of Concern," 256. See also Towns, "The (Racial) Biases of Communication."

42 Hall, "Race, the Floating Signifier," 359–60; Wynter, "Unsettling the Coloniality of Being/Power/Truth/Freedom."

43 My use of the term "raciality" follows from Denise Ferreira da Silva's "analytics of raciality," which she introduces to get beyond sociological explanations of racial subjection. Analytics of raciality describes the context of the emergence of race, "its conditions of production, and the effects of signification of the conceptual arsenal generated in scientific projects that sought to discover the truth of man." Silva, *Toward a Global Idea of Race*, xviii–xix. See also Pierre, "Racial Vernaculars of Development."

44 Williams, *Divided World*.

45 In this vein, my thinking has been particularly shaped by: Mills, *Racial Contract*; W. E. B. Du Bois, *Black Reconstruction in America*; Silva, *Toward a Global Idea of Race*; Césaire, *Discourse on Colonialism*; Morgan, *Laboring Women*; Wynter, "Unsettling the Coloniality of Being/Power/Truth/Freedom"; Thomas, *Exceptional Violence*; Williams, *Capitalism and Slavery*; Rodney, *How Europe Underdeveloped Africa*; James, *Black Jacobins*; Gilmore, "Globalisation and US Prison Growth"; Davis, *Women, Race and Class*; Hartman, *Scenes of Subjection*; Singh, "Racial Formation in an Age of Permanent War"; among many others.

46 Sexton, "People-of-Color-Blindness," 42; Vargas, *Denial of Antiblackness*, 17.

47 See, for example, Doezema, *Sex Slaves and Discourse Masters*; Kempadoo, "Modern-Day White (Wo)Man's Burden."

48 Maynard, "Do Black Sex Workers' Lives Matter?," 282. See also Hill, "Rhetoric of Modern-Day Slavery."

49 Gilmore, *Golden Gulag*, 28.

50 See, for example, Laboratory to Combat Human Trafficking, "Anti-Trafficking and Racial Justice in the Wake of George Floyd," June 2020, https://www .combathumantrafficking.org/2020/06/racial-justice-george-floyd/. Free the Slaves, "FTS Solidarity Statement on Racial Violence and Justice in the United States," June 4, 2020, https://www.freetheslaves.net/fts-solidarity-statement-on-racial -violence-and-justice-in-the-united-states/.

51 Free the Slaves, "Stop Racism and Slavery," accessed July 8, 2022, https://www .freetheslaves.net/take-action/stop-racism-slavery/. Free the Slaves, "Slavery in Mauritania," accessed July 8, 2022, https://www.freetheslaves.net/our-work/where -we-work/mauritania/.

52 Free the Slaves, "Stop Racism and Slavery," accessed August 4, 2021, https://www .freetheslaves.net/take-action/stop-racism-slavery/. See also, "Mauritania: Slavery's Last Stronghold," CNN, March 17, 2012, https://www.cnn.com/videos/world/2012 /03/17/mauritania-slavery-last-stronghold.cnn; "Modern Abolition," National Underground Railroad Freedom Center, accessed September 9, 2021, https:// freedomcenter.org/learn/modern-day-abolition/.

53 Kevin Bales writes about the difference between anti-Black racism in America and human trafficking: "[racism constitutes] the vestiges of slavery, as problems that were tough but not intractable. It was only after I moved to England in the early 1980s that I became aware of real slavery." Bales, *Disposable People*, 7.

54 See, for example, Heynen and van der Meulen, "Anti-trafficking Saviors"; Millar and O'Doherty, "Racialized, Gendered, and Sensationalized"; Chuang, "United States as Global Sheriff."

55 Cole, "White-Savior Industrial Complex"; Kempadoo, "Modern-Day White (Wo) Man's Burden"; Merry and Ramachandran, "Limits of Consent." See also Athreya, "White Man's Burden."

56 Lowe, *Intimacies of Four Continents*, 6–8, 141.

57 Wynter, "Unsettling the Coloniality of Being/Power/Truth/Freedom"; Wynter, "1492: A New World View," 7.

58 Lowe, *Intimacies of Four Continents*, 6. I am grateful for conversations with Petal Samuel who helped clarify my contribution on this point.

59 I am drawing on Lowe's discussion of the British figure of Chinese and South Asian workers as "a free race . . . who could be kept distinct from the Negroes," and as a "racial barrier" between white and Black populations, Lowe, *Intimacies of Four Continents*, 23–34.

60 Kempadoo, "Modern-Day White (Wo)Man's Burden," 13.

61 Mills, "Racial Liberalism"; Trouillot, *Silencing the Past*, 72–82.

62 I thank Dr. Thadious Davis for her guidance in working through this point in an early version of this theoretical framework. Locke, *Second Treatise of Government*; Hyde, *Bodies of Law*; Hong, "Property." See also Davis, "Object of Property."

63 Silva, *Toward a Global Idea of Race*, xiii.

64 Mills, *Blackness Visible*, 98. Also cited in Pierre, *Predicament of Blackness*, 223n3.

65 Beliso-De Jesús and Pierre, "Anthropology of White Supremacy," 67.

66 Pierre, "Racial Vernaculars of Development," 88, 95.

67 O'Connell Davidson, "Will the Real Sex Slave Please Stand Up?" 9; Kaneti, "Project Trafficking," 346.

68 O'Connell Davidson, *Modern Slavery*, 3–5; Kang, *Traffic in Asian Women*, 6–8; Bernstein, *Brokered Subjects*, 10; Doezema "Ouch! Western Feminists' 'Wounded Attachment.'"

69 On how migrant sex workers negotiate agency amid exploitation, see Mai, "'Too Much Suffering.'"

70 Sharma, "Anti-trafficking Rhetoric," 89.

71 Sharma, "Anti-trafficking Rhetoric," 89. See also Desyllas, "A Critique of the Global Trafficking Discourse."

72 Lobasz, "Beyond Border Security," 320.

73 See, for example, Lerum, "Human Wrongs vs. Human Rights"; Haynes, "Human Trafficking and Migration," 12; Desyllas, "A Critique of the Global Trafficking Discourse," 73–74; Brysk, "Rethinking Trafficking," 75.

74 Gallagher, "Two Cheers for the Trafficking Protocol," 19.

75 Musto and boyd, "Trafficking-Technology Nexus," 470–72; See also Musto, Thakor, and Gerasimov, "Between Hope and Hype."

76 Musto, *Control and Protect*, 3–4.

77 Shih, "Trafficking Deportation Pipeline," 57.

78 O'Connell Davidson, *Modern Slavery*, 25. See also Kempadoo, "Abolitionism, Criminal Justice, and Transnational Feminism," xv-xvi.

79 Kempadoo, "Women of Color and the Global Sex Trade"; Bernstein, *Brokered Subjects*; Suchland, *Economies of Violence*; Kang, *Traffic in Asian Women*.

80 Chuang, "Challenges and Perils," 146; Chuang, "Exploitation Creep," 611.

81 Hartman, *Lose Your Mother*, 6.

82 Trouillot, *Silencing the Past*.

83 Zelizer, "Reading the Past Against the Grain"; Radstone and Schwarz, *Memory*, 3–4.

84 Sharpe, *In the Wake*, 9; Scott, "Preface: Evil Beyond Repair," viii.

85 Many social causes have used the metaphor of slavery. The most prominent con-
    temporary examples are antiprison activism and antitrafficking. Historically, the
    metaphor has been used to make claims for those fighting for US independence
    from Britain in the 1770s, workers' rights for factory wage laborers in the US
    North in the 1820s, antiprostitution legislation in the 1910s, Black international
    anticolonial struggle in the 1920s, and US presidential antidrug campaigns in the
    1970–90s. In every case, the racial symbolism of the metaphor is paramount to its
    use, although in ways that uphold different political projects. See Dorsey, *Common
    Bondage*; Roediger, *The Wages of Whiteness*; Peck, "White Slavery and Whiteness";
    Getachew, *Worldmaking After Empire*.

86 McDowell and Rampersand, *Slavery and the Literary Imagination*, vii; Morrison,
    Playing in the Dark, 65.

87 Tillet, *Sites of Slavery*, 2.

88 In a striking invocation of Morrison's phrase "blessings of freedom," a promo-
    tional video for Free the Slaves claims they are "connecting those around the
    world who are struggling against modern-day slavery to those who live with the
    blessing of liberty." See *Building Bridges to Freedom*, December 29, 2014, https://
    vimeo.com/115235197.

89 Morrison, *Playing in the Dark*, 7, 13, 25, 64–65.

90 Tillet, *Sites of Slavery*; Commander, *Afro-Atlantic Flight*; Woolfork, *Embodying Ameri-
    can Slavery*; Nelson, *Social Life of DNA*.

91 Hanchard, "Black Memory versus State Memory," 61.

92 Hartman, *Lose Your Mother*.

93 Gordon, *Ghostly Matters*, 27–28.

94 McKittrick, *Demonic Grounds*, 123. For additional academic literature that inter-
    prets Sylvia Wynter's wide ranging body of work, see Bogues, *After Man, Towards
    the Human*; McKittrick, *Sylvia Wynter*; King, *Black Shoals*.

95 I find Wynter's discussion of this aspect of her work clearest in her conversation
    with David Scott. See Wynter and Scott, "Re-enchantment of Humanism."

96 Vargas and Jung, "Antiblackness of the Social and the Human," 7.

97 Wynter, "Africa, the West, and the Analogy of Culture," 42–44.

98 Wynter, "Is 'Development' a Purely Empirical Concept or Also Teleologi-
    cal?," 310.

99 Wilderson, *Red, White, and Black*, 11, 15–22.

100 Wynter, "1492: A New World View," 11; McKittrick, *Demonic Grounds*, 125.

101 Walcott, *Long Emancipation*, 10.

102 On this point, see also Woods, "Surrogate Selves," 122.

103 Du Bois, *Black Reconstruction*; Shange, *Progressive Dystopia*, 6, 10; Dilts, "Crisis,
    Critique, and Abolition," 237; Davis, *Abolition Democracy*.

104   I am grateful to Salamishah Tillet for pointing out this important distinction to me when thinking with her phrase "sites of slavery."

105   Murphy, *Economization of Life*, 47.

106   Trouillot, *Silencing the Past*, 73.

107   Lowe, *Intimacies of Four Continents*, 153.

108   Cox, *No Common Ground*, 16; King, *Black Shoals*, 119.

109   Free the Slaves post on Facebook from August 23, 2016, also available on the organization's website: Malika Metha, "How Mobile Phones Provide Hope to Slaves in India," Free the Slaves, August 23, 2016, https://www.freetheslaves.net /how-mobile-phones-provide-hope-to-slaves-in-india/.

110   This imagery also builds on the longstanding trope used in *National Geographic* photography where white people bring technology to people living in rural villages and wearing traditional colorful dress. See Lutz and Collins, *Reading National Geographic*.

111   Another variation of this narrative thematizes Chinese companies that run industrial mines in DRC as the primary culprit of corruption and enslavement and call for greater regulation of Chinese industry, which nevertheless aligns with US political and corporate interests. See, for example, Siddharth Kara, "Is Your Phone Tainted by the Misery of the 35,000 Children in Congo's Mines?" *Guardian*, October 12, 2018, https://www.theguardian.com/global-development/2018/oct/12/phone -misery-children-congo-cobalt-mines-drc. The article is featured on the *Guardian*'s antitrafficking platform, "Modern-Day Slavery in Focus."

112   Thomas, *Exceptional Violence*, 6.

113   Kempadoo, "Modern-Day White (Wo)Man's Burden," 15.

114   Tillet, *Sites of Slavery*, 17.

115   Scott, "Preface: Evil Beyond Repair."

116   Thomas, *Political Life in the Wake of the Plantation*, 213.

117   Hartman, *Lose Your Mother*, 165–70; Thomas, *Exceptional Violence*, 238; Hartman and Wilderson, "Position of the Unthought," 197–99; Lewis, *Scammer's Yard*, 150, 174.

118   Lewis, *Scammer's Yard*, 147.

119   Carole McGranahan uses this phrase in relation to covert humanitarian operations of the US State Department and the CIA. See McGranahan, "Love and Empire," 334.

120   Recent examples of this phenomenon include Murphy, *New Slave Narrative*; Bales and Trodd, *Antislavery Usable Past*.

121   Campt, *Listening to Images*.

122   Benjamin, "Discriminatory Design, Liberating Imagination," 4.

123   Carmichael, "Power and Racism," 30.

124   Robin D. G. Kelley, "Trump Says Go Back, We Say Fight Back," *Boston Review*, November 15, 2016, http://bostonreview.net/forum/after-trump/robin-d-g-kelley -trump-says-go-back-we-say-fight-back.

125   Spillers, "Mama's Baby, Papa's Maybe"; Spillers, "Whatcha Gonna Do?"; Crawley, *Blackpentecostal Breath*.

1 "Trillions Demanded in Slavery Reparations," BBC News, August 20, 1999, http://
news.bbc.co.uk/2/hi/africa/424984.stm.

2 Ticky Monekosso, "West Africa's Child Slave Trade," BBC News, August 6, 1999,
http://news.bbc.co.uk/2/hi/world/africa/412628.stm.

3 Mike Williams, "Sudan Haunted by Slavery," BBC News, August 15, 1999, http://
news.bbc.co.uk/2/hi/africa/421086.stm.

4 CARICOM Reparations Commission, "10-point Reparation Plan," accessed May 8,
2020, http://caricomreparations.org/caricom/caricoms-10-point-reparation-plan/.

5 Rowena Mason, "Slavery Reparations Call Overshadows Cameron's Visit to
Jamaica," Guardian, September 30, 2015, https://www.theguardian.com/world/2015
/sep/30/slavery-reparations-call-overshadows-david-camerons-visit-to-jamaica.

6 On the relationships among slavery, capitalism, and modernity see Wynter, "Un-
settling the Coloniality of Being/Power/Truth/Freedom"; James, Black Jacobins;
Williams, Capitalism and Slavery; Du Bois, The World and Africa; Rodney, How Europe
Underdeveloped Africa.

7 Beckles, Britain's Black Debt; Kelley, "A Day of Reckoning"; Henry, Long Overdue.
Black reparations discussion has experienced a revival in recent years. In fall
2019, US Democratic candidates for president openly endorsed Black reparations
during the primary debates on national broadcast outlets. The eventual nominee
Joe Biden, however, did not. In June 2019, a subcommittee of the House Judiciary
Committee held a hearing on bill H.R. 40, a commission to study proposals for
reparations. The willingness to revisit conversations about Black reparations
comes amid the development of the Movement for Black Lives Policy Platform,
which includes a demand for reparations, and the repopularization of the topic in
the public sphere by journalist Ta-Nehisi Coates in June 2014.

8 Doezema, "Loose Women or Lost Women?"

9 Biondi, "Rise of the Reparations Movement," 255.

10 In From Here to Equality, Darity and Mullen use the "fork in the path" metaphor to
help frame US history in relation to demands for reparations, writing, "At several
historic moments the trajectory of racial inequality could have been altered
dramatically, but at each juncture, the road chosen did not lead to a just and fair
America . . . at none of these forks was the path to full justice taken." Darity and
Mullen, From Here to Equality, 1.

11 Merry, Seductions of Quantification; Weitzer, "New Directions in Research"; Weitzer,
"Sex Trafficking and the Sex Industry"; Chuang, "United States as Global Sheriff";
Jason Szep and Matt Spetalnick, "State Department Watered Down Human
Trafficking Report," Reuters, August 3, 2015, http://mobile.reuters.com/article
/idUSKCN0Q821Y20150803?irpc=932; Carol Morello, "U.S. Drops Cuba and Malay-
sia from Human Trafficking Blacklist," Washington Post, July 27, 2015, https://www
.washingtonpost.com/world/national-security/us-drops-cuba-and-malaysia-from
-human-trafficking-blacklist/2015/07/27/e2a9bb1e-2a9d-4c88-b7c6–583eea3aa9fe
_story.html; Alliance to End Slavery and Trafficking, "U.S. State Department Fails

to Hold Countries Accountable for Human Trafficking," press release, July 27, 2015, https://endslaveryandtrafficking.org/u-s-state-department-fails-to-hold-countries -accountable-for-human-trafficking/.

12 Gallagher, "Improving the Effectiveness," 392.

13 Based on the 2001–21 TIP Reports, the official average is less than one sub-Saharan African country per year (0.71) is ranked in Tier 1. In ten of the twenty-one years surveyed, no sub-Saharan countries were ranked in Tier 1, and only in three of the twenty-one years was more than one sub-Saharan country ranked in Tier 1.

14 Trafficking in Persons Report, US Department of State, 2001, 29.

15 Trafficking in Persons Report, US Department of State, 2001, 73.

16 Trafficking in Persons Report, US Department of State, 2001, 84.

17 Trafficking in Persons Report, US Department of State, 2001, 98.

18 Grewal, *Transnational America*. The Rome Statute defines "enslavement" as a crime against humanity that can be tried in the International Criminal Court. It was ratified in 1998 and went into effect in 2002. The Lord's Resistance Army was one of the first cases in the ICC, see https://www.icc-cpi.int/uganda. For an excellent ethnographic analysis of the politics of the ICC and Africa, see Clarke, *Fictions of Justice*.

19 Trafficking in Persons Report, US Department of State, 2001, 46.

20 See also Okyere, Agyeman, and Saboro, "Why Was He Videoing Us?"

21 Trafficking in Persons Report, US Department of State, 2001, 2.

22 Quirk, *Anti-Slavery Project*, 109.

23 Joel Quirk, "Uncomfortable Silences: Slavery, Colonialism, and Imperialism," *openDemocracy*, October 22, 2015, https://www.opendemocracy.net/en/beyond -trafficking-and-slavery/uncomfortable-silences-anti-slavery-colonialism-and -imperialism/. See also Grant, *Civilised Savagery*, 42–45.

24 For the role of Christian missionaries in bringing to light the atrocities committed within the Congo Free State, see Grant, *Civilised Savagery*, chapter 2. Grant also discusses how missionary humanitarian outrage coexisted with missionary support for colonial expansion.

25 Getachew, *Worldmaking after Empire*, 64; Quirk, *Anti-Slavery Project*, 92–93.

26 Quirk, *Anti-Slavery Project*, 92.

27 Getachew, *Worldmaking after Empire*, 52–67.

28 Getachew, *Worldmaking after Empire*, 53.

29 Getachew, *Worldmaking after Empire*, 55.

30 Garvey, "The Principles of the Universal Negro Improvement Association," November 25, 1922, www.blackpast.org/african-american-history/1922-marcus-garvey -principles-universal-negro-improvement-association/.

31 Garvey, "The Principles of the Universal." For a thorough and nuanced analysis of the complexities of Garveyism and pan-Africanism in Liberia and its relationship to the United States and League of Nations' accusations of slavery in Liberia, see Sundiata, *Brothers and Strangers*.

32 In Anti-Slavery International's 2005 report titled "1807–2007: Over 200 Years of Campaigning against Slavery," the organization mentions its campaigns against forced

labor in the colonies in the late nineteenth and early twentieth centuries, and how antislavery "provided a perfect justification for colonial conquest and the exploitation of the local population," 25, but fails to note how those campaigns were also underpinned by an antiblack ideology. Mike Kaye, "1807–2007: Over 200 Years of Campaigning against Slavery," Anti-Slavery International, August 2005, https://www.antislavery .org/wp-content/uploads/2017/01/18072007.pdf.

33 Getachew, *Worldmaking after Empire*, 59.

34 Getachew, *Worldmaking after Empire*, 56.

35 Lowe, *Intimacies of Four Continents*; Wynter, "Unsettling the Coloniality of Being/ Power/Truth/Freedom."

36 Trafficking in Persons Report, US Department of State, 2002, 56.

37 Trafficking in Persons Report, US Department of State, 2009, 38.

38 Of course, post–Civil War, it was white Southern Americans who were actively trying to reenslave Black Americans. See Du Bois, *Black Reconstruction*; Hartman, *Scenes of Subjection*.

39 Government of the United States, official press release, "UN World Conference against Racism, Discrimination, Xenophobia and Related Intolerance," May 4, 2001, quoted in Beckles, *Britain's Black Debt*, 185. See also Franklin, "Commentary— Reparations as a Development Strategy," 364.

40 Quoted in "Rice Dismisses Reparations for Slavery," CNN, September 9, 2001, https://www.cnn.com/2001/ALLPOLITICS/09/09/rice.reparations/index.html.

41 For an excellent analysis of Condoleezza Rice's position as a Black woman in the visual landscape of antitrafficking and multiculturalism, see Hua, *Trafficking Women's Human Rights*, 95–119. In *Black Is a Country*, Nikhil Singh notes that Colin Powell "appears as the embodiment of America's self-transcendence of its racist past." Singh, *Black Is a Country*, 274n11.

42 Secretary Colin L. Powell, "Special Briefing on Release of Trafficking in Persons Report," US Department of State, Washington, DC, June 5, 2002, https://2001 -2009.state.gov/secretary/former/powell/remarks/2002/10748.htm.

43 Colin L. Powell, "Letter from Secretary Colin L. Powell," Trafficking in Persons Report, US Department of State, Washington, DC, June 2003, https://2009-2017 .state.gov/documents/organization/21555.pdf.

44 Condoleezza Rice, "Letter from Secretary Condoleezza Rice," TIP Report 2007, US Department of State, June 12, 2007, https://2009-2017.state.gov/j/tip/rls/tiprpt /2007/82798.htm.

45 Beckles, *Britain's Black Debt*, 176.

46 United Nations, *Declaration and Programme of Action*, 15 (my emphasis).

47 Beckles, *Britain's Black Debt*, 192.

48 Beckles, *Britain's Black Debt*, 172–93.

49 Beckles, *Britain's Black Debt*, 18. See also Franklin, "Commentary—Reparations as a Development Strategy," 364.

50 Beckles, *Britain's Black Debt*, 186.

51 United Nations, *Protocol to Prevent*, 2000, Article 3.

52 Gallagher, "Two Cheers for the Trafficking Protocol."

53 The Civil Liberties Act was signed into law by President Reagan on August 10, 1988. Yamamoto, "What's Next?," 417.

54 Darity and Mullen, *From Here to Equality*, 15. See also N'COBRA, "Legislation Strategies Commission," last accessed September 30, 2021, http://ncobra.org/commissions /Legislation.html.

55 Tillet, *Sites of Slavery*, 141–43.

56 *Cato* was dismissed on the grounds that the court did not have jurisdiction because the waiver for sovereign immunity only applies to injustices that happened after 1945. *Cato* was the first federal reparations litigation attempt since Callie House's association filed a federal class action lawsuit for ex-slaves in 1915, which was also denied by citing sovereign immunity. See Berry, *My Face Is Black Is True*, 294n27. Sovereign immunity refers to the government's right to protect itself from being sued, unless it consents to being sued. A process for instituting a waiver for sovereign immunity was implemented in 1946, and made retroactive to 1945 in order to allow victims of an American military airplane crash into the Empire State Building to sue the US government. The US government also paid reparations to victims of the September 11 terrorist attacks in order to prevent victims from suing the airlines.

57 Hillary Clinton, "Remarks for the UN Fourth World Conference on Women," September 5, 1995, https://www.un.org/esa/gopher-data/conf/fwcw/conf/gov /950905175653.txt.

58 Henry, *Long Overdue*, 78.

59 Darity and Mullen, *From Here to Equality*, 17.

60 "Aetna Acknowledges Issuing Slave Policies During 1850s, Offers Apology, Denies Reparations," *DemocracyNow!*, March 14, 2000, https://www.democracynow.org /2000/3/14/aetna_acknowledges_issuing_slave_policies_during.

61 Many colleges refused to publish the ad in the newspapers, others apologized after doing so, and some published on the grounds of "free speech." The Duke University student newspaper, *The Chronicle*, published the ad on March 19, 2001, during my freshman year of college there, and defended its publication as "the free exchange of ideas." See Gary Pessin, "Why the Chronicle Ran the Reparations Ad," *Chronicle*, March 21, 2001, https://issuu.com/dukechronicleprintarchives/docs/the _chronicle_2001-03-21. Weeks of editorial exchanges, panel debates, petitions and protests followed, as did many thoughtful interpersonal interracial conversations on whether or not "reverse racism" was a legitimate way to understand the world. My involvement in those conversations and political actions was a pivotal learning experience in my early career in multi-issue, multiracial organizing. William Darity (a Duke professor) and Kirsten Mullen also make the point that "Horowitz's platform possibly had the unintended consequence of setting off a series of heated public and private rebuttals, effectively rekindling the reparations conversation." Darity and Mullen, *From Here to Equality*, 23.

62 Beckles, *Britain's Black Debt*, 176–78; Franklin, "Commentary—Reparations as a Development Strategy," 363; International Network of Scholars and Activists for Afrikan Reparations, "Global Report," 8–9.

63 Beckles, *Britain's Black Debt*, 182–83.

64 Muntu Matsimela, interviewed by Yusuf Nuruddin. See Anderson, Matsimela, and Nuruddin, "Reparations Movement," 429.

65 Peter Viles, "Suit Seeks Billions in Slave Reparations," CNN, March 27, 2002, http://edition.cnn.com/2002/LAW/03/26/slavery.reparations/

66 Adjoa Aiyetoro, "N'COBRA's Litigation Work," *Black Reparations Times*, March 7, 2003, http://ncobra.org/resources/pdf/ViewBlackReparationsTimes.pdf; Darity and Mullen, *From Here to Equality*, 18–19.

67 Kibibi Tyehimba, "Reparations Lobbyists on Capitol Hill," *Black Reparations Times*, March 7, 2003, http://ncobra.org/resources/pdf/ViewBlackReparationsTimes.pdf, 1, 5, 12.

68 Biondi, "Rise of the Reparations Movement," 267.

69 The Afrikans and Afrikan Descendants WCAR that followed on October 2, 2002, in Barbados recommended instituting August 17 as the International Day for Reparations, in honor of Garvey's birthday.

70 Afrikans and Afrikan Descendants World Conference Against Racism, "The Bridgetown Protocol," Official Report of the Afrikan and Afrikan Descendants World Conference Against Racism, October 2–6, 2002, Bridgetown, Barbados, edited by Amani Olubanjo Buntu, 2003, 48.

71 Kelley, "Day of Reckoning," 206. Of course, demands for reparations have taken many shapes, approaches, and tactics, including initiatives that align with the imperatives and logics of capitalism and neoliberalism.

72 Biondi, "Rise of the Reparations Movement," 260.

73 Kelley, "Day of Reckoning," 219.

74 Biondi, "Rise of the Reparations Movement," 255; Balfour, "Unreconstructed Democracy?"

75 Melamed, "Racial Capitalism," 77. Ruth Wilson Gilmore uses a similar phrase in "Geographies of Racial Capitalism." See also Singh, "Racial Formation in an Age of Permanent War."

76 United Nations, *Declaration and Programme of Action*, 2002, 16.

77 United Nations, *Declaration and Programme of Action*, 2002, 16.

78 Kelley, "On Reparations and Decolonization."

79 Kelley, "Day of Reckoning," 218.

80 Bumiller, *In an Abusive State*; Hua, *Trafficking Women's Human Rights*; Sharma, "Anti-trafficking Rhetoric"; Suchland, *Economies of Violence*; Bernstein, *Brokered Subjects*; Kempadoo, "Sex Workers' Rights."

81 Davis, "Case for U.S. Reparations to African Americans," 377; Darity and Frank, "Political Economy of Ending Racism," 250–51.

82 US Congress, *Trafficking Victims Protection Reauthorization Act of 2003*. Pub. L. 108-193, 117 Stat. 2878, https://www.congress.gov/bill/108th-congress/house-bill/2620/text. The 2003 reauthorization limited the remedy to §1589, 1590, and 1591, which were all added to the chapter in 2000. The 2008 reauthorization broadened the remedy to any victim of a violation in chapter 77, but added the ten-year statute of limitation.

83 United Nations General Assembly, "Report of the Working Group."

84 United Nations General Assembly, "Report of the Working Group," 19–22.

85 Ishaan Tharoor, "U.S. Owes Black People Reparations for a History of 'Racial Terrorism' Says U.N. Panel," *Washington Post*, September 27, 2016, https://www .washingtonpost.com/news/worldviews/wp/2016/09/27/u-s-owes-black-people -reparations-for-a-history-of-racial-terrorism-says-u-n-panel/.

86 O'Connell Davidson, *Modern Slavery*, 83; Tryon Woods, "The Anti-blackness of 'Modern Day Slavery' Abolitionism," *openDemocracy*, October 10, 2014, https:// www.opendemocracy.net/en/beyond-trafficking-and-slavery/antiblackness-of -modernday-slavery-abolitionism/; Joel Quirk, "Reparations Are Too Confront- ing: Let's Talk about 'Modern Day Slavery' Instead," *openDemocracy*, May 7, 2015, https://www.opendemocracy.net/en/beyond-trafficking-and-slavery/reparations -are-too-confronting-lets-talk-about-modernday-slavery-instea/.

87 In the Preface to *Redress for Historical Injustices in the United States*, the editors Michael T. Martin and Marilyn Yaquinto relate an anecdote from the 2002 conference, The Moral Legacy of Slavery: Repairing Injustice, where an audience member challenged the claim for reparations for Black Americans because, as a woman of Jewish ancestry, she could attest to a long history of many different groups of people experiencing oppression. Martha Biondi's chapter in the collec- tion points out that in addition to Holocaust survivors receiving reparations from the German government and corporations, "Germany has also paid reparations to the state of Israel," which constitutes a redress paid to the Jewish collective, not individual victims. Biondi, "Rise of the Reparations Movement," 259. Darity and Frank make a similar point, see Darity and Frank, "Political Economy of Ending Racism," 249.

88 Liam Hogan, "'Irish Slaves': The Convenient Myth," *openDemocracy*, January 14, 2015, https://www.opendemocracy.net/en/beyond-trafficking-and-slavery/irish -slaves-convenient-myth/.

89 Hogan, "Irish Slaves."

90 Liam Hogan, "Two Years of the 'Irish Slaves' Myth: Racism, Reductionism and the Tradition of Diminishing the Transatlantic Slave Trade," *openDemocracy*, Novem- ber 7, 2016, https://www.opendemocracy.net/en/beyond-trafficking-and-slavery /two-years-of-irish-slaves-myth-racism-reductionism-and-tradition-of-diminis/.

91 Biondi, "Rise of the Reparations Movement," 261.

92 Du Bois, *Black Reconstruction*; Harris, "Whiteness as Property."

93 Irwin, "'White Slavery' as Metaphor."

94 Irwin, "'White Slavery' as Metaphor"; Doezema, *Sex Slaves and Discourse Masters*; Kempadoo, "Modern-Day White (Wo)Man's Burden"; Vance, "Innocence and Experience"; Pliley, *Policing Sexuality*; Soderlund, *Sex Trafficking, Scandal*; Joel Quirk and Genevieve LeBaron, "The Use and Abuse of History: Slavery and Its Lega- cies," *openDemocracy*, April 21, 2015, https://www.opendemocracy.net/en/beyond -trafficking-and-slavery/use-and-abuse-of-history-slavery-and-its-contemporary-leg /; Hua, *Trafficking Women's Human Rights*.

95 Doezema, *Sex Slaves and Discourse Masters*, 84; Pliley, *Policing Sexuality*, 24–25.

96 Pliley, *Policing Sexuality*, 3–5; Jessica Pliley, "Sexual Surveillance and Moral Quar-antines: A History of Anti-trafficking," *openDemocracy*, April 27, 2015, https://www.opendemocracy.net/en/beyond-trafficking-and-slavery/sexual-surveillance-and-moral-quarantines-history-of-antitrafficking/.

97 Pliley, *Policing Sexuality*, 2.

98 Blair, *I've Got to Make My Livin'*, 190–191. Blair notes, however, that Black leaders also navigated the white slavery discourse to try to protect Black girls. Cheryl Hicks notes how Black women social reformers were specifically concerned that white slavery discourse made the victimization of Black girls invisible. Hicks, *Talk with You Like a Woman*, 92–93. Muhammad, *Condemnation of Blackness*, 128–34, notes that social reformers concerned about prostitution and immigrant uplift often failed to extend these discourses to Black women who were seen as unredeemable or victims of their own deficiencies.

99 I am grateful to Dr. Shana L. Redmond for first bringing this convergence to my attention at the University of Southern California in 2016 and for encouraging me to follow its path.

100 Feimster, *Southern Horrors*, 212–33.

101 Doezema, *Sex Slaves and Discourse Masters*, 87–90; Blair, *I've Got to Make My Livin'*, 192.

102 Roberts, "Galveston's Jack Johnson."

103 Wells-Barnett, *A Red Record*.

104 Wilson, *Chicago and Its Cess-pools of Infamy*, 47. Jo Doezema's research, drawing on Frederick Grittner, *White Slavery: Myth, Ideology, and American Law* (Taylor and Francis, 1990), directed me to Wilson's tract. Both Doezema and Grittner also make note of Wilson's comparisons to Black slavery.

105 Pliley, *Policing Sexuality*, 15; Blair, *I've Got to Make My Livin'*, 190–91.

106 In *Wayward Lives, Beautiful Experiments*, Saidiya Hartman captures Ida B. Wells's efforts in this regard with profound lyricism: "As the women drank tea and ate shortbread, they planned ways to prevent such things from ever happening, collectively dreamed of a country in which they might be citizens, weighed the pros and cons of African emigration, lamented the dead. Ida Wells described the virtues of Winchester and concluded self-defense was the sole protection afforded black women." Hartman, *Wayward Lives, Beautiful Experiments*, 41–42.

107 Wilson, *Chicago and Its Cess-pools of Infamy*, 59.

108 Wilson, *Chicago and Its Cess-pools of Infamy*, 54. Presidents Lyndon Johnson, Richard Nixon, and George H. W. Bush all used the idea that drugs dealers "enslaved" their customers into lives of addiction, once again coding Black people as the enslavers of other Black people.

109 On the complex relationship between South State Street as a vice district and hub of respectable Black business in the 1910s, see Garb, *Freedom's Ballot*, 151–55.

110 Feimster, *Southern Horrors*, 215. See also Bay, *To Tell the Truth Freely*; Mariame Kaba, "Ida B. Wells and the Negro Fellowship League," April 18, 2012, https://www.usprisonculture.com/blog/2012/04/18/why-dont-we-know-more-about-the-negro-fellowship-league/.

111 Feimster, *Southern Horrors*, 226.

112 Quoted in Ida B. Wells-Barnett, *On Lynchings*, 30.

113 Quoted in Ida B. Wells-Barnett, *On Lynchings*, 29.

114 Attributed to Victor Hugo, quoted in Pliley, *Policing Sexuality*, 14.

115 Wells-Barnett, *A Red Record*; Feimster, *Southern Horrors*, 212–13.

116 Free the Slaves, "Our Model for Freedom: Slavery Today," accessed May 21, 2020, https://www.freetheslaves.net/our-model-for-freedom/slavery-today/.

117 Bales, *Disposable People*, 7.

118 Bales, *Disposable People*, 7, 10, 11.

119 Kate Hodal, "One in 200 People Is a Slave. Why?" *Guardian*, February 25, 2019, https://www.theguardian.com/news/2019/feb/25/modern-slavery-trafficking -persons-one-in-200; Bales, *Disposable People*, 10–11, 14.

120 Bales, "Exploring the Links between Slavery and Conflict."

121 Hill, "How to Stage a Raid," 42; Suchland, *Economies of Violence*.

122 Wilderson, *Red, White, and Black*, 101.

123 I follow Deborah Thomas's point that forgiveness is not reparative and certainly does not guarantee repair. See Thomas, *Exceptional Violence*, 238. See also Lewis, *Scammer's Yard*, 161.

124 Darity and Mullen, *From Here to Equality*, 264–69.

125 Boyce Davies and M'Bow, "Towards African Diaspora Citizenship," 36–41.

126 Scott, "Preface: Evil Beyond Repair," x (emphasis in original).

127 Lewis, *Scammer's Yard*, 173.

128 Hartman, *Lose Your Mother*, 165–70. Taking up the limitations of reparations, Jared Sexton reframes the conversation: "If the status quo is predicated on the historical terror of slavery, then to move toward reparations in this light is to threaten . . . total systemic collapse. What else could it mean to repair the legacy of five centuries of slavery?" Sexton, "Racial Profiling and the Societies of Control," 216n36.

129 David Scott and Jovan Lewis offer important critiques of the future-oriented position of state-led reparations initiatives. I nevertheless juxtapose antitrafficking and reparations discourses to distinguish their different political investments, both of which were being negotiated in the same policy arenas.

CHAPTER 2. BLAMING BLACK MOTHERS

1 Thomas, *Exceptional Violence*, 66; Briggs, *Reproducing Empire*.

2 James, *The Black Jacobins*; Robinson, *Black Marxism*; Buck-Morss, "Hegel and Haiti."

3 Holsey, *Routes of Remembrance*; Hartman, *Lose Your Mother*; Pierre, *Predicament of Blackness*; Commander, *Afro-Atlantic Flight*.

4 Campt, *Listening to Images*. I am grateful to conversations with Wendy Kozol that helped clarify my thinking on this point.

5 Ubelong, "'My Kids Hate Me . . . I Sold Them': Slavery and Child Labour in Ghana—in Pictures," *Guardian*, September 30, 2016, https://www.theguardian.com /global-development/gallery/2016/sep/30/ghana-slavery-child-labour-kids-hate-me -i-sold-them-in-pictures.

6 "About us," Ubelong website, accessed October 10, 2016, http://ubelong.org/about -us/. As of July 31, 2020, Ubelong was no longer operating because of the COVID-19 pandemic, and the website no longer exists.

7 As Susan Moeller points out in *Compassion Fatigue*, international news coverage in general utilizes simplistic and formulaic frames, rarely covers structural issues, and often uses sensationalizing "tidbits" to maintain readers' attention.

8 Betty Mensah and Sam Okyere, "How CNN Reported on 'Child Slaves' Who Were Not Really Enslaved," *Al Jazeera*, March 18, 2019, https://www.aljazeera.com /indepth/opinion/cnn-reported-child-slaves-enslaved-190315103733047.html.

9 Cheerful Hearts Foundation, "Stop Child Labour and Trafficking Project," accessed May 1, 2020, http://cheerfulheartsfoundation.org/stop-child-labour -trafficking-project/.

10 Cheerful Hearts Foundation, "Anti-child Trafficking Project Launched," January 28, 2016, http://cheerfulheartsfoundation.org/anti-child-trafficking-project -launched/.

11 Cheerful Hearts Foundation, "Anti-child Trafficking Project Launched."

12 Cyril, "Motherhood, Media, and Building a 21st Century Movement," 32.

13 See "The Boys Who Went to Yeji," accessed August 10, 2020, https://worldschild rensprize.org/jamesfactsandfigures. Annan is also featured as "today's freedom hero" in the National Underground Railroad Freedom Center's *Invisible: Slavery Today* exhibition.

14 Morgan, *Laboring Women*; Morgan, *"Partus sequitur ventrem"*; Roberts, *Killing the Black Body*, 23.

15 Bridges, "Intersection of Class and Race."

16 Roberts, *Killing the Black Body*, 25–26.

17 Hogarth, *Medicalizing Blackness*.

18 Roberts, *Killing the Black Body*, 31.

19 Roberts, *Killing the Black Body*, 33.

20 Roberts, *Killing the Black Body*, 43.

21 Leif Coorlim, "Child Slaves Risk Their Lives on Ghana's Lake Volta," CNN "Freedom Project," February 2019, https://www.cnn.com/interactive/2019/02/africa /ghana-child-slaves-intl/.

22 "Gang of Captives Met at Mbame's on Their Way to Tette," *Slavery Images: A Visual Record of the African Slave Trade and Slave Life in the Early African Diaspora*, accessed August 10, 2020, http://www.slaveryimages.org/s/slaveryimages/item/419.

23 Free the Slaves, "Trafficking's Footprint," 14. The limitations section of the study reports that "actual prevalence [of child trafficking] may be lower than calculated rates" because "in some instances, community members insisted that their household be 'deleted' from the social mapping since they had not been consulted before their household had been added." Such assertions of family autonomy resist being conscripted into the narratives of enslavement and the global humanitarian gaze.

24 Okyere, Agyeman, and Saboro, "'Why Was He Videoing Us?," 48.

25 In a different context, Wendy Hesford writes that the Indian mothers in *Born Into Brothels* are represented as harsh, unloving, and unmotherly, in contrast to

the white woman protagonist whose humanitarianism saves the children, in part, through building a "reasonable and nurturing relationship with the children." See Hesford, *Spectacular Rhetorics*, 165–66.

26 Pierre, *Predicament of Blackness*, 53.

27 Pierre, *Predicament of Blackness*, 54–55.

28 See Johnson, Howell, and Evered, "Where Nothing Was Before," for a description of the competing narratives of modernization, farming, and displacement in the creation of the Volta River Project.

29 Nkrumah, "READ: Kwame Nkrumah's Iconic 1963 Speech on African Unity," Speech at the Inaugural ceremony of the Organization of African Unity, Addis Ababa, Ethiopia, 1963, May 24, 2019, https://face2faceafrica.com/article/read -kwame-nkrumahs-iconic-1963-speech-on-african-unity.

30 Spillers, "Mama's Baby, Papa's Maybe," 203.

31 Shaler quoted in Muhammad, *Condemnation of Blackness*, 20.

32 Shaler quoted in Muhammad, *Condemnation of Blackness*, 21.

33 Shaler quoted in Muhammad, *Condemnation of Blackness*, 17.

34 Byrd, *Black Republic*, 5, 83.

35 Muhammad, *Condemnation of Blackness*, 24.

36 On the language of increase, see Morgan, *Laboring Women*.

37 Muhammad, *Condemnation of Blackness*, 51.

38 Wynter, "Unsettling the Coloniality of Being/Power/Truth/Freedom," 264.

39 Muhammad, *Condemnation of Blackness*, 51.

40 Hartman, *Wayward Lives, Beautiful Experiments*, 71.

41 Muhammad, *Condemnation of Blackness*, 122–23.

42 Thomas, *Exceptional Violence*, 61–66.

43 Moynihan, *Negro Family*; Collins, *Black Feminist Thought*, 75; Roberts, *Killing the Black Body*, 16; Hong, "Neoliberalism"; Hinton, *From the War on Poverty to the War on Crime*, 20; Mullings, *On Our Own Terms*, 78–79.

44 Glazer quoted in Moynihan, *Negro Family*, chapter 3.

45 Tera Hunter, *Bound in Wedlock*, offers a compelling reading of the ways that Black couples navigated and reworked what marriage meant to them during slavery and Reconstruction.

46 Collins, *Black Feminist Thought*, 76–77; Roberts, *Killing the Black Body*, 17–19, 217–25; Lubiano, "Black Ladies, Welfare Queens, and State Minstrels."

47 Collins, *Black Feminist Thought*; Spillers, "Mama's Baby, Papa's Maybe."

48 Hong, "Neoliberalism"

49 Lubiano, "Black Ladies, Welfare Queens, and State Minstrels," 335 (emphasis in original).

50 Roberts, *Killing the Black Body*, 21.

51 On gifting freedom, I am thinking with Mimi Nguyen's *The Gift of Freedom*, although in a different context of liberal intervention within US imperial formations.

52 Byrd, *Black Republic*, 195; Renda, *Taking Haiti*, 26–28.

53 Edwidge Danticat, "The Long Legacy of Occupation in Haiti," *New Yorker*, July 28, 2015, https://www.newyorker.com/news/news-desk/haiti-us-occupation-hundred -year-anniversary.

54　Hudson, *Bankers and Empire*; Dupuy, *Haiti in the World Economy*, 132–36; Dupuy, *From Revolutionary Slaves to Powerless Citizens*, 94.

55　Alex Dupuy, "One Year after Earthquake, Foreign Help Is Actually Hurting Haiti," *Washington Post*, January 7, 2011, https://www.washingtonpost.com/wpdyn/content /article/2011/01/07/AR2011010703043.html.

56　Hoffman, "Saving Children, Saving Haiti?"; Hoffman, "Slaves and Angels"; Sommerfelt, *Child Domestic Labour in Haiti*; Sommerfelt and Pedersen, "Child Labor in Haiti," 427–30.

57　Robinson, *Black Marxism*; Ortiz, *An African American and Latinx History of the United States*, 20–22, 27–32; Byrd, *Black Republic*.

58　James, "Preface to the First Edition," *Black Jacobins*, ix.

59　Trouillot, *Silencing the Past*, 70–107; Schwarz, "Haiti and Historical Time," 93.

60　Ortiz, *African American and Latinx History*, 21. This important historical event was reactivated in the public imagination through the performance artist Dread Scott's participatory "Slave Rebellion Reenactment," on November 8–9, 2019, which retraced the twenty-six-mile route of the uprising along the River Parishes in Louisiana and into New Orleans. One of the promotional materials for the event encouraged supporters to "imagine successful slave revolts."

61　Lowe, *Intimacies of Four Continents*, 23.

62　Office of the Historian, "The United States and the Haitian Revolution, 1791–1804," Office of the Historian, Foreign Service Institute, US Department of State, accessed August 21, 2020, https://history.state.gov/milestones/1784-1800 /haitian-rev.

63　Marlene Daut, "When France Extorted Haiti—the Greatest Heist in History," *Conversation*, July 9, 2021, https://theconversation.com/when-france-extorted-haiti -the-greatest-heist-in-history-137949.

64　Gaffield, "Five Myths about the Haitian Revolution," *Washington Post*, August 4, 2021, https://www.washingtonpost.com/outlook/five-myths/five-myths-about-the -haitian-revolution/2021/08/04/1cf7be4e-f3c1-11eb-a49b-d96f2dac0942_story.html. See also Gaffield, *Haitian Connections in the Atlantic World*.

65　Westenley Alcenat, "The Case for Haitian Reparations," *Jacobin*, January 14, 2017, https://www.jacobinmag.com/2017/01/haiti-reparations-france-slavery -colonialism-debt/; Beckett, *There Is No More Haiti*, 112–13. In 2003, President Aristide issued a demand that France repay Haiti this sum. A year later, there was a coup in Haiti, and the new leadership renounced the previous demand for reparations.

66　Beckett, "Ontology of Freedom."

67　Daut, *Tropics of Haiti*, 6.

68　Byrd, *Black Republic*, 6–7.

69　James, *Black Jacobins*, ix.

70　Forsdick and Høgsbjerg, *Black Jacobins Reader*, 11–12.

71　Forsdick and Høgsbjerg, *Black Jacobins Reader*, 23–25. C. L. R. James was present, along with Martin Luther King, at the 1957 Independence Day celebrations in Ghana with Kwame Nkrumah. James later wrote *Nkrumah and the Ghana Revolution*.

The links between Ghanaian independence and Haitian independence in Black struggle and intellectual history make antitrafficking's specific use of Ghana and Haiti even more concerning.

72   Scott, "Theory of Haiti," 128.

73   Scott, "Theory of Haiti," 126.

74   Madeline Kristoff and Liz Panarelli, "Haiti: A Republic of NGOs?" United States Institute of Peace Brief 23, April 26, 2010, https://www.usip.org/sites/default/files /PB%2023%20Haiti%20a%20Republic%20of%20NGOs.pdf; Kathie Klarreich and Linda Polman, "The NGO Republic of Haiti," *Nation*, October 31, 2012, https://www .thenation.com/article/archive/ngo-republic-haiti/.

75   Cadet, *Restavec*, 4.

76   See Daut, *Tropics of Haiti*.

77   Cited in Ortiz, *African American and Latinx History*, 30.

78   James, *Black Jacobins*, 14.

79   Cadet, *Restavec*.

80   Cadet, *Restavec*, 179–82.

81   Cadet, *Restavec*, 184.

82   Free the Slaves, *Haiti's Model Communities Fight Restavek Child Slavery*, 2014, accessed August 14, 2020, video, https://vimeo.com/84902894.

83   Free the Slaves, *Haiti's Model Communities Fight*.

84   Campt, *Listening to Images*, 3.

85   Campt, *Listening to Images*, 4.

86   Campt, *Listening to Images*, 57–58.

87   Campt, *Listening to Images*, 51.

88   Richardson et al., "Haiti's Model Communities," 6 (emphasis in original).

89   Richardson et al., "Haiti's Model Communities," 7.

90   Richardson et al., "Haiti's Model Communities," 13.

91   In her report on child workers in Haiti, Tone Sommerfelt writes, "By the same token, 'culture' does not motivate people to take in children or place them in domesticity. People's various needs, on the other hand, motivate them to act. In Haiti, as will be shown, these needs are related to poverty (parents' low incomes), parents' hopes of giving their children a better future, to the fact that formal education is a highly treasured value, and to priorities among 'employing' households in terms of perceived labour needs." See Sommerfelt, *Child Domestic Labour in Haiti*, 16.

92   According to the report, due to cost savings in other areas, some of the J/TIP funds were transferred to the local agency, where it was used it to hire a livelihoods expert consultant, who then trained community members on how to save money. Such maneuvers make visible the convoluted aid structures that prevent people from receiving money directly, in no small part due to racialized suspicion and paternalism. See Ferguson, *Give a Man a Fish*.

93   Richardson et al., "Haiti's Model Communities," 8.

94   Murphy, *Economizrtion of Life*, 47.

95   Quoted in Murphy, *Economization of Life*, 52.

96   Murphy, *Economization of Life*, 48.

97 Jonathon Katz and Leslie Curtis, "'Haiti Is Not a Theater of Suffering': An Interview with Jonathan Katz," *Vital*, November 2, 2016, https://the-vital.com/2016/11/02/haiti-katz/.

98 King, "Owning Laura Silsby's Shame"; Jonathon Katz, "Haiti Frees Missionary Laura Silsby," *Associated Press*, May 18, 2010, https://www.sfgate.com/news/article/Haiti-frees-missionary-Laura-Silsby-3187846.php.

99 King, "Owning Laura Silsby's Shame," 2.

100 Ginger Thompson, "Case Stokes Haiti's Fear for Children, and Itself," *New York Times*, February 1, 2010, https://www.nytimes.com/2010/02/02/world/americas/02orphans.html; Frank James, "Laura Silsby, Haiti 'Orphans' Would-Be Rescuer, Serial Rule Breaker," NPR, February 5, 2010, https://www.npr.org/sections/thetwo-way/2010/02/laura_silsby_haiti_orphans_wou.html.

101 Erica Jones, "DC's Missing Teens: What's True and What's Not," NBC News, March 24, 2017, https://www.nbcwashington.com/news/local/dcs-missing-teens-whats-true-and-whats-not/41909/.

102 Although their website no longer functions, in March 2017 Stop Modern Slavery's website (www.stopmodernslavery.org) was emblazoned with a quote by Kevin Bales, who was credited as "Lead Expert on Modern Slavery." It also featured a picture of the coalition wearing red T-shirts, with two Black people in the front carrying the organization's banner. Although he is not named, one was James Kofi Annan, the founder of the Ghanaian antitrafficking NGO Challenging Heights.

103 US Department of Justice, "D.C. Human Trafficking Task Force," accessed March 30, 2017, https://www.justice.gov/usao-dc/human-trafficking

104 Quoted in Holland, "Black Lawmakers Call on FBI to Help on Missing Black Girls," *Associated Press News*, March 23, 2017, https://apnews.com/article/ce3e97256b554c9f860d53b520622ab7.

105 Sheryl Gay Stolberg, "Missing Girls in Washington DC Widen City's Racial Divide," *New York Times*, March 31, 2017, https://www.nytimes.com/2017/03/31/us/washington-dc-missing-girls-children-trafficking.html.

106 Derrica Wilson, the director of the Black and Missing Foundation, often links the case of missing girls to human trafficking in her press commentary. The Black and Missing Foundation was started in 2008 and has not always invoked the trafficking discourse, despite always being focused on issue of racial disparities within missing persons cases. In a 2014 news article about the racial disparities in the official response between a white woman's disappearance (Hannah Graham) and a Black transwoman's disappearance (Sage Smith) in Charlottesville, for instance, the Black and Missing Foundation's cofounder Natalie Wilson discusses Sage Smith's case, including the problems with classifying Black missing persons as runaways, but does not invoke the language of trafficking. See Stuart, "Two Years after Sage Smith's disappearance, Family Wants Answers over Discrepancies in Missing Person Cases," *Cville Weekly*, November 19, 2014, http://www.c-ville.com/two-years-sage-smiths-disappearance-family-wants-answers-discrepancies-missing-person-cases/.

107 The Melanin Project, "The Black Lives Matter Movement Moves into New Territory, Confronting Human Trafficking!," April 12, 2017, https://www .themelaninproject.org/tmpblog/2017/4/10/the-black-lives-matter-movement -moves-into-new-territory-human-trafficking.

INTERLUDE. #FREECYNTOIABROWN

1 "Prison abolitionist Mariame Kaba on Cyntoia Brown, the First Step Act and NYC Building 4 New Jails," *Democracy Now!*, January 11, 2019, https://www .democracynow.org/2019/1/11/prison_abolitionist_mariame_kaba_on_cyntoia.
2 Richie, *Arrested Justice*, 18.
3 Richie, *Arrested Justice*, 133; Burrowes, "Building the World We Want to See," 390.
4 Davis, *Abolition Democracy*, 109; Camp, *Incarcerating the Crisis*, 151.
5 Critical Resistance and Incite! Women of Color Against Violence, "Gender Violence and the Prison-Industrial Complex"; Ruth Wilson Gilmore, "Ruth Wilson Gilmore Makes the Case for Abolition," *Intercept*, June 10, 2020, podcast, https://theintercept .com/2020/06/10/ruth-wilson-gilmore-makes-the-case-for-abolition/.
6 Participatory defense is a community organizing strategy where family and community members that make up an incarcerated person's support network affect the outcome of bail, sentencing, and parole hearings by packing the court with supporters, testifying to the person's character, and writing letters to the judge in support of the person, among other strategies. Participatory defense is a highly effective strategy because it holds the courts accountable by showing that community members are watching. For more description on how we used this strategy in Charlottesville, see Beutin et al., "Radical Yes," 22–23. There can also be a tension in participatory defense where letters to the judge are tactically crafted to emphasize a person's moral character in ways legible to the dominant gaze. I mention this for how it relates to "model prisoner" rhetoric but also sharply departs from it because it fundamentally sees the incarcerated person as already, inherently deserving to be free. These are the nuances of organizing *tactics* that are obscured by coverage that focuses on the effectiveness of celebrities, social media, or antitrafficking language in getting people out of jail.
7 Beutin, "The Anti-trafficking Apparatus."
8 Christal Hayes, "Cyntoia Brown Wasn't a Victim, Stole Money after Killing Johnny Allen: Prosecutors," *Newsweek*, November 21, 2017, https://www.newsweek.com/cyntoia -brown-heres-why-teen-was-sentenced-life-after-claiming-she-was-sex-718766.
9 Janice Williams, "Who Is Cyntoia Brown? 'Sex Trafficking Victim' Gets Support from Celebs on Instagram," *Newsweek*, November 21, 2017, https://www.newsweek .com/cyntoia-brown-instagram-sex-trafficking-718573.
10 A. J. Willingham, "Why Cyntoia Brown, Who Is Spending Life in Prison for Murder, Is All Over Social Media," CNN, November 27, 2017, https://www.cnn.com /2017/11/23/us/cyntoia-brown-social-media-murder-case-trnd/index.html.
11 Daniel Victor, "Why Celebrities Have Rallied behind Cyntoia Brown, a Woman Spending Life in Prison," *New York Times*, November 22, 2017.

12 Associated Press, "Cyntoia Brown Case: Celebrities Support Teen Killer, Highlight Sex Trafficking Abuse," CBS News, November 24, 2017, https://www.cbsnews.com/news/cyntoia-brown-case-celebrities-support-teen-killer-highlight-sex-trafficking-abuse/.

13 *Essence Magazine* took a different approach with a headline that immediately adopted a slavery victim framing: "Who Is Cyntoia Brown? Social Media Rallies around Child Sex Slave Sent to Prison for Killing Abuser." Danielle Kwateng-Clark, "Who Is Cyntoia Brown? Social Media Rallies around Child Sex Slave Sent to Prison for Killing Abuser," *Essence Magazine*, November 21, 2017, https://www.essence.com/news/cyntoia-brown-child-sex-slave-documentary/.

14 Max Kutner, "Sex Slaves on the Farm," *Newsweek*, February 13, 2015. The article describes how Latino middlemen traffic Mexican women into sex work and then migrant farmworkers "purchase" them for sex. The article portrays Latino men as tricky, hyper sexual, animalistic, and heartless, and Latina women as their naive and helpless victims, who are eventually freed from their enslavers (the traffickers and the farmworkers) through a US investigation led by ICE and Homeland Security that lands the traffickers in jail and the women on temporary T visas for their state cooperation (a temporary status for trafficking victims who testify against their traffickers). The fate of the farmworkers, themselves precarious migrant workers on temporary visas or without documentation, is not discussed.

15 Willingham, "Why Cyntoia Brown."

16 Cyntoia was birthed by a white woman who used alcohol during her pregnancy and who was told that her "Black baby" was an illegitimate part of her white family, although her whiteness and her family's racism are rarely mentioned in news coverage. Cyntoia was adopted and raised by a Black family. Cyntoia has described that her adoptive father was physically abusive toward her, an aspect of the story that some, but not all, news reports included. In her book *Free Cyntoia*, Cyntoia describes her early childhood with her Black adoptive parents as caring and loving. She also describes learning that she was adopted and her biological mother was an alcoholic white woman, which made her feel like she "came from trash." In the book, Cyntoia narrates her biracial identity as a source of consternation, teasing, and unbelonging. Although Cyntoia's adoptive Black mother was the stable and loving figure in her life, the racial coding of the figure of the pathological family folds back on itself, combining elements of three racial tropes: (1) the tragic mulatta, (2) the dysfunctional Black home, and (3) the unnaturalness of being poor and white, and thus poor whites' mental illness and dysfunction.

17 For a reinterpretation of Nat Turner in relation to Black women's resistance and evasion tactics, see Holden, *Surviving Southampton*.

18 Maynard, "Do Black Sex Workers' Lives Matter?"; See also Baker, "Racialized Rescue Narratives." For a biographical example of these outcomes, see "Shamere McKenzie," *End Slavery Now* (blog), January 3, 2015, https://www.endslaverynow.org/blog/articles/shamere-mckenzie.

19 McLaurin, *Celia, a Slave*.

20 Mariame Kaba also notes this historical resonance with Cyntoia Brown's story in her editorial, "Black Women Punished for Self-Defense Must Be Freed from Their Cages," *Guardian*, January 3, 2019, https://www.theguardian.com/commentisfree /2019/jan/03/cyntoia-brown-marissa-alexander-black-women-self-defense-prison.

21 The "matrix of violence" is Beth Richie's phrase, see Richie, *Arresting Justice*, 133.

22 Morgan, *Laboring Women*.

23 McKay and Smith Foster, Introduction to *Incidents in the Life of a Slave Girl* by Harriet Jacobs. I am also invoking one of my favorite sentences in John L. Jackson Jr.'s writing, which I keep on a note beside my desk: "people's stubborn recognition of their own continued worth despite external threats of devaluation and marginalization—maybe even because of those threats." Jackson, "On Ethnographic Sincerity," S279.

24 Associated Press, "Attorneys Seek New Trial for Teenage Killer," *Oklahoman*, November 13, 2012, https://oklahoman.com/article/feed/462280/attorneys-seek-new -trial-for-teenage-killer.

25 See for instance, Anita Wadhwani, "Teen Killer's Story Inspires Push to Change Tennessee Law," *Tennessean*, June 30, 2016, https://www.tennessean.com/story/news /crime/2016/06/30/ruling-offers-hope-teens-sentenced-life-but-not-tennessee /86247118/.

26 Ahuser, "Cyntoia Brown, Trafficking Victim Serving Life Sentence for Murder, Will Get Clemency Hearing," *New York Times*, May 3, 2018.

27 Dakin Andone, "Parole Board Splits on Clemency for Trafficking Victim for Killing a Man Who Picked Her Up for Sex," CNN, May 24, 2018, https://www.cnn.com /2018/05/24/us/cyntoia-brown-clemency-request/index.html.

28 Associated Press, "Cyntoia Brown: Sex Trafficking Victim in Prison for Murder Granted Full Clemency," *Guardian*, January 7, 2019, https://www.theguardian.com /us-news/2019/jan/07/cyntoia-brown-sex-trafficking-victim-murder-tennessee.

29 Kate Hodal, "Cyntoia Brown: Trafficked, Enslaved, Jailed for Life at 16—and Fighting Back," *Guardian*, October 23, 2019, https://www.theguardian.com/global -development/2019/oct/23/cyntoia-brown-long-trafficked-enslaved-jailed-for-life-at -16-and-fighting-back.

30 Stacy Case, "Fox 17 Investigates: Child Sex Slave in Nashville Prison for Killing Man Who Used Her," ABC 7 WJLA, November 16, 2017, https://wjla.com/news /nation-world/fox-17-investigates-child-sex-slave-in-nashville-prison-for-killing -man-who-used-her.

31 Mallory Gafas and Tina Burnside, "Cyntoia Brown Is Granted Clemency after Serving 15 Years in Prison for Killing Man Who Bought Her for Sex," CNN, January 8, 2019, https://edition.cnn.com/2019/01/07/us/tennessee-cyntoia-brown -granted-clemency/index.html.

32 Hodal, "Cyntoia Brown."

33 On deserving freedom, my mind wanders to Ursula K. Le Guin: "No man earns punishment, no man earns reward. Free your mind of the idea of *deserving*, the idea of *earning*, and you will begin to be able to think." Le Guin, *The Dispossessed* (New York: EOS, 2001), 358 (emphasis in original).

34 Derri Smith, founder of End Slavery Tennessee, is often quoted invoking this line in media interviews about Cyntoia Brown's case. End Slavery Tennessee is a predominately white and white woman-led faith-based organization that conforms to the general contours of the antitrafficking industry. At the time of writing, the landing page of their website featured a silhouetted young white woman whose blond ponytail was backlit and whose face was covered with the phrase "Slavery exists here. You can stop it." On her bio page, Derri Smith described herself as a survivor of child abuse who is answering God's call to end human trafficking; available at https://www.endslaverytn.org/dsmithbio.

35 Brown-Long, *Free Cyntoia*.

36 Durisin, van der Meulen, and Bruckert, "Contextualizing Sex Work."

37 Peterson, Robinson, and Shih, "The New Virtual Crackdown on Sex Workers' Rights."

38 Loyd and Gilmore, "Race, Capitalist Crisis, Abolitionist Organizing," 42–43.

39 Mariame Kaba and Brit Schulte, "Not a Cardboard Cutout: Cyntoia Brown and the Framing of a Victim." *Appeal*, December 6, 2017, https://theappeal.org/not-a -cardboard-cut-out-cyntoia-brown-and-the-framing-of-a-victim-aa61f8of9cbb/; Natasha Lennard, "Cyntoia Brown's Freedom Is a Reminder That All Sex Workers Have a Right to Self-Defense," *Intercept*, January 9, 2019, https://theintercept .com/2019/01/09/cyntoia-brown-clemency-sex-work-self-defense/.

40 Kaba and Schulte, "Not a Cardboard Cutout."

CHAPTER 3. WHEN SLAVERY'S NOT BLACK

1 Commander, *Afro-Atlantic Flight*.

2 Commander, *Afro-Atlantic Flight*, 12.

3 United Nations General Assembly, "Resolution 62/122."

4 United Nations, "UN Marks Day of Remembrance with Calls to End Modern Slavery."

5 A year earlier, the theme of the 2014 International Day of Remembrance of Victims of Slavery and the Transatlantic Slave Trade was Haiti's victory over slavery in 1804. The press release for that event noted that "slavery still stalks our planet" and that "too many children are held in servitude and are victims of child labour," a reference to the antitrafficking figure of the Haitian child restavèk, a slavery "lingering" in Haiti's present. See United Nations, "UN Marks Day of Remembrance."

6 See for instance, Kara's 2017 screenplay *Trafficked*, directed by Will Wallace (KK Ranch Productions, 2017). On Kristof, see Mathers, "Mr. Kristof, I Presume?"; and Mahdavi, *From Trafficking to Terror*.

7 Rotman, *Byzantine Slavery and the Mediterranean World*; Gann and Willen, *Five Thousand Years of Slavery*.

8 In Laura Murphy's *The New Slave Narrative*, which is an example of normative antitrafficking scholarship that upholds the central tenets of the antitrafficking discourse, she uses this exact idea to dismiss critiques of antiblackness within antitrafficking. She writes, "I contend that these critiques disregard the fact that slav-

ery has taken many forms throughout human history and that it both pre-dates and postdates the . . . institution of chattel slavery that existed in the Americas." Murphy, *New Slave Narrative*, xi–xii.

9   Ferguson and Hong, drawing on Reddy, in Ferguson and Hong, "Sexual and Racial Contradictions of Neoliberalism," 1058.

10 Hong, "Speculative Surplus," 112; Hong, "Neoliberalism," 57.

11 Commander, *Afro-Atlantic Flight*, 12.

12 Gray, "Subject(ed) to Recognition," 778.

13 Melamed, *Represent and Destroy*, 42.

14 Ferguson and Hong, "Sexual and Racial Contradictions of Neoliberalism," 1061; Melamed, *Represent and Destroy*, 40.

15 Shih, "Freedom Markets"; Suchland, *Economies of Violence*, 163–86; Page, "How Many Slaves Work for You?"

16 Sharma, "Anti-trafficking Rhetoric"; Penelope Kyritsis and Jennifer Rosenbaum, "Interview: The Struggle for Migrant Workers' Rights," *openDemocracy*, August 23, 2017, https://www.opendemocracy.net/en/beyond-trafficking-and-slavery/interview-struggle-for-migrant-workers-rights/; Peterson, Robinson, and Shih, "New Virtual Crackdown on Sex Workers' Rights"; Shih, "Duplicitous Freedom," 1078.

17 Gann and Willen, *Five Thousand Years of Slavery*. The textbook won the following awards, according to its back cover: Notable Books for a Global Society (Winner); Nautilus Book Award for Middle Grade and Teen Nonfiction (Gold Winner); *ForeWord Reviews*' Book of the Year Awards—Young Adult Nonfiction (Silver Winner); Distinguished Books of the Association of Children's Librarians of Northern California (Selected).

18 "About the Authors," accessed on June 24, 2020, https://gannwillen.com/about/.

19 Gann and Willen, *Five Thousand Years of Slavery*, 2.

20 Gann and Willen, *Five Thousand Years of Slavery*, 3.

21 Gann and Willen, *Five Thousand Years of Slavery*, 46.

22 Gann and Willen, *Five Thousand Years of Slavery*, 50.

23 Gann and Willen, *Five Thousand Years of Slavery*, 53.

24 Gann and Willen, *Five Thousand Years of Slavery*, 58–59.

25 Gann and Willen, *Five Thousand Years of Slavery*, 92.

26 Gann and Willen, *Five Thousand Years of Slavery*, 92.

27 Gann and Willen, *Five Thousand Years of Slavery*, 128.

28 Gann and Willen, *Five Thousand Years of Slavery*, 150. The white American woman who rescued Mark Kwadwo is Pam Cope. She founded the organization Touch a Life and, according to her website, after reading about Mark's story in the *New York Times*, went to Ghana to rescue Mark from modern-day slavery. Child trafficking in Ghana has now been incorporated into Touch a Life's programming under the name "Find Your Mark." Such a name lays bare the white redemptionist impulse at the heart of the organization. Although the *New York Times* journalist largely refers to the exploitation as trafficking and indentured servitude rather than slavery, the article contains an image of a Black African mother with the caption, "Poverty

forced Efua Mansah to sell her son, Kwabena, when he was 7." See Sharon La-Franiere, "Africa's World of Forced Labor, in a 6-Year-Old's Eyes," *New York Times*, October 29, 2006.

29 Gann and Willen, *Five Thousand Years of Slavery*, 156.

30 Hua, *Trafficking Women's Human Rights*, 101.

31 Ferguson and Hong, "Sexual and Racial Contradictions of Neoliberalism"; Harvey, *New Imperialism*.

32 Melamed, "Spirit of Neoliberalism," 3.

33 Sharma, "'New Order of Things.'"

34 Browne, *Dark Matters*, 57, direct quote from Patricia Hill Collins cited in Browne.

35 On antitrafficking's punitive and carceral approach, see Chuang, "Exploitation Creep," 611–12; Musto, *Control and Protect*.

36 Hua, *Trafficking Women's Human Rights*, 117.

37 "About Us," National Underground Railroad Freedom Center, accessed May 17, 2020, https://freedomcenter.org/about-us.

38 Rabinowitz, *Curating America*, 298–99.

39 Melamed, *Represent and Destroy*, 26, 35.

40 John Kiesewetter, "Civil Unrest Woven into City's History," *Cincinnati Enquirer*, July 15, 2001, https://www.cincinnati.com/story/news/blogs/our-history/2018/06/08 /civil-unrest-woven-into-citys-history/685960002/; Horton and Horton, *In Hope of Liberty*, 165.

41 Taylor, *Frontiers of Freedom*; Steinglass and Scarselli, *Ohio State Constitution*.

42 Damon Lynch and Thomas Dutton, "Cincinnati's 'Beacon,'" *Nation*, January 10, 2005, https://www.thenation.com/article/cincinnatis-beacon/.

43 King, "Letter from a Birmingham Jail." King writes, "I have almost reached the regrettable conclusion that the Negro's great stumbling block in the stride toward freedom is not the White Citizen's Counciler or the Ku Klux Klanner, but the white moderate who . . . prefers a negative peace which is the absence of tension to a positive peace which is the presence of justice."

44 Edward Rothstein, "Museum Review: Slavery's Harsh History Is Portrayed in Promised Land," *New York Times*, August 18, 2004.

45 Upon the occasion of the opening of the National Underground Railroad Freedom Center in Cincinnati, Ohio, in 2004, historian David Blight published an edited volume entitled *Passages to Freedom: The Underground Railroad in History and Memory*. Essays within *Passages* address the relationship between the legends of the Underground Railroad and the historical specificities in different cases and regions. What all commentators on the Underground Railroad tend to agree on is that the history and the mythology have mass popular appeal. David Blight is on the National Advisory Council for the National Underground Railroad Freedom Center and he is the director of Yale University's Gilder Lehrman Center for the Study of Slavery, Resistance and Abolition. Both institutions have incorporated antitrafficking discourse alongside other programming focused on the legacies of slavery.

46 The elicit/elide framework comes from Denise Ferreira da Silva, *Toward a Global Idea of Race*.

47 Foner, *Gateway to Freedom*, 15.

48 Schulz, "The Perilous Lure of the Underground Railroad," *New Yorker*, August 22, 2016.

49 In "Beyond the 'NGO Aesthetic,'" Jennifer Bajorek analyzes Sam Hopkins's art that critiques the NGO aesthetic and its influence on culture in Nairobi. According to Hopkins, the NGO aesthetic is characterized by consumerism, "bad visual metaphors," the reduction of "complex issues down to keywords," and light/dark visual metaphors that recast Western progress narratives on the African continent. The exhibition *Invisible: Slavery Today* is broken into two rooms: one dimly lit and darkly painted where stories of modern-day slavery are presented, and the other white-walled and brightly lit where stories of how to support the NGOs that sponsored the exhibition are featured as today's abolitionists.

50 In 2022, the NURFC hosted a temporary exhibition about contemporary incarceration titled *Marking Time: Art in the Age of Mass Incarceration*.

51 Coalition of Immokalee Workers, "Anti-Slavery Program," accessed July 12, 2022, https://ciw-online.org/slavery/.

52 Holmes, *Fresh Fruit, Broken Bodies*; Thompson and Wiggins, *The Human Cost of Food*; Otero, "Neoliberal Globalization, NAFTA, and Migration." Juris, *Networking Futures*.

53 Geffert, "H-2A Guestworker Program"; Holden, "Bitter Harvest."

54 The case depicted in the NURFC is based on the case *United States v. Navarrete*, which sentenced Cesar Navarrete in December 2008. CIW collaborated with the Department of Justice in the prosecution. US Department of Justice, "Four Defendants Sentenced for Roles in Scheme to Enslave Farmworkers in Florida," December 19, 2008, https://www.justice.gov/archive/opa/pr/2008/December/08-crt-1134.html.

55 Kristine Phillips, "ICE Arrests Nearly 150 Meat Plant Workers in Latest Raid in Ohio," *Washington Post*, June 20, 2018, https://www.washingtonpost.com/news/post-nation/wp/2018/06/20/ice-arrests-nearly-150-meat-plant-workers-in-latest-immigration-raid-in-ohio/.

56 On the relationship between farmworker rights movements and Black labor struggles, see Ortiz, *An African American and Latinx History of the United States*, 5, 11, 163–84. On the criminalization of Black mobility, see Walcott, *Long Emancipation*.

57 Hong, "Neoliberalism," 57.

58 "Official anti-racism" is Jodi Melamed's term, Melamed, "Spirit of Neoliberalism," 2. Although I am following Hong's argumentation here, Melamed makes a related point when she writes that neoliberalism devalues those it deems less worthy global citizens. See Melamed, *Represent and Destroy*, 44.

59 Hong, "Neoliberalism," 59.

60 Melamed, *Represent and Destroy*, 42.

61 Melamed, *Represent and Destroy*, 42.

62 "About," accessed on June 26, 2020, http://www.tipheroes.org/about/ (emphasis in original).

63 Watts and Williams, "Escaping ISIS."

64 *Yazidi: Strength and Survival*. See also Atika Shubert and Bharati Naik, "'Hundreds' of Yazidi Women Killing Themselves in ISIS Captivity," CNN, October 5, 2015,

http://www.cnn.com/2015/10/05/middleeast/yazidi-women-suicide-in-isis-captivity/index.html.

65 Andrea Mitchell, Cassandra Vinograd, F. Brinley Bruton, and Abigail Williams, "Kerry: ISIS Is Committing Genocide against Yazidis, Christians, and Shiite Muslims," *NBC News*, March 17, 2016, https://www.nbcnews.com/storyline/isis-terror/john-kerry-isis-committing-genocide-n540706.

66 See for instance, Lori Hinnant, Maya Allezeruzzo, and Balint Szlanko, "ISIS Tightens Its Grip on Its 3,000 Sex Slaves," *CBC News*, July 5, 2016, https://www.cbc.ca/news/world/isis-women-sex-slaves-1.3666253.

67 Martin Chulov, Julian Borger, Richard Norton-Taylor, and Dan Roberts, "US Troops Land on Iraq's Mt. Sinjar to Plan for Yazidi Evacuation," *Guardian*, August 13, 2014, https://www.theguardian.com/world/2014/aug/13/us-ground-troops-direct-role-evacuate-yazidis-iraq.

68 On the relationship between spectacle, affect, and media production of the Islamic State, see Kraidy, "Projectilic Image."

69 Hesford, "Trafficking American Exceptionality," 312. In the CNN footage of an Iraqi food relief mission rescuing Yazidis, the journalist is audibly aghast that "a little red-headed baby ended up in my hands." See "Dramatic Rescue as Yazidis Flee ISIS," CNN, August 11, 2014, video, https://www.cnn.com/videos/world/2014/08/11/watson-yazidis-rescue-iraq-isis-orig-mg.cnn.

70 Hua, *Trafficking Women's Human Rights*, 99.

71 Mahdavi, *From Trafficking to Terror*, 16.

72 Hesford and Shuman, "Precarious Narratives," 43.

73 Spivak, "Can the Subaltern Speak?" 296.

74 Browne, *Dark Matters*, 9.

75 A21, "Who We Are," accessed June 29, 2020, https://www.a21.org/content/who-we-are/gnihwo.

76 A21, "2019 Freedom Report," accessed June 29, 2020, https://www.a21.org/content/freedom-report-2019/gq5aps.

77 A21, "Can You See Me? Campaign," YouTube, May 22, 2018, https://www.youtube.com/watch?v=keaXpoZmE6I.

78 Videos and still images of these scenarios are available on A21's website: https://www.a21.org/content/can-you-see-me/gnsqqg.

79 In the video "Can you see me? Campaign," Staca Shehan, executive director of the National Center for Missing and Exploited Children, uses the language of empowerment specifically. She states that the A21 campaign, "provides the public with real life examples to empower them with education and give them an action-oriented response so that they know where to make reports."

80 Browne, *Dark Matters*, 132–33.

81 I encountered this sign at a Delta gate on January 31, 2018 (my emphasis). Notably, Delta Airlines was also the lead sponsor of the National Underground Railroad Freedom Center's 2019 gala entitled, "2019 Everyday Freedom Hero Awards Presented by Delta Air Lines," accessed June 29, 2020, https://freedomcenter.org/EFHA2019.

82 A21, "Can you see me? Campaign."

83 The news story is taken from Maura Furfay, "My Mexican Husband Was Accused of Trafficking Our Daughter on a United Flight," *Huffington Post*, April 17, 2017, http://www.huffingtonpost.com/entry/my-mexican-husband-was-accused-of -trafficking-our-daughter_us_58f4adade4b01566972250cf.

84 Airline Ambassadors International, "2018 Annual Report," accessed June 30, 2020, https://airlineamb.org/2018-annual-report/, 6.

85 Airline Ambassadors International, "TIP Line App," July 2, 2019, https://airlineamb .org/tip-line-app/.

86 Airline Ambassadors International, "Human Trafficking," training slides posted July 11, 2015, https://www.slideshare.net/airlineamb/basic-humantraffickingtraining forweb715.

87 Mahdavi, *From Trafficking to Terror*, 17.

88 Browne, *Dark Matters*, 134.

89 Sexton, "Racial Profiling and the Societies of Control," 202.

90 Sexton, "Racial Profiling and the Societies of Control," 207.

91 This incident occurred in Toronto Pearson Airport on November 8, 2019. I was traveling to the United States to witness Dread Scott's Slave Rebellion Reenactment in New Orleans. The confluence puts in stark relief my research question: To what ends do we put the memory of slavery and its abolition—racial profiling at the border or embodied revolutionary action?

92 Department of Homeland Security, "Indicators of Human Trafficking," accessed June 29, 2020, https://www.dhs.gov/blue-campaign/indicators-human-trafficking.

93 Juan González, "Juan González: There Are Refugees in Desperate Need of Help in Airports across the United States," *DemocracyNow!*, June 26, 2019, https://www.democracynow.org/2019/6/26/juan_gonzalez_migrants_chaos_at _airports#transcript.

94 Donald Trump, "State of the Union Address," February 5, 2019, https://www .whitehouse.gov/briefings-statements/president-donald-j-trumps-state-union -address-2/.

95 "President Trump on Human Trafficking," C-SPAN, February 1, 2019, https://www .c-span.org/video/?457491-1/president-trump-delivers-remarks-human-trafficking -southern-border.

96 On paramilitary vigilantism, see Shih, "Not in My 'Backyard Abolitionism,'" 59.

97 Operation Underground Railroad, "Why the Underground Railroad," accessed May 15, 2020, https://ourrescue.org/about#ugr. As of July 12, 2022, the content at this link has been changed.

98 In one of the organization's high-profile raids in Haiti, a Black Haitian sex worker is figured as the "kingpin" trafficker. In such an example, Ballard draws on Black women abolitionist heroes of the past to justify the criminalization of Black women in the present. The video "Haiti Rescue Report: Operation Toussaint" is available at: https://www.youtube.com/watch?v=LLnaSioV4Is. I analyze this example in a forthcoming article entitled "There's a Trafficking Jam on the Underground Railroad."

99 Sexton, "People-of-Color-Blindness," 42.
100 Commander, *Afro-Atlantic Flight*.
101 Browne, *Dark Matters*, 21.
102 Browne, *Dark Matters*, 47–49.

CHAPTER 4. DECEPTIVE EMPIRICISM

1 *Disposable People* was first published in 1999, a revised version with a new preface was published in 2004, and another in 2012. In the 2012 edition, Bales responds to scholarly criticism that he received for his claims by stating that the initial version of *Disposable People* is "full of assertions" and "some readers took the assertions as facts," but after even more years of research he is now sure that the cheaper price of slaves today is, indeed, a fact.

2 The CNN "Freedom Project: Ending Modern-Day Slavery," accessed May 12, 2017, http://thecnnfreedomproject.blogs.cnn.com. "The Numbers" sidebar was a part of the website's initial launch in 2011 and remained in place until the website was replaced with a new version at cnn.com/freedom in 2015. The original website still exists, although as of 2020 it has not retained its formatting.

3 Free the Slaves, "Modern Slaves Are Cheap and Disposable," accessed July 7, 2020, https://www.freetheslaves.net/our-model-for-freedom/slavery-today/.

4 The historical projection that it was not in one's financial interest to hurt one's slaves is challenged by the high rate of slaves worked to death on sugar plantations. Notably, Eric Williams argued that "racial differences made it easier to justify and rationalize Negro slavery," but the origin of racial slavery was based on economics: "the Negro slave was cheaper" than the white indentured servant. Williams, *Capitalism and Slavery*, 19.

5 Lowe, *Intimacies of Four Continents*, 11–12. Walter Rodney also notes that the "bourgeois scholars [who] have tried to suggest that the trade in slaves did not have worthwhile monetary returns" are an example of the "distortions of which white bourgeois scholarship is capable." Rodney, *How Europe Underdeveloped Africa*, 96.

6 Frank Wilderson, drawing on Saidiya Hartman, aims to correct "the notion that the profit motive is the consideration in the slaveocracy that trumps all others," by emphasizing that the constituent elements of slavery are not "exploitation and alienation but accumulation and fungibility." Wilderson, *Red, White, and Black*, 14. In *Black Reconstruction*, W. E. B. Du Bois famously named the psychological and symbolic wages of whiteness that accrue to poor whites. Ella Myers offers what she calls "whiteness as dominion" as what accrues to whites in her reading of Du Bois's writings. See Myers, "Beyond the Psychological Wage," 1.

7 Bales, "Slavery Today," video, accessed July 14, 2020, https://www.futurelearn.com /info/courses/slavery/0/steps/24383.

8 @Freedom_Fund, "The average modern-day slave is sold for $90–100 compared to the equivalent of $40,000 some 200 years ago, says @kevin_bales via @TR_Foundation," Twitter, November 23, 2017, 10:05 a.m., https://twitter.com/Freedom_Fund /status/933713016666894336. Kevin Bales is on the board of the Freedom Fund.

9   Thomson Reuters Foundation, "Human Trafficking and Modern-day Slavery," accessed July 6, 2020, https://www.trust.org/media-development/areas-of-focus/?sfid =a15D0000018xNdwIAE.

10 Musto, Thakor, and Gerasimov, "Between Hope and Hype."

11 Free the Slaves home page, accessed November 20, 2019, https://www.freetheslaves .net.

12 Silva, *Toward a Global Idea of Race*, xiii.

13 Benjamin, "Discriminatory Design, Liberating Imagination," 4.

14 O'Connell Davidson, *Modern Slavery*, 7; Neil Howard, "Modern Slavery Policy Does Not Set People Free," *Al Jazeera*, December 2, 2019, https://www.aljazeera.com /indepth/opinion/modern-slavery-policy-set-people-free-191130160248387.html.

15 Bales, "Exploring the Links between Slavery and Conflict." The talk was hosted by International Institute for Strategic Studies (IISS). The IISS is part of the Council of Councils, a project of the Council of Foreign Relations, both of which are funded by the Robina Foundation. The Robina Foundation also funded Yale's Gilder Lehrman Center Working Group on Modern Day Slavery and Human Trafficking from 2016 to 2019.

16 Bales, "The Most Resistant Slavery."

17 Bales, "The Most Resistant Slavery."

18 Bales, "The Most Resistant Slavery."

19 Roberts, *Killing the Black Body*, 88–98.

20 Siddharth Dube, "Minding Their Business: The Unfinished Battle for Sex Workers Rights," *Caravan*, June 1, 2020, https://caravanmagazine.in/reportage/unfinished -battle-sex-workers-rights. In this article about early progress and success in sex worker organizing in India in 1997, the author writes, "On that afternoon, it would have seemed just as fanciful to imagine a reversal—with the United States government, celebrity feminists, and Christian and Hindutva obscurantists joining hands to blight the movement, and to imprison countless sex workers in the name of rescuing them. Yet that, tragically, is what soon came to be."

21 I am grateful to conversations with Cal Biruk for helping me reframe the research question that undergirds this chapter in this way.

22 "Editorial: The Peculiar Institution," 8.

23 "Editorial: The Peculiar Institution," 8.

24 Bales, "The Social Psychology of Modern Slavery," 80–81.

25 Bales, "The Social Psychology of Modern Slavery," 82.

26 Bales, "The Social Psychology of Modern Slavery," 83.

27 Bales, "The Social Psychology of Modern Slavery," 86.

28 Bales, "The Social Psychology of Modern Slavery," 86.

29 George Musser, in Bales, "The Social Psychology of Modern Slavery," 84 (sidebar). The "hard to count" narrative justifies both the need for more money for more antitrafficking NGO research and insulates those projects from critiques about data inaccuracy. Vigneswaran, "Methodological Debates in Human Rights Research," analyzes how one social scientist team addressed the "hidden" claim by developing a creative and responsive sampling method. When those researchers found

little evidence of the scale of prevalence of trafficking that NGOs were claiming, antitrafficking advocates largely ignored their results or simply continued to insist it was inaccurate because of its clandestine nature.

30 Benjamin, "Discriminatory Design, Liberating Imagination," 4.

31 "Editorial: The Peculiar Institution," 8.

32 Wynter, "Unsettling the Coloniality of Being/Power/Truth/Freedom," 264.

33 Wynter, "Unsettling the Coloniality of Being/Power/Truth/Freedom," 266.

34 Wynter, "Unsettling the Coloniality of Being/Power/Truth/Freedom," 264.

35 Wynter, "Unsettling the Coloniality of Being/Power/Truth/Freedom," 280–81.

36 In 1735, natural scientist Carl Linnaeus published his order of the genus Homo into four separate groups based on capacity for self-knowledge. The groups were classified and marked by physical characteristics and cultural traits: white European (ruled by law), red American (ruled by custom), yellow Asian (ruled by opinion) and black African (ruled by dominion). Let me emphasize: scientific knowledge asserted that Black Africans were biologically characterized by their natural proclivity to be mastered by others. Roberts, *Fatal Invention*, 28–30; on Linnaeus's use of "capacity for self-knowledge" in his taxonomy, see Müller-Wille, "Linnaeus and the Four Corners of the World."

37 Snorton, *Black on Both Sides*, 17–53; Hogarth, *Medicalizing Blackness*; Rusert, "Naturalizing Coercion," 26.

38 Muhammad, *Condemnation of Blackness*, 35–39; Roberts, *Fatal Invention*, 35.

39 Hinton, *From the War on Poverty to the War on Crime*, 3.

40 Roberts, *Fatal Invention*, 27–28.

41 Browne, *Dark Matters*; Scannell, "This Is Not Minority Report."

42 Bales quoted in "Editorial: The Peculiar Institution," 8.

43 "Genevieve LeBaron and Kevin Bales on Forced Labor and Modern Slavery," *Slavery and Its Legacies*, Yale University, March 5, 2018, podcast, https://slaveryanditslegacies.yale.edu/news/genevieve-lebaron-and-kevin-bales-forced-labor-and-modern-slavery

44 Rogers cited in Chuang, "Giving as Governance?," 1528.

45 Cited in Chuang, "Giving as Governance?," 1535.

46 At the time of writing, the 2018 report was the most recent. According to Walk Free Foundation's website, the next Global Slavery Index will be released in 2022. Accessed March 25, 2022, https://www.walkfree.org/projects/the-global-slavery-index/

47 Chuang, "Giving as Governance?," 1550; Anne Gallagher, "Unravelling the 2016 Global Slavery Index, Part 2," *openDemocracy*, June 28, 2016, https://www.opendemocracy.net/en/5050/unravelling-2016-global-slavery-index-part-two/; Gallagher, "The Global Slavery Index: Seduction and Obfuscation," *openDemocracy*, December 4, 2014, https://www.opendemocracy.net/en/5050/global-slavery-index-seduction-and-obfuscation/. Thomson Reuters Foundation's website justifies its antitrafficking journalist training program by citing the Global Slavery Index: "According to the Global Slavery Index, 45.8 million people are trapped in some form of slavery today. Journalists around the world play an instrumental role in

shedding light over this largely under-reported issue," accessed July 10, 2020, www
.trust.org/media-development/areas-of-focus.

48 Rights Lab home page, accessed November 11, 2019, www.nottingham.ac.uk
/research/beacons-of-excellence/rights-lab/index.aspx.

49 "U21 Early Career Researcher Workshop 2020 (online)—call for nominations,"
email announcement.

50 Bethany Jackson and Jessica Wardlaw, "Slavery from Space," *Rights Lab* (blog),
University of Nottingham June 1, 2017, https://blogs.nottingham.ac.uk/rights/2017
/06/01/walkfree5/.

51 Bales, "Unlocking the Science of Slavery," 5–6.

52 For an excellent analysis of the history of legal definitions of slavery and their
relationship to antitrafficking, see O'Connell Davidson, *Modern Slavery*, chapter 2.
For a critique of Bales's definition of slavery, see Patterson, "Trafficking, Gender,
and Slavery." For a revision to the legal definition of slavery written by Members
of the Research Network on the Legal Parameters of Slavery (of which Bales is a
member), see "Bellagio-Harvard Guidelines on the Legal Parameters of Slavery,"
March 3, 2012, https://glc.yale.edu/sites/default/files/pdf/the_bellagio-_harvard
_guidelines_on_the_legal_parameters_of_slavery.pdf.

53 BRE Group press release, accessed January 3, 2019, https://www.bregroup.com
/press-releases/2018-annual-uk-top100-corporate-modern-slavery-influencers-index
-rankings-announced/.

54 Bales, "Speech: Day 1 Keynote—Kevin Bales."

55 Keith Feldman names aerial surveillance technologies used within the US war on
terror "racialization from above" technologies. Using satellites within antitrafficking advocacy is one example of how antitrafficking operates as the discursively
humanitarian arm of US imperial antiterrorism military schemes. See Feldman,
"Empire's Verticality," 330.

56 Quoted in Sarah Scoles, "Researchers Spy Signs of Slavery from Space," *Science*,
February 19, 2019, https://www.sciencemag.org/news/2019/02/researchers-spy-signs
-slavery-space.

57 Okyere, "Are Working Children's Rights?"

58 Bales, "Speech: Day 1 Keynote—Kevin Bales."

59 Okyere, "Are Working Children's Rights?," 83.

60 Okyere, "Moral Economies and Child Labour," 238.

61 Okyere, "Moral Economies and Child Labour," 243.

62 On how algorithms reproduce racial bias, see Noble, *Algorithms of Oppression*; Kris-
tian Lum and William Isaac, "To Predict and Serve?" *Significance*, October 7, 2017,
https://doi.org/10.1111/j.1740-9713.2016.00960.x.

63 Broussard, *Artificial Unintelligence*, 8.

64 In *Prisoners of Freedom*, Harri Englund demonstrates how poverty is seen as a
technical problem, not a structural one: "Poverty was, in the official rhetoric,
essentially a technical problem, a result of dysfunctions in local and global
markets." Englund, *Prisoners of Freedom*, 13. See also Ferguson, *Anti-politics
Machine*.

65 Agarwal, "Can We Really Spot Slavery from Space?" *openDemocracy*, June 3, 2019, https://www.opendemocracy.net/en/beyond-trafficking-and-slavery/can-we-really-spot-slavery-space/.

66 International Justice Mission, "2020 Year in Review," 16, accessed October 14, 2021, https://www.ijm.org/2020-year-in-review-full-report.

67 Quoted in Kieran Guilbert, "Satellites and Science Turn Tide in Fight to End Slavery: Expert," *Reuters*, November 15, 2017, https://www.reuters.com/article/us-slavery-conference-global-science/satellites-and-science-turn-tide-in-fight-to-end-slavery-expert-idUSKBN1DF1SA.

68 "The Antislavery Usable Past," Arts and Humanities Research Council, accessed July 14, 2020, https://ahrc.ukri.org/research/case-study-archives/the-antislavery-usable-past/.

69 The content of the course is publicly accessible without registering for it at www.futurelearn.com/info/step-course/ending-slavery-strategies-for-contemporary-global-abolition.

70 UK Research and Innovation, "Using Insights from Antislavery Movements to Inform Modern Policy," August 1, 2019, accessed July 12, 2022, https://www.ukri.org/about-us/how-we-are-doing/research-outcomes-and-impact/ahrc/using-insights-from-antislavery-movements-to-inform-modern-policy/.

71 "Slavery Today," accessed July 13, 2020, https://www.futurelearn.com/info/courses/slavery/0/steps/24383.

72 Bales, "Slavery Today," accessed July 14, 2020, https://www.futurelearn.com/info/courses/slavery/0/steps/24383.

73 Murphy, *The Economization of Life*; Cyril, "Motherhood, Media, and Building a 21st-Century Movement," 32; Sasser, *On Infertile Ground*, 33–34, 51–70.

74 Monti Datta, "Measuring Slavery," accessed July 14, 2020, video, https://www.futurelearn.com/info/courses/slavery/0/steps/24386 (my emphasis).

75 Chuang, "Giving as Governance?," 1550.

76 Biruk, *Cooking Data*. In the Harvard report that assesses one of Free the Slaves' programs, the researchers discuss how diligent they were in training the interviewers, but sometimes interviewers still skipped questions or otherwise didn't follow the protocol which led the Harvard researchers to have to discard those data where they "had doubts about whether questions had been administered according to protocol," 53. Biruk describes how "culture" in these cases is both the explanation for the intervention and the reason it fails. Biruk also reads such instances of going off script as moments of fieldworker expertise that can actually help preserve research projects' relationships with communities, even though they are discarded or dismissed as unreliable data.

77 Gallagher, "The Global Slavery Index Is Based on Flawed Data—Why Does No One Say So?," *Guardian*, November 28, 2014, https://www.theguardian.com/global-development/poverty-matters/2014/nov/28/global-slavery-index-walk-free-human-trafficking-anne-gallagher. In addition to the embedded logic of civilizational hierarchy based in racialized difference displayed here, what exactly can "like Africa" mean for such a large and diverse continent?

78   Arthur Torrington, "Making Freedom," accessed July 14, 2020, video, https://www
     .futurelearn.com/info/courses/slavery/o/steps/24413.

79   "The Community-based Model," accessed July 13, 2020, https://www.futurelearn
     .com/info/courses/slavery/o/steps/24414.

80   Kevin Bales and Zoe Trodd, email message to participants, November 15, 2016.

81   Englund, *Prisoners of Freedom*, 9.

82   Lowe, *Intimacies of Four Continents*, 6.

83   Kosmatopoulos, "The Birth of the Workshop," 535.

84   Williams, *Divided World*, xxvi.

85   Howard, *Child Trafficking*; Howard, "Accountable to Whom?"

86   Dottridge, "Effects of Anti-trafficking Policies on Migrants," 417.

87   Gausman et al. "When We Raise Our Voice," 12.

88   Gausman et al. "When We Raise Our Voice," 55.

89   Gausman et al. "When We Raise Our Voice," 12.

90   Biruk, "The Invention of 'Harmful Cultural Practices,'" 352.

91   Biruk, drawing on Steven Epstein, in Biruk "The Invention of 'Harmful Cul-
     tural,'" 352.

92   O'Connell Davidson, *Modern Slavery*, 11.

93   Clarke and Thomas, *Globalization and Race*.

94   Merry, Davis, and Kingsbury, *Quiet Power of Indicators*; Adams, "Metrics of the
     Global Sovereign," 25.

95   Merry, *Seductions of Quantification*, 9–10.

96   In *The Good Project*, Monika Krause argues that the main objective of NGO pro-
     grams is to reproduce themselves.

97   Snyder, "From Slavery to Freedom," 14.

98   Merry, *Seductions of Quantification*, 1.

99   Snyder, "From Slavery to Freedom," 15.

100 Snyder, "From Slavery to Freedom," 34.

101 Free the Slaves, *Community-Based Model for Fighting Slavery Report*, appendix 2.

102 Free the Slaves, *Community-Based Model for Fighting Slavery Report*, appendix 2.

103 That rights training is a mechanism counted as freeing slaves is further obscured
     by the fact that Free the Slaves also counts and reports the number of people
     reached by rights training (which refers to those who did not meet the criteria for
     being enslaved prior to the training) as a separate output, which is far higher than
     the number freed. Across several indicator reports over several years, measuring
     freedom for Free the Slaves very often comes down to counting the number of
     rights training sessions, awareness sessions, and arrests and prosecutions that Free
     the Slaves and its local partners participate in.

104 Bales, *Ending Slavery*, 223.

105 Merry, *Seductions of Quantification*, 3.

106 "The Community-based Model," accessed July 14, 2020, https://www.futurelearn
     .com/info/courses/slavery/o/steps/24414.

107 "A Slavery-Free World," accessed July 14, 2020, video, https://www.futurelearn
     .com/info/courses/slavery/o/steps/24422.

108 "A Slavery-Free World."

109 "Corker: Bill to Launch End Modern Slavery Initiative to Become Law," Press Release, US Senate Committee on Foreign Relations, December 8, 2016, 2020, https://www.foreign.senate.gov/press/chair/release/corker-bill-to-launch-end -modern-slavery-initiative-to-become-law.

110 Free the Slaves, "Community Liberation Initiative," accessed January 2, 2020, https://www.freetheslaves.net/our-model-for-freedom/community-liberation -initiative/

111 Snyder, "From Slavery to Freedom," 34.

112 "A Slavery-Free World."

113 Bales, *Ending Slavery*, 226.

114 Thomas, *Political Life in the Wake of the Plantation*; Gilmore, *Golden Gulag*; Camp, *Incarcerating the Crisis*; Singh, *Black Is a Country*; Robinson, *Black Marxism*; Shange, *Progressive Dystopia*; Richie, *Arrested Justice*.

115 "The Combahee River Collective Statement," reprinted in Taylor, *How We Get Free*, 23.

116 Sharpe, *In the Wake*; Du Bois, *Black Reconstruction*.

INTERLUDE. #CHARLOTTESVILLE

1 Zyahna Bryant, "Opinion/Letter: Lee Statue a Symbol of Pain and Suffering," *Daily Progress*, March 26, 2016; Zyahna Bryant, "Petition: Change the Name of Lee Park and Remove the Statue," accessed November 8, 2021, https://www.change .org/p/charlottesville-city-council-change-the-name-of-lee-park-and-remove-the -statue-in-charlottesville-va.

2 John Edwin Mason describes why he favored the commission's recommendation to transform, rather than remove, the monuments, but then changed his mind after Heather Heyer was killed in August 2017. He writes that it "added another layer of meaning to the statue. It is now covered in blood. It always had been, of course, but the metaphor had been a distant one." Mason, "History, Mine and Ours," 22.

3 City of Charlottesville, "Blue Ribbon Commission on Race, Memorials, and Public Spaces, Report to City Council," December 19, 2016, 19 and Appendix L, 2.

4 Citizen Justice Initiative, *The Illusion of Progress: Charlottesville's Roots in White Supremacy*, (Charlottesville: University of Virginia, 2017), accessed June 3, 2020, https://www .arcgis.com/apps/Cascade/index.html?appid=a31f53ca6a54439087085d6c313758a5.

5 Sophie Abramowitz, Eva Latterner, and Gillet Rosenblith, "Tools of Displacement: How Charlottesville, Virginia's Confederate Statues Helped Decimate the City's Historically Successful Black Communities," *Slate*, June 23, 2017, https:// slate.com/news-and-politics/2017/06/how-charlottesvilles-confederate-statues -helped-decimate-the-citys-historically-successful-black-communities.html.

6 Citizen Justice Initiative, *The Illusion of Progress*, chapter 3.

7 Charlottesville City Council, "RFI# 22–06 Acquisition ONE (1) or TWO (2) Confederate Statues," June 7, 2021, https://www.charlottesville.gov/DocumentCenter

/View/5814/RFI-22–06-Acquisition-ONE-1-or-TWO-2-Confederate-Statues-PDF
?bidId=139.

8 Max Marcilla, "6 Bids Made for Charlottesville's Confederate Statues," WHSV,
October 19, 2021, https://www.whsv.com/2021/10/20/6-bids-made-charlottesvilles
-removed-confederate-statues/. The Jefferson School was granted its bid by the
City Council in December 2021.

9 My thinking on ethnographic sensibilities has been shaped by Jackson, *Thin Description*; Cerwonka and Malkki, *Improvising Theory*; Weston, "'Real Anthropology'
and Other Nostalgias."

10 Madison, *Critical Ethnography*, 179.

11 Madison, *Critical Ethnography*, 14–15.

12 Allen and Jobson, "The Decolonizing Generation"; Harrison, *Decolonizing
Anthropology*.

13 Allen and Jobson, "The Decolonizing Generation," 135.

14 Shange, *Progressive Dystopia*, 7. Audre Lorde writes, "We can train ourselves to
respect our feelings and to transpose them into a language so they can be shared."
Lorde, "Poetry Is Not a Luxury," 37.

15 Lorde, "The Uses of Anger," 130.

16 Jackson, *Thin Description*, 52.

CHAPTER 5. HISTORY IS ANTIBLACKNESS

1 Sharpe, *In the Wake*, 21.

2 Precision Air operates the majority of flights from Dar es Salaam, Tanzania, to Stone
Town, Zanzibar. I came across this edition of the magazine on my flight to Zanzibar
in July 2017.

3 Loveland, "Rattling the Chains."

4 Loveland, "Rattling the Chains," 16.

5 Loveland, "Rattling the Chains," 19.

6 Du Bois, *World and Africa*, 43.

7 Du Bois, *World and Africa*, 42.

8 Lowe, *Intimacies of Four Continents*, 45.

9 Hill, "Rhetoric of Modern-Day Slavery."

10 Trouillot, *Silencing the Past*, 54.

11 Rodney, *How Europe Underdeveloped Africa*, 109.

12 Rodney, *How Europe Underdeveloped Africa*, 109.

13 "Summer 1964: White Folks Project," SNCC Digital Gateway, accessed December 31, 2018, https://snccdigital.org/events/white-folks-project/.

14 "Summer 1964: White Folks Project."

15 "MLK50: A Legacy Remembered," National Civil Rights Museum, accessed June 5,
2020, https://www.civilrightsmuseum.org/mlk50-a-legacy-remembered.

16 "Human Trafficking," Center for the Study of Slavery and Justice at Brown University, accessed November 4, 2021, https://www.brown.edu/initiatives/slavery-and
-justice/human-trafficking.

17   For years Polaris promoted its campaigns to shutter massage businesses and specifically used racial categories as indicators of trafficking victims, such as "recently
arrived from China or South Korea," and "speaks little or no English." In the
aftermath of the Atlanta shooting, Polaris removed all its webpages related to this
program, but I used the Wayback Machine to retrieve them. See also Samantha
Cole, "Anti-trafficking Group Deletes Massage Parlor Fear-Mongering after Shooting," *Vice*, March 22, 2021, https://www.vice.com/en/article/7k9gb9/anti-trafficking
-polaris-massage-parlors-atlanta-shooting.

18   The narrator of the video introduces the three organizations as "crusaders on the
front lines of today's civil rights movement." The three profiled organizations are
Black Girls Code, Polaris (human trafficking), and CHIRLA (an immigrant rights
organization in Los Angeles), in that order.

19   On the cannibalization of memory see Zelizer, "Cannibalizing Memory in the Global
Flow of News"; Beutin, "Black Suffering for/from Anti-trafficking Advocacy."

20   Du Bois, *Black Reconstruction*, 711.

21   Rodney, *How Europe Underdeveloped Africa*, 94.

22   Du Bois, *Black Reconstruction*, 711–13.

23   Du Bois, *Black Reconstruction*, 713.

24   On historical recursion, see Stoler, *Duress*, 31–32.

25   Trouillot, *Silencing the Past*, 106.

26   Trouillot, *Silencing the Past*, 75.

27   Trouillot, *Silencing the Past*, 76.

28   Wynter, "Unsettling the Coloniality of Being/Power/Truth/Freedom," 293–95.
Trouillot, Silencing the Past, 77. Wynter, "1492: A New World View," 11 (emphasis
in original).

29   Wynter, "Unsettling the Coloniality of Being/Power/Truth/Freedom," 295.

30   Wynter, drawing on Quijano, in Wynter, "Unsettling the Coloniality of Being/
Power/Truth/Freedom," 296.

31   Wynter, "Unsettling the Coloniality of Being/Power/Truth/Freedom," 301,
281–82.

32   Trouillot, *Silencing the Past*, 76–77.

33   Mignolo, "Sylvia Wynter," 113.

34   Du Bois, *Black Reconstruction*, 727.

35   Pierre, "Racial Vernaculars of Development," 87.

36   Eudell, "Modernity and the 'Work of History,'" 14.

37   Trouillot, *Silencing the Past*, 73 (my emphasis).

38   Ansfield, "Still Submerged," 137.

39   Hesford, *Spectacular Rhetorics*, 57.

40   Mensah and Okyere, "How CNN Reported on 'Child Slaves' Who Were Not Really
Enslaved," *Al Jazeera*, March 18, 2019, https://www.aljazeera.com/indepth/opinion
/cnn-reported-child-slaves-enslaved-190315103733047.html.

41   Sharpe, *In the Wake*, 116–17. Sharpe writes, "By considering the relationship between
imaging and imagining in the registers of Black annotation and Black redaction,
I want to think about what these images calls forth. And I want to think through

what they call on us to do, think, feel in the wake of slavery. . . . What might practices of Black annotation and Black redaction offer?"

42 Walcott, *Long Emancipation*, 43.
43 See also Sexton, "Abolition Terminable and Interminable."
44 Walcott, *Long Emancipation*, 52.
45 Sharpe, *In the Wake*, 53–57.
46 Walcott and Abdillahi, *BlackLife*, 22.
47 Boyce Davies and M'Bow, "Towards African Diaspora Citizenship," 14.
48 Sharpe, *In the Wake*, 21; Ray, "Afterlives of Slavery, Epistemologies of Race," 61.
49 Fatma Naib, "Sweden: 'Torture, Rape, and Slavery in Libya Must Stop,'" *Al Jazeera*, accessed October 30, 2021, https://interactive.aljazeera.com/aje/2017/sweden
-protests-libya/index.html.
50 Shih, "Not in My 'Backyard Abolitionism'"; Batstone, *Not for Sale*, 8.
51 "Action for Humanity: Public Statement on the Repatriation of Gambian Women from Lebanon," September 5, 2020, accessed October 22, 2021, https://d-infodigest
.com/action-for-humanity-public-statement-on-the-repatriation-of-gambian
-women-from-lebanon/; US Department of State, *2021 Trafficking in Persons Report*,
246.
52 Sharpe, *In the Wake*, 21.
53 Sharpe, *In the Wake*, 21.
54 Stoler, *Duress*, 25.
55 Sharpe, *In the Wake*, 11.
56 Thomas, *Political Life in the Wake of the Plantation*, 1; Jackson, *Thin Description*,
239–40.
57 Sharpe, *In the Wake*, 131, 116.
58 Trouillot, *Silencing the Past*, 148.

AFTERWORD

1 Free the Slaves, "FTS Solidarity Statement on Racial Violence and Justice in the United States," June 4, 2020, https://www.freetheslaves.net/fts-solidarity-statement
-on-racial-violence-and-justice-in-the-united-states/.
2 Free the Slaves, "Child Labor Is Child Abuse," June 11, 2020, accessed July 12, 2022, https://www.freetheslaves.net/child-labor-is-child-abuse/.
3 I thank Elena Shih for her insights on this point.

Bibliography

Adams, Vincanne. "Metrics of the Global Sovereign: Numbers and Stories in Global Health." In *Metrics: What Counts in Global Health*, edited by Vincanne Adams, 19-56. Durham, NC: Duke University Press, 2016.

Allen, Jafari Sinclaire, and Ryan Cecil Jobson. "The Decolonizing Generation: (Race and) Theory in Anthropology since the Eighties." *Current Anthropology* 57, no. 2 (2016): 129-48.

Ansfield, Bench. "Still Submerged: The Uninhabitability of Urban Redevelopment." In *Sylvia Wynter: On Being Human as Praxis*, edited by Katherine McKittrick, 124-41. Durham, NC: Duke University Press, 2015.

Anderson, Sam, Muntu Matsimela, and Yusuf Nuruddin. "The Reparations Movement: An Assessment of Recent and Current Activism." In *Redress for Historical Injustices in the United States*, edited by Michael T. Martin and Marilyn Yaquinto, 427-46. Durham, NC: Duke University Press, 2007.

Appadurai, Arjun. *Modernity at Large: Cultural Dimensions of Globalization*. Minneapolis: University of Minnesota Press, 1996.

Athreya, Bama. "White Man's Burden and the New Colonialism in West African Cocoa Production." *Race/Ethnicity: Multidisciplinary Global Contexts* 5, no. 1 (Autumn 2011): 51-59.

Bajorek, Jennifer. "Beyond the 'NGO Aesthetic.'" *Social Text* 34, no. 2 (June 2016): 89-107.

Baker, Carrie. "Racialized Rescue Narratives in Public Discourse on Youth Prostitution and Sex Trafficking in the United States." *Politics and Gender* 15 (2019): 773-800.

Bales, Kevin. "Day 1 Keynote." Speech at Trust Conference, November 15, 2018. http://www.trustconference.com/videos/i/?id=446815ec-0536-45b6-ba1a-187b99fc8ad2&confYear=2018.

Bales, Kevin. *Disposable People: New Slavery in the Global Economy*. 3rd ed. Berkeley: University of California Press, 2012.

Bales, Kevin. *Ending Slavery: How We Free Today's Slaves*. Berkeley: University of California Press, 2007.

Bales, Kevin. "Exploring the Links between Slavery and Conflict." Recorded talk. International Institute for Strategic Studies, May 16, 2019. https://www.iiss.org/events/2019/05/slavery-and-conflict.

Bales, Kevin. "The Most Resistant Slavery: Slavery in War." Conference presentation at "Roundtable: Fighting Modern Slavery—What Works?," Yale University, November 3, 2018. https://glc.yale.edu/events/conferences/2018-annual-conference/schedule.

Bales, Kevin. "The Social Psychology of Modern Slavery." *Scientific American* 286, no. 4 (April 2002): 80–88.

Bales, Kevin. "Unlocking the Science of Slavery." *Slavery Today* 1, no. 1 (February 2014): 1–9.

Bales, Kevin, and Zoe Trodd, eds. *The Antislavery Usable Past: History's Lessons for How We End Slavery Today*. Nottingham, UK: The Rights Lab, University of Nottingham, 2020.

Balfour, Lawrie. "Unreconstructed Democracy? W. E. B. Du Bois and the Case for Reparations." *American Political Science Review* 97, no. 1 (2003): 33–44.

Batstone, David. *Not for Sale: The Return of the Global Slave Trade—and How We Can Fight It*. Rev. ed. New York: Harper Collins Publishers, 2010.

Bay, Mia. *To Tell the Truth Freely: The Life of Ida B. Wells*. New York: Hill and Wang, 2010.

Beckett, Greg. "The Ontology of Freedom: The Unthinkable Miracle of Haiti." *Journal of Haitian Studies* 19, no. 2 (2013): 54–74.

Beckett, Greg. *There Is No More Haiti*. Berkeley: University of California Press, 2019.

Beckles, Hilary. *Britain's Black Debt: Reparations for Caribbean Slavery and Native Genocide*. Kingston, Jamaica: University of the West Indies Press, 2013.

Beliso-De Jesús, Aisha M., and Jemima Pierre. "Anthropology of White Supremacy." Special section, *American Anthropologist* 122, no. 1 (March 2020): 65–75.

"Bellagio-Harvard Guidelines on the Legal Parameters of Slavery." March 3, 2012. https://glc.yale.edu/sites/default/files/pdf/the_bellagio-_harvard_guidelines_on_the_legal_parameters_of_slavery.pdf.

Benjamin, Ruha. "Introduction: Discriminatory Design, Liberating Imagination." In *Captivating Technology: Race, Carceral Technoscience, and Liberatory Imagination in Everyday Life*, edited by Ruha Benjamin, 1–22. Durham, NC: Duke University Press, 2019.

Bernal, Victoria, and Inderpal Grewal, eds. *Theorizing NGOs: States, Feminisms, and Neoliberalism*. Durham, NC: Duke University Press, 2014.

Bernstein, Elizabeth. *Brokered Subjects: Sex, Trafficking, and the Politics of Freedom*. Chicago: University of Chicago Press, 2019.

Berry, Mary Frances. *My Face Is Black Is True: Callie House and the Struggle for Ex-Slave Reparations*. New York: Penguin Random House, 2005.

Beutin, Lyndsey. "Black Suffering for/from Anti-trafficking Advocacy." *Anti-Trafficking Review* 9 (2017): 14–30.

Beutin, Lyndsey. "The Anti-trafficking Apparatus Has a Racial Justice Problem." In *White Supremacy, Racism and the Coloniality of Anti-Trafficking*, edited by Kamala Kempadoo and Elena Shih, 47–63. London: Routledge, 2022.

Beutin, Lyndsey, Cherry Henley, B. Esi Okesanya, and Sally Williamson. "The Radical Yes: A Constellation of Mutual Aid Projects in Charlottesville." *Southern Cultures* 27, no, 3 (Fall 2021): 18–30.

Biondi, Martha. "The Rise of the Reparations Movement." In *Redress for Historical Injustices in the United States*, edited by Michael T. Martin and Marilyn Yaquinto, 255–69. Durham, NC: Duke University Press, 2007.

Biruk, Cal (Crystal). *Cooking Data: Culture and Politics in an African Research World.* Durham, NC: Duke University Press, 2018.

Biruk, Cal (Crystal). "The Invention of 'Harmful Cultural Practices' in the Era of AIDS in Malawi." *Journal of Southern African Studies* 46, no. 2 (2020): 339–56.

Blair, Cynthia. *I've Got to Make My Livin': Black Women's Sex Work in Turn-of-the-Century Chicago.* Chicago: University of Chicago Press, 2010.

Blight, David, ed. *Passages to Freedom: The Underground Railroad in History and Memory.* Washington, DC: Smithsonian Books, 2004.

Boellstorff, Tom. *Coming of Age in Second Life: An Anthropologist Explores the Virtually Human.* Princeton, NJ: Princeton University Press, 2008.

Bogues, Anthony, ed. *After Man, Towards the Human: Critical Essays on Sylvia Wynter.* Kingston, Jamaica: Ian Randle Publishers, 2006.

Boyce Davies, Carole, and Babacar M'Bow. "Towards African Diaspora Citizenship: Politicizing an Existing Global Geography." In *Black Geographies and the Politics of Place,* edited by Katherine McKittrick and Clyde Woods, 14–45. Cambridge, MA: South End Press, 2007.

Bridges, Khiara. "The Intersection of Class and Race: Imagining an Ethnography of the Reproductive Lives of Class-Privileged Women of Color." Public lecture at Oberlin College, May 7, 2019.

Briggs, Laura. *Reproducing Empire: Race, Sex, Science, and U.S. Imperialism in Puerto Rico.* Berkeley: University of California Press, 2002.

Broussard, Meredith. *Artificial Unintelligence: How Computers Misunderstand the World.* New York: NYU Press, 2019.

Browne, Simone. *Dark Matters: On the Surveillance of Blackness.* Durham, NC: Duke University Press, 2015.

Brown-Long, Cyntoia. *Free Cyntoia: My Search for Redemption in the American Prison System.* With Bethany Mauger. New York: Atria Books, 2019.

Brysk, Alison. "Rethinking Trafficking: Human Rights and Private Wrongs." In *From Human Trafficking to Human Rights: Reframing Contemporary Slavery,* edited by Alison Brysk and Austin Choi-Fitzpatrick, 73–85. Philadelphia: University of Pennsylvania Press, 2013.

Buck-Morss, Susan. "Hegel and Haiti." *Critical Inquiry* 26, no. 4 (2000): 821–65.

Bumiller, Kristin. *In an Abusive State: How Neoliberalism Appropriated the Feminist Movement against Sexual Violence.* Durham, NC: Duke University Press, 2008.

Buntu, Amani Olubanjo, ed. *The Bridgetown Protocol: Official Report of the Afrikans and Afrikan Descendants World Conference against Racism, October 2–6, 2002, Bridgetown, Barbados:* Afrikans and Afrikan Descendants World Conference against Racism, 2003.

Burrowes, Nicole. "Building the World We Want to See: A Herstory of Sista II Sista and the Struggle against State and Interpersonal Violence." *Souls* 20, no. 4 (2018): 376–98.

Byrd, Brandon. *The Black Republic: African Americans and the Fate of Haiti.* Philadelphia: University of Pennsylvania Press, 2020.

Cadet, Jean-Robert. *Restavec: From Haitian Slave Child to Middle-Class American.* Austin: University of Texas Press, 1998.

Camp, Jordan. *Incarcerating the Crisis: Freedom Struggles and the Rise of the Neoliberal State.* Berkeley: University of California Press, 2016.

Campt, Tina. *Listening to Images*. Durham, NC: Duke University Press, 2017.

CARICOM Reparations Commission. "10-Point Reparation Plan." Accessed May 8, 2020. http://caricomreparations.org/caricom/caricoms-10-point-reparation-plan/.

Carmichael, Stokely. "Power and Racism." In *Stokely Speaks: From Black Power to Pan-Africanism*, edited by Bob Brown, 17–30. Chicago: Lawrence Hill Books, 2007.

Cerwonka, Allaine, and Liisa Malkki. *Improvising Theory: Process and Temporality in Ethnographic Fieldwork*. Chicago: University of Chicago Press, 2007.

Césaire, Aimé. *Discourse on Colonialism*. Translated by Joan Pinkham. New York: Monthly Review Press, 2000. First published 1955 by Editions Présence Africaine.

Chapkis, Wendy. "Trafficking, Migration, and the Law: Protecting Innocents, Punishing Immigrants." *Gender and Society* 17, no. 6 (December 2003): 923–37.

Chuang, Janie. "The Challenges and Perils of Reframing Trafficking as 'Modern Day Slavery.'" *Anti-Trafficking Review* 5 (2015): 146–49.

Chuang, Janie. "Exploitation Creep and the Unmaking of Human Trafficking Law." *American Journal of International Law* 108, no. 4 (October 2014): 609–49.

Chuang, Janie. "Giving as Governance? Philanthrocapitalism and Modern-Day Slavery Abolitionism." *UCLA Law Review* 62, no. 6 (2015): 1516–56.

Chuang, Janie. "The United States as Global Sheriff: Using Unilateral Sanctions to Combat Human Trafficking." *Michigan Journal of International Law* 27, no. 2 (2006): 437–94.

Citizen Justice Initiative. *The Illusion of Progress: Charlottesville's Roots in White Supremacy*. Charlottesville: University of Virginia, 2017. Accessed June 3, 2020. https://www.arcgis.com/apps/Cascade/index.html?appid=a31f53ca6a54439087085d6c313758a5.

Clarke, Kamari. *Fictions of Justice: The International Criminal Court and the Challenge of Legal Pluralism in Sub-Saharan Africa*. Cambridge: Cambridge University Press, 2009.

Clarke, Kamari, and Deborah Thomas, eds. *Globalization and Race: Transformations in the Cultural Production of Blackness*. Durham, NC: Duke University Press, 2006.

CNN. *Yazidi: Strength and Survival*. CNN "Freedom Project," 2015, video.

Cole, Teju. "The White-Savior Industrial Complex." *Atlantic*, March 21, 2012. https://www.theatlantic.com/international/archive/2012/03/the-white-savior-industrial-complex/254843/.

Collins, Patricia Hill. *Black Feminist Thought: Knowledge, Consciousness, and the Politics of Empowerment*. New York: Routledge, 1991.

"Combahee River Collective Statement." 1977. In *How We Get Free: Black Feminism and the Combahee River Collective*, edited by Keeanga-Yamahtta Taylor, 15–27. Chicago: Haymarket Books, 2017.

Commander, Michelle. *Afro-Atlantic Flight: Speculative Returns and the Black Fantastic*. Durham, NC: Duke University Press, 2017.

Cox, Karen. *No Common Ground: Confederate Monuments and the Ongoing Fight for Racial Justice*. Chapel Hill: University of North Carolina Press, 2021.

Crawley, Ashon. *Blackpentecostal Breath: The Aesthetics of Possibility*. New York: Fordham University Press, 2016.

Critical Resistance and Incite! Women of Color Against Violence. "Gender Violence and the Prison-Industrial Complex." In *The Color of Violence: The Incite! Anthology*, 223–26. Cambridge, MA: South End Press, 2006.

Cyril, Malkia A. "Motherhood, Media, and Building a 21st-Century Movement." In *Revolutionary Mothering: Love on the Front Lines*, edited by Alexis Pauline Gumbs, China Martens, and Mai'a Williams, 32–35. Toronto: Between the Lines Press, 2016.

Danewid, Ida. "White Innocence in the Black Mediterranean: Hospitality and the Erasure of History." *Third World Quarterly* 38, no. 7 (2017): 1674–89.

Darity, William, Jr., and Dania Frank. "Political Economy of Ending Racism and the World Conference against Racism." In *Redress for Historical Injustices in the United States*, edited by Michael T. Martin and Marilyn Yaquinto, 249–54. Durham, NC: Duke University Press, 2007.

Darity, William A., Jr., and A. Kirsten Mullen. *From Here to Equality: Reparations for Black Americans in the Twenty-First Century*. Chapel Hill: University of North Carolina Press, 2020.

Daut, Marlene. *Tropics of Haiti: Race and the Literary History of the Haitian Revolution in the Atlantic World, 1789–1865*. Liverpool, UK: Liverpool University Press, 2015.

Daut, Marlene. "When France Extorted Haiti—the Greatest Heist in History." *Conversation*, July 9, 2021. https://theconversation.com/when-france-extorted-haiti-the -greatest-heist-in-history-137949.

Davis, Adrienne. "The Case for U.S. Reparations to African Americans." In *Redress for Historical Injustices in the United States*, edited by Michael T. Martin and Marilyn Yaquinto, 371–78. Durham, NC: Duke University Press, 2007.

Davis, Angela. *Abolition Democracy: Beyond Empire, Prisons, and Torture*. New York: Seven Stories Press, 2005.

Davis, Angela. *Women, Race and Class*. New York: Vintage Books, 1983. First published 1981 by Random House.

Davis, Thadious. "The Object of Property." In *Games of Property: Law, Race, Gender, and Faulkner's "Go Down, Moses."* Durham, NC: Duke University Press, 2003.

De Genova, Nicholas. "The 'Migrant Crisis' as Racial Crisis: Do *Black Lives Matter* in Europe?" *Ethnic and Racial Studies* 41, no. 10 (2018): 1765–82.

Desyllas, Moshoula Capous. "A Critique of the Global Trafficking Discourse and U.S. Policy." *Journal of Sociology and Social Welfare* 34, no. 4 (December 2007): 57–79.

Dilts, Andrew. "Crisis, Critique, and Abolition." In *A Time for Critique*, edited by Bernard E. Harcourt and Didier Fassin, 230–51. New York: Columbia University Press, 2019.

Doezema, Jo. "Loose Women or Lost Women? The Re-emergence of the Myth of 'White Slavery' in Contemporary Discourses of 'Trafficking in Women.'" *Gender Issues* 18, no. 1 (2000): 23–50.

Doezema, Jo. "Ouch! Western Feminists' 'Wounded Attachment' to the Third World Prostitute." *Feminist Review* 67 (2001): 16–38.

Doezema, Jo. *Sex Slaves and Discourse Masters: The Construction of Trafficking*. London: Zed Books, 2010.

Dorsey, Peter. *Common Bondage: Slavery as Metaphor in Revolutionary America*. Knoxville: University of Tennessee Press, 2009.

Dottridge, Mike. "Effects of Anti-trafficking Policies on Migrants." In *Routledge Handbook of Migration and Development*, edited by Tanja Bastia and Ronald Skeldon, 409–20. New York: Routledge, 2020.

"Dramatic Rescue as Yazidis Flee ISIS." CNN, August 11, 2014. Video. https://www.cnn
.com/videos/world/2014/08/11/watson-yazidis-rescue-iraq-isis-orig-mg.cnn.

Du Bois, W. E. B. *Black Reconstruction in America, 1860–1880*. New York: Free Press, 1998. First published 1935 by Harcourt, Brace and Company.

Du Bois, W. E. B. *The World and Africa*. Edited by Henry Louis Gates Jr. New York: Oxford University Press, 2007.

Dupuy, Alex. *From Revolutionary Slaves to Powerless Citizens: Essays on the Politics and Economics of Underdevelopment, 1804–2013*. New York: Routledge, 2014.

Dupuy, Alex. *Haiti in the World Economy: Class, Race, and Underdevelopment Since 1700*. New York: Routledge, 2018.

Durisin, Elya, Emily van der Meulen, and Chris Bruckert. "Contextualizing Sex Work: Challenging Discourses and Confronting Narratives." In *Red Light Labour: Sex Work, Agency, and Resistance*, 3–24. Vancouver: UBC Press, 2018.

"Editorial: The Peculiar Institution." *Scientific American* 286, no. 4 (April 2002): 8–9.

Englund, Harri. *Prisoners of Freedom: Human Rights and the African Poor*. Berkeley: University of California Press, 2016.

Eudell, Demetrius. "Modernity and the 'Work of History.'" In *After Man, Towards the Human: Critical Essays on Sylvia Wynter*, edited by Anthony Bogues, 1–24. Kingston, Jamaica: Ian Randle Publishers, 2006.

Fassin, Didier. *Humanitarian Reason: A Moral History of the Present*. Translated by Rachel Gomme. Berkeley: University of California Press, 2011.

Feldman, Keith. "Empire's Verticality: The Af/Pak Frontier, Visual Culture, and Racialization from Above." *Comparative American Studies* 9, no. 4 (2011): 325–41.

Feimster, Crystal. *Southern Horrors: Women and the Politics of Rape and Lynching*. Cambridge, MA: Harvard University Press, 2009.

Ferguson, James. *The Anti-politics Machine: "Development," Depoliticization, and Bureaucratic Power in Lesotho*. Minneapolis: University of Minnesota Press, 1994.

Ferguson, James. *Give a Man a Fish: Reflections on the New Politics of Distribution*. Durham, NC: Duke University Press, 2015.

Ferguson, Roderick A., and Grace K. Hong. "The Sexual and Racial Contradictions of Neoliberalism." *Journal of Homosexuality* 59, no. 7 (2012): 1057–64.

Foner, Eric. *Gateway to Freedom: The Hidden History of the Underground Railroad*. New York: W. W. Norton, 2015.

Forsdick, Charles, and Christian Høgsbjerg. Introduction to *The Black Jacobins Reader*, edited by Charles Forsdick and Christian Høgsbjerg, 1–52. Durham, NC: Duke University Press, 2017.

Franklin, V. P. "Commentary—Reparations as a Development Strategy: The CARICOM Reparations Commission." *Journal of African American History* 98, no. 3 (2013): 363–66.

Free the Slaves. *Community-Based Model for Fighting Slavery*. Report, June 19, 2015.

Free the Slaves. "Trafficking's Footprint: Two-Phase Baseline Study of Child Trafficking in 34 Communities in 6 Districts in Ghana." April 2018. https://www.freetheslaves.net/wp-content/uploads/2018/04/Traffickings-Footprint-in-Ghana-April-2018.pdf.

Gaffield, Julia. *Haitian Connections in the Atlantic World: Recognition after Revolution*. Chapel Hill: University of North Carolina Press, 2015.

Gallagher, Anne. "Two Cheers for the Trafficking Protocol." *Anti-Trafficking Review* 4 (2015): 14–32.

Gallagher, Anne. "Improving the Effectiveness of the International Law of Human Trafficking: A Vision for the Future of the US Trafficking in Persons Reports." *Human Rights Review* 12, no. 3 (2011): 381–400.

Gann, Marjorie, and Janet Willen. *Five Thousand Years of Slavery.* Toronto: Tundra Books, 2015.

Garb, Margaret. *Freedom's Ballot: African American Political Struggles in Chicago from Abolition to the Great Migration.* Chicago: University of Chicago Press, 2014.

Garvey, Marcus. "The Principles of the Universal Negro Improvement Association." November 25, 1922. https://www.blackpast.org/african-american-history/1922-marcus-garvey-principles-universal-negro-improvement-association/.

Gausman, Jewel, Miriam Chernoff, Angela Duger, Jacqueline Bhabha, and Hillary Chu. "When We Raise Our Voice: The Challenge of Eradicating Labor Exploitation: An Evaluation of a Community Empowerment Intervention in Uttar Pradesh, India." Boston: François Xavier Bagnoud Center for Health and Human Rights at Harvard University, 2016.

Geffert, Garry. "H-2A Guestworker Program: A Legacy of Importing Agricultural Labor." In *The Human Cost of Food: Farmworkers' Lives, Labor, and Advocacy,* edited by Charles Thompson and Melinda Wiggins, 113–36. Austin: University of Texas Press, 2002.

Getachew, Adom. *Worldmaking after Empire: The Rise and Fall of Self-Determination.* Princeton, NJ: Princeton University Press, 2019.

Gilmore, Ruth Wilson. "Geographies of Racial Capitalism." *Antipode,* June 1, 2020. https://antipodeonline.org/geographies-of-racial-capitalism/.

Gilmore, Ruth Wilson. "Globalisation and US Prison Growth: From Military Keynesianism to Post-Keynesian Militarism." *Race and Class* 40, no. 2–3 (1999): 171–88.

Gilmore, Ruth Wilson. *Golden Gulag: Prisons, Surplus, Crisis, and Opposition in Globalizing California.* Berkeley: University of California Press, 2006.

Gordon, Avery. *Ghostly Matters: Haunting and the Sociological Imagination.* Minneapolis: University of Minnesota Press, 2008.

Grant, Kevin. *A Civilised Savagery: Britain and the New Slaveries in Africa, 1884–1926.* New York: Taylor and Francis, 2004.

Gray, Herman. "Race, Media, and the Cultivation of Concern." *Communication and Critical/Cultural Studies* 10, no. 2–3 (2013): 253–58.

Gray, Herman. "Subject(ed) to Recognition." *American Quarterly* 65, no. 4 (2013): 771–98.

Grewal, Inderpal. *Transnational America: Feminisms, Diasporas, Neoliberalisms.* Durham, NC: Duke University Press, 2005.

Hall, Stuart. "Race, the Floating Signifier: What More Is There to Say about 'Race'?" In *Stuart Hall: Selected Writings on Race and Difference,* edited by Paul Gilroy and Ruth Wilson Gilmore, 359–73. Durham, NC: Duke University Press, 2021.

Hall, Stuart. "The West and the Rest: Discourse and Power." In *Stuart Hall Essential Essays.* Vol. 2, *Identity and Diaspora,* edited by David Morley, 141–84. Durham, NC: Duke University Press, 2019.

Hall, Stuart. "The Work of Representation." In *Representation: Cultural Representations and Signifying Practices,* edited by Stuart Hall, 13–74. London: Sage, 1997.

Hanchard, Michael. "Black Memory versus State Memory: Notes toward a Method." *Small Axe* 26 (June 2008): 45–62.

Harris, Cheryl. "Whiteness as Property." *Harvard Law Review* 106, no. 8 (1993): 1707–91.

Harrison, Faye V., ed. *Decolonizing Anthropology: Moving Further toward an Anthropology for Liberation*. Washington, DC: American Association of Anthropology, 1991.

Hartman, Saidiya. *Lose Your Mother: A Journey along the Atlantic Slave Route*. New York: Farrar, Straus and Giroux, 2007.

Hartman, Saidiya. *Scenes of Subjection: Terror, Slavery, and Self-Making in Nineteenth-Century America*. New York: Oxford University Press, 1997.

Hartman, Saidiya. *Wayward Lives, Beautiful Experiments*. New York: W. W. Norton, 2019.

Hartman, Saidiya, and Frank B. Wilderson. "The Position of the Unthought." *Qui Parle* 13, no. 2 (Spring/Summer 2003): 183–201.

Harvey, David. *The New Imperialism*. Oxford: Oxford University Press, 2005.

Haynes, Dina Francesca. "Human Trafficking and Migration." In *Human Rights in Crisis*, edited by Alice Bullard, 111–28. Aldershot, UK: Ashgate, 2008.

Henry, Charles P. *Long Overdue: The Politics of Racial Reparations*. New York: NYU Press, 2007.

Hesford, Wendy. *Spectacular Rhetorics: Human Rights Visions, Recognitions, Feminisms*. Durham, NC: Duke University Press, 2011.

Hesford, Wendy. "Trafficking American Exceptionality." *Women's Studies in Communication* 41, no. 4 (2018): 310–14.

Hesford, Wendy, and Amy Shuman. "Precarious Narratives: Media Accounts of Islamic State Sexual Violence." In *Precarious Rhetorics*, edited by Wendy Hesford, Adela Licona, and Christa Teston, 41–61. Athens: Ohio State University Press, 2018.

Heynen, Robert, and Emily van der Meulen. "Anti-trafficking Saviors: Celebrity, Slavery, and Branded Activism." *Crime, Media, Culture: An International Journal*, April 22, 2021.

Hicks, Cheryl. *Talk with You Like a Woman: African American Women, Justice, and Reform in New York, 1890-1935*. Chapel Hill: University of North Carolina Press, 2010.

Hill, Annie. "The Rhetoric of Modern-Day Slavery: Analogical Links and Historical Kinks in the United Kingdom's Anti-trafficking Plan." *philoSOPHIA* 7, no. 2 (2017): 241–60.

Hill, Annie. "How to Stage a Raid: Police, Media, and the Master Narrative of Trafficking." *Anti-Trafficking Review* 7 (2016): 39–55.

Hinton, Elizabeth. *From the War on Poverty to the War on Crime: The Making of Mass Incarceration in America*. Cambridge, MA: Harvard University Press, 2016.

Hogarth, Rana. *Medicalizing Blackness: Making Racial Difference in the Atlantic World, 1780-1840*. Chapel Hill: University of North Carolina Press, 2017.

Hoffman, Diane. "Saving Children, Saving Haiti? Child Vulnerability and Narratives of the Nation." *Childhood* 19, no. 2 (2012): 155–68.

Hoffman, Diane. "Slaves and Angels: The Child as a Developmental Casualty in Haiti." *Autrepart* 4 (2014): 95–109.

Holden, Christopher. "Bitter Harvest: Housing Conditions of Migrant and Seasonal Farmworkers." In *The Human Cost of Food: Farmworkers' Lives, Labor, and Advocacy*, edited by Charles Thompson and Melinda Wiggins, 169–94. Austin: University of Texas Press, 2002.

Holden, Vanessa. *Surviving Southampton: African American Women and Resistance in Nat Turner's Community*. Urbana: University of Illinois Press, 2021.

Holmes, Seth. *Fresh Fruit, Broken Bodies: Migrant Farmworkers in the U.S.* Berkeley: University of California Press, 2013.

Holsey, Bayo. *Routes of Remembrance: Refashioning the Slave Trade in Ghana.* Chicago: University of Chicago Press, 2008.

Hong, Grace K. "Property." In *Key Words for American Cultural Studies,* edited by Bruce Burgett and Glenn Hendler. New York: NYU Press, 2007. https://keywords.nyupress.org/american-cultural-studies/essay/property/.

Hong, Grace K. "Neoliberalism." *Critical Ethnic Studies* 1, no. 1 (Spring 2015): 56–67.

Hong, Grace K. "Speculative Surplus: Asian American Racialization and the Neoliberal Shift." *Social Text* 36, no. 2 (2018): 107–22.

Horton, James, and Lois Horton. *In Hope of Liberty: Culture, Community and Protest Among Northern Free Blacks.* New York: Oxford University Press, 1998.

Howard, Neil. "Accountable to Whom? Accountable for What? Understanding Anti-child Trafficking Discourse and Policy in Southern Benin." *Anti-Trafficking Review* 1 (2012): 43–59.

Howard, Neil. *Child Trafficking, Youth Labour Mobility and the Politics of Protection.* London: Palgrave Macmillan, 2017.

Hua, Julietta. *Trafficking Women's Human Rights.* Minneapolis: University of Minnesota Press, 2011.

Hudson, Peter. *Bankers and Empire: How Wall Street Colonized the Caribbean.* Chicago: University of Chicago Press, 2017.

Hunter, Tera. *Bound in Wedlock: Slave and Free Black Marriage in the Nineteenth Century.* Cambridge, MA: Harvard University Press, 2019.

Hyde, Alan. *Bodies of Law.* Princeton, NJ: Princeton University Press, 1997.

International Network of Scholars and Activists for Afrikan Reparations. "Global Report." United Nations International Decade for People of African Descent (IDPAD), September 2019. https://www.inosaar.llc.ed.ac.uk/sites/default/files/atoms/files/inosaar_global_report_sept_2019_final.pdf.

Irwin, Mary Ann. "'White Slavery' as Metaphor: Anatomy of a Moral Panic." *Ex Post Facto: The History Journal* 5 (1996). Accessed May 10, 2020. https://www.walnet.org/csis/papers/irwin-wslavery.html.

Jackson, John L., Jr. *Thin Description: Ethnography and the African Hebrew Israelites of Jerusalem.* Cambridge, MA: Harvard University Press, 2013.

Jackson, John L., Jr. "On Ethnographic Sincerity." Supplement, *Current Anthropology* 51 (October 2010): S279–87.

James, C. L. R. "Preface to the First Edition." *The Black Jacobins: Toussaint L'Ouverture and the San Domingo Revolution.* 2nd ed. New York: Vintage Books, 1989. First published 1938 by The Dial Press.

James, C. L. R. *The Black Jacobins: Toussaint L'Ouverture and the San Domingo Revolution.* 2nd ed. New York: Vintage Books, 1989.

Johnson, Laura, Jordan Howell, and Kyle Evered. "'Where Nothing Was Before': (Re)Producing Population and Place in Ghana's Volta River Project." *Journal of Cultural Geography* 32, no. 2 (2015): 195–213.

Juris, Jeffrey. *Networking Futures: The Movements against Corporate Globalization.* Durham, NC: Duke University Press, 2008.

Kaneti, Marina. "Project Trafficking: Global Unity in Addressing a Universal Challenge?" *Human Rights Review* 12 (2011): 345–61.

Kang, Laura Hyun Yi. *Traffic in Asian Women*. Durham, NC: Duke University Press, 2020.

Kelley, Robin D. G. "'A Day of Reckoning': Dreams of Reparations." In *Redress for Historical Injustices in the United States*, edited by Michael T. Martin and Marilyn Yaquinto, 203–21. Durham, NC: Duke University Press, 2007.

Kelley, Robin D. G. *Hammer and Hoe: Alabama Communists During the Great Depression*. Chapel Hill: University of North Carolina Press, 1990.

Kelley, Robin D. G. "On Reparations and Decolonization." Lecture presented at York University, June 29, 2021.

Kempadoo, Kamala. "Introduction: Abolitionism, Criminal Justice, and Transnational Feminism: Twenty-First-Century Perspectives on Human Trafficking." In *Trafficking and Prostitution Reconsidered: New Perspectives on Migration, Sex Work, and Human Rights*. 2nd ed. Edited by Kamala Kempadoo, Jyoti Sanghera, and Bandana Pattanaik, vii–xlii. Boulder, CO: Paradigm Publishers, 2012.

Kempadoo, Kamala. "The Modern-Day White (Wo)Man's Burden: Trends in Anti-Trafficking and Anti-Slavery Campaigns." *Journal of Human Trafficking* 1 (2015): 8–20.

Kempadoo, Kamala. "Sex Workers' Rights Organizations and Anti-trafficking Campaigns." In *Trafficking and Prostitution Reconsidered: New Perspectives on Migration, Sex Work and Human Rights*. 2nd ed. Edited by Kamala Kempadoo, Jyoti Sanghera, and Bandana Pattanaik, 149–58. Boulder, CO: Paradigm, 2012.

Kempadoo, Kamala. "Women of Color and the Global Sex Trade: Transnational Feminist Perspective." *Meridians* 1, no. 2 (Spring 2001): 28–51.

King, Martin Luther, Jr. "Letter from a Birmingham Jail." April 16, 1963. https://www.africa.upenn.edu/Articles_Gen/Letter_Birmingham.html.

King, Shani. "Owning Laura Silsby's Shame: How the Haitian Child Trafficking Scheme Embodies the Western Disregard for the Integrity of Poor Families." *Harvard Human Rights Journal* 25, no. 1 (2012): 1–47.

King, Tiffany Lethabo. *The Black Shoals: Offshore Formations of Black and Native Studies*. Durham, NC: Duke University Press, 2019.

Kleinman, Julie. *Adventure Capital: Migration and the Making of an African Hub in Paris*. Berkeley: University of California Press, 2019.

Kosmatopoulos, Nikolas. "The Birth of the Workshop: Technomoral, Peace Expertise, and the Care of the Self in the Middle East." *Public Culture* 26, no. 3 (2014): 529–58.

Kraidy, Marwan. "The Projectilic Image: Islamic State's Digital Visual Warfare and Global Networked Affect." *Media, Culture, and Society* 39, no. 8 (2017): 1194–209.

Krause, Monika. *The Good Project: Humanitarian Relief NGOs and the Fragmentation of Reason*. Chicago: University of Chicago Press, 2014.

Lerum, Kari. "Human Wrongs vs. Human Rights." *Contexts* 13, no. 1 (Winter 2014). https://contexts.org/articles/selling-people/#lerum.

Lewis, Jovan Scott. *Scammer's Yard: The Crime of Black Repair in Jamaica*. Minneapolis: University of Minnesota, 2020.

Lobasz, Jennifer K. "Beyond Border Security: Feminist Approaches to Human Trafficking." *Security Studies* 18 (2009): 319–44.

Locke, John. *Second Treatise of Government*. 1690. https://www.gutenberg.org/files/7370/7370-h/7370-h.htm.

Lorde, Audre. "Poetry Is Not a Luxury." In *Sister Outsider: Essays and Speeches*, 36–39. Berkeley, CA: Crossing Press, 2007.

Lorde, Audre. "The Uses of Anger: Women Responding to Racism." In *Sister Outsider: Essays and Speeches*, 124–33. Berkeley, CA: Crossing Press, 2007.

Loveland, Rachel. "Rattling the Chains: East African Slavery." With Wycliffe Muga. *PAA Tanzania* 85 (March 2017): 14–19.

Lowe, Lisa. *The Intimacies of Four Continents*. Durham, NC: Duke University Press, 2015.

Loyd, Jenna, and Ruth Wilson Gilmore. "Race, Capitalist Crisis, Abolitionist Organizing: An Interview with Ruth Wilson Gilmore." In *Beyond Walls and Cages: Prisons, Borders, and Global Crisis*, edited by Jenna M. Loyd, Matt Mitchelson, and Andrew Burridge, 42–54. Athens: University of Georgia Press, 2012.

Lubiano, Wahneema. "Black Ladies, Welfare Queens, and State Minstrels." In *Race-ing Justice, En-Gendering Power: Essays on Anita Hill, Clarence Thomas, and the Construction of Social Reality*, edited by Toni Morrison, 323–63. New York: Pantheon, 1992.

Lutz, Catherine, and Jane Collins. *Reading National Geographic*. Chicago: University of Chicago Press, 1993.

Madison, D. Soyini. *Critical Ethnography: Method, Ethics, Performance*. 2nd ed. New York: Sage Publications, 2011.

Mahdavi, Pardis. *From Trafficking to Terror: Constructing a Global Social Problem*. New York: Routledge, 2013.

Maher, Stephanie. "Historicizing 'Irregular' Migration from Senegal to Europe." *Anti-Trafficking Review* 9 (2017): 77–91.

Mai, Nicola. "'Too Much Suffering': Understanding the Interplay between Migration, Bounded Exploitation and Trafficking through Nigerian Sex Workers' Experiences." *Sociological Research Online* (2016). https://www.socresonline.org.uk/21/4/13.html.

Mason, John Edwin. "History, Mine and Ours: Charlottesville's Blue Ribbon Commission and the Terror Attacks of August 2017." In *Charlottesville 2017: The Legacy of Race and Inequity*, edited by Louis P. Nelson and Claudrena N. Harold, 19–36. Charlottesville: University of Virginia Press, 2018.

Mathers, Kathryn. "Mr. Kristof, I Presume? Saving Africa in the Footsteps of Nicholas Kristof." *Transition* 107 (2012): 14–31.

Maynard, Robyn. "Do Black Sex Workers' Lives Matter? Whitewashed Anti-Slavery, Racial Justice, and Abolition." In *Red Light Labour: Sex Work, Regulation, Agency, and Resistance*, edited by Elya Durisin, Emily van der Meulen, and Chris Bruckert, 281–92. Vancouver: UBC Press, 2018.

McDowell, Deborah E., and Arnold Rampersand. Introduction to *Slavery and the Literary Imagination*, vii–xiii. Baltimore: Johns Hopkins University Press, 1989.

McGranahan, Carole. "Love and Empire: The CIA, Tibet, and Covert Humanitarianism." In *Ethnographies of U.S. Empire*, edited by Carole McGranahan and John F. Collins, 333–49. Durham, NC: Duke University Press, 2018.

McKay, Nellie, and Frances Smith Foster. Introduction to *Incidents in the Life of a Slave Girl*, by Harriet Jacobs. New York: W. W. Norton, 2001.

McKittrick, Katherine. *Demonic Grounds: Black Women and the Cartographies of Struggle*. Minneapolis: University of Minnesota Press, 2006.

McKittrick, Katherine, ed. *Sylvia Wynter: On Being Human as Praxis*. Durham, NC: Duke University Press, 2015.

McLaurin, Melton. *Celia, a Slave*. Athens: University of Georgia Press, 1991.

Melamed, Jodi. "Racial Capitalism." *Critical Ethnic Studies* 1, no. 1 (2015): 76–85.

Melamed, Jodi. *Represent and Destroy: Rationalizing Violence in the New Racial Capitalism*. Minneapolis: University of Minnesota Press, 2011.

Melamed, Jodi. "The Spirit of Neoliberalism: From Racial Liberalism to Neoliberal Multiculturalism." *Social Text* 24, no. 4 (2006): 1–24.

Merry, Sally Engle. *The Seductions of Quantification: Measuring Human Rights, Gender Violence, and Sex Trafficking*. Chicago: University of Chicago Press, 2016.

Merry, Sally Engle, Kevin E. Davis, and Benedict Kingsbury, eds. *The Quiet Power of Indicators: Measuring Governance, Corruption, and the Rule of Law*. Cambridge: Cambridge University Press, 2015.

Merry, Sally Engle, and Vibhuti Ramachandran. "The Limits of Consent: Sex Trafficking and the Problem of International Paternalism." In *Paternalism beyond Borders*, edited by Michael Barnett, 224–55. Cambridge: Cambridge University Press, 2016.

Mignolo, Walter. "Sylvia Wynter: What Does It Mean to Be Human?" In *Sylvia Wynter: On Being Human as Praxis*, edited by Katherine McKittrick, 106–23. Durham, NC: Duke University Press, 2015.

Millar, Hayli, and Tamara O'Doherty. "Racialized, Gendered, and Sensationalized: An Examination of Canadian Anti-trafficking Laws, Their Enforcement, and Their (Re)Presentation." *Canadian Journal of Law and Society* 35, no. 1 (April 2020): 23–44.

Miller, Daniel, and Don Slater. *The Internet: An Ethnographic Approach*. London: Routledge, 2000.

Mills, Charles. *Blackness Visible: Essays on the Philosophy of Race*. Ithaca, NY: Cornell University Press, 1998.

Mills, Charles. "The Illumination of Blackness." In *Antiblackness*, edited by Moon-Kie Jung and João H. Costa Vargas, 17–36. Durham, NC: Duke University Press, 2021.

Mills, Charles. *The Racial Contract*. Ithaca, NY: Cornell University Press, 1997.

Mills, Charles. "Racial Liberalism." *PMLA* 123, no. 5 (2008): 1380–97.

Moeller, Susan. *Compassion Fatigue: How the Media Sell Disease, Famine, War and Death*. New York: Routledge, 1999.

Morgan, Jennifer. "*Partus sequitur ventrem*: Law, Race, and Reproduction in Colonial Slavery." *Small Axe* 22, no. 1 (2018): 1–17.

Morgan, Jennifer. *Laboring Women: Reproduction and Gender in New World Slavery*. Philadelphia: University of Pennsylvania Press, 2004.

Morrison, Toni. *Playing in the Dark: Whiteness and the Literary Imagination*. Vintage, 1993.

Moynihan, Daniel Patrick. *The Negro Family: The Case for National Action*. Washington, DC: Office of Policy Planning and Research, US Department of Labor, March 1965. https://www.dol.gov/general/aboutdol/history/webid-moynihan.

Muhammad, Khalil. *The Condemnation of Blackness: Race, Crime, and the Making of Modern Urban America*. Cambridge, MA: Harvard University Press, 2010.

Müller-Wille, Staffan. "Linnaeus and the Four Corners of the World." In *The Cultural Politics of Blood, 1500–1900*, edited by Kimberly Anne Coles, Ralph Bauer, Zita Nunes, and Carla L. Peterson, 191–209. Basingstoke, UK: Palgrave Macmillan, 2015.

Mullings, Leith. *On Our Own Terms: Race, Class, and Gender in the Lives of African American Women*. New York: Routledge, 1997.

Murphy, Laura. *The New Slave Narrative: The Battles over Representations of Contemporary Slavery*. New York: Columbia University Press, 2019.

Murphy, Michelle. *The Economization of Life*. Durham, NC: Duke University Press, 2017.

Musto, Jennifer. *Control and Protect: Collaboration, Carceral Protection, and Domestic Sex Trafficking in the United States*. Berkeley: University of California Press, 2016.

Musto, Jennifer, and danah boyd. "The Trafficking-Technology Nexus." *Social Politics* 21, no. 3 (2014): 461–83.

Musto, Jennifer, Mitali Thakor, and Borislav Gerasimov. "Editorial: Between Hope and Hype: Critical Evaluations of Technology's Role in Anti-trafficking." *Anti-Trafficking Review* 14 (2020): 1–14.

Myers, Ella. "Beyond the Psychological Wage: Du Bois on White Dominion." *Political Theory* 47, no. 1 (2019): 6–31.

Nelson, Alondra. *The Social Life of DNA: Race, Reparations and Reconciliation after the Genome*. Boston: Beacon Press, 2016.

Nguyen, Mimi. *The Gift of Freedom: War, Debt, and Other Refugee Passages*. Durham, NC: Duke University Press, 2012.

Nkrumah, Kwame. "READ: Kwame Nkrumah's Iconic 1963 Speech on African Unity." Speech at the inaugural ceremony of the Organization of African Unity, Addis Ababa, Ethiopia, 1963. May 24, 2019. https://face2faceafrica.com/article/read-kwame-nkrumahs-iconic-1963-speech-on-african-unity.

Noble, Safiya. *Algorithms of Oppression: How Search Engines Reinforce Racism*. New York: NYU Press, 2018.

O'Connell Davidson, Julia. *Modern Slavery: The Margins of Freedom*. London: Palgrave Macmillan, 2015.

O'Connell Davidson, Julia. "Will the Real Sex Slave Please Stand Up?" *Feminist Review* 83 (2006): 4–22.

Okyere, Sam. "Are Working Children's Rights and Child Labour Abolition Complementary or Opposing Realms?" *International Social Work* 56, no. 1 (2013): 80–91.

Okyere, Sam. "Moral Economies and Child Labour in Artisanal Gold Mining in Ghana." In *Revisiting Slavery and Antislavery: Towards a Critical Analysis*, edited by Laura Brace and Julia O'Connell Davidson, 231–60. Cham, Switzerland: Palgrave Macmillan, 2018.

Okyere, Sam, Nana Agyeman, and Emmanuel Saboro. "'Why Was He Videoing Us?': The Ethics and Politics of Audio-Visual Propaganda in Child Trafficking and Human Trafficking Campaigns." *Anti-Trafficking Review* 16 (2021): 47–68.

Operation Underground Railroad. "Why the Underground Railroad." Accessed May 15, 2020. https://ourrescue.org/about#ugr.

Ortiz, Paul. *An African American and Latinx History of the United States*. Boston: Beacon Press, 2018.

Otero, Gerardo. "Neoliberal Globalization, NAFTA, and Migration: Mexico's Loss of Food and Labor Sovereignty." *Journal of Poverty* 15, no. 4 (2011): 384–402.

Page, Allison. "'How Many Slaves Work for You?' Race, New Media, and Neoliberal Consumer Activism." *Journal of Consumer Culture* 17, no. 1 (2014): 46–61.

Parreñas, Rhacel. *Illicit Flirtations: Labor, Migration, and Sex Trafficking in Tokyo*. Palo Alto, CA: Stanford University Press, 2011.

Patterson, Orlando. "Trafficking, Gender, and Slavery: Past and Present." In *The Legal Understanding of Slavery: From the Historical to the Contemporary*, edited by Jean Allain, 322–59. Oxford: Oxford University Press, 2012.

Peck, Gunther. "White Slavery and Whiteness: A Transnational View of the Sources of Working-Class Radicalism and Racism." *Labor: Studies in Working-Class History of the Americas* 1, no. 2 (2004): 41–63.

Perkowski, Nina. "Deaths, Interventions, Humanitarianism and Human Rights in the Mediterranean 'Migration Crisis.'" *Mediterranean Politics* 21, no. 2 (2016): 331–35.

Peterson, Meghan, Bella Robinson, and Elena Shih. "The New Virtual Crackdown on Sex Workers' Rights: Perspectives from the United States." *Anti-Trafficking Review* 12 (2019): 189–93.

Pierre, Jemima. *The Predicament of Blackness: Postcolonial Ghana and the Politics of Race*. Chicago: University of Chicago Press, 2013.

Pierre, Jemima. "The Racial Vernaculars of Development: A View from West Africa." *American Anthropologist* 122, no. 1 (2019): 86–98.

Pliley, Jessica. *Policing Sexuality: The Mann Act and the Making of the FBI*. Cambridge, MA: Harvard University Press, 2014.

Quirk, Joel. *The Anti-Slavery Project: From the Slave Trade to Human Trafficking*. Philadelphia: University of Pennsylvania Press, 2011.

Rabinowitz, Richard. *Curating America: Journeys through Storyscapes of the American Past*. Chapel Hill: University of North Carolina Press, 2016.

Radstone, Susannah, and Bill Schwarz. Introduction to *Memory: Histories, Theories, Debates*, edited by Susannah Radstone and Bill Schwarz, 1–9. New York: Fordham University Press, 2010.

Ransby, Barbara. "Henry Louis Gates' Dangerously Wrong Slave History." *Colorlines*, May 3, 2010. https://www.colorlines.com/articles/henry-louis-gates-dangerously -wrong-slave-history.

Ray, Sohomjit. "Afterlives of Slavery, Epistemologies of Race: Black Women and Wake Work." *WSQ: Women's Studies Quarterly* 48, no. 1/2 (Spring/Summer 2020): 60–63.

Renda, Mary A. *Taking Haiti: Military Occupation and the Culture of U.S. Imperialism, 1915–1940*. Chapel Hill: University of North Carolina Press, 2001.

Richardson, Laurie, Cara Kennedy, Fondasyon Limyè Lavi, and Free the Slaves. "Haiti's Model Communities: Ending *Restavèk* Child Domestic Servitude." March 2014. https://www.freetheslaves.net/wp-content/uploads/2015/03/HaitiReport_Mar2014 _Mar21_-English_Final_web_small.pdf.

Richie, Beth. *Arrested Justice: Black Women, Violence, and America's Prison Nation*. New York: NYU Press, 2012.

Roberts, Dorothy. *Fatal Invention: How Science, Politics, and Big Business Re-create Race in the Twenty-First Century*. New York: New Press, 2011.

Roberts, Dorothy. *Killing the Black Body: Race, Reproduction, and the Meaning of Liberty*. New York: Vintage Books, 2017. First published 1997 by Pantheon.

Roberts, Randy. "Galveston's Jack Johnson: Flourishing in the Dark." *Southwestern Historical Quarterly* 87, no. 1 (1983): 37–56.

Robinson, Cedric. *Black Marxism: The Making of the Black Radical Tradition*. Chapel Hill: University of North Carolina Press, 2000. First published 1983 by Zed Press.

Rodney, Walter. *How Europe Underdeveloped Africa*. New York: Verso, 2018. First published 1972 by Bogle-L'Ouverture Publications.

Roediger, David. *The Wages of Whiteness: Race and the Making of the American Working Class*. London: Verso, 1991.

Rose, Gillian. *Visual Methodologies: An Introduction to the Interpretation of Visual Materials*. 2nd ed. London: Sage, 2007.

Rotman, Youval. *Byzantine Slavery and the Mediterranean World*. Cambridge, MA: Harvard University Press, 2009.

Rusert, Britt. "Naturalizing Coercion: The Tuskegee Experiments and the Laboratory Life of the Plantation." In *Captivating Technology*, edited by Ruha Benjamin, 25–49. Durham, NC: Duke University Press, 2019.

Saucier, P. Khalil, and Tryon P. Woods. "Ex Aqua: The Mediterranean Basin, African on the Move and the Politics of Policing." *Theoria: A Journal of Social and Political Theory* 61, no. 141 (December 2014): 55–75.

Sasser, Jade S. *On Infertile Ground: Population Control and Women's Rights in the Era of Climate Change*. New York: NYU Press, 2018.

Scannell, R. Joshua. "This Is Not Minority Report: Predictive Policing and Population Racism." In *Captivating Technology*, edited by Ruha Benjamin, 107–29. Durham, NC: Duke University Press, 2019.

Schwarz, Bill. "Haiti and Historical Time." In *The Black Jacobins Reader*, edited by Charles Forsdick and Christian Høgsbjerg, 93–114. Durham, NC: Duke University Press, 2017.

Scott, David. "Preface: Evil Beyond Repair." *Small Axe* 55 (2018): vii–x.

Scott, David. "The Theory of Haiti: The Black Jacobins and the Poetics of Universal History." In *The Black Jacobins Reader*, edited by Charles Forsdick and Christian Høgsbjerg, 115–38. Durham, NC: Duke University Press, 2017.

Sexton, Jared. "Abolition Terminable and Interminable." In *Revisiting Slavery and Antislavery*, edited by Laura Brace and Julia O'Connell Davidson, 305–25. London: Palgrave Macmillan, 2018.

Sexton, Jared. "People-of-Color-Blindness: Notes on the Afterlife of Slavery." *Social Text* 28, no. 2 (2010): 31–56.

Sexton, Jared. "Racial Profiling and the Societies of Control." In *Warfare in the American Homeland: Policing and Prison in a Penal Democracy*, edited by Joy James, 197–218. Durham, NC: Duke University Press, 2007.

Shange, Savannah. *Progressive Dystopia: Abolition, Antiblackness, and Schooling in San Francisco*. Durham, NC: Duke University Press, 2019.

Sharma, Nandita. "Anti-trafficking Rhetoric and the Making of a Global Apartheid." *NWSA Journal* 17, no. 3 (2005): 88–111.

Sharma, Nandita. "'The New Order of Things': Immobility as Protection in the Regime of Immigration Controls." *Anti-Trafficking Review* 9 (2017): 31–47.

Sharpe, Christina. *In the Wake: On Blackness and Being.* Durham, NC: Duke University Press, 2016.

Shih, Elena. "Duplicitous Freedom: Moral and Material Care Work in Anti-trafficking Rescue and Rehabilitation." *Critical Sociology* 44, no. 7–8 (2018): 1077–86.

Shih, Elena. "Freedom Markets: Consumption and Commerce across Human-Trafficking Rescue in Thailand." *Positions: Asia Critique* 25, no. 4 (2017): 769–94.

Shih, Elena. "Not in My 'Backyard Abolitionism': Vigilante Rescue against American Sex Trafficking." *Sociological Perspectives* 59, no. 1 (2016): 66–90.

Shih, Elena. "The Trafficking Deportation Pipeline: Asian Body Work and the Auxiliary Policing of Racialized Poverty." *Feminist Formations* 33, no. 1 (Spring 2021): 56–73.

Silva, Denise Ferreira da. *Toward a Global Idea of Race.* Minneapolis: University of Minnesota Press, 2007.

Singh, Nikhil. *Black Is a Country: Race and the Unfinished Struggle for Democracy.* Cambridge, MA: Harvard University Press, 2004.

Singh, Nikhil. "Racial Formation in an Age of Permanent War." In *Racial Formation in the Twenty-First Century,* edited by Daniel Martinez HoSang, Oneka LaBennett, and Laura Pulido, 276–301. Berkeley: University of California Press, 2012.

Snorton, C. Riley. *Black on Both Sides: A Racial History of Trans Identity.* Minneapolis: University of Minnesota Press, 2017.

Snyder, Karen. "From Slavery to Freedom: Three-Year Field Test of the Free the Slaves Community Model." Community Liberation Initiative. Free the Slaves, 2018.

Soderlund, Gretchen. *Sex Trafficking, Scandal, and the Transformation of Journalism, 1885–1917.* Chicago: University of Chicago Press, 2013.

Sommerfelt, Tone, ed. *Child Domestic Labour in Haiti: Characteristics, Contexts and Organisation of Children's Residence, Relocation and Work.* Oslo: FAFO Institute for Applied Social Science, 2002.

Sommerfelt, Tone, and Jon Pedersen. "Child Labor in Haiti." In *The World of Child Labor: An Historical and Regional Survey,* edited by Hugh D. Hindman, 427–30. New York: M. E. Sharpe, 2009.

Sundiata, Ibrahim. *Brothers and Strangers: Black Zion, Black Slavery, 1914–1940.* Durham, NC: Duke University Press, 2003.

Spillers, Hortense. "Mama's Baby, Papa's Maybe: An American Grammar Book." In *Black, White, and in Color: Essays on American Literature and Culture,* 203–29. Chicago: University of Chicago Press, 2003.

Spillers, Hortense. "'Whatcha Gonna Do?'—Revisiting 'Mama's Baby, Papa's Maybe: An American Grammar Book': A Conversation with Hortense Spillers, Saidiya Hartman, Farah Jasmine Griffin, Shelly Eversley, and Jennifer L. Morgan." *Women's Studies Quarterly* 35, no. 1–2 (2007): 299–309.

Spivak, Gayatri. "Can the Subaltern Speak?" In *Marxism and the Interpretation of Culture,* edited by Cary Nelson and Lawrence Grossberg, 271–313. Urbana: University of Illinois Press, 1988.

Steinglass, Steven, and Gino Scarselli. *The Ohio State Constitution: A Reference Guide.* Westport: Praeger Publishers, 2004.

Stoler, Ann Laura. *Duress: Imperial Durabilities in Our Times.* Durham, NC: Duke University Press, 2016.

Suchland, Jennifer. *Economies of Violence: Transnational Feminism, Postsocialism, and the Politics of Sex Trafficking.* Durham, NC: Duke University Press, 2015.

Tagg, John. *The Burden of Representation: Essays on Photographies and Histories.* Minneapolis: University of Minnesota Press, 1988.

Taylor, Nikki. *Frontiers of Freedom: Cincinnati's Black Community 1802–1868.* Athens: Ohio University Press, 2005.

Thomas, Deborah. "The End of the West and the Future of Us All." *African Diaspora* 11 (2018): 123–43.

Thomas, Deborah. *Exceptional Violence: Embodied Citizenship in Transnational Jamaica.* Durham, NC: Duke University Press, 2011.

Thomas, Deborah. *Political Life in the Wake of the Plantation.* Durham, NC: Duke University Press, 2019.

Thompson, Charles, and Melinda Wiggins, eds. *The Human Cost of Food: Farmworkers' Lives, Labor, and Advocacy.* Austin: University of Texas Press, 2002.

Ticktin, Miriam. *Casualties of Care: Immigration and the Politics of Humanitarianism in France.* Berkeley: University of California Press, 2011.

Tillet, Salamishah. *Sites of Slavery: Citizenship and Racial Democracy in the Post–Civil Rights Imagination.* Durham, NC: Duke University Press, 2012.

Towns, Armond. "The (Racial) Biases of Communication: Rethinking Media and Blackness." *Social Identities* 21, no. 5 (2015): 474–88.

Trodd, Zoe. "Am I Still Not a Man and a Brother? Protest Memory in Contemporary Antislavery Visual Culture." *Slavery and Abolition* 34, no. 2 (2013): 338–52.

Trouillot, Michel-Rolph. *Silencing the Past: Power and the Production of History.* Boston: Beacon Press, 1995.

United Nations. *Protocol to Prevent, Suppress and Punish Trafficking in Persons Especially Women and Children, Supplementing the United Nations Convention against Transnational Organized Crime.* United Nations Human Rights Office of the High Commissioner, November 15, 2000. https://www.ohchr.org/en/professionalinterest/pages/protocoltraffickinginpersons.aspx.

United Nations. "UN Marks Day of Remembrance with Calls to End Modern Slavery." *UN News,* March 25, 2015. https://news.un.org/en/story/2015/03/494362-un-marks-day-remembrance-calls-end-modern-slavery.

United Nations. "UN Marks Day of Remembrance with Calls to Tackle Slavery's Lingering Consequences." *UN News,* March 25, 2014. https://news.un.org/en/story/2014/03/464662-un-marks-day-remembrance-calls-tackle-slaverys-lingering-consequences.

United Nations. *World Conference Against Racism, Racial Discrimination, Xenophobia, and Related Intolerance: Declaration and Programme of Action.* New York: United Nations Department of Public Information, 2002. https://www.ohchr.org/Documents/Publications/Durban_text_en.pdf.

United Nations General Assembly. "Report of the Working Group of Experts on People of African Descent on Its Mission to the United States of America." August 18, 2016. https://daccess-ods.un.org/tmp/2590324.87869263.html.

United Nations General Assembly. "Resolution 62/122. Permanent Memorial to and Remembrance of the Victims of Slavery and the Transatlantic Slave Trade." December 17, 2007. https://undocs.org/A/RES/62/122.

US Department of State. *2001 Trafficking in Persons Report*. June 2001. https://2009-2017 .state.gov/j/tip/rls/tiprpt/2001/index.htm.

US Department of State. *2002 Trafficking in Persons Report*. June 2002. https://2009-2017 .state.gov/j/tip/rls/tiprpt/2002/index.htm.

US Department of State. *2003 Trafficking in Persons Report*. June 2003. https://2009-2017 .state.gov/j/tip/rls/tiprpt/2003/index.htm.

US Department of State. *2007 Trafficking in Persons Report*. June 2007. https://2009-2017 .state.gov/j/tip/rls/tiprpt/2007/index.htm.

US Department of State. *2009 Trafficking in Persons Report*. June 2009. https://2009-2017 .state.gov/j/tip/rls/tiprpt/2009/index.htm.

US Department of State. *2010 Trafficking in Persons Report*. June 2010. https://2009-2017 .state.gov/j/tip/rls/tiprpt/2010/index.htm.

US Department of State. *2011 Trafficking in Persons Report*. June 2011. https://2009-2017 .state.gov/j/tip/rls/tiprpt/2011/index.htm.

US Department of State. *2012 Trafficking in Persons Report*. June 2012. https://2009-2017 .state.gov/j/tip/rls/tiprpt/2012/index.htm.

US Department of State. *2013 Trafficking in Persons Report*. June 2013. https://2009-2017 .state.gov/j/tip/rls/tiprpt/2013/index.htm.

US Department of State. *2015 Trafficking in Persons Report*. July 2015. https://2009-2017 .state.gov/j/tip/rls/tiprpt/2015/index.htm.

US Department of State. *2018 Trafficking in Persons Report*. June 2018. https://www.state .gov/reports/2018-trafficking-in-persons-report/.

US Department of State. *2021 Trafficking in Persons Report*. June 2021. https://www.state .gov/reports/2021-trafficking-in-persons-report/.

Vance, Carole. "Innocence and Experience: Melodramatic Narratives of Sex Trafficking and Their Consequences for Law and Policy." *History of the Present* 2, no. 2 (Fall 2012): 200–18.

Vargas, João H. Costa. *The Denial of Antiblackness: Multiracial Redemption and Black Suffering*. Minneapolis: University of Minnesota Press, 2018.

Vargas, João H. Costa, and Moon-Kie Jung. "Antiblackness of the Social and the Human." In *Antiblackness*, edited by Moon-Kie Jung and João H. Costa Vargas, 1–14. Durham, NC: Duke University Press, 2021.

Vigneswaran, Darshan. "Methodological Debates in Human Rights Research: A Case Study of Human Trafficking in South Africa." In *Contemporary Slavery: Popular Rhetoric and Political Practice*, edited by Annie Bunting and Joel Quirk, 179–201. Vancouver: UBC Press, 2017.

Walcott, Rinaldo. *The Long Emancipation: Moving toward Black Freedom*. Durham, NC: Duke University Press, 2021.

Walcott, Rinaldo, and Idil Abdillahi. *BlackLife: Post-BLM and the Struggle for Freedom*. Winnipeg: ARP Books, 2019.

Watts, Edward, and Evan Williams, producers. *PBS Frontline*. Season 2015, episode 12, "Escaping ISIS." Aired July 14, 2015. https://www.pbs.org/wgbh/frontline/documentary /escaping-isis/.

Weitzer, Ronald. "Human Trafficking and Contemporary Slavery." *Annual Review of Sociology* 41 (2015): 223–42.

Weitzer, Ronald. "New Directions in Research on Human Trafficking." *The Annals of the American Academy of Political and Social Science* 653, no. 1 (2014): 6–24.

Weitzer, Ronald. "Sex Trafficking and the Sex Industry: The Need for Evidence-Based Theory and Legislation." *Journal of Criminal Law and Criminology* 101 (2011): 1337–70.

Wells-Barnett, Ida B. *On Lynchings*. New York: Dover Publications, 2014.

Wells-Barnett, Ida B. *A Red Record: Tabulated Statistics and Alleged Causes of Lynching in the United States*. Chicago: Donohue and Henneberry, 1895. https://www.gutenberg.org /files/14977/14977-h/14977-h.htm.

Weston, Kath. "'Real Anthropology' and Other Nostalgias." In *Ethnographica Moralia: Experiments in Interpretive Anthropology*, edited by Neni Panourgiá and George Marcus, 126–37. New York: Fordham University Press, 2008.

Wilderson, Frank. *Red, White, and Black: Cinema and the Structure of U.S. Antagonisms*. Durham, NC: Duke University Press, 2010.

Williams, Eric. *Capitalism and Slavery*. Chapel Hill: University of North Carolina Press, 1994. First published 1944 by University of North Carolina Press.

Williams, Randall. *The Divided World: Human Rights and Its Violence*. Minneapolis: University of Minnesota Press, 2010.

Wilson, Samuel Paynter. *Chicago and Its Cess-pools of Infamy*. 16th ed. Project Gutenberg, 2020. Accessed July 13, 2022. http://www.gutenberg.org/files/61836/61836-h/61836-h .htm. First published 1910.

Woods, Brian, and Kate Blewett, dirs. *Slavery: A Global Investigation*. True Vision, 2000. Film. https://truevisiontv.com/films/details/90/slavery-a-global-investigation.

Woods, Tryon P. "Surrogate Selves: Notes on Anti-trafficking and Anti-blackness." *Social Identities* 19, no. 1 (2013): 120–43.

Woolfork, Lisa. *Embodying American Slavery in Contemporary Culture*. Urbana: University of Illinois Press, 2008.

Wynter, Sylvia. "Africa, the West, and the Analogy of Culture: Cinematic Text after Man." In *Symbolic Narratives/African Cinema: Audiences, Theory and the Moving Image*, edited by June Givanni, 25–76. London: British Film Institute, 2000.

Wynter, Sylvia. "1492: A New World View." In *Race, Discourse, and the Origin of the Americas*, edited by Vera Lawrence Hyatt and Rex Nettleford, 5–57. Washington, DC: Smithsonian Institution Press, 1995.

Wynter, Sylvia. "Is 'Development' a Purely Empirical Concept or Also Teleological? A Perspective from 'We the Underdeveloped.'" In *Prospects for Recovery and Sustainable Development in Africa*, edited by Aguibou Yansané, 299–316. Westport, CT: Greenwood Press, 1996.

Wynter, Sylvia. "Unsettling the Coloniality of Being/Power/Truth/Freedom: Towards the Human, After Man, Its Overrepresentation—An Argument." *CR: The New Centennial Review* 3, no. 3 (2003): 257–338.

Wynter, Sylvia, and David Scott. "The Re-enchantment of Humanism: An Interview with Sylvia Wynter." *Small Axe* 8 (September 2000): 119–207.

Yamamoto, Eric. "What's Next? Japanese American Redress and African American Reparations." In *Redress for Historical Injustices in the United States*, edited by Michael T. Martin and Marilyn Yaquinto, 411–26. Durham, NC: Duke University Press, 2007.

Zelizer, Barbie. "Cannibalizing Memory in the Global Flow of News." In *On Media Memory: Collective Memory in a New Media Age*, edited by Motti Neiger, Oren Meyers, and Eyal Zandberg, 27–36. London: Palgrave Macmillan, 2011.

Zelizer, Barbie. "Reading the Past against the Grain: The Shape of Memory Studies." *Critical Studies in Mass Communication* 12, no. 2 (June 1995): 214–39.

Zelizer, Barbie. *Remembering to Forget: Holocaust Memory through the Camera's Eye*. Chicago: University of Chicago Press, 1998.

Index

Page numbers in italics refer to figures and maps.

Englund, Harri, 229n64
Enke, Stephen, 87
#ethnographersheart, 169–71, 184–85; as method, 175
ethnography, 170–71, 187–88
Equiano, Olaudah, 174

family planning, 87–88
Farmer-Paellmann, Deadria, 45, 46
farmworkers, Latinx, 2, 104, 108, 121–22; in *Invisible: Slavery Today*, 112–15, *114*; NAFTA and, 113
Fassin, Didier, 198n24
FBI (Federal Bureau of Investigation), 108
feminism, transnational, 48–49
Five Thousand Years of Slavery (Gann and Willen), 102, 104–9, 221n17, 221n28
Floyd, George, 193
Foner, Eric, 111
forced labor: colonialism and, 38–39, 205n32; in Haiti, 78. *See also* slavery
forced sterilization, 139
Franklin, John Hope, 110
#FreeCyntoiaBrown, 26, 94, 96, 99
freedom: in antitrafficking discourse, 161–63; Black capacity for, 25, 82, 182, 185; Free the Slaves model of, 152–59, 202n88; gifting of, 78, 213n51; Haitian, 20–21, 86; Haitian mothers and, 20–21; of Indian workers, 21; migration and, 115; modernity and, 21; NGO model of, 149; white supremacy and, 11
freedom, Black, 162–63; modernity and, 61
Freedom Fund, 144, 145
Free the Slaves, 5, 6–7, 22, 51, 160, 198n23, 229n76; antireparations rhetoric of, 57; Black Lives Matter solidarity statement, 193–95; Community Vigilance Committees, 155–56; data collection of, 231n103; "Freedom for Haiti's Children" report, 86–87, 215n92; Ghanaian children video, 67–68, 69; *Haiti's Model Communities Fight Restavek Child Slavery* video, 84–86; model of freedom, 152–59, 202n88; promotional films, 153–55; race and, 56; "racial justice" rhetoric of, 11; technological approach, 134–35. *See also* Bales, Kevin

Gallagher, Anne, 15, 34
Garvey, Marcus, 39, 208n69
genocide: Indigenous, 107; Yazidi, 119

Getachew, Adom, 38
Ghana, 7; antitrafficking policy and, 37; Black mothers in, 26, 61–71; child slavery in, 37, 71–72, 187, *188*; child "trafficking" in, *63*, 63–66, *64*, 71–72, 212n23, 221n28; mining in, 146–48; neocolonialism in, 73; slavery in, 17–18, 37, 107, 146–48; working age in, 63–65
globalization, 4, 155; movements against, 104; reparations and, 47–48, 176; slavery and, 59–60; slavery discourse and, 54, 160, 185
Global Slavery Index, 144–45, 151, 174, 228nn46–47
González, Juan, 128–29, 130
Gordon, Avery, 18
Graham, Hannah, 216n106
Grono, Nick, 145
Guardian: Cyntoia Brown coverage, 99; Ghanaian child labor coverage, 63, *63*, *64*, 65

Haiti, 7; Black mothers in, 26, 61–62; "child slavery" in, 78; class in, 81–82; development in, 78; forced labor and, 78; independence of, 79–80, 214n71; NGO intervention in, 81, 88–89; restavèk system, 20–21, 40, 78–79, 81–87, 112, 182; slavery in, 82; US occupation of, 78, 80
Haitian Revolution, 21, 43, 152, 220n35; Black radical tradition and, 79–80; legacy of, 74–75; self-determination and, 80–81, 96
Hamer, Fannie Lou, 138–39, 149
Hartman, Saidiya, 75, 210n106; afterlives of slavery, 18
Haslam, Bill, 98–99
Hassan, Ameena, 119
Hassan, Khalil, 119
Hesford, Wendy, 212n25
Heyer, Heather, 167–68, 232n2
Hicks, Cheryl, 210n98
Hill, Anita, 77
Hoffman, Frederick L., 75
Hogan, Liam, 51–52
Hong, Grace K., 76–77, 116, 223n58
Hopkins, Sam, 223n49
Horowitz, David, 45–46, 207n61
Hua, Julietta, 109, 120
humanism: antiblack, 184; liberal, 18–19
Humanity United, 63, 144

slavery, 1; afterlives of, 4, 17–19, 174–75, 190, 192; antitrafficking and, 1–2; antitrafficking discourse and, 167, 175; as beyond racial, 112; Black mothers and, 68–69; blame for, 23, 25, 105; colonialism and, 59–60; contemporary, 107; costs of, 134–35, *135*, 141, 149, 150, 226nn4–5, 226n8; definitions of, 141; deportation and, 1, 5; in DRC, 22–23, 203n111; in Ghana, 17–18, 37, 71–72, 107, 187, *188*, 146–48; globalization and, 54, 59–60, 160, 185; in Haiti, 82; the Human and, 57–58; human trafficking as, 169–70; incarceration and, 1; in India, 21, 22, 140–41, 146–48, 153–54, 157–58, 167; as intraracial phenomenon, 130; in Mauritania, 11–12; memory of, 17–18, 115, 168; as metaphor, 202n85; modernity and, 7, 40, 56; multiculturalism and, 106–7, 108, 121, 131; multiculturalizing of, 25, 27, 171; naturalizing of, 41–42; in present-day Africa, 105, 167; pre-transatlantic slave trade, 105; redress for, 21, 28; "science" of, 137, 142; settler colonialism and, 7; US inculpability for, 103, 120–22, 130–31; white inculpability in, 82
slavery, American: as "mild," 74–75
slavery, transatlantic: antiblackness and, 7; antitrafficking discourse and, 5–6; dispossession and, 14; immigration and, 4; memory of, 102
Slavery: A Global Investigation, 5–6, 198nn20–23
slave trade: in Africa, 38–39, 174–78; Arabs and, 3, 11, 175–78; Libyan, 1–2, 190; in West Africa, 31–32
Smith, Adam, 134
Smith, Derri, 220n34
Smith, Sage, 216n106
Snell, Jeremy, 187
social justice, 98; antitrafficking advocacy and, 194, 218; antitrafficking discourse and, 193; movements for, 48, 97, 111, 117
Sommerfelt, Tone, 215n91
Sörnäs, Clara, 173–74
sovereign immunity, 207n56
Spillers, Hortense, 73
Stop Modern Slavery, 90, 216n102
Student Nonviolent Coordinating Committee (SNCC), 179
Suchland, Jennifer, 197n5
Sundiata, Ibrahim, 3, 205n31

surveillance, 104; antiblack, 132; antiterrorism and, 122, 126; antitrafficking and, 122–23; of migrants, 4; of sex workers, 15–16; unfreedom and, 8

Taylor, Breonna, 193
technochauvinism, 148
Thomas, Clarence, 77
Thomas, Deborah, 7, 23, 211n123
Thomson Reuters Foundation, 135, 145, 228n47
Tillet, Salamishah, 24
Torrington, Arthur, 152
Touch a Life, 221n28
Trafficking in Persons (TIP) Reports, 34–36, 39–40, *41*, 102, 120, 191; modern-day slavery rhetoric in, 42–44; reparations and, 49; "slave-like conditions" in, 40; tier rankings, *35*, *36*, 205n13
trafficking laws, 108; Mann Act, 7; Trafficking Victims Protection Act (TVPA), 32–33, 44, 46, 89
Trafficking Victims Protection Act (TVPA), 32–33, 44, 89; 2003 reauthorization, 49–50, 208n82
Trodd, Zoe, 144, 145; MOOC course, 149–54, 159
Trouillot, Michel-Rolph, 21, 183, 184, 185
Trump, Donald, 130–31, 167
TSA (Transportation Security Administration): trafficking identification methods, 127
Tubman, Harriet, 131
Tulsa massacre of 1921, 46, 50
Turner, Nat, 96

Ubelong, 63, 212n6
Underground Railroad, 115, 222n41; in antitrafficking discourse, 109, 118, 131; interracial cooperation framing, 109–12; range of significations, 111; rhetoric of NURFC, 118–19
Underground Railroad rhetoric: Yazidi women and, 119, 121
unfreedom, 8, 189; as Black pathology, 21
United Nations: human trafficking protocol, 5, 15; World Conference on Racism (WCAR), 42–44, 46
United States v. Navarrete, 223n54
US State Department: antitrafficking discourse, use of, 25; antitrafficking policies, 33, 37–38, 81, 86, 109, 215n92; antitrafficking projects,

www.ingramcontent.com/pod-product-compliance
Lightning Source LLC
Chambersburg PA
CBHW071734270326
41928CB00013B/2675